Looking to Jesus

—

Thinking More Often and Deeply of Christ

Nelson P. Miller

Looking to Jesus: thinking more often and deeply of Christ.

Miller, Nelson P.

Published by:

Crown Management LLC – January 2016

1527 Pineridge Drive
Grand Haven, MI 49417
USA

ISBN: 978-0-9905553-9-1

All Rights Reserved
© 2016 Nelson P. Miller
c/o 111 Commerce Avenue S.W.
Grand Rapids, MI 49503
(616) 301-6800 ext. 6963

For those wanting to draw more closely to Jesus.

*Dedicated to Bruce, Bob, and Chris, as
effective leaders in discipleship.*

Summary Table of Contents

Looking to Jesus 1

1   **His Heralding** 6

2   **His Coming** 28

3   **His Calling** 57

4   **His Ministry** 115

5   **His Miracles** 190

6   **His Sacrifice** 255

7   **His Resurrection** 318

8   **His Revelation** 352

Conclusion 366

Epilogue 368

Table of Attributes 369

Table of Citations 374

Detailed Table of Contents

Looking to Jesus 1
1 **His Heralding** 6
   1 Word 7
   2 Priest 8
   3 Guest 10
   4 Contender 12
   5 Lawgiver 14
   6 Commander 16
   7 Deliverer 18
   8 Avenger 20
   9 Crowned 21
   10 Protector 23
   11 Responder 25
2 **His Coming** 28
   12 Conceived 29
   13 Flesh 31
   14 Swaddled 32
   15 Proclaimed 34
   16 Named 36
   17 Consecrated 38
   18 Consolation 40
   19 Redeemer 42
   20 King 44
   21 Alien 46
   22 Insurgent 48
   23 Returned 50
   24 Aware 52
   25 Grown 54
3 **His Calling** 57
   26 Immersed 58
   27 Baptized 60
   28 Fasted 62
   29 Tested 64
   30 Powered 66
   31 Centered 68
   32 Supported 70
   33 Passionate 73
   34 Anointed 75

35	Judge	77
36	Revealer	79
37	Fulfillment	81
38	Family	83
39	Inscrutable	85
40	Life	88
41	Christ	90
42	Shepherd	92
43	Joyous	94
44	Builder	96
45	Interpreter	98
46	Good	99
47	Celebrated	101
48	Authoritative	103
49	Scriptural	105
50	Path	107
51	Vine	109
52	Glorifying	111
53	Commissioner	113

4 His Ministry 115

54	Leader	116
55	Preacher	118
56	Teacher	120
57	Unschooled	122
58	Surprising	124
59	Worshiper	126
60	Warrior	128
61	Participant	130
62	Signifier	132
63	Harvester	134
64	Appointer	136
65	Convener	138
66	Dispatcher	141
67	Resting	143
68	Intercessor	145
69	Partaker	147
70	Expositor	149
71	Counteractive	151
72	Liberator	154
73	Allegorical	155
74	Egalitarian	158

75	Inclusive	160
76	Childlike	162
77	Pursuer	164
78	Forgiving	166
79	Divider	168
80	Defender	170
81	Verified	172
82	Calming	174
83	Persistent	176
84	Ready	178
85	Shrewd	180
86	Savior	182
87	Serving	184
88	Friend	186
89	Restorer	187
5	**His Miracles**	**190**
90	Healer	191
91	Rescuer	193
92	Facilitator	195
93	Testifier	198
94	Celebrant	200
95	Visitor	202
96	Willing	204
97	Knowing	206
98	Drawing	208
99	Astonished	210
100	Compassionate	212
101	Astonishing	214
102	Fearsome	216
103	Vanquisher	218
104	Responding	221
105	Accessible	223
106	Merciful	226
107	Secretive	228
108	Provider	230
109	Testing	232
110	Terrifying	234
111	Receptive	236
112	Therapeutic	238
113	Superior	240
114	Dutiful	242

	115 Worker	244
	116 Fruitful	246
	117 Humble	248
	118 Restorative	250
	119 Unequivocal	252
6	**His Sacrifice**	255
	120 Denouncing	256
	121 Refusing	258
	122 Offending	260
	123 Persecuted	263
	124 Refugee	265
	125 Prophetic	267
	126 Resolute	269
	127 Watchful	271
	128 Threatened	273
	129 Besieged	275
	130 Guarded	277
	131 Condemned	279
	132 Weeping	281
	133 Troubled	283
	134 Hated	285
	135 Betrayed	287
	136 Broken	289
	137 Poured	290
	138 Abandoned	292
	139 Arrested	294
	140 Tried	296
	141 Convicted	298
	142 Sentenced	300
	143 Appealed	302
	144 Scourged	304
	145 Burdened	306
	146 Crucified	308
	147 Separated	310
	148 Mourned	312
	149 Pierced	314
	150 Buried	315
7	**His Resurrection**	318
	151 Living	319
	152 Transient	321
	153 Conferrer	323

¹⁵⁴	Glorified	325
¹⁵⁵	Announced	327
¹⁵⁶	Appearing	329
¹⁵⁷	Disguised	331
¹⁵⁸	Doubted	334
¹⁵⁹	Rebuking	336
¹⁶⁰	Greeting	338
¹⁶¹	Conversing	340
¹⁶²	Opposed	342
¹⁶³	Physical	343
¹⁶⁴	Identifiable	345
¹⁶⁵	Functional	347
¹⁶⁶	Ascended	349

8 His Revelation 352

- ¹⁶⁶ Transfigured 353
- ¹⁶⁷ Returning 355
- ¹⁶⁸ Unexpected 356
- ¹⁶⁹ Impersonated 358
- ¹⁷⁰ Gathering 360
- ¹⁷¹ Enthroned 362
- ¹⁷² Rewarding 364

Conclusion 366
Epilogue 368
Table of Attributes 369

Looking to Jesus

What do you think of Jesus? Or more to the point, what do you think *about* when you think of Jesus? The question for the longtime, committed Christian is no longer one of salvation. Those who know Jesus as their Lord and Savior have settled that most-important point, maybe settled it recently or long ago, but in any case settled it. The question remains, though: what does the committed Christian, the follower or even disciple of Christ, think about when thinking about Jesus? The question raises no small point. Jesus left little doubt that he wants us *obeying* him, which one might also express as *following* him. Obeying Jesus in the strict submission sense is clearly one good thing to do, one very important and valuable commitment and concept. To *follow* Jesus is quite a bit like *obeying* him because one would only then go where he goes and do what he does. Yet to obey or to follow Jesus first implies *thinking about* him, getting a picture in one's mind about who he is and what he does. A traditional way of characterizing to obey, follow, or even think about Jesus is to *look to* him. One *looks to* Jesus as a longtime, committed disciple more so than simply obeying him. Why can *looking to* be a more-powerful construct than mere obedience for longtime followers? Obedience, while critically important, is too easily misconstrued as an invitation to legalism, to a system of rules, even self-improvement principles, those things that, again while laudable at times, can dry out and weary a follower. One might at times even question who needs Jesus, when we have his rules, when we can simply perform through obedience.

That unfortunate temptation to legalistic error may be precisely the point why Jesus urges us not merely to obey him but also to *look to* him. Obeying may be one thing while *looking to* may be a slightly or even significantly different thing. They may indeed be Mary versus Martha things with Mary looking and loving while Martha merely obeyed. Jesus wanted the disciples and others to understand him, to logically digest what he said, take it to heart, and carry it out. Yet he also wanted the disciples and others to look to him as in to regard him, trust him, and rely on his presence. Each of these things, regarding, trusting, and relying, requires *thinking of* him. You may have had a very popular or very funny, strong, courageous, smart, swift, rich, or powerful friend when you were young and first cognizant of friends, someone to whom you looked up. This special friend may in some sense have favored and blessed you or at least made you feel better just thinking about this friend. Jesus may in part simply want us to regard him in similar manner, to turn our minds toward him not for rules but for his presence. Remember one of the most-difficult, indeed most-awful Gospel events, when to the putative followers who allegedly performed miracles in his name Jesus said that he never *knew* them? He wants us to *know* him, not merely to do as he says.

In short, the antidote to a book of rules is a book on relationship, not simply to obey Jesus but to know him. Some may question how one can know a person with whom one has not directly interacted and lived. If you said that you knew someone famous, when to the contrary you had never even met the person, then others would regard you as a fabricator, name dropper, and exaggerator. Yet we do speak of *knowing* someone in a different sense of having so thoroughly immersed ourselves in the study of that person's recorded sayings, writings, works, and life as to become in some way imbued with the person's spirit. In that way, a literary scholar might legitimately claim to know Shakespeare or Austen just as a scientist would know Einstein or McClintock, physician know Harvey or Curie, politician know Churchill or Thatcher, philosopher know Socrates or Wollstonecraft, or historian know Joan of Arc or Lincoln. The *knowing* would only be true when the study was so deeply reflective that the scholar had captured within the scholar's own spirit something of the figure's essence. Although this analogy informs, yet when the subject comes to knowing Jesus, we need not be scholars. Fortunately, Jesus is just as likely, indeed probably much more likely, to acknowledge knowing a humble soul than anyone claiming to be his scholar.

Jesus certainly gave us the events, stories, images, and scenes to know him. The surprising and immensely satisfying thing to those who have long followed Jesus but who wish more confidently to *know* him is that he gave us so much more to know him than we routinely appreciate. Even devoted followers may think superficially that they have few deeply reflective images of Jesus, certainly the crucifixion and resurrection but maybe only a few more, when to the contrary he gave us dozens of images, even hundreds. Within each grand stage of Jesus's earthly life, from his heralding to his coming, calling, ministry, crucifixion, resurrection, and revelation, we have many discrete descriptions of subtly profound events, everything from miracles of many kinds and extraordinary supernatural encounters to ordinary interactions that his divine presence turned profound. Jesus gave us so many of these scenes and events that we could take a lifetime exploring and reflecting on them, which may be exactly what he hopes and expects us to do in order for us to claim in the end to have known him.

In that very respect of coming to know him across a lifetime, Jesus had good reason to describe himself as the groom and his Church as the bride. Imagine yourself at the end of a long married life. Wouldn't you expect to know nearly everything about your spouse? Shouldn't it surprise you to hear your spouse describe to a friend something that you had not heard, did not know, or at least could not recall about your spouse? We get to know a spouse so richly and deeply that they seem a part of us, as if every event of their life was an event of our life even when we were not actually present for some of those events. We just become so familiar with a spouse that their character and presence imbues us. This familiarity, closeness, and presence may be much of what Jesus intended to convey in his bride-to-groom, groom-to-bride analogy that we would be that close to him. Both ancient and modern cultures give marriage a transactional cast, as in a covenant and exchange of vows, property, rights, and obligations. Don't mistake Jesus's groom-to-bride analogy, though, as intending primarily a transactional meaning. Rather, both ancient and modern cultures have also seen marriage as an intimate and sacramental relationship. And so in some sense, Jesus may want to know each of us, and each of us to know him, with the intimate familiarity of a spouse.

The many images of himself that Jesus gives us, on which we may reflect deeply in order to know him, are in their ready effect in fact deeply instructive. We can learn so much simply from what occurred to and around Jesus and how he responded to those events. Thus each small section of this book begins with a paragraph drawing on the Bible's text to describe an event in Christ's life. We must first know about each Christ event itself, most of them thoroughly familiar to us as part of the story of Jesus and the Bible text even if not always marked out as a discrete event. Count and recount those rich and numerous events. Each small section's second paragraph then describes what the event might mean to us as it occurs to us throughout the day and we turn even momentarily to reflect on it. Consider in these second paragraphs how reflection on Christ through each event might inform our heart, mind, and soul. Each of this book's small sections then concludes with an application suggesting how each event of Christ's life might inform, shape, and guide a life forward. The Bible is not history but life. We are part of its story.

Yet again, even as valuable as instruction in and from the events of Christ's life might be, instruction is not exactly the central point of recounting Christ events and images. *Relationship* is instead the central point. To know someone is to have a relationship with someone. So while one might organize these images of Jesus thematically, perhaps around themes like perseverance, love, service, and so on, the point of knowing someone instead seems more to be to know their life as a whole. To know someone's life as a whole is to know the life from beginning to end in the order in which it developed. This book thus takes Jesus's life in chronological order, grouping each discrete event first as the foretelling or heralding of Jesus, then Jesus's coming followed by his calling, ministry, sacrifice, resurrection, and revelation. Jesus is eternal, meaning that his story is without beginning and without end, but his earthly life, to which we have so many witnesses, principally but not exclusively the Gospel witnesses, had these stages. He gave us this plain record of the birth, development, implementation, and completion of his earthly ministry through which to know him. We could not know him without recognizing that the images of him lie within this profound structure of heralding, coming, calling, ministry, sacrifice, resurrection, and revelation.

Of course, head knowledge of the events of Jesus's life may not be getting any closer to knowing him than would be following everything that he said to do or not do. Constructs of the mind, or even commitments of the will, are not entirely things of the heart. We are instead filled of God, filled by God, the Holy Spirit inhabiting our bodies including our hearts, minds, and souls as God once inhabited the Israelites' tabernacle and temple. One only hopes that God's habitation through his indwelling Holy Spirit grows when we fix our mind on the life of Christ. God's only Son clearly pleases the Father. The Father's mind is always on the Son just as the Son's mind is always fixed on the Father. Wouldn't we please Father and Son, indeed join richly in the Holy Trinity, by fixing our own minds on the Son? Consider, then, not an imaginary Jesus but the authentic One, exactly as history recorded him. Know the life of the Son.

1
His Heralding

Word. *John 1:1.* **Priest.** *Genesis 1:26.* **Guest.** *Genesis 18:1.* **Contender.** *Genesis 32:22.* **Lawgiver.** *Exodus 24:9.* **Commander.** *Joshua 5:13.* **Deliverer.** *Judges 6:11.* **Conqueror.** *Judges 13:1.* **Crowned.** *Ezekiel 1:26.* **Protector.** *Daniel 3:1.* **Responder.** *Daniel 10:4.*

Jesus was a long time coming. In his coming, Jesus left us many resplendent records of discrete events our reflection on which draws us closer to him. Those events do not merely include his miraculous conception and celestial and angelic heralds of his virgin birth. As if those events were alone not sufficiently unprecedented and extraordinary, the Bible in addition gives us 1,500 years of the foreshadowing and prefiguring of Christ's birth. Jesus's coming was easily the longest awaited, most precisely predicted, most profoundly prefigured, and most achingly anticipated of events in human history. We do not fully appreciate Jesus's coming unless we first appreciate the great herald that preceded it and thus the great anticipation that it held. The Old Testament fills with what some construe as theophany or Christophany but which any may just as readily accept as mysterious types prefiguring Christ, God not having chosen to make his revelation any clearer. Only after having committed our wonder to the unprecedented Old Testament record, may we then fully appreciate the poignancy and perfection of Jesus's actual birth. What a rich record God has given us on which to dwell in anticipation of the glorious coming of his magnificent Son, whom God's word also assures us, was with the Father in the beginning.

1 **Word.**

John 1:1; *see also* Genesis 1:26.

Genesis begins with God creating the heavens and earth, at first dark and formless with only God's Spirit hovering over the emptiness. God then let light banish darkness and gave creation shape filled with vegetation and animals. God did each of these things first by speaking and then blessing, day by day. Then for the first time referring to himself and his actions using the first-person plural, God said let *us* make humankind in *our* image and likeness so that humans would rule the new kingdom. God then blessed the man and woman whom they—God in plural—created in their—again, God in plural—image, seeing that all was good. Written a millennium and a half later, the Gospel of John begins again with the beginning, with creation, but with a perspective on genesis that was both new and yet very old. John tells followers that the Word, Jesus, was with God in the beginning, and that the Word, Jesus, was God. Jesus though was not just already in the Trinity, Father, Son, and Holy Spirit, at creation in the beginning. Jesus was also the agent through whom God created. God made all things through Jesus because Jesus held life as the light of all humankind. Jesus's light shone through the darkness in a way that the darkness could not overcome.

The creation story of Genesis, in which God says let *us* make humankind in *our* image and *our* likeness, foreshadows John's revelation of Jesus as the Word with God in the beginning. The account of Jesus as the Word of, with, and as God in the beginning is a follower's core Jesus image. For the follower, everything must begin with this image of the pre-existent Jesus in Trinitarian communion with the Father and his Holy Spirit. That the full revelation of Jesus as the Word with God in the beginning came not in the Old Testament account of Genesis but instead with John's glorious Gospel in no sense contradicts, diminishes, or alters the Genesis account of the great creator God and his hovering Holy Spirit, with its plural-God suggestion of his image-carrying Son. We read Genesis and John together, as one must always construe all parts of the Bible together. Reading the Bible's literal beginning in Genesis together with the beginning of the last of the four

Gospels takes only a little discipline, as one must read any text wholly and with discipline to construe it accurately and fairly. The point, though, is not how followers obtain this first and foundational image of Jesus. Rather, the question is what we make of this mind-shattering image. And while Trinitarian doctrine is plenty clear for profound reflection, the answer almost seems to be that followers have not much more to do with Jesus's first image than to stand, kneel, or submit in awe.

She studied God's word often and enjoyably, in groups and alone. She certainly appreciated sound doctrine, even feeling that she could after a lifetime of studies sense unsound doctrine from a mile away. The more often one looks at a picture and its parts, the easier distinguishing alterations becomes. She could tell when the tiniest thing was out of place in her kitchen, bathroom, bedroom, and wardrobe, so why would she not tell when the tiniest thing was out of place in her beloved word of God? Yet for all of her interest, reflection, and study, she was not fundamentally a rational follower. Oh, she was highly rational, just as God's word was perfectly principled even while profound. She just did not require of God that he make all sense to her, reveal him fully to her, or justify his awe. She knew enough to accept what understanding, clarity, and revelation that he gave her as riches beyond compare. If he withheld a little more or a lot more for others or for himself, then she knew that he did so for her benefit. Indeed, she treasured the unknown and unknowable things that he withheld, knowing as she did that the withheld things only fueled her awe. And for her, the first of those gloriously unfathomable images would always be Jesus with the Father and Holy Spirit in the beginning, Jesus as the pre-existent, creator Word of God.

2 Priest.

Genesis 1:26; *see also* Genesis 14:18; Psalm 110:4; Hebrew 5:6; Hebrew 7:11.

After Jesus with the Father in the beginning, followers must then know Jesus as the great High Priest, possessing the purity, holiness, power, and authority of the creator-ruler God. Abram and Lot had come up out of Egypt to the Jordan River and plain together. There they decided to separate, Lot to the plain of Sodom and Gomorrah while Abram to the hills of Canaan. Lot though fell captive to four kings who defeated the rulers of the plain. Hearing of Lot's capture, Abram gathered his men to fight and defeat the four conquering kings. The king of Sodom came to thank and reward Abram for regaining his lands. Yet just then the mystery happened. Melchizedek, known only as the king of Salem and priest of God Most High, appeared with the sacrificial bread and wine to bless Abram in the name of God Most High. Recognizing Melchizedek's standing as priest of God Most High, Abram gave Melchizedek a tithe of everything that he had recovered from the conquering kings. From the king of Sodom, though, Abram took no reward. God alone would make Abram rich, not the king of Sodom. A millennium and a half later, the Apostle Paul, quoting a Psalm, would write of Jesus that he is the eternal priest in Melchizedek's order, the perfect sacrifice of an indestructible life for the salvation of all who obey him. For as Jesus himself said, "Before Abraham was born, I am."

Abram's encounter of Melchizedek, whose name means *my king is righteousness*, is a mysteriously wondrous event that helps us think of Jesus's peculiar pre-existence as both a holy priest and powerful king while also a sacrificial savior. God of course created us in his own image, saying precisely so, "Let us make mankind in our image, in our likeness," with the purpose that mankind would rule. Yet in so saying, God spoke of *us* as he might speak of Father and Son or even the Trinitarian Father, Son, and Holy Spirit pre-existing his creation. We have no specific need of resolving whether Melchizedek, the mysterious priest-king of God Most High, who arose from his own order in the power of an indestructible life rather than a documented priestly lineage, who like Christ offered the sacrificial bread and wine, and to whom even the patriarch Abram tithed, was Christ himself or a type or prefiguring of Christ. Melchizedek's appearance and communion casts our thoughts of Jesus back to the earliest of times, to the primordial Ancient of Days who was present at creation itself, history's end we certainly know but also its *beginning*.

Sometimes, indeed fairly often, something about Jesus made the hair on the back of his neck stand up. That *something*, he had learned, was a supernatural, mystical, or numinous quality that persons attribute to divinity generally but that he had not found in much of anything or anyone other than Christ himself. Oh, he had rarely experienced, almost by accident and always to his distaste, the weirdness of the occult. The world could certainly seem odd or inhabited at times, especially when any number of people and programs foisted that weirdness on an unsuspecting public. He resisted that foisting quite effectively. He had no interest whatsoever in experiencing anything darkly magical, no conjuring or séance for him. Instead, he read the Bible clearly and consistently, certainly for its moral lessons, certainly also for the salvation story of Jesus, and also for the movement of the Holy Spirit, but also for its *historicity*, the authenticity of its ancient and panoramic record. Jesus, though, pierced and brought to instant life that record, knitting God's otherworldliness with every human image. He thought often of Jesus not only as incarnate man-God but as pre-existent God-man, just often enough not to lose the sense of the hair standing up on the back of his neck. He feared that losing that numinous sense of Jesus might just cost him his life.

3 Guest.

Genesis 18:1.

We should also welcome and revere Jesus as an honored guest who brings both immediate blessing and ultimate judgment. Abraham had received God's blessed promise that he would have ancestors as numberless as the sand on the seashore. He had obeyed God with the circumcision of his male family members. Yet he was now 99 years old and his only wife Sarah, with whom Abraham had no children, well beyond child-bearing age, and thus a broken old man who had instead borne a son by his wife's maidservant. Abraham and Sarah would die, it seemed, with none of the promised children to reflect, receive, and carry on God's blessing. Abraham simply sat in the heat of the day with Sarah hidden behind him deep in their tent, when the Lord suddenly appeared. Abraham at first saw not one Lord but three men to whom Abraham bowed low, offering food, rest, and ceremonial washing of their feet. When the three accepted his offer, Abraham rushed Sarah and his servant to prepare the best that they could muster, and then stood near as the three ate. Finally, they asked Abraham where Sarah was, to which he replied that she was in the tent. One then promised to return in a year by which time Sarah would have a son. The eavesdropping Sarah laughed to herself that she would have no such pleasure after being all worn out, but the Lord, perceiving her thoughts, corrected her that nothing was too hard for the Lord and that she would indeed have a son. Two of the men then headed down to investigate the great sins of Sodom, while Abraham pleaded with the Lord to spare it for the few righteous they would find there. The two men, identified now as angels of the Lord, indeed found the men of Sodom demanding that Abraham's nephew Lot let them have sex with the two visitors. The Lord then spared Lot's family while destroying Sodom and Gomorrah. And within a year, Sarah bore the promised son.

Jesus as honored guest carrying both blessing and judgment is a powerful image. The word tells us to treat every guest as honored lest we entertain angels. How strange but perfectly arranged that the Lord would appear to the fully broken Abraham as one of three honored guests, the other two later identified as angels, to confirm and convey his promised blessing. Again, one need not know with certainty that Jesus, who himself said that he existed before Abraham, was actually the one who appeared at the entrance to Abraham's tent or whether the figure to whom Abraham referred as the Lord was instead the Father, an angel, or an apparition. Jesus is the Father's image, as Jesus himself said. One might even think of the three men together who appeared at Abraham's tent entrance as a Trinitarian three, Father, Son, and Holy Spirit, except that the account later describes the other two as angels. The Bible provides us with just what we need to know, which in this instance may be precisely these allusions without intending that we construe them with any certainty. We know, though, that Jesus pre-existed Abraham, Jesus is Lord, and Jesus is the Father's incarnation and image. One image of Jesus that we can and should reliably accept is his presence with and influence over the great patriarch Abraham. Jesus was no Johnny-come-lately to the patriarch party but the life-giving Lord himself.

As so many other parents had done, they gave their tiny newborn the name of the great patriarch's laughing wife, the one who bore at such late age the promised child. Mother and father probably each had their own inspiration for giving their child the matriarch's name. Such is likely often the case with naming newborn infants, mother and father coming to the choice from different perspectives. Here, though they both knew the precious story of the laughing matriarch. Their common inspiration was then at least in part that they hoped their child would, like the matriarch, laugh and especially be able to laugh at herself. They also prayed that Jesus would hear and share in their daughter's laughter, indeed that he would appear at the entrance to *her* tent as the Lord had stood at the entrance to Abraham's tent. They prayed also that she would receive Jesus as Abraham had received the Lord, bowing deeply to him and serving him her best. They knew and trusted that if she did so, then this loving Lord whom they also knew so well and equally trusted would bless her as he had blessed Abraham. And so their child grew in delight, laughing often, laughing at herself when appropriate, laughing with children, and before too long laughing, walking, and talking with Jesus. That their child especially laughed with and about other children became the parents' special delight. God blesses, and God blesses especially through laughing children. Jesus knows those who laugh.

4 Contender.

Genesis 32:22.

We also have the privilege of knowing Jesus as the God with whom we may wrestle for blessings. Jacob had cheated his brother Esau out of his birthright, having to flee to his uncle in another land as a consequence. There Jacob had married his uncle's daughter, indeed two of his uncle's daughters when his uncle tricked him into working twice as long for the marriage, much as Jacob had tricked Esau. Jacob, though, managed to cheat his uncle, too, and so also fled his uncle as a consequence, in the course of which his beloved wife stole the uncle's treasures. With nowhere but home to go, the trickster Jacob braced to meet Esau whom he knew would still have it in for him. So Jacob divided his flocks and servants, sending one contingent ahead as a gift to mollify Esau. He also sent the other contingent, the one with his wives and children, ahead, leaving Jacob alone. Yet Jacob was not alone, for a man appeared, wrestling with Jacob until morning. When the man was unable to overpower Jacob, he simply touched Jacob's hip, wrenching it out of joint so that Jacob could do nothing other than lie holding onto the man, who told Jacob to let him go. Jacob refused unless the man would first bless him. So the man gave Jacob the new name Israel, meaning that he had wrestled with God to overcome. Jacob named the site the *place of God* for his having seen God face to face. God changed the heart of Esau, who spared Jacob.

The image of Jesus as one with whom we may wrestle and contend for blessings presents such an extraordinary opportunity. Religions often conceive of gods as remote, barely concerned with human affairs. Yet here we have our incarnate God whom we can physically grasp and with whom we can literally as well as figuratively wrestle for blessings. As a tradesman working with wood and stone, Jesus was certainly a strong man. That he kept perfectly to God's will through mortal beating, scourging, and crucifixion better proves his incomparable strength. Fully divine, though, he was still fully human. If Jacob wrestled literally with God incarnate, and with Jesus the Father's likeness and incarnate God, then one might construe that Jacob wrestled with Jesus, although again, the Bible is far from clear on that point, and no need arises to prove, disprove, or dispute the point. The account of Jacob wrestling with God nonetheless gives followers a powerful way of thinking about Jesus. Jesus desires that we are anything other than lukewarm toward him. He desires our passion, which is not always settled, gentle, and cool. We wrestle with things, indeed wrestle with God, cheaters and tricksters just like Jacob but still earnest in the passion of our fears, loves, desires, yearning, and insecurities. Jacob recognized when he had need of God and was alone with God. He then seized God, struggled mightily with him, even let God injure him, and still held onto God for his blessing. Do we cling to Jesus with the same intensity for his blessing?

He gradually came to realize that he had several things, maybe even many things, over which to wrestle with God. He had long thought himself content. God had called, blessed, and provided, and he trusted God to continue to call, bless, and provide. His own desperate situation, already so fully resolved through the awful magnificence of the work of Christ, compelled him little. He knew himself to be wretched, poor, pitiful, blind, and naked but still fully covered and appropriately anointed by Christ. Why should he then wrestle with God? Yet he could see things around him that bore wrestling, things for which he would willingly sacrifice. Those things had mostly to do with the condition of others' souls, not that his soul's condition was any better but simply that he felt it fully committed or at least on the steady way to full commitment to Christ. Maybe he should wrestle more over himself, he thought, but instead he wrestled with God for others. His wrestling for a long time showed no effect until a great breakthrough, so like Jacob's dawn. That dawn emboldened him to wrestle again and wrestle more. He might be a sad and sodden trickster and fake like Jacob, but one thing that he could do was to hold on. He grasped the image of himself lying at Jesus's feet, hip wrenched out of socket like Jacob's, but still holding on for the blessing of others. Jesus, set my people free.

5 Lawgiver.

Exodus 24:9; *see also* Genesis 49:10; Acts 2:36; James 4:12.

The Old Testament also prefigures Jesus as the great lawgiver, carrier of his Father's authority both to give law and judge obedience to it. Moses had led the nation of Israel out of Egypt, into the desert, and through its wilderness toward the strangely spiritual Mount Sinai. Mount Sinai, at about 7,500 feet in height and a three-hour climb, is otherwise ordinary among that desert's wilderness mountains except that there Moses would meet God. Moses and his brother Aaron and Aaron's sons Nadab and Abihu led Israel's seventy elders up Mount Sinai, where they met and saw God. The Old Testament account leaves little doubt that they saw God not as a cloud or other apparition but *in human form*. God indeed stood *with his feet* on bright blue pavement like one made of precious stone and, though the elders must have feared harm, the account says raised *no hand* against them. The elders were in no dream or trance, for the account also says that they ate and drank there. Once again, readers have no need of judging with any certainty whether Jesus himself stood before Moses, Aaron, Aaron's sons, and Israel's seventy elders, or whether the elders merely saw a prefiguring or type of the coming Messiah who in one was to be lawgiver, judge, and savior. The Bible gives us what we need, letting us leave aside disputes over precise meanings. No one can know all of God, and none has standing to demand his greater clarity. Readers have enough in knowing that when one sees Jesus, one sees the Father in human form, and that our precious Trinity of Father, Son, and Holy Spirit is the three-person God in one. We know also that Moses received the Ten

Commandments carved into stone tablets, and received elaborate accompanying regulations, from God on Mount Sinai, the same God who would later judge Nadab and Abihu most harshly for offering fire against those regulations. God's word is law, even as God's Son is also judge and savior.

The image of Jesus as lawgiver is such an important one today in a postmodern age leaving us each to construct our own truth, rule, order, and meaning. We know Jesus as savior, just as we should. Salvation is its own wonder and critically important to each of us. Do we, though, know Jesus as lawgiver, one who reveals life-giving rules for attitudes, relationships, and behaviors? Lawgivers expect obedience. Can one even *know* a ruler and authority like God without perceiving, recognizing, and accepting demands for obedience? Some would construe Jesus as an all-forgiving and never-judging Messiah, but the Old Testament refers to the scepter not departing from Judah until the Messiah to whom it belongs comes to rule all nations. Jesus's brother James then refers to the *one* Lawgiver who both saves *and destroys*, whom the physician Luke also identifies in Acts as Jesus both Messiah *and Lord*. Messiahs we eagerly await, but to lords we necessarily submit. Humans have great need for forgiveness and equally great need for salvation, occupying as we do such temporary and torn tents. Yet we also have great need for a Lawgiver, the corruption of our tents alone proving that great need for life-giving rule, order, and regulation. Indeed, one can hardly conceive meaningfully of Messiah, Savior, and salvation without also discerning Lawgiver, Judge, and Lord. The tender baby whom Mary would eventually bear in humble cave is the same great Lawgiver whose finger carved law into tablets of Mt. Sinai stone. Thank God for the image of Jesus as Lawgiver.

Some might have thought it odd that such a generally encouraging, friendly, and gentle person as she would actually draw on Jesus just as much for his hard rule and regulation as for his soft sensitivity and salvation. She knew that some regarded the church as a place primarily or even solely for women looking for the Savior's spiritual intimacy. Yet she also saw the church as a place to learn and draw on the Lawgiver's clarity of role, rule, and regulation. She didn't see that clarity as legalistic. Indeed to the contrary, she was seldom particularly certain about the application of Jesus's directions, which while clear were simultaneously much more often general rather than specific. Still, she drew on the image of Jesus not only as the gentle Savior but the firm

Lawgiver. She knew her need for authority and found that need fully satisfied in Jesus. For her, he had not so much freed her from law including the Ten Commandments as fulfilled law for her including embodying those Commandments. Apart from Jesus, she had little sense of how any Old Testament regulation might govern her. She certainly was not keeping closely to food, cleaning, dress, or other regulation. Instead, the power and purpose that she drew from law, rule, and regulations were in the full Spirit of her savior Lawgiver. Like others may have thought about her, she sometimes also thought it odd that Christianity would hold so much more meaning for her because of its sure relationship to law rather than solely because of its prospect for salvation. She only knew her need for the order, power, and purpose of the one great Lawgiver whom she knew through and as Jesus.

6 Commander.

Joshua 5:13; *see also* Revelation 19:13.

The Old Testament also prefigures Jesus as the commander of God's army, not only a holy and authoritative figure but also a figure of power. Joshua was Moses' trusted lieutenant who had advocated that Israel obey the Lord by entering and taking the promised land of Canaan from its inhabitants. When the frightened fighting men of Israel refused, the Lord sent Israel on forty years of wandering in the desert until those men had died. Joshua then led Israel across the Jordan River and into Canaan, preparing first to take the fortified city of Jericho. Just as Joshua approached Jericho, though, he encountered a figure standing ahead of him with a drawn sword in his hand. As the nation's courageous leader, Joshua approached asking the figure whether he was on Israel's side or the side of Israel's enemies. The figure's mysterious response was that he was neither for Israel nor for Israel's enemies but had instead come as commander of the army of the Lord. Joshua made appropriate response falling to his face in reverence while asking what message the commander had for his servant. The commander responded that the reverently prostrate Joshua should also remove his sandals because he was on holy ground, which Joshua promptly did. The Lord then gave

Joshua the well-known instruction to march around Jericho once each day for six days and then seven times on the seventh day after which trumpet blasts would bring down Jericho's fortified walls. Joshua and the Israelites thus possessed the Promised Land.

The image of Jesus as commander of heaven's armies is a powerful magnifier of what his incarnation meant then and means today. Although he might have looked like any other newborn, and his birth in the full inn's humble stable would have made him appear especially defenseless, the incarnate-divine infant actually came in incomparable power as the still-commanding head of God's own army. He could have called legions down to his side at every threat including the threats to which he so awfully but temporarily succumbed in his torture and crucifixion. We could not have fully known Jesus as the Father's Son and image if Jesus had not always been his Father's commander, as any king turns to his eldest or only son for military leadership. A king's son must first prove himself worthy of the throne. Sons do so through battles. The Book of Revelation describes the Word of God, whom followers know as Jesus, as leading the armies of heaven. As the Father's eternal Son, Jesus has led and will continue to lead those armies forever. Precisely whom Joshua encountered outside Jericho may be another one of those intended mysteries, although who other than God himself has no sides to take for or against Israel? Israel like all others must choose and take God's side. Joshua did so in prostrate reverence, forgetting only to remove his sandals to perfect his prostration in such holy presence. The very ground on which we stand becomes holy when we stand before God. Know and embrace Jesus's image as commander of God's armies.

The world frightened her, no doubt. Such horrible things happened on such large scope with such regularity, whether wars, genocides, murders, torture, frauds, or famines. While some of the horror had natural origin, the vast majority of it had human origin, all of it had human dimension, and human corruption accelerated, exacerbated, and worsened all of it. The awful things that people did to one another, individually and collectively, just staggered her, so much so that she hardly knew what to do with the thought of such evil. That huge struggle between good and evil was a large part of her need and respect for Jesus. Somewhere, somehow, deep down, she knew Jesus not just for his spiritual solace and intimacy but as a resolute and prevailing warrior. The battle between good and evil was over, and good had won, she knew full well in the victory of Jesus. God had legions at his command that he had commanded so surely that Jesus had overcome his own most-horrible death. Jesus now commanded those legions. The only struggles were ones that God permitted only for a time and with the ultimate outcome in his favor already indisputably determined. While Jesus had not chosen sides, for his side was the only side that mattered, she though had long ago chosen Jesus's side, the side of the one great commander. Every time that the world shocked her again with its brutality, she remembered the ultimate victory of Jesus.

7 Deliverer.

Judges 6:11.

The Old Testament also foreshadows Jesus as deliverer. The Israelite Gideon was separating the wheat harvest inside of a winepress, of all places, to hide his little bounty from the occupying Midianites. Although in that circumstance he hardly seemed like a mighty warrior, the angel of the Lord appeared to Gideon calling him precisely that, saying also that the Lord was with him. Gideon's comical retort, for which he even more comically asked the angel's pardon, was that if the Lord was with them, then why was he hiding his paltry harvest in a winepress, from an occupying enemy? The account, which initially describes the mysterious figure as the *angel* of the Lord, resumes saying that the *Lord* turned to Gideon telling him to go save the Israelites, sent by the Lord. Gideon once again asked a gently satirical pardon in asking how he could possibly save the nation when Gideon was the weakest member of the weakest clan. The Lord's answer was simply that he, the Lord, would be with Gideon. Gideon then prepared for the Lord an offering of meat and bread without yeast, placing them on a rock before the Lord. Here, the account ends with the angel of the Lord touching the rock with the staff in his hand, fire flaring from the rock to consume the offering, and the angel of the Lord disappearing. Gideon despaired, finally realizing that he had indeed seen the angel of the Lord *face to face*, but the Lord spoke to him, saying that he would not die. Gideon would instead free the nation in the power of the delivering Lord.

The image of Jesus as deliverer from long before, indeed eternally before, his birth holds such power for his followers. Gideon's condition, fearing enemies even in winnowing his bare subsistence provision, is so often our own condition. No matter how rich or poor our actual material condition, we sense a meagerness and vulnerability about our lives, as if what much or little we have enemies of all kinds, natural, artificial, and supernatural, may at any moment take from us. We *are* vulnerable, like grass withering in the dry heat. We are also so commonly anxious about our vulnerability. Rather than glorying in the goodness of God and the rich bounty of his harvest, we hide, hoard, and protect what much or little that we have so that even that which we have we enjoy, savor, and share too little. Yet this miserliness is our condition only until we embrace the full character of Jesus. Jesus is not merely a spiritual savior who will on our earthly demise lift up our souls cleansed to the Father in the sky. Jesus is the full deliverer, powerful now naturally as well as forever supernaturally. Jesus gives us kingdom access and fullness of spirit from the moment that we meet him, even if our capacity to receive that fullness remains imperfect for a time. His power delivers us from our Midianites, letting us reap openly and share generously. The Jesus we know as the Christmas infant and crucified King of the Jews is also and always has been the One who delivers.

He knew deliverance. Oh, he had acquaintances whose deliverance was probably more obvious to others than his own deliverance, although one never really knows what others think. Maybe others could see just as plainly as he could feel that he was in full need of deliverance. He didn't have the painfully obvious addictions, crimes, and convictions that others had overcome through Jesus's deliverance, although again he was quite closely familiar with the fact and power of those other deliverances. As crazy as it sounded, he sometimes almost wished that he had such obvious and correctible corruptions because the subtle corruptions that he knew that he harbored were so difficult to discern, acknowledge, face, and overcome, and still just as deadly as the more-obvious addictions, crimes, and convictions. Yet even without the obvious recovery of an addict or liberation of a prisoner, he nonetheless knew that he had Jesus's deliverance from the anxiety, emptiness, nihilism, miserliness, and other deep and fatal corruptions of his spirit. He could sense Jesus's deliverance just as powerfully as if he had walked out of a literal prison, as indeed he had occasionally done on jail-ministry visits, each door opening wide before him before clanging shut behind him, leading him to the incredibly sweet smell of a rainy summer night's freedom. Thank God for the deliverance of Jesus.

8 Avenger.

Judges 13:1.

The Old Testament also foreshadows Jesus as an avenger. The Israelite nation had suffered forty years at the hands of the ruling Philistines. Among the suffering Israelites was a man Manoah whose wife was unable to bear children. To that wife appeared the angel of the Lord, telling her that she would bear a son dedicated to God, who would deliver Israel from the Philistines. Manoah's wife told Manoah about this awe-striking angel of God who had appeared to her to announce the Israelites' avenger. Manoah prayed that the man of God would appear once again, which he did, repeating that Manoah's wife must do as he said in bearing the child without drinking any wine. Manoah offered to prepare a meal for the angel of the Lord, but the angel directed only a burnt offering to the Lord. When Manoah asked the angel's name, the reply came that the name was *beyond understanding*. The angel then ascended in the flame of Manoah's burnt offering, Manoah crying out that they would now die for having seen God. Manoah's wife reasoned soberly that if God had meant for them to die, then he would not have announced that she would bear the avenging child. Manoah's wife indeed conceived, bearing the brute Samson in whom the Spirit of the Lord stirred ever greater in vengeance over the Philistines. In Samson's heroic death pulling down the temple on the Philistine rulers, he finally avenged Israel.

The image of Jesus as avenger satisfies a significant need. We must forgive others to ourselves receive forgiveness. What happens though to those offenses, whether by or against us, and to the evil that drove them? Creation must not be indifferent to evil because then it must also be indifferent to good. Christian truth so rooted in struggle cannot be too like Buddhist nirvana where both suffering and desire disappear. The world certainly has both suffering and desire, both good and evil. Ignoring them doesn't make them go away. Christ as avenger satisfies that conundrum that truth must address, defeat, and resolve evil without evil corrupting truth in the encounter. How does the soldier in battle not become too much like the enemy when each wars violently at one another? Jesus's simultaneous ability to defeat evil, pay for its wrong, and redeem the wrongdoer once again sets the world in order. Rather than ignoring chaos to pretend nirvana, we struggle with Christ as Samson struggled, yet while knowing that Christ has prevailed and that his victory will manifest itself in the end to struggle. We have less need of avenging ourselves when we stand with the ultimate Avenger. Jesus has always held the power that briefly possessed Samson. He simply relinquished that power for a time when he chose the role of incarnate divine infant. Followers should be glad for the powerful redress we find through Jesus.

He knew that the meekness that he so easily and characteristically exhibited had to have its counterpart in courage, strength, and conviction. Humility, indeed docility, could only go so far. He could turn his cheek most of the time, but some situations simply demanded a stand. He was seldom very sure of what those situations were and was instead generally willing to back away and back down from most stands. Yet the world had to have aspects of truth and justice, or all seemed lost. To never take a stand seemed almost as bad as to participate in the world's many atrocities. The challenge though was how to stand without turning due retribution into undue revenge and retaliation, without becoming too like the wrongdoer. He knew that he needed a model, hero, and mentor that the world in its own ways could not provide. The comic superhero was indeed as captured and corrupted by the world as its darker portrayals depicted. He knew that he needed a supernaturally transcendent hero, one whom he found to perfection in the resurrection-avenging Jesus.

9 Crowned.

Ezekiel 1:26.

The Old Testament also foreshadows Jesus as the spectacular reigning king on heaven's throne. Ezekiel prophesied to the nation of

Israel in exile in Babylon. The shock of exile must have been great, the horror of exile's enslavement multiplied by Israel's devastating detour from God's plan as his favored people. Ezekiel's vision began with the heavens opening to images of God. An immense cloud of flashing lightning surrounded by brilliant light carried four human figures at the center of a fire like glowing metal. The figures, though human in form, had calf-like feet gleaming like burnished bronze. Each figure had four faces and wings with hands under the wings. The faces were not just human but also lion, ox, and eagle. The figures, looking like burning coals or torches, sped back and forth like lightning with fire flashing between them. Awesomely high intersecting wheels rimmed entirely with eyes whirled next to each figure as it moved. A huge vault stretched above the fearsome figures, with a voice coming from a throne high above the great vault. The figure of a man was on the throne, his upper body glowing like metal while his lower body looked like fire. Brilliant light and rainbow surrounded him. Ezekiel recognized the man as the *appearance of the likeness of the glory of the Lord*. The voice then sent Ezekiel with the Lord's message to his exiled people.

The image of Jesus as a spectacular reigning king must be our vision of him if we are to know him as fully God in the Father's human form. What does *Jesus as incarnate God* mean if not that he embodies, carries, and represents magisterially God's full powers? While seeming oddly outlandish, so much so as to approach the mythical or fictional, the very wildness of Ezekiel's vision is also perfectly necessary. No vision of the full powers of God could be ordinary. The vision must be spectacular, freshly seen, and supernaturally extraordinary because God's powers are so perfectly vast. Ezekiel's vision is also necessarily more than just of the brilliantly glowing enthroned being. Followers of Jesus benefit from also having a vision of the workings of God. The enormously fearsome, magically complex, and lightning-swift actions of the four figures seems precisely what one must anticipate of God in his providence. How, one often wonders, does he accomplish all that he does? Yet contemplating the four figures that Ezekiel saw in his vision, those whom God in the image of the Son of Man directs from heaven's throne, makes one wonder how we do not see more of all that he accomplishes. The profusion of the four speeding figures' potent actions represents perfectly God's constant magnificent works. Ezekiel's vision seems precisely how Jesus must appear in his full reign directing his breathtakingly numerous and profound works.

She wasn't a great deal for science fiction. Her literary and entertainment tastes were more grounded, sensitive, and restrained. Even so, she occasionally sensed the universe's wildness, vastness, awfulness, and magnificence, and surmised that the creator God must work spectacularly within and without that universe. She tended very much to connect Jesus with the best of her refined tastes. She knew him to be the completely grounded Lord whose every word and act soaked and balanced her in sensibility, truth, and wisdom. Never did she imagine Jesus as so magnificently grand of visage and active in role as to direct multiple complex whirling beings at the speed of lightning flashes. Yet when she thought for the first time about it deeply, she realized that her own necessity alone nearly warranted such fearsome action. How could he accomplish all that she alone needed, not to mention his simultaneously fulfilling the needs of so many others, in the vast wildness of her own little corner of the planet, without such grand form? She needed an extravagantly conceived and formed Jesus, one who indeed glowed like molten metal far above the complex providences of angelic beings, above the huge vault enthroned.

10 Protector.

Daniel 3:1.

The Old Testament also foreshadows Jesus as companion protector. Daniel, himself an exiled Jew, had coached Shadrach, Meshach, and Abednego into leadership positions in their strange Babylon home. They had been careful, though, not to serve Babylon's foreign gods and worship its idolatrous images. Indeed, the strange land's astrologers pointed out to its king Nebuchadnezzar that Shadrach, Meshach, and Abednego were not at horn's call falling down to worship the huge image of gold that Nebuchadnezzar had set up on the plain. A furious Nebuchadnezzar had them hauled before him where he threatened to throw them into a blazing furnace if they continued to refuse. Refusing the order, Shadrach, Meshach, and Abednego merely replied that God would save them from the furnace if he wished. So three of Nebuchadnezzar's strongest soldiers tossed the firmly bound Shadrach,

Meshach, and Abednego into a furnace heated seven times hotter than normal, those soldiers dying from the flames in the process. But Shadrach, Meshach, and Abednego simply walked unbound and unharmed around in the fire with a mysterious fourth figure that Nebuchadnezzar proclaimed looked like a son of the gods. Nebuchadnezzar commanded the three to come out of the furnace, which they did without so much as a singed hair and with no smell of smoke on their bodies. And Nebuchadnezzar gave praise to the Most High God, ordered the death of anyone who criticized that God, and promoted Shadrach, Meshach, and Abednego.

The pre-incarnation image of Jesus as companion protector is a powerful addition to the later Gospel message of salvation that his incarnate life conveyed. Salvation is wondrous. Followers have every reason to look eagerly forward to God's kingdom welcome, although still, some help along the way would be nice. Jesus provides that help as a companion protector. The challenge may be small, or the challenge may be as great as a seven-times-hotter fiery furnace. Jesus doesn't merely direct his angels in protective ministrations but may enter the fires and flood waters with us. He walks with followers today, as he walked around in the fire with Shadrach, Meshach, and Abednego. Jesus is no fair-weather companion but instead one who is most present in the greatest challenge. He is no weak companion but instead one who is all powerful. The size of the challenge doesn't matter to his ability to bring a follower through and out of it without any stench of it remaining. His protection is not purely defensive, not only a rear-guard action that leaves one whole but in the lurch. When Jesus protects, he also promotes, as his protection led to Nebuchadnezzar's promotion of Shadrach, Meshach, and Abednego. Followers see so much of Jesus's power, presence, and purpose in his Old Testament types and representations. Know Jesus as the ancient companion protector.

Like anyone, he had been on both sides of wrongs, both perpetrator and victim. The victim side he didn't like any more than the perpetrator side. The whole binary thing of wrongdoer and wronged was so repetitive, depressing, and hopeless, going from one to the other and back again. As an unsuspecting and regretful perpetrator of all kinds of insensitivity, he knew that he needed obedience to a Lord's reform, an obedience that he also knew the Lord's Holy Spirit would best convey at the most-opportune moments. The thought didn't seem all that masculine, but what he felt that he needed to avoid being a *victim* was a powerful protector, one who could accompany him through nearly equally powerful wrongs. Time and again, he found that his own equanimity and modest strength was simply not enough to carry him through challenges that seemed designed to strike him right where he had no armor. Maybe that was so, he thought, that the challenges were showing him that he had weaknesses that he barely knew, could not alone remediate, and needed a protector to overcome. He had of course heard of Jesus as a companion protector but had not until recently fully realized his need for that protection. He had wanted to be a protector more so than the protected. Yet he was also realizing that Jesus had been protecting him all along. He was passing through challenges without serious wounds, not even offended or bitter. The fires had not burned. He had a powerful companion protector.

11 Responder.

Daniel 10:4.

The Old Testament also foreshadows Jesus as responding to prayer, revealing himself and his plan to those who pursue him. Daniel had been captive in Babylon since age eighteen, his God-favored wisdom having lifted him to great power at the right hand of Nebuchadnezzar and later Darius over the whole of the known world. Daniel had such wisdom because he had so much of God, having pursued him in person-to-person prayer through every challenge and trial. Prayer defined Daniel both privately and publicly. He had indeed stood so surely by God in prayerful relation as to cost him a night in the den of lions. Yet even as he had known God through prayer, he had not seen God. Then late in life, at the end of three weeks of God-pursuing self-denial, Daniel saw in a vision a man dressed in linen with a gold belt, body like topaz, and face like lightning. The man's eyes were like torches, arms and legs like bronze, and voice like a multitude. The account that the man gave to Daniel of directing God's angels over the rulers of nations made it clear that he spoke as God. The man recounted to Daniel what the Book of Truth recorded about the coming ages, including the rise and fall of nations, and the end times long coming. Among the multitude of dead, those whose names were in the book would rise to everlasting life, while those whose names the book omitted would fall to everlasting contempt. The man shared that the Messiah would come at a specific time, long after he had appeared here to Daniel.

The image of Jesus as responding personally to prayer, revealing himself and his plan, is a fitting final image or representation of Christ that the Old Testament supplies before unfolding the story of his advent. To know God, to know Christ, is a follower's goal, the ultimate pursuit. A follower does not pray to abstractions or ideals. A follower prays to God, to a person, to Christ. Daniel prayed ultimately not for elevating wisdom, not for the freedom of his captive people, but that he and others would know God. Our conditions are not as important as our relationships, and no relationship is more important than relationship with God. Prayer is the best of that relationship until God himself appears in Christ's person, when we have relationship with God in full. Daniel sought God, and God rewarded him with a vision of Christ. Daniel came to know Christ through that vision in which the man spoke of the Book of Truth and of everlasting life. Christ does not come to pass the time in idle talk. To know Christ is to know his plan for the ages and for the souls of those whose names are in his Book of Life. Daniel pursued God, and God responded. Followers have their greatest satisfaction in knowing a God who responds to prayer and responds with the greatest possible reward, which is to be eternally in his glorious presence. Jesus is the God who hears, listens, and responds.

Despite the presence of family, friends, and others in her life, she had a strong sense of being alone. That sense was not something that she sought but rather that she feared. Too often, she felt trapped in her mind, trapped in her soul, apart from and unlike others. On one hand, she knew that these feelings were not true. She was much like others and also close to others. On the other hand, she knew that these feelings represented a sort of truth. As close and alike as she was to others, she was nevertheless ultimately alone in her soul and spirit. No one else could reach her spirit, not where she felt that she needed her spirit in reach. Here, in the deepest reaches of her soul, where her deepest essence and spirit lay alone, was where she met Jesus, not the Jesus of rules or righteousness but the Jesus of spirits and souls. She knew that this extraordinary Jesus, this keeper of souls, could at any moment bring her an exquisite vision, or actually not at any moment but only at moments when she was most alone. Her realization that she was closest to Jesus when she was most alone, made her realize the grand lie of loneliness. She was never alone. When she felt alone was when she was most in reach of Jesus, nearest that grand vision that he would bring her of her eternal future in his filling presence. Just then and just there was where she learned to weep and not in mourning but in joy as the Spirit of Jesus touched her soul. She ever after treasured that touch of Jesus.

2

His Coming

Conceived. Luke 1:30. ***Swaddled.*** Luke 2:6. ***Proclaimed.*** Luke 2:10. ***Named.*** Luke 2:21. ***Consecrated.*** Luke 2:22. ***Consolation.*** Luke 2:25. ***Redeemer.*** Luke 2:36. ***King.*** Matthew 2:1. ***Alien.*** Matthew 2:14. ***Insurgent.*** Matthew 2:16. ***Returned.*** Matthew 2:16. ***Aware.*** Luke 2:49. ***Grown.*** Luke 2:52.

Having committed our wonder to the Old Testament record prefiguring Christ, we may then appreciate the poignancy and perfection of Jesus's birth, the long-heralded coming of the incarnate Messiah. Followers cannot fully appreciate the calling and ministry of Christ without first embracing his advent. For the image and Word of God to walk, talk, and teach among us, not to mention to miraculously make wine and bread, walk on water, calm the storm, raise the dead, instantly heal, and perform other miracles, requires a paradigm-shattering breaking through. God is Spirit, not ordinarily flesh. Many believe in a spiritual god without acknowledging the historic fact that God took on human form, character, and constitution. God could have done much without having taken human form and fallibility. Creation and all sorts of other miracles would still have been possible. Yet God could not have done as he did without taking human form. He could not have subjected himself to human temptation, given himself to human ridicule, and risen alive from a very horribly human death. God could not have set the perfect example before us to give us not only the complete teaching but the complete model and pattern for human life and form. Advent, coming, incarnation made these things not only possible but also compelling and compelled. By taking human form, God predestined, fulfilled, and accomplished all that the Old Testament heralded, New Testament documented, and subsequent ages proved. That precious Christmas spirit is true. Followers in some sense have all that they need in Jesus's coming. What a rich and satisfactory record God has given us on which to dwell over the coming of his glorious Son.

12 Conceived.

Luke 1:30; *see also* Matthew 1:20.

The account of Jesus's birth begins with the description of Jesus as Spirit conceived. Elizabeth was already six months pregnant with the child who would become John the Baptist. God then sent the angel Gabriel to tell Elizabeth's young relative Mary that God so favored her that she would bear the savior Jesus. Gabriel told Mary that Jesus would be Son of the Most High, reigning in an endless kingdom. Though initially frightened, even stunned, Mary only wanted to know how she would conceive the incarnate Son of God when she was a virgin already betrothed to Joseph. Gabriel answered that the power of the Most High would overshadow Mary when the Holy Spirit came to Mary, so that Mary would indeed bear the Son of God as Spirit conceived. Gabriel also told Mary that her older relative Elizabeth who had long been barren was already six months pregnant, just as an angel had told Elizabeth's priest husband Zechariah, proving again that God's word never fails. Mary replied simply that she was the Lord's servant, inviting that God fulfill Gabriel's word, upon which Gabriel disappeared. Mary promptly visited the pregnant Elizabeth whose unborn child John leapt in the womb at hearing the voice of the mother of the Savior whom John would grow to herald. Filled with the Holy Spirit, Elizabeth prophesied to Mary that Mary would indeed bear the Lord, while Mary burst into song glorifying the Lord.

While some shy away from the virgin birth, the image of Jesus as Spirit conceived is critical to sound reflection on him. Jesus's divinity is at the core of what distinguishes him from any great philosopher-martyr. Yes, Jesus's many miracles, particularly but not exclusively his raising the dead, indicated that he was from God. Yet Jesus has not been the only one to perform miracles. The New Testament records other miracles through the apostles Peter and Paul, and even the Damascene Ananias who healed Paul's blindness. While Jesus had to be fully human to complete his redemptive work, he also had to be fully divine to be the Son and exact representation of God. The only possible way to resolve that seeming contradiction is that a virgin would conceive through God's own Holy Spirit. The divine child would then be both human and divine, carrying at least the figurative DNA, whether also the literal DNA, of both divine Father and human mother. Jesus as incarnate God was both perfectly like us and perfectly unlike us, in a sense like any child is perfectly like and unlike its own biological mother. As man, Jesus could feel every human temptation and endure every human suffering but yet, in full divinity, maintain his perfect stance toward the will of the Father as the exact representation of the Father's being. A follower must know Christ's nature and origin. The Gospel record gives the follower both, exactly as much as required.

While he knew that others rejected the virgin birth as foolhardy and preposterous, even after genetic study and captivity appeared to confirm rare virgin births at least in animals, he could hardly think of Jesus without trusting in Jesus's virgin birth. Jesus's origin in human mother and divine Spirit made so much sense for who Jesus was and what he accomplished. He knew Jesus as both fully human and fully God, the only way *to* know Jesus if one was to reconcile all that he said and did. Jesus could not be part one and part the other, of which one could hardly make any sense in any case. God is either God or man, not part one and part the other, because to be part anything other than God would not to be God. Likewise, man is either man or not man, not part man and part something other, because to be part anything other than man would not to be man. To suffer the full temptation of man, Jesus had to be fully human. To perform such miracles and accomplish his redemptive work, Jesus had to be divine. Immaculate conception simply wasn't something that myth would have generated to resolve such a difficult but perfect puzzle, to herald a sacrificially redemptive Son of God. For him, the virgin birth made the full Gospel story all the more real rather than any more imagined. It solved the insoluble puzzle. He knew and embraced that Mary's conception by the Holy Spirit became the world's portal to the divine. God had broken into the world's enemy territory through the Most High's overshadowing of a humble virgin, exactly, he felt, like any Supreme Power would enter its own universe.

13 Flesh.

John 1:14.

After conception, comes flesh. The three Gospels of Matthew, Mark, and Luke, we know as the *synoptic* Gospels because they relate similar stories from similar though also different views. Matthew gives Jesus's genealogy and conception story. Mark says nothing specific of Jesus's conception and birth. Luke gives the greatest detail of both conception and birth. Following sections recount the images that Matthew and Luke give us of Jesus's conception and birth. John, though, treats the spiritual dimensions of Jesus's birth. John gives followers the critical account of Jesus as the Word become flesh, the glorious Son full of grace and truth who came from the Father to dwell among us. Do not miss the striking image that John's account gives us: conception turned Word into flesh. Mary conceived through God's Holy Spirit, just as the angel's word said, making the Word into living, breathing, and altogether *human* flesh. As John put the never-before, never-again event, conception brought the true light into the world that God had made through him and that *was his own*. John continued that although the world neither recognized nor received him, Jesus made those who did receive him *children of God*, indeed, *born* of God.

John's account provides followers with multiple striking images. The image of Jesus as the Word become flesh gives followers endless depths to plumb. To many, God is merely a theological construct, a mere concept for study or, just as bad or worse, to ignore. Well then, in Jesus, the *concept* became *flesh*, a living and breathing incarnate God in human form, walking, talking, and acting among us. Of course, God is no mere concept but the very creator of both the material and beings that he together with his Word of God Son first conceived. They, Father and Son, talked about it and then God *made it happen*. He spoke the words, and humans existed. He then sent his angel to speak again, and the Word who was his image and the embodiment of all that he would speak and will, became flesh. In direct sense, with the conception and birth of Jesus, the creator became the conceived, the maker becoming the made. John's Gospel describes something that, stunning that it can happen at all, must then happen only once. Imagine the designer becoming the design, the engineer becoming the engine. God *broke through* in Jesus, turning the heavenly dilly-dallying of mythic gods into an earthbound reality that was all his own. And in the name of Jesus, that reality became a saving *mission* all his own. History had suddenly hinged or unfolded. The Book of Life was now open for anyone to study God's now-in-the-flesh Word.

He had often puzzled over word becoming flesh, or in this one divine instance, *the Word* becoming flesh. Just what could a word or moreover the Word *becoming flesh* possibly mean? He had a sense both of the power and superfluity of words. Words were all at once essential and profound in creating and carrying meaning while simultaneously empty, trite, or too-often twisted, and therefore meaningless. People needed *actions*, not words, even if without words actions would themselves be purposeless and meaningless. Yet then he thought that maybe, just maybe, what the world needed was for a word to become *flesh with a truth mission*, and not just any word, any flesh, or any mission, but *the* Word become *immaculate* flesh on a *saving* mission. Maybe, just maybe, the thought of thought itself (for what are words but thoughts?) *becoming* something, or indeed becoming some*one* on history's one critical mission was an especially important thought. And what was history's one critical mission other than to give *saving meaning* to humankind's existence? So maybe, he thought again, this Word-become-flesh image was the single most profound thought possible for all humankind. Maybe this Word-become-flesh thing wasn't just an idle or entertaining thought but instead the one thing that anyone who cared to think must think if they just once give full attention to deep and authentic thought. That moment was when he realized that in Jesus as Word-become-flesh, he finally had embraced the origin and end of thought.

14 Swaddled.

Luke 2:6.

A central image of Jesus's coming, known by all and adored by many in the Christmas spirit, is the divine infant as a swaddled-in-the-manger babe. Joseph and Mary were already pledged for marriage when Mary conceived of the Holy Spirit. Learning of Mary's pregnancy before they had any intimacy, Joseph thought of divorcing her quietly, but an angel appeared to Joseph in a dream, confirming that the child she bore was the Holy Spirit's. So Joseph took Mary as his wife, avoiding any union until she should deliver the baby whom they were to name Jesus, meaning *he who saves*. Mary would not, though, deliver Jesus in the comfort and security of their Nazareth home. Rome had ordered a census. Mary and Joseph had to travel to the town of David, Bethlehem, to register there because Joseph was of Israel's great king's ancestral line. With the census crowds filling Bethlehem, Mary and Joseph had no place to stay, even when Mary began to deliver the baby Jesus. The Bible account says that Mary gave birth, wrapped the baby Jesus in cloths, and placed him in a *manger*, the stone trough or wood rack or box for livestock feed, particularly hay, straw, or other loose material. From the manger account, Mary must have given birth in livestock quarters, which for the location and period were typically in caves or other low or excavated areas beneath or away from human quarters. Mary may have laid the swaddled Jesus in the manger for the drying and sheltering warmth of the loose animal feed.

The image of Jesus as a swaddled babe is powerfully evocative, especially in its tenderness and the vulnerability with which it first represents the incarnate Lord. We see Jesus first as a baby, ordinary in appearance but extraordinarily humble in presentation. The Bible need not have described Mary swaddling Jesus and laying him in a manger. It need not have told the world that the inns were full so that Mary delivered Jesus in cave-like animal quarters. Jesus could have come to a ruler's house or at least could have been born in moderate comfort and security, and with the usual family fanfare, like so many other newborn babes. He was not. His birth was instead socially ignominious, inhospitably low, almost mockingly humble, likely physically desperate, and from the world's standpoint utterly unheralded. No trumpets sounded, no joyful relatives visited, and no birth announcements went out. The image of Jesus as a swaddled babe lying in a manger stands in utter contrast to the miraculous, spectacular, and magnificent appearances prefiguring and post-figuring the incarnate, glowing-metal, brilliant-light Lord. What we have here in the image of the manger-laid infant is the wholly human character of the incarnated Divine. Jesus was still right then the King of kings and Lord of lords, the almighty and eternal Word of God and Holy One. Yet he was making himself so utterly human and humble that at his coming, followers could do nothing other than weep in infant-tendered awe.

He had little doubt that he had come to Jesus through Jesus's virgin birth, through the mystery, wonder, and majesty of what children know as simply *Christmas*. His earliest and strongest sense of the divine presence was in that Christmas image of the Spirit-conceived babe in the manger, an image that so warmed his heart, secured his spirit, and enlarged his mind. So many representations and traditions of Christmas, from advent calendars with tiny hidden gifts to Nativity scenes and midnight services basked in candle and song, felt soaked in that divine presence centered so acutely on the manger-cradled infant. He treasured every one of those representations of the swaddled infant because in the image he felt closest to the divine. God held every fear for him that God should hold for every person. Every person sins, while God countenances no sin. He knew that judgment was coming for him as for everyone. Yet how could he or anyone fear a swaddled infant lying in a manger? God had made himself available to all, his availability most evident not in the teacher Jesus, the healer Jesus, or the crucified Jesus but in the swaddled Jesus. An infant wound in cloth can do nothing other than share most generously his tiny but magnificent presence. That image gave him the strong sense that when in very old age all other inspiration failed him and he had precious little faith left to which to cling, he would lay his weary head in the manger next to that tiny divine infant. Jesus's virgin birth would forever remain his polestar reflection.

15 Proclaimed.

Luke 2:8.

A next image of Jesus to which sensitive followers sometimes look is that of the shepherds visiting the newborn infant still lying swaddled in the manger. Shepherds of that day lived in nearby fields, watching over their sheep at night. These shepherds would have had no natural reason to leave their flocks to visit a newborn baby. Doing so would leave the flock unprotected. Yet this night, the Lord's glory shone brightly about them as the Lord's angel appeared to address them. The angel's appearance of course terrified the shepherds until the angel reassured them that he brought good news, indeed such good news that all the people would soon rejoice. A woman in Bethlehem had just given birth to the Savior, Messiah, and Lord, wrapping him in cloths and laying him in a manger. As if that appearance and announcement were not enough for the shepherds, a great heavenly company suddenly appeared with the angel to praise God and assure peace to those on whom God's favor rests. The shepherds had no choice but to seek out this Savior Bethlehem child, finding him exactly as the angel had said. The shepherds then told others what they had learned and seen of the infant Messiah, amazing everyone whom they told. The Bible account concludes with the shepherds returning to their fields praising God that they had seen things just as the angel had told them.

The account of the angel announcing the Christ child to the stunned shepherds makes an important contribution to a follower's image of the coming of the savior Jesus. The moment of Christ's birth was extraordinary in every supernatural respect if to the contrary quite ordinary in natural respects. Divinity on earth, not humanity on earth, is extraordinary. Christ's birth should thus have had and indeed did have a supernatural rather than natural announcement. Angels do not just appear for any reason for common communication. The angel's appearance to ordinary shepherds at their ordinary field work late at night was especially unusual. These most-credible witnesses to the divine birth had no prior stake in the matter. They were much more like the ordinary bystander eyewitness, certainly not esteemed religious officials who would have had much for which to contend over seeing and hearing an angel. Equally so, confirming the baby in the manger must have been odd to the shepherds, just as the manger story would sound odd to us if we didn't know the story of Jesus's birth so well. Babies lie in baby beds, not generally in mangers. One doesn't see a baby in the manger every night. That the angel described the baby Jesus in that precise if unusual respect presumably confirmed for the shepherds that they had witnessed exactly what the angel reported. They were the first other than mother and father to see the incarnate Messiah. Their response, to amaze everyone with the news while praising God, was perfect. History offered only one birth of the Savior

Lord. The shepherds were the ones to receive and share its supernatural announcement and first ones to see him.

She had from the story of Jesus's birth the strongest sense of parity, equity, access, and opportunity. The circumstances of his birth told her that she had access to God while assuring her that no one had any greater or lesser access than she did. Parity meant something to her. She had a visceral reaction against the thought of insiders and outsiders, never having wanted to be a member of any special club that excluded others. She wasn't even sure what had made her feel that way, but she knew how firmly she did feel that way. Of course, she saw Jesus's birth as extraordinarily humble. Yet its humility was not only in the location and circumstances of the actual birth. She especially identified with the humble circumstances of and shocking revelation to the shepherds. The realization had come to her later rather than earlier in life, probably from reading or hearing a message. Yet no matter the source, she now often felt as if she was one of those shepherds. She just generally went along doing her ordinary work like the shepherds had been doing their work late that night, when at times the thought would suddenly occur to her that God had broken into the universe. Sometimes, the sensation was almost as strong as if an angel had appeared to remind her that the Savior was born, *her* Savior as much as anyone else's Savior. She could be an ordinary shepherd, just doing her ordinary work, and still be the first to share the news of this glorious Savior. God didn't make clubs. God made people, and he made them to announce and celebrate the Savior. She would then return to her figurative flock, singing God's praises so gladly.

16 Named.

Luke 2:21.

The account of Jesus's circumcision and naming, although brief, is nonetheless valuable to followers. The Bible account states simply that when on the eighth day after his birth the time came to circumcise the infant, he was named Jesus. The brief account does not identify who presented Jesus or who circumcised him. Very likely, Mary's husband

Joseph, putatively the father even though here instead the husband of the child-bearing virgin Mary, would have presented the newborn Jesus to a priest in Bethlehem eight days after the infant's birth for his circumcision and naming. We have already seen that in the earlier account of the dream of Mary's husband Joseph, an angel appeared telling Joseph to accept the Spirit-conceived infant. The angel was more specific and forthcoming about the infant's name. Joseph was to name the infant *Jesus* specifically because he would save his people from their sins. The name *Jesus* means and sounds like *he saves*. In the Jewish law and tradition, the eighth day was when the parents would have a priest circumcise their male newborn. Circumcision's symbolic purpose was clear. God had instructed Abraham to circumcise males as a sign of their belonging to God. Circumcision thus connected Jesus to Old Testament law and covenant, although Jesus came to fulfill the law rather than simply be subject to it. Just as Christians celebrate Jesus's birth on December 25th, Christian tradition has at times and in places celebrated the circumcision and naming of Jesus on January 1st, New Year's Day, as the Feast of Circumcision.

The naming of Jesus holds so much power, meaning, and relationship for followers. The name's meaning is instant and unmistakable. Jesus *saves*. Oh, you mean Jesus? *He saves.* The Father sent an angel to Joseph with the name that the Father had chosen for his Son. Joseph dutifully named the infant *Jesus*. Given the Son's salvation message and mission, the Father could hardly have named the Son anything other than he-saves Jesus, which others know or prefer as Joshua, Yehoshua, or Yeshua in other languages, translations, or interpretations. The names all mean the same simple but abundantly and critically profound thing. The Father gave his only Son that whoever believed in him would not die but would instead live eternally. The Son came not to judge the world but to save it through him. Jesus is a world saver, the world's Savior. This salvation is not alone some intimate and deeply personal thing but also the defining movement in all of history, the great Act around which all history hinges and the world turns. Followers know and fully appreciate the profound meaning of the name *Jesus*. The Father's communication of that name through an angel to the faithful Joseph, and Joseph's dutiful carrying out of the naming eight days after Christ's birth at Christ's covenant- and law-honoring circumcision, are events that followers can and should return to, reflect on, and treasure.

He had taken long, likely far too long, to appreciate Jesus's name as fully as he ought to have done so. Before committing in earnest to following Jesus, he had regarded the name as curious, even a slight obstacle to the kind of intimate respect and devotion that he had already sensed that he wanted with this strangely attractive Lord. That faintly negative association with the name *Jesus* may have come from the culture's subtle indoctrination against the name, from the rough parodies of fictional followers using the name in obviously silly, trite, or offensive ways. He had first to get past those parodies to begin to understand and respect the name. Fortunately, he soon did so, first from appreciating the name's direct meaning so perfectly associated with the Gospel message that Christ embodied, then more gradually afterward. He gradually came to appreciate a kind of deeper meaning for names in general and for Jesus's name in particular, connected with the kingdom of heaven, the Book of Life, and eternity. His own name, he realized, had its own spiritual meaning that he could now see God had mysteriously connected with what he now perceived was his eternal destiny. From Genesis to Revelation, names were so important. His name and Jesus's name each had their deeper eternal meanings, the sort of *I am* meanings that define more than the person and person's destiny but also the person's relationship with God. With this understanding, he found that Jesus's name came to take on a sweetness and intimacy that he had once thought not possible. Oh, how glad he was for that name.

17 Consecrated.

Luke 2:22; *see also* Exodus 13:2, 12.

Like the brief account of Jesus's naming, the brief account of Jesus's consecration, mentioned in Luke's Gospel as if only in passing, holds substantial value for followers' reflection. Joseph and Mary were clearly following Jewish law in caring for the infant Jesus. They had him circumcised exactly according to Moses's law and of course named him as the Father himself had commanded. They next provided for Jesus's consecration to God exactly as Moses's law required for the firstborn son in any family. The Jews devoted and sacrificed the firstborn of their livestock and first fruit of the harvest to God in dedication, blessing, and gratitude. Other area religions compelled child sacrifice. Egypt's Pharaoh had condemned male Jewish children, Herod slaughtered the children of Bethlehem in an effort to kill Christ, and nations today abort tens of millions of children, but the Jews of Jesus's day would of course not literally sacrifice a firstborn child or any other child. They instead consecrated firstborn males to the Lord in a purification ceremony at Jerusalem, sacrificing only a pair of doves or pigeons while celebrating the child's dedication to the Lord. Joseph and Mary dutifully made the trek to Jerusalem with the newborn Jesus to accomplish Jesus's consecration in just that law-required fashion. Jesus's consecration, though, was unique. Jesus was to be God's unique Son, as two consecration events described in the following sections further confirmed.

Followers probably seldom think of the specific image of Jesus's consecration to God in purification rites at Jerusalem. After all, he was the Son of God, so peculiarly conceived of the Holy Spirit and thus already so fully and closely tied to the Father as to make redundant a traditional purification and dedication rite. That we seldom reflect on Jesus's consecration may be an unfortunate oversight. If the law required consecration of a firstborn son, as it clearly did, then Jesus would himself have likely insisted on it if he had been of age and his parents had hesitated, knowing even then what they already did of his peculiar savior-Son relationship to his divine Father. Jesus himself would later insist on his baptism by John as appropriate to law and religious order. He came not to contradict or alter the law but to fulfill the law. His consecration was appropriate and important. What followers may too-often miss is why it was so important. Spirit conception, law circumcision, holy naming, and other divine markers and events were also important. Yet at some moment, a child's parents, family, mentor, pastor, or other representative and advocate may have to stand directly before God to give the child into his full care for a lifetime's holy mission, if the child is to follow and fulfill that mission. Such, at least, was the sense and symbolism, and accepted effect, of consecration rites. As odd as it may seem at first thought, Jesus may have needed but in any case clearly had and received his due consecration, one that had a spectacular result like no other.

She began to sense her consecration to the Lord at just the moment that she sensed her first strong need for a life's mission. Maybe, she thought later, she should have had a consecration ceremony. Maybe she had missed an important rite. She knew though that her parents had indeed devoted her to the Lord, if not in ceremonial act, then in frequent prayer and by example. The old-fashioned way that she and others sometimes said it was that her parents had *raised her right.* Yet what they really meant is that her parents had given her over to the Lord. Parents may have some influence over a child's character development, she believed, in part through discipline and more largely through example, but she also felt that parents have little real power over the course and future of a child. She had seen too often kids from solid families go badly wrong but also kids from not-so-solid families go very right. She believed that parents depend on God's shelter, care, protection, and discipline for a child to come out right. In her personal sense of consecration, then, she was relying more and more on God. And he in turn was giving her a greater and greater sense of devotion to him. He was placing examples and opportunities before her while also protecting and caring for her in just the way that she needed. She was learning to treasure the image of Jesus's consecration as the best example of her own.

18 Consolation.

Luke 2:25.

The account of the infant Jesus as consolation to Israel is, like the account of his consecration to God, likely one that followers do not often recall for productive reflection. The devout and righteous Simeon had waited in Jerusalem to see the consolation of Israel, indeed waited so long and earnestly that the Holy Spirit was on him, informing him, promising him that he would not die before seeing God's Messiah. The same Spirit moved him to enter the temple courts just as Joseph and Mary brought Jesus in for purification rites and consecration. Simeon took the infant Jesus in his arms, praising God as he did so. Utterly consoled and knowing that his life was now complete, Simeon praised aloud that God could now dismiss him in peace because he had seen salvation's light for revelation to the Gentiles and the simultaneous glory of Israel. Simeon then blessed the marveling parents Joseph and Mary, although his blessing included a caution that the infant would cause the rise and fall of many. Many would speak against Jesus, who would thus reveal their thoughts and hearts. Simeon also had a warning for Mary that through the infant a sword would pierce her own soul, too. The account of Jesus as Israel's consolation has many details to recommend it to followers for productive reflection.

The image of Simeon taking Jesus in his arms as Israel's consolation—imagine that!—may be the most precious of all reflections for Christ's most intimate followers. Mary held the infant Jesus in her arms, as Joseph also must often have done so, but they were the child's parents and so were doing as any parent would have done. Simeon though was a stranger to the family and only knew this infant as the savior Son of God and consolation of Israel. Yet he *held the Son of God in his arms*. How he must have later wept over his fortune not just to have heard of the Savior's coming, not just to have seen that coming, but to have *held the Savior* in his own most-human arms. The Bible account calls this infant the *consolation* of Israel, while in Simeon we see how instantly and deeply the infant consoled. As Simeon had waited a lifetime for the answer to his yearning and reward for his faith, Israel had for a millennium and a half sought its own consolation for its struggle with God. Israel's consolation, its reward and relief, came just as instantly with the appearance of Christ as Simeon found instant relief in holding the infant in his own arms. Not all of Israel would recognize and accept Jesus as Christ, but Israel's continued struggle with God would not change that Jesus was indeed Israel's consolation. Simeon knew and spoke that truth through none less than the Holy Spirit.

He struggled, he knew. He found that it helped to admit his struggles, to himself at least. No one else seemed much interested in hearing about them, just as he wasn't that much interested in sharing them. Sharing struggles sounded too much like whining and complaining, in which he had no interest. He didn't even want to whine or complain to himself. Instead, he found that admitting to himself his own struggles had a way of helping him look forward to consolation. Initially, he wasn't sure what that consolation might be. Some consolations were short term, like putting one's sore feet up at night. Yet gradually he found that the kind of consolation toward which his struggles pointed him was not a creature-comfort consolation, like a quiet hour in front of mindless television. Rather, the consolation toward which his heart seemed to point him was deeper, spiritual, and even eternal. He found that he didn't mind struggling as long as he struggled *for* something, or maybe instead the deeper truth was that he needed to struggle for *someone*, even *with* someone. That realization was it, then. He needed both a human and divine consolation, both a short- and long-term consolation, both a spiritual and practical consolation. That reward would be true salvation, one which he was increasingly finding only in Jesus. As he read the consolation story once again, he began to identify much more deeply with Simeon. He began to embrace Jesus fully not just as needed savior but also as needed relief, solace, and reward.

¹⁹ Redeemer.

Luke 2:36.

Luke's Gospel in the same place gives us the helpful account of Jesus coming as redeemer. Just as Simeon had waited in Jerusalem for the consolation of Israel, the prophetess Anna made the great temple her home. The account says that she *never left* the temple, instead worshiping, fasting, and praying there both day and night. The account does not exactly say whether, like Simeon, Anna was waiting in Jerusalem for something or someone specific, only that she was always at the temple in worship, fast, and prayer. She may have been at the temple for very long because the account says that she was *very old*, indeed specifically eighty-four years old. She likely had little to distract her, having been widowed after just seven years of marriage. If married at around sixteen years as could easily have been the case from the custom, then Anna may have been widowed for sixty-one years. If she spent most or all of those widowed years at the temple, then she may have been at the temple for roughly three generations, a fixture of devotion if ever there was one. Unlike with the account of Simeon, we do not know what moved Anna, although such timely and timeless devotion must, as we know in the case of Simeon, have been the Holy Spirit's work. At the very moment that Simeon had taken the infant Jesus in his arms, praised God, and blessed Joseph and Mary, Anna also approached the parents. She, too, thanked God. Anna, though, spoke about Jesus to all who were looking forward to *redemption* rather than consolation. Jesus had another role and another great figure of devotion to announce it to all who were looking for it.

The image of Jesus as redeemer marks an important shift from Christ as consolation. Israel had waited long for the Messiah, making Jesus sure consolation for that wait. As God's chosen who had wandered, worshipped, exiled, and waited so long, Israel might claim to have earned the Messiah as consolation. Yet Israel, indeed the world, needed more than mere consolation. Something had long been terribly wrong with both Israel and the wider world. While humankind might claim progress, history was in fact a long hall of horrors. The chosen nation and wider race had both offended God deeply, constantly, and endlessly. Human corruption was obviously so deep and constant, and human character so hopelessly twisted, that progress, if it had in fact occurred at all, had not occurred at anything like a necessary pace. Progress could not eradicate the deep and embedded stain in any case. Only transformation could save Israel and save the world. The Gospel account does not tell the reader what Anna had seen over her eighty-four years to know that humankind needed redemption. Losing a husband after just seven years before spending widowed generations witnessing broken souls cry out to God at the temple would be an obvious answer. Worship has a way of revealing the need for redemption. Praise God that Anna saw redemption come.

From her earliest memory, she had sensed her need for something that she only much later learned was *redemption*. She had always felt just a little broken and sometimes more than just a little. Everyone struggled in the world, she knew, and not just against the world but against something within themselves that made things even harder for them in an already-hard world. Yes, the world held spectacular beauty and tenderness, and people could also be amazingly generous and kind. Yet the world also held an awfulness that infected people, and vice versa that people far too often held an awfulness that infected the world. She knew that she was not immune from the infection and infecting. She almost felt as if she had two selves, the good one and the bad. And she just didn't like the bad. The hard thing about the bad stuff that she involuntarily brought into the world was not just that it was hard immediately but that it left things hard later, in fact forever. She had a hard time forgiving herself, if forgiving one's self was even possible. She knew that her problem was that she had offended a very holy, very loving God. Her brokenness and corruption kept her a distance from God, and the distance hurt, drying out her spirit like a hot wind until she felt brittle and ready to crack. That brittleness was how she came to know Jesus so well. For in the end, her only way out of the hard place in the hot sun was in her Savior's sheltering redemption. That rich, spirit-easing redemption became the engine of her passion for worship.

20 King.

Matthew 2:1; *see also* Micah 5:2.

The beloved account of the Magi, or wise men, visiting the infant Jesus as Israel's newborn king ranks with followers right alongside the treasured image of the swaddled infant Jesus in the manger. Whatever may be the popular telling of the story, the account in Matthew's Gospel makes clear that the Magi first visited Jerusalem to find out where they might locate the Jews' newborn king to worship him. The account states that they had seen the newborn king's star, suggesting that they were astrologers, but needed help from Israel's people to locate their newborn king. Their questions alerted King Herod, disturbing him along with the rest of Jerusalem. The chief priests and law teachers whom Herod called together told Herod that Bethlehem would be the Messiah's birthplace according to the Old Testament. Herod in turn met secretly with the Magi to find out just when they had seen the star, conscripting them to find the child in Bethlehem and report back to him. Herod told the Magi that he, too, wanted to worship the newborn ruler but in fact had opposite designs in mind. The star indeed led the overjoyed Magi right to Mary with the infant Jesus, to whom the Magi bowed in worship and gave their gifts of gold, frankincense, and myrrh. The Magi did not report back to Herod, though, a dream having warned them of Herod's evil intentions for the child. They instead fled home, avoiding Jerusalem.

Followers probably have several reasons to treasure the richly complex image of the Magi worshipping the infant Jesus in Bethlehem as Israel's newborn king. Centrally, its theme simply confirms what

Joseph, Mary, the shepherds, Simeon, Anna, and many others by then already knew, which was that Jesus was the Messiah. Confirmation can come in many forms, though. Lowly shepherds honoring the infant is one thing, while mysterious astrologer-wise men from the East doing so is quite another. The otherworldly source of the Magi's insight, from their celestial studies and the extraordinary star that they followed, lends a supernatural quality to the account, as does their standing as wise men. That their celestial studies worked in tandem with the Old Testament prediction further confirms that the divine ordained the moment and place of Christ's coming. Yet those wonders merely serve as backdrop for the royally mystic quality of the event itself with the worshipfully bowing wise men giving the infant Christ the symbolic gold, frankincense, and myrrh gifts. Followers know the symbolism. The precious metal gold represents Christ's kingship; the frankincense perfume was for Christ as high priest; and the anointing-oil myrrh prefigured his embalming following his crucifixion death. The Magi account so well represents our glorious, sacrificial high-priest Christ the King.

He loved the story of the wise men worshipping the infant Christ, as he supposed that everyone did. The little crèche scenes just confirmed the tenderness, mystery, and strange majesty of the nearly surreal event. He realized as he reflected on the event that its attraction came in large part because wise men don't ordinarily worship an infant. Wise men today, he thought, make a point of not worshipping anything other than themselves and their own wisdom. While he, too, had the ambition to be wise, like so many others whom he knew had the same ambition, he simultaneously felt that worldly wisdom wearied one more than worldly wisdom secured and satisfied. For all of the bad consequences from foolishness, he knew that he would rather be wise than foolish. Yet he suspected that the wisdom of the worldly wise was more like foolishness. What he wanted was a wisdom that recognized its limitations, one that submitted itself and its owner to truth. That truth character seemed to be just the curious majesty of the Christ infant who in his Word-personifying coming both personified *and* personalized truth. The wise men were indeed wise to submit in worship to the Christ infant. They, just like Simeon and Anna from slightly different perspectives, knew that in Christ, wisdom had reached the fulfillment of its story. He, too, felt his wisdom grow rather than recede when submitting likewise to Christ's worship, and not just in worship of the mature and insightful Christ but also to the Christ infant. God's foolishness is indeed far greater than human wisdom.

21 Alien.

Matthew 2:14; *see also* Hosea 11:1.

Followers may too-often overlook the power and apparent purpose of the account of Joseph and Mary escaping with the infant Jesus from Bethlehem to Egypt. Just after the Magi had left, the Lord's angel appeared to Joseph in a dream. The angel told Joseph to wake and escape to Egypt with Mary and the infant Jesus. Joseph was to remain in Egypt until the angel summoned him because Herod was searching for Jesus in order to kill him. Joseph of course complied. He got right up in the night, leaving with Mary and Jesus for Egypt immediately. The account does not tell the reader where in Egypt they resided or how their sojourn treated them. Followers do not know the fear that might have gripped the young couple, their midnight flight's hardship on the new mother and newborn infant, their means or route of transport, or the circumstances and insecurity of their Egyptian stay. How, other than in hardship, does a new family take up residence as aliens in a foreign land? Did Joseph find work for the family's provision? Did they stay among Jews with whom they shared a language and traditions or among Egyptians with whom they had no affinity and whom they may have justly feared? One hopes that they found sufficient kindness of the sort that young families can attract even in foreign lands. Yet in any case, there Joseph, Mary, and Jesus remained until Herod had died, Herod's threat passing with him. The account ends by saying that in this manner, Joseph and Mary fulfilled what the Lord's prophet Hosea had said, which was that the Lord would call his son out of Egypt.

The image of Jesus as an alien in Egypt first becomes an important one for followers in just that respect. Jesus's coming was fulfilling Old Testament prophecy. His birth had to be in Bethlehem, and so hence Rome's decree for a census required Joseph and Mary to travel to Joseph's ancestral home of Bethlehem. Yet the Lord must also call his Son out of Egypt, and so hence Herod's threat, Joseph's dream, and the flight of Mary and Joseph to Egypt. Herod may thus in part have been only the Lord's instrument so that the Lord would fulfill prophecy by calling his Son Jesus out of Egypt. To be the Messiah, Jesus must fulfill Messiah prophecy, which he now could in coming out of Egypt. Yet the out-of-Egypt prophecy had its own symbolism beyond confirming the identity of Christ. Egypt had been a place of refuge for the Israelites from the famine, just as it became a place of refuge for Joseph, Mary, and the infant Jesus. But Egypt provided only temporary, even false, refuge, soon enslaving the Jews. Whether refuge or prison, Egypt was a foreign land to the Jews initially, just as it would have been for Joseph, Mary, and the infant Jesus. Egypt was also largely secular—about human knowledge, power, and works—rather than God fearing. Pharaoh had met Moses miracle for miracle until Pharaoh no longer could, human works always falling short of God's powers. God must draw Jesus out of the world and to him, just as God endeavors to draw us out of the world and to him through Jesus. The world has many attractions. Even Egypt had its charms. Many Jews had protested when God used Moses and his brother Aaron to draw them out of Egypt. Humans possess some power in the world, power that too-often seems just enough for the creature comforts that we too-much desire but that never quite satisfy. Followers can draw much from the image of Jesus called out of Egypt. We, too, hear God's call when recognizing that we reside in an alien land.

The achievement had taken a long time, much longer than she later wished. Yet she had very gradually developed a sense of the difference between the world with God and without God, and moreover, a sense of when she was operating in the without-God world. The achievement was important to her pilgrim's progress. She long knew that she needed God, needing not only his redemption and salvation but also his purpose, guidance, strength, comfort, and sanctification. While she knew her strong and many needs for God, she had lacked a clear enough sense of when she was or wasn't drawing on him to fulfill them. She knew that he worked even when she didn't know his workings, but she also knew that her attention to and joyful participation in his workings might accelerate them in her. She wanted to live in his kingdom moment to moment, hour to hour, feeling its assurance, security, purity, and strength. Oddly, the strongest clue that made possible her achievement in recognizing when she was more in his kingdom or less came from the Bible's stories about the literal Egypt as thematic reference to the figurative Egypt-like secular world. She needed to identify the Godless world with a place. While today's world gave her many candidates, she didn't want to label as Godless any familiar place where she might instead find many God pursuers. Biblical Egypt thus became for her that historical place that helped her identify her own figurative Egypt. From that reference, she could more and more often tell when she was living apart from God and could also more and more hear his call that she was to return to him. The image of God calling his Son out of Egypt became for her an important marker of her own maturing.

22 Insurgent.

Matthew 2:16; *see also* Jeremiah 31:15.

Followers seem generally to know of the account of Herod giving orders to kill all newborn boys in Bethlehem just after the escape of Joseph and Mary to Egypt with the infant Jesus. The account indeed follows that of Joseph and Mary's flight to Egypt. The Magi had outwitted Herod in leaving Bethlehem by another route rather than returning to Jerusalem to report to Herod how they found and worshipped the infant Messiah, newborn King of the Jews. The account tells the reader that Herod was furious. Herod's fury was presumably because he was not accustomed to the sort of duplicitous treatment in which he himself had just engaged in enlisting the Magi in his plot to locate the infant King. Despots like Herod do not endure fury lightly, particularly when their rage is over being foiled in protecting their own tyranny. In any case, Herod had not heard from the Magi for some time after having enlisted them to locate the newborn King. While the account does not say so directly, Herod may instead have learned of the Magi's flight. He may also have heard of the celebration of the shepherds and wise men of the newborn Messiah. So in his fury, and calculating from the time he had heard from the Magi, Herod took the almost incomprehensibly horrible action of ordering the murder of all boys under two years old in and around Bethlehem, one of whom he presumed must be the infant Messiah. Yet once again in doing so, Herod was only fulfilling another Old Testament prophecy, this one that the region of Ramah, the place of the Messiah's birth, would somehow hear great weeping and mourning for her children who were no more.

The image of the infant Jesus as an extraordinarily fortunate survivor of a horrible despot's broad campaign for his murder is a sobering but important reflection for followers. The account of Jesus's coming must temper its rich tenderness, communicated so perfectly in the manger, shepherd, and wise-men stories, with the realization that many would strongly and violently oppose the Messiah and his followers. Tyrannical governments like that of the despot Herod, driven by the evil and destructive spirit, especially oppose the incarnate-divine King. Jesus brought not only love, mercy, forgiveness, salvation, and healing, but also a great struggle of spiritual forces, supreme good against entire evil. The account of Herod's murdering the children of the region is brutal reminder of the depth of that evil. Herod's effort to murder the infant Jesus also reminds readers of evil's awful imperative to oppose and defeat good, particularly and specifically the goodness that the Son of God personified and brought fully into the world. The historic coming that the manger birth, shepherd welcome, and wise men gifts made look so beautiful and benign also had a fabulously hard edge to it, hard like crystal is hard in its clarity, transparency, and purity. Jesus was about to expose wrong things at the top of the religious and governmental order while forgiving wrong things at society's powerless bottom. His coming was about to reorder the world, when the world's powerful had no interest in reordering. Evil would oppose Jesus, indeed crucify Jesus, although that, too, was only carrying out God's glorious plan through his coming. Never underestimate the awful power of evil, as Herod's murder of the children proved and history has since then proven again repeatedly. Yet never underestimate the infinitely greater power of the insurgent Jesus.

The account of Herod's murder of the children had shocked him the first time that he had read it, a shock that never wore off with each successive reading. The event seemed so utterly barbaric that he could make little out of it beyond its shock value. Herod had feared the Messiah's coming so greatly and the effect that another Jewish king might have on his own jealous rule that he was willing to kill children to hold onto his own power. Jesus was then an infant, which was why Herod had killed the children. Jesus though was also one who loved children, wanted his followers to be like children, and wanted his followers to let little children come to him. Children apparently had a place in Jesus's kingdom that children did not fully have in the world, certainly not Herod's world, but in some respects not either in the modern world. People today still literally sacrifice children to lifestyle but also figuratively do so, giving their own children up to the pursuit of power, pleasures, and lifestyles. The world's way destroys children, turning parents' hearts to worldly things, while Jesus turns parents' hearts toward children and indeed into the hearts of children. He realized, too, that he must turn his own heart toward Jesus if he was not to sacrifice his own family and child for power, productivity, and other worldly things. In this way, thinking of the parents Joseph and Mary spiriting Jesus away while Herod slaughtered the remaining children became a sort of metaphor for his own daily control of temper, appetite, and ambition, bending his own strong will to the will of Jesus for the love and care of children.

23 Returned.

Matthew 2:23; *see also* Luke 2:39.

The account of Joseph and Mary bringing the young Jesus back to Israel from Egypt occupies its own special place in the account of the Messiah's coming. With Herod's death, at least some of the mortal risk in Israel to Jesus abated. Angels had appeared to Joseph in dreams first involving Mary's pregnancy and then the necessity of the family's flight to Egypt to escape the murderous Herod. An angel appeared to Joseph in a dream yet again, this time telling Joseph to take Mary and Jesus back to Israel because those who had tried to kill Jesus were now dead. Joseph of course complied, taking Mary and Jesus back to Israel. Their problem, though, was where in Israel were they to settle? Joseph naturally thought of returning to his ancestral lands in Judea, but Herod's son Archelaus now reigned there. Joseph had sound cause to fear a continuing threat that new leaders would attempt to murder Jesus, as a dream once again warned Joseph. So Joseph instead returned to the out-of-the-way town of Nazareth in the district of Galilee, which was the former home of both Joseph and Mary. Although something like a backwater or working town, Nazareth nonetheless had important distinctions. First, Old Testament prophecy was that the world would know the Messiah as a Nazarene. Joseph's choice of a Nazareth residence fulfilled that important prophecy. Some scholars hold that Nazarene may also be a Greek reference to the Hebrew word for *branch* understood as *Messiah* or instead to Samson's people the Nazirites who took vows of consecration to the Lord. Jesus was to be a Nazarene.

Followers can draw fruitfully from the image of Jesus as returning to Israel from Egypt as a Nazarene. Aren't we all returnees? Shouldn't all followers have the sense of having been called out of the world and into the promised kingdom? We must leave the falsely attractive, secular Egypt, just as Jesus left Egypt, to return to that place for which God made us, a place that his proximity defines as his kingdom. Yet Jesus's coming out of Egypt was not simply about his return but also about his return to a particular place, Nazareth, that was to be the Messiah's home. Jesus had to fulfill the prophecy for Israel to recognize him as the Messiah. The prophecy that he would be a Nazarene, though, had its own meaning. Although conceived, born, and destined for kingship, Jesus would grow up within the community of a humble backwater town. He would be the people's eternal King, a Nazarene, not the elite's next king. Scholars, teachers, rulers, authorities, and other Judean elites would look down on anyone coming from the rural Nazareth, even while that arrogant attitude of the elites would cause the poor and downtrodden people whom Jesus came to serve and rescue to look up to and champion Jesus. Jesus would need, have, and want no trappings of majesty. An ordinary figure in every worldly respect, the divine Christ would instead carry into the world majesty itself. Jesus had to come from Nazareth.

She loved the democracy, the populist and mainstream character, of Jesus's coming. For her, Christianity had always been robust, accessible, and real rather than ephemeral, distant, and abstract. To her, Jesus was so genuinely human, so *like her* in so many respects, even though pure and divine. She had never really thought of why she felt that way about him until she reflected more deeply on the events of Christ's coming. Yes, wise men had honored him as a newborn king, but first he was born in an animal shelter, his young mother had placed him a humble manger, and equally humble shepherds had rejoiced at and announced his birth. After his dedication to the Lord and circumcision, his parents had fled with him to another land. On his return, his parents had taken him to a backwater rural town where he grew up, not to an urban seat of power, cosmopolitan style, and scholarly learning. Except for the strange, prophetic events confirming his Messiah status, his basic birth story would have suggested that he was quite ordinary, maybe even another hidden and uncounted child of poverty destined for a short life of material hardship. Yet she absolutely knew that he was indeed the Son of God and personal savior. She was so glad that such an egalitarian hero had rescued and led her. While she treasured the profundity of Christ's teaching, she was nonetheless glad that it was so straightforward, unadorned, and even rustic. She knew that she would not have followed a teacher who used big words to describe arcane, complex concepts. She felt that she, too, had come from a figurative Nazareth and was therefore so glad to follow a fellow Nazarene.

24 **Aware.**

Luke 2:49.

The account of Jesus at age twelve in Jerusalem's temple courts, saying that he was in his *Father's house*, provides followers with precious insight into Jesus's early awareness of his nature, mission, and role. Joseph and Mary traveled every year from Nazareth to Jerusalem with their relatives to celebrate the Passover festival, according to custom. Jesus accompanied his parents and relatives to Jerusalem when he was twelve years old. Apparently, though, no one kept a close eye on the young Jesus in Jerusalem. His parents and relatives traveled a day heading home before they even realized that they had left him behind. They then spent three more days back in Jerusalem trying to find him. When they did, Jesus was listening to the teachers in the temple courts and asking them questions. He was more than a mere listener and questioner, though. His words were instead having profound effect. The Gospel account says that Jesus was both understanding *and answering*. So apparently, the teachers were asking Jesus questions even as Jesus asked questions of them. Jesus's words were also having profound effect insofar as the Gospel account says that his understanding and answers *amazed everyone*. The sight of Jesus listening and speaking in the temple courts also astonished his parents

Joseph and Mary. When they told Jesus how anxiously they had searched for him, Jesus's response that he had to be *in his Father's house* confounded them. Jesus nonetheless returned obediently to Nazareth with his parents and relatives, while his mother Mary remembered and treasured these confounding mysteries in her heart.

The image of the twelve-year-old Jesus questioning the teachers in Jerusalem's temple courts while amazing everyone who listened is an especially precious one to followers. Any who have reflected on Jesus at length will have wondered when and how, as his infant's mind grew to cognizance, he came to realize his Son-of-God nature, mission, and role. This one extraordinary account gives followers the only clear glimpse into Jesus's maturation from the time of his infancy until his calling to public ministry at around age thirty. The scene's revelation, the statement of which every believer must take instant note, is that Jesus knew the temple as *his Father's* house from at least as early as age twelve. Although he may well have known from his first formed thought in infancy, the Gospel account confirms that Jesus knew God as his Father from at least when he was still a relatively young boy. How often and how much earlier he had conversed and communed with his Father through the Holy Spirit we simply do not know. Followers instead draw from this account only that at a still-tender age twelve, Jesus already knew his Son relationship to his Father. Followers can also infer that Jesus knew the words of his Father because his understanding and answers were amazing everyone including the temple teachers. Twelve-year-old children do not generally amaze their elders with their insight into theological concepts. Jesus had clearly already communicated so extensively with his Father as to have what his law-teacher hearers understood to be a finely formed theology. The temple teachers who heard Jesus those few days when he was age twelve would in good time see more-substantial direct evidence that he was whom he claimed to be, the Son of God. If they had heard and understood what he told his parents that the temple was *his Father's* house, then they might have misconstrued the twelve-year-old boy's assertion as blasphemy. When Jesus said the same thing more directly in his public ministry about twenty years later, the religious leaders had him crucified for it. Jesus was in any case both precocious and prescient even at age twelve, which should give any follower cause for tender and encouraging reflection. He knew early on that he was the Son of God.

She thought often of having her own room in the Father's house, a room that Jesus was preparing for her. She had deeply loved her father, who had been a good husband, father, provider, and man. Her childhood home had been a safe, secure, even warm place, just as the home in which she was now the mother and wife was also safe, secure, and warm. So her natural association for an eternal home was a strongly positive one for her, even while she recognized that earthly homes were not such warm, safe, secure, and positive places for less-fortunate persons. The thought though of living in the Father's house warmed and heartened her to a much greater degree than the thought of any earthly home could. She loved and trusted the Father that much, anticipating his closeness, security, and inspiration far beyond anything that the world, including even a decent earthly husband and father, could offer. She soon realized that these warming reflections on her eternal home were what made the young Jesus's statement about needing to be in his Father's house so deeply encouraging to her. She didn't have to wait for her eternal home. She could dwell in that kingdom now, as Jesus did in both literal and figurative sense when staying behind from his family to be in the temple courts communing with the Father. While she went about her day, like Jesus accompanying his family through its daily and seasonal routines, she could at any time turn slightly inward, deep into that temple that God had made of her and into which he had placed his Holy Spirit. She could be in her Father's house, no less attentive to her own and her family's needs, but still enjoying the Father's love and proximity.

25 Grown.

Luke 2:52; *see also* Luke 2:40.

These several detailed accounts of Jesus's coming end with three simple statements about his development and growth. The first of those statements says that Jesus *grew in stature* and *became strong*. As we have just seen, Jesus grew through boyhood and into adulthood in the rural Nazareth. As a boy growing to manhood in Nazareth, Jesus would likely have gotten plenty of physical labor and exercise, plenty enough to make him larger in stature and strong. A later account indicating that he was a carpenter would confirm his physical strength, especially insofar as carpenters of the day and region would have labored not just with wood but also with stone. Given the time, nature, and location of his upbringing and trade, and that the Gospel account specifically calls him *strong*, Jesus may well have been considerably more virile, hardy, and strong than the average American today. The same account, though, also says that he was *filled with wisdom*. Jesus was wise out of place and time, wise in Nazareth rather than a center of learning and wise at a young age rather than in old age or his prime. Finally, and clearly most significantly, the same account says that the *grace and favor of God* were on Jesus. God was showing Jesus favor as he grew, extraordinary favor, treating Jesus as his glorious Son. Given the Gospel account, others must have witnessed his God-favored status. Indeed, the account also says that he grew in favor *with man*, meaning that the grace of God was not merely some hidden interior thing but rather outward and evident. Although he grew in stature as an ordinary man, Jesus also had God's grace and favor upon him.

The Gospel account gives it only a couple of sentences, but the image of Jesus as grown into the fullness of human form is an extraordinary one. If Herod's murderous plan had succeeded, then the world still would have seen something revolutionary in God entering his world to take infant human form. Yet Herod failed, and so the Spirit-conceived Jesus grew into adulthood. The fullness of God took the fullness of human form. One could nearly stop the Gospel accounts right there in fully satisfactory reflection, the glory of God dwelling in *and as* a strong, wise, and grace-filled man. Oh, how much seeing the grown Jesus in the flesh must have meant to any who knew his divine identity. Knowing that God entered the world briefly in any form would be knowledge that utterly transformed what we think of the world. Here, though, was Jesus, fully God while fully human, living and growing stronger day to day, month to month, and year to year. What did he look like and how did he act as a boy or as a teen? A follower would give everything to have seen. How did Jesus reflect the wisdom and grace of God in his early and mid-twenties? A follower would not for a moment be able to look away. Thank God that the Gospels give us nothing more of these years than a sentence that he grew in strength, grace, and wisdom because the very thought of knowing more of Jesus's growth and ways makes living one's own life so much less. The Gospel account is right, though, of course. The ultimate point of Jesus's coming was that he was grown. God's mission for his Son now stood before him. Watch out, world. Jesus was here.

He drew such deep encouragement from the image of Jesus grown in strength, wisdom, and grace. Christianity probably would have been something different to him if Christ had not been a strong grown man, one skilled in and accustomed to trade work. He wasn't sure how Christianity would be different if Christ had instead been a contemplative and bookish scholar, but he thought probably more philosophical, certainly less gritty and real. Jesus must have strained and sweated in his labor, even if with God's grace. In his own labors, he drew constant encouragement from the thought of God's Son in labor. As he observed his own child and other children growing up both gracefully and awkwardly, he thought of Christ growing up among other children. The mere image of Christ growing in size, strength, and wisdom lent new dignity to those difficult formative adolescent years. No matter how awkward one might be, neither boy nor girl need have any doubt of their God-given image and form. Christ had once been an adolescent. That God had taken adolescence upon himself had changed adolescence forever, just as it had changed every stage of growth into adulthood. He needed to think more often and more deeply about Christ growing up. He also needed to think more often and more deeply about Christ fully grown. Human capacity must be so astonishingly greater after God took infant form and then grew. His body was indeed a Christ temple.

3

His Calling

Immersed. Mark 1:9. *Baptized.* Luke 3:22. *Fasted.* Matthew 4:2. *Tested.* Mark 1:12. *Powered.* Luke 4:14. *Centered.* Luke 4:42. *Supported.* Mark 15:41. *Passionate.* John 2:17. *Judge.* John 5:22. *Revealer.* Matthew 11:27. *Fulfillment.* Luke 4:18. *Family.* Matthew 12:46. *Inscrutable.* Matthew 13:1. *Life.* John 6:52. *Christ.* Matthew 16:16. *Shepherd.* John 10:9. *Joyous.* Luke 10:21. *Builder.* Matthew 16:18. *Interpreter.* Luke 12:54. *Good.* Matthew 19:17. *Celebrated.* Matthew 21:9. *Authoritative.* Matthew 21:23. *Scriptural.* Matthew 22:37. *Path.* John 14:6. *Vine.* John 15:1. *Glorifying.* John 17:4. *Commissioner.* Matthew 28:19.

The long prefiguring of Christ, tenderness of Jesus's Bethlehem coming, and power of Christ's mature ministry are all palpable stages of Christ's life to followers. Followers may not have quite as strong a sense of the *calling* of Jesus that fell between his coming and ministry, even though followers very likely do know several compelling scenes within Christ's calling. Why would Christ need a calling from God when he was already the *Son of* God? That mystery confounded even John the Baptist who was initially reluctant to baptize Christ. Jesus knew better. The Gospels may not tell the reader fully why Jesus went through what became a fairly elaborate stage of calling before embarking on his full ministry. One has almost to reflect on each rich scene of that calling to appreciate why God revealed it as an important part of the Gospel record. The glory of Jesus's calling emerges bit by bit, as if to prepare us to accept and embrace his full nature. Indeed, the unfolding of that revelation, the reader's process of internalizing and adjusting to the idea of the incarnate God, may be exactly why the Bible gradually reveals Christ's call within a sort of emergence of his full ministry. Jesus's mother, brothers, and community, even his new disciples, had also to adjust to the active ministry of their divine King. Followers do well to reflect frequently and deeply on the several profound and compelling scenes of Christ's calling in order also to internalize and adjust to the fullness of the incarnate divine King.

26 Immersed.

Mark 1:9; *see also* Matthew 1:13.

Followers properly take the account of John the Baptist immersing Jesus in the Jordan River in baptism as a momentous and defining event. Consider first the immersion itself. John of course was the son of Mary's cousin Elizabeth and the one who had leapt in Elizabeth's womb at the voice of Mary who carried Jesus. John much later in maturity fulfilled his prophetic leap by taking on the extraordinary role of the celebrated Baptist, clad in camel-hair clothes and leather belt, fed of locusts and wild honey. John had for some time preached in the Judean Desert around the Jordan River to prepare for the coming Lord. While doing so, John also baptized the many who came to him, submerging each penitent briefly in the Jordan's waters. John preached that his baptism represented repentance, a figurative drowning and cleansing, and literal turning away, from the sin that corrupted both believer and non-believer. John simultaneously railed against the religious leaders who came to listen to him, for not having produced the good fruit of repentance. His greater message, though, was that One was coming who would baptize not merely with water but with the Holy Spirit's winnowing fire. When Jesus first approached John at the Jordan's waters for his own baptism, John promptly recognized Jesus as the One, although John resisted baptizing the sinless Jesus, asking instead for his own Holy Spirit baptism from Jesus. Jesus insisted on John's water baptism as proper for all righteousness, to which John relented, baptizing Jesus as he had so many others before him. One Gospel concludes this first part of the baptism account, having to do with Jesus's immersion, with Jesus *coming up out of the water*, strongly suggesting that his immersion was total.

The image of John immersing Jesus in the Jordan River has special value for followers who reflect on its propriety and meaning. John explained water baptism's purpose to submerge the old self, destroy the old sin life, and prepare the way for the new life of the Lord's Holy Spirit. We have great need for such cleansing new life. Anyone pursuing a self-improvement plan with vigor knows in candor the fruitlessness of reforming the old self. Try as we might, reform is at best only a partial plan and one that can never produce the whole transformation that access to God requires. The sinless Father and Son will not sit down in eternity with a still-corrupt but improved sinner. The hope of the Christ-dependent life is not in reform but in transformation, in new life rather than in better life. While Jesus had no need of submergence, of literal or figurative drowning in favor of new life, we have every such need. Yet as the Son of God, to receive in full propriety and signal event the Holy Spirit, Jesus was first to receive his own immersion. Anything less would have been out of the divine and prophetic order that was Jesus's order. Jesus could not alter or contradict that order any more than he could contradict the Father whose image he was. Followers face the same opportunity as Jesus to quit the old life through water baptism in order to prepare for the Holy Spirit's new life. Followers have the same opportunity as Jesus to mark and celebrate their own water baptism preparing for the Spirit's baptism. And like Jesus, followers begin their kingdom service in earnest when leaving behind the old with water baptism and beginning the new with the Holy Spirit. God's natural, prophetic, symbolic, and spiritual order, including water baptism, constructs, defines, structures, and guides the follower's new life in Jesus.

Jesus's water baptism, his full immersion in the Jordan's waters, fascinated him. For him, the scene had so many elements to draw him closer to Jesus. The event at once combined the natural, human, social, religious, historic, symbolic, prophetic, and miraculous. The world's greatest playwright could not have constructed more exquisitely the few spare Gospel lines that tell the whole baptism story. He thought often of the wildness and passion of the desert John, the parade of penitents seeking John's strange immersion, and the sneaking and scoffing religious leaders, each constituent set in strange place solely to frame the gargantuan event that was about to shatter the world. Jesus was about to receive his call, indeed about to receive not just his call but his *Caller*, marked by the majestic descent of the Holy Spirit sent by his glorious Father. In his own feebly human way, he too had come to long for the Holy Spirit, for a counselor and guide to help him on his journey into God's kingdom. Desperate to know how he could receive and recognize the Spirit, he began to turn increasingly to the spectacular and perfectly arranged scene of Jesus's baptism. He kept seeing visions of the equally desperate penitents submerging their old selves in the Jordan's wilderness at the hands of Jesus's wild herald. He thought increasingly of his own immersion, the drowning of his old self, and coming up out of the water ready, fully and properly ready now to receive, recognize, and embrace the gorgeous Spirit. His anticipation grew, and with its growth, his senses sharpened. Baptism had prepared him for his own momentous event when God would show him that he, too, could receive and recognize the Holy Spirit.

27 Baptized.

Matthew 3:16; *see also* Luke 3:22; Mark 1:10.

For the follower of Jesus, the account of Jesus receiving the Holy Spirit, the extraordinary event that concluded the scene of his baptism in the Jordan River, marks the turning of the great ages. John had just immersed Jesus in the Jordan. The three Gospel accounts supply slightly different details of what followed. One account states that Jesus *went up out of the water* as soon as John had baptized him, at the moment of which *heaven opened*. Another account records that as Jesus came up out of the water, he saw heaven *torn open*. The third account records Jesus *praying* as heaven opened. Each account records that as heaven opened, the Spirit descended on him. While one account says that *Jesus* saw the Spirit descend, the two other accounts clearly suggest that witnesses also observed the Spirit descending, especially insofar as they record the Spirit's specific form in descent. Two of the accounts record that the Spirit descended *like a dove*. The third account adds the detail that the Spirit descended *in bodily form* like a dove. One of the accounts adds that the Spirit *lighted on him*, one supposes as a bird might light on a branch. All three accounts then record that a voice came from heaven. Each account records the voice saying precisely the same things that *you are my Son whom I love* and *with you I am well pleased*. The Father had confirmed for observers in spectacular and direct fashion the nature and propriety of the baptism on which the Son had insisted. The event must have stunned and enthralled observers, especially insofar as it concluded as quickly as it began. One Gospel account concludes that *at once* the Spirit sent Jesus out into the desert.

The image of heaven opening for the Spirit's descent on Jesus feeds the hungry follower who reflects on it. Jesus would send the Holy Spirit to followers after his earthly ministry concluded, after his resurrection. The Spirit descended on the believers at Pentecost, ushering in the new church age. Yet first, at his baptism Jesus would himself receive the Spirit so that he could then carry the Spirit during his earthly ministry. Following his baptism, Jesus would have the Spirit's constant indwelling and, with it, the Spirit's guidance, consolation, strength, and power. How that extraordinary event of Jesus receiving the Holy Spirit happened is part revelation and part mystery, the mystery resolved only in part but also accentuated in the record that heaven somehow opened for the Spirit's descent. The fact that one account records Jesus as praying while heaven opened should be no surprise insofar as Jesus was naturally in constant communion with his Father and surely would have been especially so at such a special moment. Having sent the Spirit to Jesus at that moment of his prayer, the Father then declared Jesus to be his Father-pleasing Son, both clarifying and confirming what perceptive observers might have deduced even without the Father's declaration. Yet what does *heaven opening* mean, who is the Spirit, what is the Spirit's role, and why would the Spirit take dove-like form? Subsequent Gospel teachings and events suggest important answers to these and other profound questions.

Every time that he thought of Jesus's baptism with the Holy Spirit, he could hardly get past the thought of heaven opening. Certainly, the Spirit's descent in dove-like form, alighting on Jesus, defined the baptism story for him, as much as it did for so many others. If a human, albeit the one God-incarnate man Jesus, could receive the Holy Spirit alighting on him in dove-like form, then indeed the Spirit just might also be available to him, exactly as Jesus offered in fulfillment of John's prophecy. Yet before he could fully digest that endlessly rich thought, he had first to grasp this account of heaven opening. He fully appreciated that God's home, his glorious kingdom of heaven, was its own realm, which was pretty much the problem. How could the two realms, God's so glorious and his so humble, possibly connect? The thought of the Spirit or of angels moving between realms made some sense, just as humans move between their own physical worlds, whether all locally in the workplace, social or recreational gatherings, or the home, or geographically in moving between and among locales. But the heavenly realm was not just another physical place, like the many physical places that humans move between. The heavenly realm then held the Father and his Holy Spirit, and legions of other heavenly beings, while it now also holds the Son and those whom he embraces. The heavenly realm is also somehow proximate, close, near us, perhaps in some unusual respect even within us, and available. As he thought again of heaven opening at the Jordan River, just suddenly opening as Jesus prayed, and the Holy Spirit descending from heaven's opening in dove-like form, he began to long for that opening.

28 **Fasted.**

Matthew 4:2; *see also* Exodus 34:28; 1 Kings 19:8; Mark 1:12; Luke 4:2.

The Gospels next give readers the account of Jesus heading straight from his Jordan River baptism into a forty-day time in the wilderness. The three parallel accounts say that the Spirit led or sent Jesus into and around the desert wilderness, indicating that the Father intended the Son's wilderness time and testing. Jesus's forty days in the desert were a true wilderness test, one account saying that Jesus was *with the wild animals*. While the desert wilderness isolated Jesus from others, he may not have been entirely alone during the whole experience. One Gospel account says simply that *angels attended him*. Yet a more-elaborate Gospel account makes no mention of angels until after Jesus's forty-day fast and concluding tempting in the wilderness, when the account says that angels *came and attended him*, suggesting that their ministrations solely followed the fast rather than in any respect eased it. In any case, the record makes clear that Jesus had no food for those forty days, two accounts saying only that he fasted but the third confirming explicitly that *he ate nothing*. Beyond that clarity, the Gospels give no details of the fast, only to say that when the forty days ended, Jesus was hungry. Jesus's forty-day fast echoes the forty days that Moses fasted on the mountain with God when receiving the Ten Commandments and the forty days that Elijah traveled without food on his journey to the mountain of God. Peter, James, and John would later see the transfigured Jesus conversing with Moses and Elijah. Jesus's forty-day fast also touches on the forty years that Israel spent wandering in the desert, although God fed Israel during its wandering, even while the Israelites whined over the monotony of their food during their wandering. The Gospels record no complaint from Jesus, only obedience to the Spirit's leading.

The image of Jesus fasting for forty days in the wilderness is a powerful one for a follower's reflection. Anyone who has fasted even for a short time, even as short as a day or two, can attest to a fast's purifying power. Food attracts and energizes. Its allure leads us on, and its nutrition sustains us. The absence of food forces us to rely on other things, in a voluntary spiritual fast on the sustenance and power of God. In fasting, the follower turns from natural nutrition to spiritual sustenance. Jesus proved fasting's value. The Spirit wanted to confirm for Jesus his total reliance, both physical and mental, both natural and spiritual, on God before Jesus faced one of his great challenges. A forty-day fast is beyond natural capability. Mimickers have died trying. Jesus would grow hungry in his forty day fast, but he would not die, the Father instead sustaining him. Fasting connects the physical with the spiritual. It restores the body and the body's appetites to the soul, spirit, will, and mind. Fasting may have weakened Jesus into hunger, exposing him to the following testing. But fasting also prepared Jesus for that testing, throwing Jesus entirely back on God. While a follower would not wisely attempt a forty-day fast, in Jesus's forty-day fast followers can taste of the power and purity of Godly reliance. Followers may be saved and sanctified, but for delivery they may also need to prepare. Look not to the next meal or drink but to God. Rely on him in all things, natural and spiritual.

She had tasted of the fortifying power of fasting, although not as a practice or discipline but as a surprisingly reliable route to God. She felt quite firmly that fasting had no power in itself. In fact, fasts always seemed to weaken her in ways that she did not want to be weak. Fasts revealed her dependence on food and drink. They made her woozy, hungry, and fatigued. They forced her to change habits that she found were tied to pursuing food and drink. Fasts also gave her surprising amounts of time, and not just time to *do* things but time to *think*. They made her realize how often she thought about food and drink. During a fast, she had to force herself to think about something other than food or drink, especially at her habitual times for food and drink. She found that the only reliable way to continue a fast was to immerse herself in something during those times, especially to occupy her *mind* with things, and not just aimless things but things about which she cared most deeply. Fasts forced her to find her inspiration source, the things that made her want to persevere. Fasting, like illness or injury, confirmed for her that when the natural was not available, the supernatural remained available. When food was not around, God was still around. Her closeness to God did not happen every time she fasted, and sometimes she only realized later the proximity and intimacy that she had found during the fast. But just thinking of Jesus communing with the Father during his forty days in the wilderness made her want to fast again.

29 **Tested.**

Mark 1:12; *see also* Matthew 4:3.

Followers who reflect on Jesus's forty days in the wilderness may reasonably feel that the central purpose of that time lay not in Jesus's wilderness deprivation and isolation, or even his daunting forty-day fast, but instead in his meeting head-on and overcoming the devil's temptation. While the Gospel accounts say generally that the Spirit led or sent Jesus into the desert wilderness, one account does so clearly indicating that the Father intended the Son's testing. Jesus's testing, though, was not simply the demands of an extraordinary forty-day fast. Jesus also faced direct tempting in a momentous encounter with his demon opponent. Jesus and one Gospel account name the encountered tempter *Satan*, while another more-elaborate Gospel account calls the tempter *the devil*. In one account, the devil Satan takes Jesus to the top of the temple and then to the pinnacle of a very high mountain, giving followers spectacular settings for their momentous encounter. The two longer Gospel accounts show the devil tempting Jesus first with food, then to test God, and finally with the world's splendor. As followers know well, each time Jesus quoted scripture back to his tempter, *it is written*. Jesus thus deployed the power and protection of God's own word, even when the devil tried the similar tactic of misquoting scripture to Jesus. In the third and final tempting, Jesus commanded Satan away from him after quoting scripture. Significantly, Satan obeyed, although one Gospel account says that Satan left only until another *opportune time*. As indicated in the prior section, angels came to attend to the hungry Jesus as soon as Satan left.

The account of Jesus resisting the devil confirms for followers Jesus's complete devotion to the will of his Father, even when deeply weakened. Followers probably fully appreciate the attraction that they would feel to Satan's offer of food, God's help, and the world's splendors, particularly when Satan would quote scripture in justification. The account's point may indeed be that who but Jesus would have resisted? Yet the scene of Jesus's testing teaches followers attributes not only of Jesus but of the one who opposes him. While anyone knows the awful nature of evil, we very seldom see direct accounts of the appearance, words, strategies, character, and intent of personified evil. God personifies love in Jesus, just as the devil Satan who opposes Jesus personifies evil. The evil one made grand offers to Jesus, offers that many if not all others would not have resisted. Followers know better than to underestimate the opposition, relying not on their own strength of character but on the prayer that Jesus taught followers to pray for the protection of the Father. The Father knew that his Son would resist the offers of evil. The Father knows the much more-limited extent to which we are willing to resist evil. The forty fasting wilderness days had surely weakened Jesus at least in the sense that one account says that he was hungry. By offering Jesus bread, the tempter promptly seized on that weakness, as is the tempter's strategy. Jesus's command for Satan to flee, and Satan's obedience to that command, confirms for followers the power that Jesus holds over evil. When one Gospel account says that Satan left only until another opportune time, it reinforces Satan's wily character and strategy to monitor for weakness. Followers should draw from the account not just Jesus's utter devotion but also the character and strategies of opposing evil.

He sometimes wondered how the Gospels' authors learned of Jesus's momentous encounter with the devil. Jesus well might, he surmised, have shared the account with the disciples, or perhaps the authors received the account by other inspiration. In any case, for him, the tempting account was more than about its lessons on the opposing character of Jesus and Satan. The account's value had just as much or more to do with the image of Jesus facing Satan directly. Evil so often seems so subtle, he thought, that to have an account of its personification would be an important aid to recognizing and resisting it. To see Jesus doing so, though, meant so much more than any such psychological advantage. To draw the strength to resist temptation, he had only to think of Jesus standing on the point of the temple or pinnacle of the mountain, still resisting the devil's wiles. He had seen wonderful graphic and artistic depictions of the image that fed and fired the inspiration that he drew from the written account. Thinking of Jesus speaking back to the devil from the temple's spire or mountaintop seemed to him like praying for the Father's own protection from temptation. He wasn't sure whether prayer included just thinking of inspiring images of Jesus like the tremendously powerful image of Jesus ordering Satan away from him on the mountaintop, but he sensed that the Father might accept these portrait-prayers when they included his glorious Son. So he silently continued to collect, catalog, and contemplate powerful images of the Son.

30 Powered.

Luke 4:14; *see also* Luke 8:42.

The Gospels' unfolding account of Jesus's calling to public ministry thus begins with his immersion in the Jordan River followed by the Spirit's descent as he came up out of the water and then his fasting and testing in the Judean desert. The account then records a fascinating result of his having received and participated so fully and perfectly in his long-awaited, prophetic calling. What could or would possibly be next for Jesus, following the dramatic, historic, and transcendent event of heaven's opening to allow the dove-like Spirit to alight on him as his

Father's voice thundered in appreciation? The Gospel accounts first record that Jesus returned to his home in Galilee. In indicating that Jesus returned to his Nazareth home by the Sea of Galilee only *when Herod put John in prison*, one account appears to suggest that Jesus may have lingered with or near John for a time in the Judean wilderness. If so, then one can picture the cousins in deepest fellowship discussing Jesus's emerging mission. While readers can only guess how Jesus heard of John's imprisonment and whether they might have been together leading up to it, the Gospel account does indicate that Jesus did not remain in Nazareth on his return to Galilee but instead lived in another Galilean village Capernaum. In doing so, Jesus fulfilled yet another prophecy that the people of that particular region, living in darkness in the shadow of death, would see his great light. These details though, if they were all that the accounts offered readers, would be an incomplete denouement to the profundity of Jesus's Spirit baptism. Instead, one Gospel account adds the critical observation that when Jesus returned to Galilee after his baptism, he did so *in the Spirit's power*. Indeed, Jesus returned in such Spirit-filled condition that the account also records that news of him spread *everywhere* and that *everyone* praised him. Jesus was different after his baptism with the Spirit, just as he should have been. People could see the difference, which then made them hear of him and praise him.

Although many followers probably overlook its brief mention, the image of Jesus returning to Galilee filled with the Spirit's power indeed should inspire followers who meditate on it. Something big should happen when heaven opens and the Spirit descends and alights on a person, ignoring for a moment that the person was none less than Jesus. Spirit-filling should change a person in a way that is evident not only to the person changed but to others who observe the person. Followers at least want Spirit-filling to be that way. Who wouldn't want to see evidence of the Spirit's filling in one's self or, if the huge fortune should befall another, then see the power in that other? People often sense power in others, even if only the power of position, authority, fame, reputation, physical strength, or wealth. Here, though, Jesus now carried God's own Holy Spirit, a filling that one would certainly hope others would see, which indeed they did so powerfully that *everyone everywhere* in that region heard of and praised Jesus. If a reader takes the Gospel account literally, then the Father had not simply *empowered* Jesus as if to grant him some delegated authority but had instead *powered* him with the Holy Spirit. The Holy Spirit is not some permission to speak or act in God's name in order to do this or that. The Spirit instead powers those whom the Spirit touches, as if energy flowed in, around, through, and out. That evident power, obvious power, effective power is what the Gospel account indicates Jesus carried into Galilee. Now filled with the Spirit's power, Jesus's calling was complete.

She had finally come to the point that she felt that she had a constant need for God's power. Early in her life and even into mid-life, she had felt a natural vitality carry her into and out of days with their many good and bad situations, although not that she had ever really felt that her own power was sufficient. On many days and in many situations, even early in her life, her own power was clearly not enough. She, like anyone, would stumble and even drag her way into and out of things, sensing all the while that she had far too little of her own gumption to get her in properly or to get her out having accomplished what she should. As she looked back, even in mid-life, she could see that she had already been relying in good part not on her own quite-limited power but on God's power. She knew her reliance on God to be true in part because she had committed herself to it. She had long prayed for God to sustain her in whatever she encountered, as Jesus's prayer said, to give her the daily bread that she would need. She also knew her reliance on God to be true because of the generally upward course of her inward life. She had no reason to think that her own energy had somehow enabled her to navigate her life's many inward and outward twists and turns, as any life has twists and turns, in such a way as to have her end up so blessed as she was, not though that she claimed to be any better than anyone else. The evidence of her own weakness and God's power so obvious now to her absolutely convinced her that from the moment that she had embraced Jesus as a young woman, his Spirit had, at least to the degree that her small but always-growing faith had allowed it, filled, guided, and powered her. She wept in inspired satisfaction, thinking of Jesus walking through Galilee in the fullness of the Spirit's power.

31 **Centered.**

Luke 4:42; *see also* Matthew 14:13; Luke 5:16.

Sprinkled among the Gospel accounts of Jesus's many different actions are brief references to Jesus seeking out solitary times and places. Yes, the Father called the Son to public ministry in a river baptism and Spirit anointing. The Son fasted, passed the evil one's wilderness testing, and returned to Galilee for ministry in the Spirit's power. Yet throughout that ministry, indeed *often* as the Gospel plainly records, Jesus sought solitude to pray to his heavenly Father. Those times when Jesus withdrew from the crowds and even from the disciples into solitude came at different times including late at night, in the middle of the night, and in the early morning at daybreak. Sometimes, Jesus withdrew in response to specific events, such as with news of Herod's murder of John the Baptist. Yet even then, crowds pressed him, followed him, and sought him out from his solitude. One Gospel account records that when people would discover the places to which he had withdrawn, he would rise to leave again to renew his solitude, but the people who had found him would then try to keep him from leaving them again. Accounts also record clearly that Jesus's intent in these solitary times was to be alone *in order to pray*. He was not withdrawing solely out of weariness, although he may well often have been weary. He was not withdrawing out of irritation or in refusal to preach, teach, and heal. Jesus withdrew to commune with his Father, as he did in the Garden of Gethsemane, most earnestly to pour his heart out to the Father in prayer.

The image of Jesus praying in solitude to the Father witnesses powerfully to the follower of the need continually to center the heart, mind, and soul on God. That Jesus would withdraw in solitude to pray to the Father seems almost counterintuitive given that he is the Father's image, at all times knowing the Father's mind. Yet the high frequency with which he sought solitude to pray, together with the Gospel record that he often sought to leave again those who searched for and found him, confirm for the reader Jesus's need to pray. Even Jesus, the very Son of God, needed time alone to center his heart, mind, and soul on the Father. If Jesus had that urgent need, then how much more urgently must his followers have that need? How often and earnestly should we be withdrawing into solitude to pray? We have every bit as great a need to center our heart, mind, and soul on Jesus and the Father. The follower may long ago have felt and answered the Father's call, may be so closely acquainted with and committed to God's word and will as to leave no doubt of that calling, and yet the follower must do as Jesus did so often, which is to withdraw into solitude and pray. The image of Jesus praying alone to the Father is a precious scene stimulating the follower into like action, seeking like relationship with both the Son and Father.

One of his favorite meditations was on Jesus praying. His own prayers had long seemed to him to be few, brief, and distracted, even when he had succeeded in finding the time and solitude to pray. He later discerned that his obstacle was in part in having no clear image, model, or pattern for when, where, and how he should pray. Oh, he knew the prayer that Jesus taught his followers to pray and fully appreciated that it was the profound and perfect prayer pattern. He had also read several books on prayer and heard several more accounts of how and how often various Christian saints down through the ages had prayed. He also had close acquaintances whom he knew to be great prayer models and mentors. In those respects, he had no excuse for failing to pray effectively, earnestly, and often. Yet something had still seemed amiss or absent in his urge, will, and discipline to pray, until he had finally focused on Jesus withdrawing into solitude to pray. He could hardly see himself praying, indeed often could hardly *stand* himself praying. The very thought of it seemed somehow too presumptuous that the Father would bear to listen to his trite and petty prayers. But he could see Jesus praying and the Father listening. Nothing in the image of Jesus praying appeared to him at all odd or incongruous. He knew that the Father would listen in rapt attention to every word of Jesus's prayer. He also knew his need to pray and the need of others for his prayer. So as he prayed, he wrapped himself in the image of Jesus praying. And finally, at more-frequent moments, he sensed God close and prayer as natural and intrinsic, like breathing sweet morning air while walking close to Jesus.

32 Supported.

Mark 15:41; *see also* Luke 7:38, 8:3; John 12:3.

The Gospels record Jesus receiving the care and support of the women who accompanied him. While the Gospels indicate that many women followed Jesus, Mark's account refers specifically to Mary Magdalene, Mary the mother of James the younger, and Salome, when stating that *these women had followed him and cared for his needs.* Luke's Gospel names Mary Magdalene, Joanna who managed Herod's household, and Susanna, as having helped to support Jesus and the disciples out of their own means. Jesus presumably received the care of these or other women throughout his public ministry. Someone would have needed to provide for him. The disciples doubtless also did so from time to time, whether in picking grains, going into town for provisions purchased out of funds that the lost disciple Judas kept, or preparing a last supper. Yet the Gospels do refer specifically to the care of the women. The accounts do not indicate precisely what the women made their habit or practice of doing for Jesus as he moved widely about preaching, teaching, and healing, although followers know well the account of one such woman, a Samaritan, whom Jesus asked to draw water for him at the well. Followers are also familiar with the accounts, further addressed in another section below, of one woman wiping Jesus's feet with her hair while anointing his feet with perfume and her tears, and another woman Mary anointing Jesus's head with perfume shortly before his crucifixion. The women's care thus clearly included more than simply providing and preparing food and drink. One can also easily imagine the women and others washing and caring for Jesus's clothes and caring for his blisters, sores, wounds, and hair, to say nothing yet of his washing, treatment, and wrapping following his crucifixion death.

The image of Jesus receiving the support and care of the women can be a surprising one for the follower. As the all-powerful Son of God, Jesus, one would think, needed no care. He had an army of angels at his call. After fasting for forty days, angels attended to his needs. His Father would surely provide for his every need. Yet Jesus, while fully divine, was also fully human. He faced every temptation humans knew. Those temptations would have included hunger and thirst, the kind of very human need that women of the households that Jesus visited could have readily met just as they did for far less-esteemed guests. Jesus also slept at times, the Gospel account records, suggesting that he might have felt the kind of daily weariness that any other human feels, again the kind of need that households could readily have met with an empty couch, rug, or bed. Jesus's calling, his ability to move about freely and efficiently to preach, teach, and heal, apparently depended on care and support of others, particularly from women. His calling might not have been humanly possible, or at least not so swiftly effective in the short span of three years, if he had not had their support and care. Followers search today for deserving ministries, studying and praying to discern whom best to support with the time and treasures with which God blesses us. Imagine the richness of the opportunity to provide and care not only for Jesus's followers but also for Jesus himself. The image of Jesus's followers providing for his care and support should inspire care for those who carry out his ministry today.

She cared often and much for her family, indeed so often and so much that she always seemed to have more to do. *Chores*, she often thought of those many constantly repeated activities, *when will they ever end?* She hardly had to think of them as she did them because they had long ago grown so automatic, routine, and predictable. Then one day she again came across the account of the women caring for Jesus. She tried to imagine what doing so would have been like. She would have had no problem with motivation, she suspected. Would the care, though, have grown routine? Would she have grumbled doing her part over and over again, or doing another's part when she had already done her part? Somehow, she could not imagine being anything other than grateful to do whatever she could have done for Jesus. Indeed, she imagined relishing the duties even more so as they were more routine. As she imagined doing over and over for Jesus the many mundane little things that life really takes for any decent degree of comfort, she thought again of the few spectacular things that the women had done for Jesus in caressing his feet with their tear- and perfume-soaked hair. Would she have thought of something equally vivid and demonstrative of the care she felt for Jesus? She pulled her family's clothes from the dryer and began folding them once again while still dreaming of something far more expressive that she might have done for Jesus. Carrying the folded clothes through her house to their familiar closet and drawer destinations as she imagined making a home for Jesus, she suddenly realized that out of the constant cry of her heart she had already done exactly that, made of her heart and home the most spectacular expression of Jesus love of which God had made her capable.

33 Passionate.

John 2:17; *see also* Matthew 21:12; Luke 19:45.

The Gospels record Jesus's zeal in carrying out his calling, particularly his passion for his Father and his Father's holiness. No scenes mark Jesus's zeal more than his driving the markets and money changers from the temple courts. Early in his public ministry, just before the Passover celebration, Jesus left his mother, brothers, and disciples in Capernaum for Jerusalem. There Jesus found the usual sellers of cattle, sheep, and doves, and money changers sitting at tables, in the courts outside the temple, a scene that had likely existed and repeated itself for many hundreds of years. Jesus had himself likely seen the scene before on visits with his family to Jerusalem. Yet in this instance, Jesus did something that the temple courts had likely never before seen. Filled with zeal that the prophets had centuries earlier predicted, Jesus made a whip out of cords with which to drive the livestock from the area. He tipped over the money changers' tables, scattering their coins across the temple courts, while he shouted at the sellers of doves to *get them out of here*, adding *how dare you turn my Father's house into a market!* The disciples who witnessed Jesus's passion remembered the prophets saying that zeal for his Father's house would consume the Messiah. The religious leaders, though, demanded that Jesus show them a sign that he had authority to do as he had just done. During the Passover celebration, Jesus would show others many miraculous signs but not here to the religious leaders. He instead answered them with a veiled reference to his coming crucifixion and resurrection, a reference that no one understood at the time but that his disciples would recall and understand later. Another Gospel records Jesus clearing the temple courts of money changers again at the end of his public ministry.

The image of Jesus driving the markets and money changers from the temple courts startles followers who first confront it. The culture represents Jesus as a gentle man of love and peace. When the subject came to his Father's holiness, though, Jesus's calling made him a man of zeal and passion. Making and using a whip to drive animals out of the temple courts while shouting at their sellers is not a peace-inspiring action. Turning over tables, spilling coins across the temple courts, is not a peacemaking act. Jesus could act and did act with disruptive passion when the occasion called for it. Readers must then appreciate why this moment in the temple courts called so deeply for Jesus's passionate action. After his baptism, Jesus's first entry into the temple courts at the time of Passover would have been a momentous occasion. Passover celebrated the angel of death's passing by the Jews who had marked their homes with the blood of the lamb's sacrifice. Jesus was now the Lamb of God, come to fulfill all sacrifice, come in effect to end the old sacrificial system. The veiled reference to his crucifixion and resurrection with which Jesus explained his authority to clear the temple courts thus made perfect sense. Jesus, not animal or coin offerings, was the sacrifice that would redeem and restore followers to God's grace. Jesus's coming for sacrifice and calling to resurrection made the sellers and money changers irrelevant. Jesus had to clear away the old sacrificial system because he fulfilled and completed it. Although none at the time fully understood it, Jesus had just announced his calling.

He sometimes wondered about the place if any that passions, especially righteous anger and fury, had in these things of faith. His readings showed him so many cautions against ire and rage that he felt that adopting the cultural Jesus, the safe and sentimental god-is-love Jesus, was the much-more-prudent thing. Yet he also read occasionally of a sort of *heated* side of Jesus, of his shouting in anger and turning over tables. Jesus often had a way of getting everyone, especially the religious leaders, *stirred up*, and not just stirred up over anything but stirred up *against him*. This darker side of Jesus's actions puzzled and even frightened him. Were his followers also supposed to be angry? Were we supposed to be turning over tables and shouting down those whom we felt engaged in sacrilege and desecrated his house? Why hadn't Jesus just preached to the sellers and money changers in the temple courts as he had to so many others so often? He kept looking closer at the event to see if he could generalize anything from it to govern his own conduct, to see if Jesus seemed to be sanctioning his own ire and rage. He kept sorting through the times that he had been angry and had even wanted to express his rage over real wrongs or perceived insults, but none of them seemed to fit anything like what Jesus had been conveying in the temple courts. To the contrary, Jesus had instead been especially constrained even at his arrest, trial, sentencing, and crucifixion, precisely when his own reputation and person were most assaulted. Reacting violently or even vehemently to wrongs just didn't seem like Jesus or like what Jesus wanted from his followers. He remained completely unable to generalize lessons from Jesus's temple-court outbursts other than that Jesus most jealously guarded his sacrificial mission. Maybe that was it, he decided. Jesus's passion seemed most to flare when someone seemed to suggest that he need not be the savior that his Father had intended, that someone or something else would instead accomplish it. And so he decided that the one thing that he could safely be passionate about was *his own* commitment to faith, not the practices or commitments of others. No, he would avoid ire and rage as far as he humanly could, except when he saw or sensed temptation to step away from his own commitment. He would let his own passion flare solely to extinguish that temptation, not to put out the light or passions of others.

34 Anointed.

Luke 7:38; *see also* Matthew 26:6.

A calling also needs an anointing. Jesus's baptism with the Holy Spirit in the Jordan River was itself a necessary anointing for all that Jesus would do so perfectly consonant with the Father's will. Yet the Gospels also record a remarkable event in which a woman anoints Jesus's feet with her tears and perfume. The event occurred not at the beginning of Jesus's public ministry but further in when the religious leaders had already come to know of Jesus's ministry. One of those leaders invited Jesus to his house for dinner. While Jesus reclined at the low table characteristic of such houses then, a woman with a sinful past stood behind Jesus weeping in such a way as to wet his feet with her tears. The woman then knelt down to wipe Jesus's feet with her hair, kissing his feet as she did so. She then poured perfume on Jesus's feet from an alabaster jar that she had brought with her. The religious-leader host, though, grumbled to himself at the sinful woman's touching Jesus's feet. Jesus responded to the religious leader's thought with a lesson in forgiveness that the one forgiven much loves much, while the one forgiven little loves little. The woman had shown Jesus the exquisite honor, indeed given him a most-precious anointing, that the religious leader had not. Jesus then turned to the woman to tell her that he forgave her sins, adding that her faith in him had saved her. The attending religious leaders only grumbled further at Jesus's last words of forgiveness. Another account records a woman pouring perfume on Jesus's head shortly before his arrest and conviction. Jesus knew his calling while also recognizing his due anointing.

The scene of the sinful woman anointing Jesus's feet with her tears and perfume, and kissing his feet while wiping them with her hair, is among the most precious of images on which a follower might meditate. The woman's heart and actions depict, as much or more than any other scene, an appropriate approach toward Jesus. We all have reason to anoint Jesus's feet with our tears, kiss those feet, and wipe them with our hair, in a posture of due abasement. Followers who appreciate and pursue the woman's remarkable stance gain hugely valuable insight, authenticity, and attitude. No other posture reflects equivalent candor, clarity, honesty, and truth, and in those things no greater strength and power. How purifying that physical act must have been for the woman when Jesus then uttered the precious words of her forgiveness. The Holy Spirit had guided the woman's heart to help her find the courage to enter the religious leader's home and the right posture to honor and anoint Jesus at the right moment. Jesus is certainly due the anointing, and everyone, not just a certain sinful woman, owes him that anointing. The woman's anointing Jesus with perfume from an alabaster jar could also have broadly foreshadowed Jesus's frighteningly violent and sorrowful death, as Jesus's subsequent anointing by another woman Mary just days before his crucifixion more clearly did so. Jesus's calling was not just to an extraordinary public ministry of teaching, preaching, and healing but also to a sacrificial death and redemptive resurrection. Jesus had a calling like no other, and he would require and was due an equal-to-the-task anointing.

She had no more-favorite image of Jesus than one in which she saw little more than his feet through her tear-soaked eyes, up very close as she wiped those feet with her hair and kissed those feet. She had taken a long road to reaching this point of abject humility before Jesus, but she very much welcomed the point. She had no false illusion about her standing on merit before Jesus. The very thought of her standing before Jesus had something uncomfortable about it, or if not uncomfortable (for anyone should wish to be in Jesus's presence), then something *incongruous*. Just as famous figures like Moses before the burning bush and Joshua confronted by the commander of the Lord's army had reason to abase themselves in the divine presence, so too she felt a similar need. The fact that Jesus had walked, talked, eaten, and lived with the many who followed him made that kind of physical subjugation difficult, awkward, and inappropriate or at least unexpected. Yet like the woman in the religious leader's house, she felt that need to align herself properly to the divinity and purity of Jesus. The scene of the woman in the religious leader's house gave her the sufficient image. Indeed, more than merely sufficient, the scene gave her a soul satisfaction that seldom failed to bring her to tears. She wished that she, too, could have anointed Jesus with her tears, although maybe he was accepting her tears right now in the same manner, while granting her the same forgiveness.

35 Judge.

John 5:22; *see also* Matthew 28:18; John 3:35; John 13:3; 2 Corinthians 5:10.

The Gospels also record that Jesus's calling included making judgments, expressly stating that he had his Father's authority to do so. Jesus as judge is an image of which followers must take account. In one Gospel account, Jesus tells his listeners that rather than the Father judging anyone, the Father *entrusted all judgment to the Son.* That record further records Jesus as saying that the Father entrusted judgment to the Son because he is the *Son of Man* and also specifically in order that all would honor the Son as they must also honor the Father. The way to honor the Father, Jesus added, is to honor the Father's Son because to reject the Son is to reject the Father who sent the Son. The judgment that Jesus then passed was that those who heard and accepted his words *as the words of the Father who sent him* have no condemnation, indeed no death, but instead eternal life. Jesus told his listeners that the dead were hearing the Son of God's voice and living because of it, the Father having given the Son life not from any natural source but *in himself.* God the Father holds life within him and gave that in-him life to the Son. This judgment, though, that Jesus would pass would not be his own judgment to please himself but the just judgment that he heard from the Father. One of the Apostle Paul's letters then confirms that which we must construe from Jesus's calling as judge, which is that we must strive to please Jesus before whom we will each appear for judgment.

The image of Jesus's calling to serve as his Father's judge is a vital image for followers. While Jesus as judge may seem a daunting figure, who really would want to follow a god who shows no discernment, who makes no distinction among any whether they respect, obey, and follow that god or not? Judging is essential to authority just as judging is essential to trust, confidence, and respect. Confidence in Jesus as judge should be especially easy and sound when we recognize the distinct basis for his judging. Thank God that *Jesus does not judge on merit.* Jesus's judgment is not that the works of one of us are worthy while the works of another one of us are not. If it were so, then indeed every one of us should fear his judgment for can any one of us truly claim with confidence that we are better than the rest? Jesus's judgment is instead whether we honor him as the Father's Son. Jesus judges belief in him, reliance on him, and recognition of him as the essential savior. The simplicity, clarity, and *availability* of that belief is the reason why none should fear and all should instead trust his judgment, even as all should continually examine the heart, mind, and soul to embrace ever more fully that trustworthy belief. The reward, which is self-vitalizing life within and in him, is greater than anything that the follower can earn or conjure in natural life. The life within him that the Father held himself and gave to Jesus is an extraordinary resurrection life, a self-vitalizing life that first suffuses the natural life and later raises and transforms the natural body after its sin-obligated death. Judges both convict the suspect *and freely redeem* the convicted. Jesus called to judge is the follower's essential image.

He had never had the fear and loathing of divine judgment that others often expressed. His confidence in Jesus as judge, though, had nothing to do with believing himself free from guilt, as he suspected most people believed themselves to be. For him, the realization was exactly the contrary. He had known since his earliest thought that God justly condemned him for the naturally corrupt nature of his own hard heart, selfish mind, and broken soul. Who should fear condemnation when condemnation is perfectly due? The world would be a much worse place if anything else were true, he had concluded. He expected, wanted, and needed that judgment. On the other hand, he had also long known that God was not a harsh but rather a merciful judge. He had a way out of this judgment thing, he had always suspected and before too long fully knew. While properly being a judging God, the Father had revealed in his Son Jesus the plan that he must have fashioned even before humankind's great fall from grace. He would restore all who acknowledged his beloved but plan-laden Son. His Son would be both judge and sentence, both executioner and executed, in order that the Father could remain both just and merciful. As he reflected again on this extraordinary plan and its superlative gift, his appreciation for the image of Jesus as judge grew further.

36 Revealer.

Matthew 11:27; *see also* John 10:15, 14:9, 17:26; Hebrews 1:3; Colossians 1:15.

The Gospels several times record Jesus disclosing, most directly to his disciples in private while less directly to the listening crowds, that core part of his calling that as the image of God and the Father's only Son, Jesus reveals the Father to those whom Jesus chooses. Matthew's Gospel records Jesus speaking to the Father, praising him for hiding who Jesus was from the wise while revealing who Jesus was to little children, at the Father's pleasure. Jesus continued that not only had the Father committed all things to Jesus but also that no one other than the Son knows the Father, and those to whom the Son *chooses to reveal* the Father. Jesus decides whether to show God to one or another. Likewise, John's Gospel records Jesus telling the disciples that the Son knows the Father just as the Father knows the Son, and later that anyone who sees the Son *has seen the Father*. To see Jesus is to see God. Later still, John's Gospel records Jesus speaking to the Father, for the disciples' benefit telling the Father aloud that while the world does not know the Father, Jesus knows the Father, and the disciples now know that the Father sent Jesus. Jesus continues speaking to the Father for the disciples' benefit, saying that Jesus has shown the disciples the Father and will continue to do so. Jesus even reveals his purpose in showing the Father to the disciples, which is to see the Father's love for the Son in the disciples, indeed for Jesus himself to be in the disciples. Revealing the Father to the disciples and, through them, to the world was at the core of Jesus's calling.

The concept and calling of Jesus as the *radiance of God's image* and *exact representation of his being* is of course a central one on which followers should reflect. Jesus's calling had more than a salvation purpose to it. His calling also involved revealing his Father's nature, character, and image to both the saved and unsaved. Humans had forever speculated on the character of an invisible God. Recognize then how significant having a visible image of God would be to understanding, appreciating, and accepting God's exquisite character. While humans could never know the full character of an infinite, eternal, and limitless God, the fullest revelation of God's nature that humans could know would be to see and experience God *in human form*. God could have revealed his nature in many ways, as indeed he did in a burning bush, parted sea, snake on a pole, water-gushing rock, manna from heaven, and other images that the Old Testament records. Yet the entirely human image of Jesus, from infant to cross and beyond in all of the recorded dramatic, demonstrative, and poignant events of his life, reveals so vastly much more of God. Followers and indeed seekers and rejecters of God need not guess at the attributes of God when they see them illustrated in Jesus so clearly across the many events and actions of his life while also hearing them reflected in Jesus's words. When followers meditate on Jesus as the image of God, they embrace an image that so fully informs their faith as utterly to define it. One either believes Jesus to be the Son of God or doesn't believe it. One either believes that God could and did take human form, or one doesn't believe it. The difference defines and distinguishes followers. Followers might dwell fruitfully forever on that one image that the Son represents the Father in radiant being, the Father having given full life and perfect form to his one and only Son. Jesus's central calling for which God cast him was to represent and take on the image of the Father.

If he had one image of Jesus on which he meditated more often than any other, and always beneficially, then that image was that of Jesus as God in human form. The concept never exhausted him and instead always led him on in his thinking, prayer, appreciation, and sensitivity. He recognized that God taking human form was a difficult concept for many to accept and indeed was such a stumbling block as to lead to failure in faith for too many. Unfortunately, those many who could not reconcile a vast God with his incarnate form in Jesus included acquaintances quite close to him. On the other hand, he knew that the Gospels and letters that followed were unmistakable in their conclusion that Jesus was exactly that. Jesus himself had said it as clearly as anyone could express it. And so being the consistent Bible reader that he was, and knowing what Jesus said about himself, he had long ago faced the challenge of reconciling the eternal-spirit-creator qualities of God with Jesus as God incarnate including, most difficult of all, God as baby Jesus in the manger. God had somehow inhabited or imbued a wind in the treetops, burning bush, dark shadow, and pillar of fire, he thought. Then why not inhabit and imbue human form when humans are God's highest creation? He could have relied for proof of Jesus's divinity on Jesus's long prophetic foreshadowing, Jesus's miracles, and Jesus's resurrection, all of which helped. Yet he also felt that he needed no particular proof that God would take human form, first of all because Jesus said it, but also because it made such sense. God wanted to reveal himself, to share his radiance, and did so in perfect design in Jesus's coming and calling.

37 Fulfillment.

Luke 4:18; *see also* Matthew 21:4; Luke 19:29.

The Gospels unmistakably record Jesus fulfilling his calling and prophetic role. Jesus consistently intimated and sometimes even directly declared that he was prophecy's fulfillment. The early Gospel account recording the occasion when Jesus went into Nazareth's synagogue after his baptism and wilderness test is one clear example of Jesus expressing that he was prophecy's fulfillment. On that occasion, Jesus stood to read from the scroll the words of the prophet Isaiah. He deliberately chose to read that the Lord's Spirit was *on him*, moreover that the Lord had *anointed him* to preach the Gospel, proclaim freedom, restore sight, release the oppressed, and proclaim the Lord's favor. While these words were Isaiah's, and Jesus might just have been reading as anyone would read, by recording that everyone *fastened their eyes on him* as he finished and sat to give the customary interpretation, the account clearly suggests that his listeners suspected that something much more significant was up. Indeed, Jesus declared the scripture *fulfilled in your hearing.* Amazed at his gracious words, all at first spoke well of Jesus but *as Joseph's son.* They still saw Jesus as a local boy grown to adulthood who, though gracious in word and deed, remained no different or greater than any of them. So Jesus continued to indicate his prophetic role, this time not so graciously but instead critically, saying that a hometown honors no prophet, not even the great prophets Elijah and Elisha whose miracles instead benefited believing outsiders. As another example, late in his public ministry, Jesus told the disciples to go bring a donkey's colt to him to ride in entry into Jerusalem to the crowd's shouts of *Hosanna,* all to fulfill another Old Testament prophecy. Jesus fulfilled prophecy, knew that he was doing so, and clearly expressed it.

Followers may rarely overlook but never forget the image of Jesus fulfilling Messiah's prophetic role. *Being* the Messiah, Good News, Son of God, and Christ is obviously Jesus's central image. Recognize, though, that in fulfilling that central role, Jesus need not necessarily have *announced* or even *known* it. Film and other forms of fiction often have a central figure curiously unaware of the figure's critical, heroic, or savior status, even when others around the figure are quite well aware that the figure must accept the role if society is to progress or persist. History itself has examples of groundbreaking figures in science, conflict, art, or other expression or thought who at the time of their inventive work had little or no clue of the watershed that it and they represented. Jesus was instead from the first plainly self-aware that he fulfilled the world's longest and greatest prophecy. Happenstance is one thing, while conscious and deliberate fulfillment is quite another. One can just barely imagine a certain individual just happening to be in the right place at the right time with the right skills and disposition to accomplish something great and historic as if by chance. Jesus wasn't that individual. He instead had great understanding of just who he was and what his coming represented, so much greater than those around him that their ignorance seems almost willful or in some instances even malicious. Jesus knew who he was, while others mostly didn't. The realization that Jesus was the fulfiller of all messianic prophecy came painfully slowly even to his closest followers. Jesus knew his Father's mind, certainly well enough to know his Savior role. Jesus then accepted and carried out that role to its perfect conclusion. Followers have much to draw from the power of Jesus's glorious fulfillment.

She had always felt that the fact of Jesus's coming was something *big*. She supposed that Christmas had a lot to do with it. From the time that she was a little child, she had always had a rich sense that Jesus *fulfilled* something, *completed* something, *accomplished* something for which God had made the universe, indeed for which God had made *her*. She respected the wise and learned, appreciated the peacemaker and healer. Miracles impressed her as they impressed anyone else, and she could adore a saint, too. Yet no matter how holy anyone might look or sound, today or in days long gone, for her Jesus had always been someone utterly distinct. She knew, too, that it was his prophetic fulfillment that made him so. For her, as for many of her friends in fellowship, Jesus's prophetic fulfillment made all the difference in his preeminence, all the difference in his priority, all the difference in her utter commitment to him in profound appreciation and complete belief. She loved that he was the fulfillment of all for which the Father had created the universe, populated it with humankind, and allowed humankind the independence to fall. Because Jesus was the fulfillment, for her he need not have also been so wise, even though he was. He need not have been so kind, even though he was. He need not have been the miraculous healer, the great warrior, the one who fed thousands, or the one who walked on water and shone like the sun, even though he was all of those persons, too. She treasured him for all of those things but most of all as love's fulfillment.

38 Family.

Matthew 12:46; *see also* Luke 8:21.

During the time of his public ministry, Jesus did not live with his natural family but instead lived with the disciples and others who welcomed him into their homes as he lived the itinerant life of a traveling teacher and preacher. In doing so, Jesus could have done what most of us would do when away from family for an extended time, which would have been to indicate just that he was *away from his family*. Instead, though, the Gospels record Jesus declaring almost precisely the opposite. Jesus had been speaking indoors to yet another crowd when his mother Mary approached outside with Jesus's brothers, wanting to speak to Jesus. One of those brothers presumably included James who well after Jesus's resurrection would author the profound Bible epistle of the same name, in which James confessed Jesus as Christ. The family's intentions in this instance, though, may not have been anything of the sort. When one of the crowd called to Jesus's attention that his mother and brothers were outside wanting to speak to him, Jesus first questioned whether they really were his mother and brothers. Pointing instead to the disciples who had followed him throughout his increasingly hazardous and arduous public ministry to that point, Jesus said instead that *here are my mother and brothers*. To make his point even more clear, Jesus added that those who *do the will of his Father* were his brother, sister, and mother. God had called Jesus into a new family, one that grew as Jesus attracted new followers into doing the will of his Father.

The image of Jesus as calling followers into his family, indeed identifying followers as his mother, brothers, and sisters, should deeply encourage every follower. One of the great mysteries of our Trinitarian faith is that it involves family not simply as a value or commitment but in relationship at its core. God through a Spirit anointing called and held Jesus in Son relationship to the Father, forming family at the heart of faith. We do not simply obey and follow Christ. Rather, we join in the familial relationship of Father, Son, and Spirit at the faith's core. When we accept Christ, we also join his family of faith in fellowship with other followers, whom Christ brings together as his brothers and sisters. In the above account, the crowd, or at least its one member who addressed Jesus about his mother and brothers waiting to speak to him outside, appeared to expect Jesus to respond to the call of his natural mother and brothers. Family involves familiarity, loyalty, trust, confidence, respect, love, care, and, with all of those things, mutual obligation. We respond to the wish of a mother, instruction of a father, and will of a family. So why wouldn't a man, even this extraordinary man Jesus, go speak to his waiting family? His listeners might have reasonably assumed that Jesus owed his family more than he owed any members of the crowd including his disciples. Yet Jesus had a different understanding, a deeper spiritual conception going beyond the merely natural, biological, and social understanding, of family. He had a heavenly Father who was creating and extending his own family. His disciples and any other members of the crowd who did his Father's will had become his brothers and sisters, even mothers. We are Jesus's family, his royal family, when doing his Father's will.

He kept turning over in his mind this thought of Jesus as brother. He had a natural brother, one whom he loved and respected, even if that brother was not a declared follower of Jesus. His natural brother was familiar to him, warm, and comforting. Having grown up sharing every significant experience with his brother, he liked his brother in ways that he could not really like any others. They shared so much, even if what they shared was increasingly old history for both of them. His brother was also loyal and respectful to him in ways that he didn't expect others to be. He had no natural claim for respect, love, care, or obligation from anyone other than his brother. He kept turning over in his mind this fraternal familiarity and commitment as he thought again of Jesus as his brother. Could he really be as familiar, close, and trusting with Jesus as he was with his natural brother? He knew to a certainty that Jesus was reliable, loving, caring, and resourceful in so many ways that no one else could be, even his brother. Yet Jesus was, well, *Jesus*, indeed Jesus *Christ*, which meant that he was also King of kings, Lord of lords, and incomparable Savior. As hard as he tried, *brother* implied a familiarity that he simply could not equate with Jesus's divinity and majesty, until he began to realize that the equating was probably exactly the point. God didn't want him thinking that Jesus was less than divine, less than the only begotten Son of the eternal Father, and more like his natural and quite mortal brother. Rather, God wanted him thinking that he could be familiar, indeed heart-intimate like brothers sharing their blood, with divinity. God wanted followers in his divine realm as family. Jesus hadn't come to the world to be of the world but to draw followers into God's own kingdom.

39 Inscrutable.

Matthew 13:1; *see also* Mark 4:10; Luke 8:9, 10:21.

An unusual attribute of Jesus's calling, one on which followers may less often reflect than they profitably could, has to do with his frequent inscrutability. The Gospels record Jesus teaching in parables having varying degrees of clarity as to their meaning. Indeed, Jesus so frequently taught in parables the meaning of which was less than obvious, or even plainly ambiguous, that the disciples once asked Jesus why he did so. Matthew's Gospel relates that Jesus on one occasion taught such a large crowd by the shore that he sat in a boat to be seen and heard. Jesus taught then in parables, just as he commonly did at other times. Jesus's parable in this instance was that of the farmer scattering seeds on different soils, only the seeds falling on good soil producing a crop of thirty, sixty, or a hundredfold. *He who has ears, let him hear*, Jesus concluded in apparent reference to the parable's potential inscrutability. Indeed, Jesus's parable may have had no obvious meaning to his listeners, not even one that the disciples could properly appreciate, because the account next records that the disciples came to Jesus asking why he spoke in parables. Jesus explained that he had already shared with the disciples *secrets of the kingdom of heaven* that he had not yet shared, at least openly, with the people. His parables alluded to those secrets. Jesus continued that those who had the soft heart, seeing eyes, listening ears, and open mind to recognize the kingdom about which he spoke would receive even more abundance than they had already received. Those with hard hearts would keep their eyes shut, refuse to hear, and accordingly lose everything. The account further records Jesus intimating, but only intimating, that he would heal anyone who heard, saw, understood, and turned toward Jesus, who (the account further intimated) was the Messiah and Word whom prophets and righteous persons had longed to see and hear. Jesus then explained plainly how his seeds-and-soils parable illustrated the willingness of hearers to accept the message of the heavenly kingdom. On other occasion, Jesus spoke of how his Father had hidden truths from the wise and learned while revealing them to little children. In accepting his calling, Jesus was often inscrutable as to meanings that he nonetheless clearly intended, as his Father hid those meanings from the wise but revealed them to the unlearned.

The image of Jesus teaching in parables that left hearers uncertain of his plain meaning becomes hugely important for the follower when considering the Gospel's core message, just alluded to in the above section, that God adopts followers into his family for access to his glorious kingdom. Following Jesus is a choice, not a compulsion. Jesus attracts followers to his Father's kingdom not by threat and force, and not even by argument, but instead by exquisite love to the point of his complete and brutal sacrifice. Jesus had no plan or desire to *argue* or perhaps even to *reason* with anyone but instead to *invite* everyone. Yes, Jesus had the soundest of rationales for his exquisite offer, one that powerfully attracts the reasonable person. Yet Jesus made perfectly clear by teaching in parables and explaining why he did so that he desired *relationship* over reason. Indeed, Jesus disguised his reasoning specifically in order to ensure that persons approached him through soft hearts that desired relationship over reason. The reasons were certainly there. God has an unparalleled kingdom of riches to offer, by far the greatest of those riches being his own presence. God has a particular, singular, and perfect plan for the redemption that entry into his kingdom requires. His kingdom and plan, formed and implemented in the person of Jesus Christ, should compel reasonable persons to follow, except that God could compel persons to follow without any such plan and reason. God instead desires our free choice out of which to draw welcome and intimate relationship. Jesus's frequent inscrutability was the necessary light that attracted the moth, one that while losing a moth's life in the light's flame would gain God's eternal paradise in glorified body more like the most-beautiful butterfly.

He had not taken long to appreciate Jesus's willingness, or maybe even Jesus's *necessity*, to appear and be inscrutable. He had always retained a sense that Jesus was and should be *mysterious*. In doing so, in keeping Jesus at least a little *other-worldly*, he realized that he may have been too attracted to mystics and mysticism. Yet he also knew that God revealed only small parts of his majesty and that no one other than the Son of God could know God fully. He accepted that God needed no explanation, indeed that explaining God anything close to fully would reduce God to something or someone other. Jesus should be inscrutable to a large degree, he concluded, or he would want to find a larger god, of which he knew he wanted none other than Jesus. So he found Jesus's impenetrability crucially important. The other important thing that he had fairly quickly realized about the often ambiguous way in which Jesus taught or even acted, such as when performing miracles, is that each event's ambiguity forced him in advance to choose whether he would understand, accept, and follow Jesus. He would have found plain meaning too plain too often in order to make choice any part of his response to Jesus's words and actions. When instead Jesus left words and actions open to interpretation, Jesus left him with the personal authority to choose a follower's interpretation. Not surprisingly then, he found himself on occasion interpreting Jesus's actions to those who were not yet following Jesus and instead resisted the parables and scriptures, he hoped out of misunderstanding rather than hardness. Even as he did so, though, he sensed the uselessness of reason, explanation, and interpretation against a heart not yet softened by humility, fear, awe, loss, or love, and recognition of one's utter dependency on God for every good thing. He finally had a good grasp, he felt, of why Jesus was willing to remain inscrutable at least to some if not also to many.

40 Life.

John 6:52.

In another nearly inscrutable revelation, one that his hearers promptly misunderstood, Jesus disclosed that his calling included to be for others the *source of life*. The Gospels record Jesus describing himself not just as the source of guidance or encouragement but of a follower's *eternal life*. Jesus had just fed five thousand and then walked on water to join his disciples in crossing the lake, while the usual crowd pursued in boats. Jesus soon met the crowd, gathering them in a Capernaum synagogue for another profound and, to many of them inscrutable, revelation. Jesus told the assembled crowd members that for eternal life, they should eat the food that he would give them. When the crowd asked what exactly that food was that they should eat, perhaps like the manna that had come down from heaven in their ancestor's desert wanderings, Jesus replied that *he* was the Father's bread of life come down from heaven. When they began arguing among themselves about how they could possibly *eat his flesh* as Jesus had also indicated, Jesus replied that they would need to both eat his flesh and *drink his blood* for him to give them eternal life. If they did so, Jesus would then raise them up at the last day. *He* was the real food and drink come down from heaven, Jesus continued, by which humans live. Without him, they had no life, while with him, having eaten his flesh and drunk his blood, they had eternal life. Jesus is a follower's eternal life by which the follower will dwell forever in the kingdom of heaven.

The image of Jesus disclosing to the confused crowd his calling as the *source of life* is a profoundly rich one for followers on which to meditate. The crowd's confusion over what Jesus meant by *eating his flesh* and *drinking his blood* can fairly reflect a follower's own confusion. Some followers today might simply look away from what Jesus said, especially when taking what he said too limitedly and literally as the crowd clearly did. Literally, to eat a man's flesh and drink a man's blood would of course be no sustenance at all but a horrible offense against everything. Jesus, though, was no ordinary man, and his words carried no ordinary meaning, things that the crowd still did not fully appreciate. His blood would indeed run at his scourging and crucifixion, but it would do so specifically to redeem followers' wrongs, as the blood of those followers would otherwise have to run. Jesus's flesh is also available for our consumption when we commune with him in rich relationship in faith. That consumptive relationship through which Jesus lives in us and we live in Jesus then sustains us not just temporarily but eternally. Jesus can in these transformative, redemptive, and resurrecting ways provide us with an eternal kingdom life that we would not otherwise gain by any natural means. We know the limitation to natural means. Natural thirst and hunger do not end, only finding brief satisfaction. Natural life ends despite every effort to sustain and prolong it. Yet life in Jesus does not end, indeed cannot end, because Jesus is life incarnate, not simply the power of life but its source. While life could end, the source of life cannot end. Taking the source of life in you, and placing yourself within the source of life, brings eternal life, which was Jesus's calling.

She had her reasons to seek eternity, she supposed as anyone did. One, she sensed eternity all around her and indeed within her. If eternity was all around and within, then why couldn't she in some way connect with it? Two, she felt that eternity was where she belonged. She understood the world's material things, dealing with them every moment of every day. Yet she was also acutely aware of eternal things including love, awe, order, creativity, magnificence, generosity, forgiveness, grace, mercy, and beauty. She was so acutely aware of these eternal things that she felt more at home in them than in the material world, although she only knew eternal things through the material things that represented them. That compelling connection between the material and eternal was her third reason to seek eternity. She had the strongest sense that what she saw and touched would someday soon marry the eternal. That separation that she felt she simply knew would someday come together. She supposed that in so thinking, she was referring to the coming of the *kingdom of heaven*.

That kingdom was coming, she could just feel it in her bones, as her grandmother and mother would both have said. Her final reason for seeking eternity, though, was in exactly what Jesus said. Jesus had revealed eternity to her. Jesus had described the action that he would take and then actually took, and the relationship that he expected with her, for her to join him and others in eternity. Her seeking eternity was thus not something philosophical, not a Platonic conception or new-age yearning. Her seeking eternity was instead something obedient, demonstrated, and compelled. Jesus had called her, she knew. And she was *definitely* answering his call to eternity.

41 Christ.

Matthew 16:16.

The Gospels of course also record Jesus acknowledging his calling as Christ, the Son of the living God. Followers know well the scene at Caesarea Philippi. There, Jesus turned to his disciples to ask them who people thought that he was. In asking the disciples this central question, Jesus referred to himself as the Son of Man. The disciples answered factually that the people seemed confused, some saying that Jesus was his cousin John the Baptist, while others thought that he was the ancient prophet Elijah or perhaps Jeremiah or some other prophet. Jesus then asked the disciples that most-important question, which was not what others thought but what *they* thought. *Who do you say I am?* Jesus asked the disciples. Followers know that Peter was the disciple who answered boldly and correctly that Jesus is *the Christ, Son of the living God*. Jesus promptly confirmed that Peter was correct, indeed that Jesus's Father in heaven had revealed this truth to the disciples. Because the disciples accepted that world-shaking truth, Jesus told them that he would give them the *keys to the kingdom of heaven*. Yet right then in the midst of what must have been a momentous confirmation and cause for wonder and celebration, Jesus promptly warned the disciples not to tell anyone what the disciples now knew clearly that he was indeed the Christ. Jesus explained that Jerusalem's religious leaders would first need to make him suffer to the point of killing him so that

God could raise him on the third day. Peter, the very disciple who had just proclaimed Jesus as the Savior Lord, attempted to rebuke Jesus that he must never suffer and die, but Jesus replied in the firmest manner that he would instead do just as God planned.

Followers find hugely significant the Gospel's scenes like the above one of Jesus acknowledging his calling as the Messiah, meaning the Anointed or Chosen One. That Jesus knew and expressly acknowledged his calling as humankind's Savior leaves followers with no doubt. Everything including the prophecies and their fulfillment, and Jesus's teaching, authority, and miracles, pointed to Jesus as the Savior. The very name *Jesus* and the name's earlier variants Joshua or Yeshua translate literally as He Who Saves. Salvation itself refers to the Israelites' God Jehovah as one who brings humankind back into relationship with him through the only means possible, which would be his own actions in himself. Yet even with all of that circumstantial evidence, Jesus's own declaration reassures followers that those circumstances support truth. Jesus said that he was the Messiah who had come to redeem humankind through his own sacrifice. Jesus then carried out that calling. Followers can dwell productively on the scenes of Jesus acknowledging his salvation calling. Jesus is the Christ, Messiah, and Anointed One. Praise God that we have Jesus as Savior, and praise God again that Jesus acknowledges to us his salvation role. While at times to certain crowds or persons he may have been intentionally inscrutable, at other times to others he was crystal clear in acknowledging his momentous calling.

As much as he appreciated Jesus's subtlety, the way in which Jesus could tease out meaning and faith using inscrutable responses and queries, he also treasured the certainty with which Jesus spoke on special occasion. Sometimes, he valued examination and introspection, commentary and query, but other times he simply needed clarity, indeed certainty and guarantee. He needed to know who *Jesus* thought Jesus was, not who the religious leaders thought he was, or the disciples, or the crowds, or even who *he* thought Jesus was. At times, he just wanted to hear *Jesus* on Jesus, not even Jesus on what he thought of the religious leaders, or of the disciples in their frequent foolishness, or of the pursuing, believing, and then suddenly doubting and even murderous crowds in all of their quick-turning facileness. Sometimes, he just tired of all of the questions about Jesus and all of the topsy-turvy drama that went with those questions. At those times, he turned to the sure scenes of Jesus saying who Jesus was. When Jesus spoke clearly, he was fully ready to listen. He might frequently miss the subtle meaning of many of Jesus's parables and round-about teachings. He might not get the context, word usage, reference, allegory, or allusion. In those instances of momentary doubt, when he tired of earnest enquiry, he always had a solacing scene of Jesus on Jesus. As much as he appreciated the mysteries of God and never wanted to plumb them fully, which he knew that he couldn't, he nonetheless also liked having a God of clarity and certainty.

42 Shepherd.

John 10:9.

The Gospels record Jesus depicting himself in his calling as shepherd of this great flock of followers, another attribute on which followers may draw in reflection. Late in his ministry, Jesus addressed a crowd in the temple courts using figures of speech that the account says the crowd did not understand. Jesus described a sheep pen with a watchman who opened the gate to call in the sheep who recognized his voice. The pen would protect the sheep against predator and thief. The watchman would call the sheep in at night and lead them out by day using his familiar and trustworthy voice, going on ahead of his flock as their shepherd. Because the crowd did not understand, Jesus explained that he was the gate, watchman, and shepherd. Those who expect to enter to be saved from the thief, who would otherwise kill and destroy, must do so through Jesus, the gate, who also gives life to the full as the shepherd, one who lays down his own life to save and protect the sheep. Hired hands scatter when the wolf attacks because they care nothing for the sheep, but the good shepherd fights to the death. Jesus told the crowd plainly that he is the good shepherd who knows his sheep. He also told them plainly that while he lays his life down for his sheep, the very reason that his Father loves him, he does so voluntarily and with authority to take it up again. As often happened, Jesus's words divided the crowd, some saying that he was *raving mad* while others defended him. Jesus plainly, though, represented his calling to be the great gatekeeper shepherd.

The image of Jesus as a gatekeeper shepherd powerfully informs the follower who reflects on it deeply. If as we know he is the Christ, the Messiah come to save the world, then he is necessarily the figure to whom we must turn, knowing that those who do not do so, who instead reject the Savior, lose his salvation and protection. As Jesus himself said in the above address to the crowd, those who hope to enter the protection of the sheep pen by ways other than the gatekeeper shepherd are only thieves who threaten the flock. A shepherd has both a role beneficial to the sheep but also detrimental to the wolf or thief. As Jesus himself said in the above address, the shepherd cannot protect the flock without opposing the wolf even unto death. While followers may reflect more often on the shepherd's beneficial role to the sheep that by day he leads and feeds them, followers would also do well to reflect on the shepherd's detrimental role toward the wolf and thief that the shepherd opposes them to the point of precluding entry. Jesus is watchman and gatekeeper as much as shepherd of the sheep. Life carries deadly opposition about which followers should know and that they should communicate to others, sharing Jesus's good-news-shepherd message in its truest light surrounded by the love, forgiveness, and service that he mandates.

She had a memory of sheep from her grandmother's farm that made Jesus's shepherd image especially powerful to her. As a young girl, she had seen firsthand how precious sheep were. Her family album even included an old photograph of her lifting and clutching a helpless sheep, with her own eyes half closed and with the biggest smile. Yet as endearing as sheep were, she supposed in just the way that Jesus felt about humans made in his Father's image, she also knew how confused, clueless, and vulnerable sheep were. They seemed to live in a dark world, one filled in their own minds with many dire threats. They easily mistook friends for enemies but also enemies for friends. While they seemed to know that they could at any moment face the fateful wolf, and thus tended to bunch and scurry at the slightest provocation, they also seemed at times to be naïve about or oblivious to what were very real threats to their welfare and existence. Despite the care and management that her grandmother and helpers showered on the sheep, the sheep would still get separated and lost easily, wander away to fall into pits or get tangled in fences, or get savaged by strange dogs.

Something was always happening to the sheep, which to her just made them all the more endearing. What her grandmother's sheep needed was a good-shepherd protector like Jesus. She could almost remember thinking exactly that she wished to be the sheep's Jesus as she hugged that sheep so long ago and someone, probably her grandmother, snapped the photo.

43 Joyous.

Luke 10:21.

The Gospels record Jesus fully accepting his calling that, while magnificent in glorifying both himself and his Father, was also awful in its isolation, torment, and physical, mental, emotional, and spiritual difficulty. Yet the Gospels nonetheless record Jesus accepting his arduous, even horrible calling with great joy. One Gospel account records that well into Jesus's ministry, with the awful time of his arrest, conviction, and crucifixion fast approaching, Jesus took time to celebrate his relationship with his Father. The account begins with seventy-two disciples returning joyfully to tell Jesus of the miracles that they had performed in his name. Jesus replied that they should indeed rejoice because he had written their names in heaven. The account then specifically states that the Holy Spirit *filled Jesus with joy* at that same time. As if he could not contain that joy, Jesus broke out in praise for his Father and his Father's *good pleasure* in revealing his good news not to the learned but to little children. Jesus then confirmed his calling, speaking to his Father with the disciples listening, saying that only he, the Son, knew the Father, and those to whom Jesus chose to reveal the Father. Jesus then turned to the disciples, calling them blessed for seeing and hearing what many prophets and kings had hoped to see and hear. Jesus knew joy within his magnificent but arduous calling.

The image of a joyous Jesus, one who could celebrate his relationship with his Father even while anticipating his coming arrest, torture, and crucifixion, should encourage followers deeply. Like Jesus, no matter the dread followers might feel for whatever awaits them, they may still find joy when the Holy Spirit fills them with knowledge of their relationship with Jesus. That dread is nothing more than the short drive to a beloved grandparent's home for Christmas, or a brisk walk in the cold to reach the warm fire and hot drink of a cozy shelter, or the darkest part of night just before the glorious dawn. Followers might notice that Jesus's joy, while the Spirit's product, expressed itself in conversation with the Father, Jesus sharing his knowledge of the Father while recognizing the Father's knowledge of him. In our knowledge of the Son and his knowledge of us, we find expression for the joy that the Spirit brings us, even as we anticipate joining the Son in his kingdom. The Spirit causes us to speak joyfully of the work of Jesus. Even while realizing something of the agony that Jesus endured around the cross, followers may also draw more often on the joyous Jesus who delighted then, delights now, and rejoices forever in relationship with his Father. The cross was but a brief even if utterly dark and wholly necessary dot in an eternity of joyful relationship. Reflect on the joyous Jesus.

She delighted in all manner of things, mostly small things but generally anything that had any quality of large or small delight in it. Sometimes her delight was something funny that someone said, not as in a deliberate joke but just an odd and amusing way of putting a thing, even a mistaken thing. Other times her delight was in something that someone did, but again not in something deliberately funny but unintentionally so, when some happenstance showed an amusing lightness to life and circumstance. Yet other times, her delight was just in something amusing about a person or thing, again showing the levity, creativity, originality, and boundlessness of life. These small delights just seemed to her to peek through what was otherwise pretty mundane stuff, too often tiresome or even difficult stuff, heavy stuff that seemed to drain life. Then she would think of the joy of Jesus, how little children flocked to him, how he must have smiled at their lightness and how they had no guile, hiddenness, or inwardness about them. She imagined that when Jesus said to let the little children come to him and that only those who are like little children enter his kingdom, he meant that his kingdom was a place of perpetual delight. She sensed that the delight in her, that capacity of hers that noticed the small delights of life, was his Spirit in her delighting in the things of heaven. She hoped that it was so. She wanted and expected heaven with Jesus to be constant joy and delight.

†

44 Builder.

Matthew 16:18.

The Gospels record Jesus acknowledging that his mission included building his church, indeed while he also proclaimed that not even hell would prevail against it. Jesus had a calling, and fully embraced his calling, as a builder of something hugely important and meant to last. Jesus was a builder. Followers will recall that when at Caesarea Philippi, Peter acknowledged Jesus as the Messiah, Son of the living God, Jesus had not only confirmed the truth of Peter's acknowledgment but added that *on this rock I will build my church*. Jesus had something to build, something to fashion or construct, and what Jesus would construct would be a spiritual institution, making Jesus a builder but a special kind of builder of a spiritual structure. Jesus said specifically that he would build on *this rock*, implying something solid and immovable. Then to elaborate on the fixed and permanent nature of his construction, Jesus added that hell would not overcome what he built. While followers are well aware of Jesus's intent to build his church as an immovable institution, which he expressed so clearly at Caesarea Philippi, fewer may recall that Jesus also added that he would give those who confessed Jesus as Messiah the keys to the kingdom of heaven. He would build and then give the keys to the building. The account of Jesus as builder ends with his order that the disciples not tell anyone yet that he was the Messiah.

The image of Jesus as builder informs, guides, and encourages followers who reflect on it deeply. Jesus's public ministry was so short and yet his impact on existing religious institutions so tremendous that one hardly has a moment to think of Jesus as a builder. Jesus as *disrupter* comes more to mind than Jesus as *builder*. Yet Jesus was clearly both the greatest possible agent for institutional change while also the greatest possible institution builder. Jesus laid a new foundation for human institution, and that foundation was confession of him as Savior, Lord, and Christ. While his church, that spiritual institution founded solely on his confession and for his glorification, would last eternally as bride of Christ, humankind could now build temporal institutions so aligned to his church, so founded on him, that they too would endure at least for a greater time than they would without such a rock at the foundation. Not just local churches and worldwide denominations, and not just hospitals, relief agencies, and other foundations and charities, but even commercial enterprises founded in whole or part on confession of Jesus as Lord, would form and thrive. With Jesus as builder, followers would also naturally build when embracing Jesus as Christ. With Jesus, spiritual things need not be ephemeral, transitory, or imaginary. They could express themselves in form, institution, and structure, growing and developing in generative and creative union with the Lord who vitalizes them. Jesus as builder is a hugely important image for the committed follower.

He loved that Jesus built things. He loved that Jesus's Spirit seemed to promote human activity in that it grow, accumulate, organize, and take shape. He rejoiced at all the institutions in one way or another formed of faith in Christ, all the way from the very small ministries of one or two followers to the very large, indeed worldwide, organizations promoting and supporting activities in some way related to the faith. Oh, he knew of their impermanence and even of their very human distortion and corruption. He had no illusion that everything was perfect in organizations formed around faith. Yet he just found it special to be a part of that constant building and growing, those things that made faith so much more than an inner sanctuary, more like an outer sanctuary open to all whether for shelter or to contribute. He would occasionally laugh inwardly at the faith's huge worldwide outward expression, thinking *this Jesus thing is big*. He of course treasured the intimacy of inner faith with Jesus, but he found that he also took joy in the big outer things of faith, not so much in the distorted human institutions but in the great movement of the Spirit that one could see behind those institutions. Enormous social and political reforms, things that saved and liberated whole populations, seemed a frequent part of those Spirit movements, but so too did economic and commercial movements bringing relief and prosperity, and even scientific insights bringing wonder and medical breakthroughs against disease. He decided that when Jesus said that he would build, Jesus meant something consequential, permanent, and world-changing. He decided that he liked being part of something *big*.

45 Interpreter.

Luke 12:54.

The Gospels record Jesus effectively observing, reading, and interpreting the times, knowing the views, expectations, and inclinations of the crowds before they declared them. Far from a cloistered cleric, Jesus instead knew culture, worldview, and behavior, in the sense of being aware or streetwise. Jesus also urged his followers to do and be likewise. Later in his public ministry, Jesus addressed the crowd first with allegory, saying that they could tell from the clouds and wind direction whether it was going to be wet or dry, or hot or cold. Calling them *hypocrites*, Jesus then asked them why, when they were so good at interpreting natural causes, at reading the coming weather, they could be so bad at seeing the signs of the times? They could predict rain but not predict behavior, when they had the signs of behavior right in front of them. Jesus continued with an instruction to judge for themselves what is right, presumably rather than leaving that judgment to the untrustworthy religious leaders. He ended with a lesson to reconcile with one's adversary before going before the judge, in case the judge would jail one until one paid the last penny. Jesus read and interpreted people, predicting their behaviors and actions, and wanted his followers doing so, too.

The image of Jesus seeing the signs of the times, knowing how people and crowds would behave from the observations that he made of their beliefs and attitudes, and then acting accordingly, should encourage followers to do the same, as Jesus also instructed. People tend to respond as the day and age teaches them to respond. Few stand apart from the times because they have nothing on which to stand other than the times. The culture and views of the day become their culture and views. Jesus saw how commerce, culture, education and leadership affected attitudes and behaviors. He read the signs of the times in the sense of seeing how popular worldviews influenced actions. He could predict what the religious leaders would do, what the law experts would do, and how crowds and individuals would behave, because he could interpret their beliefs into their actions. To interpret the times, one must to a degree stand apart from the times. One doesn't see the air that one breathes until the air changes, only then one just sensing it before once again becoming accommodated to it. Jesus stood entirely apart from the times. He was not simply a part of culture and history but changed culture and the course of history because he knew, indeed was, its ultimate source. Jesus wanted his followers taking the long view, long enough at least to read the signs of the times, not just the weather, or maybe sports or traffic, but why people behaved as they did especially when it came to *following Jesus*.

He knew that he was nearly as captivated by the times, influenced by the times, controlled by the times, as anyone else was, even though he wished it wasn't true. He often felt like he would rather have been borne in ancient times, of course when Jesus was here, but maybe even in the hundreds of years afterward, as the faith grew first by word of mouth and house churches until gradually institutionally and even in the academies. Maybe then the signs of the times might not have been so prevalent and powerful, before mass media and entertainment. Maybe then, he could have immersed himself more completely in life with Christ, with more solitude, service, worship, and prayer. Now, he could hardly get away from the times, not that he tried particularly hard. He wasn't even sure that *getting away* from the times was what Jesus had meant when he spoke of *interpreting* the times. Rather, he figured that Jesus had himself been at least somewhat immersed in the times, traveling from largest town to smallest village and back again, so often in crowds, in both rich and humble homes, and just generally with people. Yet Jesus had also stood apart from the times, interpreted the times, *known* the times and their effect on people, how those times either supported or opposed his mission. He decided that he didn't want to hide from the times after all but simply to see how they influenced his relationship with Jesus and Jesus's relationship with others. He wanted a *Jesus* worldview, the one reliable foundation from which to interpret the movements of culture and the world.

46 Good.

Matthew 19:17; *see also* Mark 10:18.

Jesus's calling also included to be the One who is *good*. Nearly everyone wants at some time to be good or thought of as good. Jesus was the lone one who accomplished that ambition, even while he also urged that ambition on his followers. The Gospels record a well-known account of a rich young man approaching Jesus with the question of what *good thing* he must do for eternal life. Jesus first rejoined why the young man had asked about what is good when *only One is good*. Yet Jesus then answered that the young man should obey the commandments. The young man replied that he had in fact done so. Jesus then told the young man that if he wanted to be perfect and have treasure in heaven, then he should give everything that he had for the benefit of the poor, while following Jesus. When the young man left sad because he was unwilling to give up his great wealth, Jesus told his disciples that the rich have a hard time entering the kingdom of heaven. The disciples were at first concerned that no one might enter heaven, but Jesus reassured them that God made all things possible. Peter then declared that the disciples had left behind everything to follow Jesus, to which Jesus replied that the disciples who followed him would sit on thrones in heaven. When one leaves things behind for Jesus, they receive a hundred times as much with eternal life in heaven. No one but Jesus has the goodness to enter heaven, but those who give up things to pursue Jesus enter heaven with him.

The image of Jesus as good, indeed as the only One who is good, provides an important marker on which followers can reflect. Goodness attracts. We both want to be good and want to be around goodness. We want to be virtuous, blameless, and without fault, and moreover part of a community of noble and good people who do right things while helping one another prosper. We want the reputation of decency, civility, and morality. We want these things because they will also mean that life is good and that we will enjoy life's blessings. Goodness both satisfies a human need to be judged fit and acceptable, while also leading to other satisfactions. Goodness satisfies both inherently and extrinsically, inherently because something within us desires to be right with the things and also extrinsically because then we justly expect a good person's reward. Although people may today seldom really think and speak frequently and consistently about goodness, good and our need for it nonetheless play significant roles in shaping our attitudes and influencing our behavior. The rich young man reflected that need for goodness. He had goodness as his ambition. Jesus, though, showed the rich young man that we attain to goodness only through the One who is truly, consistently, completely, and perfectly good. The rich young man discovered that without Jesus, goodness is an impossible standard, something to which no one could genuinely aspire because none could genuinely achieve it. Goodness demands an intermediary, a perfect go-between, the One who is Jesus.

She had a strong desire to be thought right and good. She didn't let it influence her unduly, but she still recognized that her desire was there. She also thought often of how to deal with it, how to pursue that desire in a way that actually made sense. The more that she thought about it, the more that she realized that Jesus was exactly right, as he was always right, that she could not achieve it, could not reach the level of goodness to which she aspired. She realized that she wanted to be *good enough* for heaven, good enough to just make it to someplace that she had always wanted to go, that place that she had always wanted to end up. Yet she knew to a certainty that heaven was far too special for *good enough* to get her in. If entering the kingdom were a matter of being just good enough, maybe having done just enough good, then she probably wouldn't really want entry. That kind of standard would change her life into a labor rather than a love. The kingdom would be an economy rather than a relationship. She really only had one way that she wanted to enter heaven, which was through Jesus. She now knew that Jesus was not claiming to be some special portal into heaven but instead was revealing heaven to be the only meaningful way that it could be, a place so special that its economy was all glorious relationship, not rules and labor but relationship to the Son and, through him, with the Father.

47 Celebrated.

Matthew 21:9; *see also* Mark 11:1; Luke 19:29; John 12:12.

All four Gospels record Jesus celebrated publicly in grand spectacle on his triumphal entry into Jerusalem, fulfilling his calling as the Messiah and coming King. When Jesus and the disciples returned to Jerusalem for the last time, on the eve of his arrest during the week of Passover, Jesus had two disciples go ahead to bring a donkey's colt to him, to fulfill the Old Testament prophecy that Israel's king would come *gentle and riding on a donkey's foal.* The accounts record that a very large crowd spread their cloaks and palm branches over the road to cover Jesus's path into Jerusalem. The crowd shouted *Hosanna to David's Son* and *blessed is he who comes in the Lord's name* as Jesus made his final entry into Jerusalem. The accounts further record that the spectacle of Jesus's parade entry was so extraordinary as to stir all of Jerusalem. Everyone in the city asked who the crowds were honoring in such grand fashion during Passover Week, to which the crowds answered that they honored *the prophet Jesus of Nazareth*. Children would later continue to shout *Hosanna to David's Son* when they saw Jesus in the temple courts. Although the crowds honored Jesus as the Messiah, which was his calling, few in the crowds may have fully understood the kind of Savior Messiah for which the prophecies had called. As events later that week showed, many in the crowds may have desired or expected a conventional king, meaning a national, political, or military leader to relieve them from Roman domination. Most of the religious leaders desired no king at all, despite Jesus's prophetic calling.

The image of Jesus making his triumphal entry into Jerusalem indeed provides a grand spectacle for reflection. Few moments in Jesus's public ministry permit the follower to celebrate fully who Jesus was and what he was accomplishing. His triumphal entry is one of those moments. No matter the crowds' misguided motivation or prophetic misunderstanding, Jesus received due honor from what the accounts record were *very large* crowds. That Jesus received such honor in Jerusalem during the week of Passover in a way that stirred the whole city fit perfectly his prophetic and historic role. The triumphal entry is for the follower a brief moment when the prior tensions of Jesus's ministry and gathering darkness of his coming arrest resolved into light. The world should have honored Jesus most grandly rather than crucified him so ignominiously, and in the triumphal entry, the world briefly did. That the world may have done so out of mischievous motive and misbegotten intent simply reflects the world in which we live. Jesus briefly had his due honor from Jerusalem, in which the follower can at least briefly rejoice. Palm Sunday, which is today's observance of Jesus's triumphal entry, has exactly that cast to it of an oddly ominous but nonetheless significant celebration. Let the follower often so reflect.

He had some time ago gotten the feeling that he had an accurate sense of what Palm Sunday meant. He could feel the real cheer that everyone would want to share that Jesus had due honor. He imagined carrying a palm branch toward Jerusalem, waving it in Jesus's honor before throwing it on the road in his honor. He hoped that he would have been one of those many who threw on the road not just a palm branch but also his cloak over which Jesus could then ride in his triumphal entry into Jerusalem. He imagined wanting to shout with the rest of the crowd in the greatest excitement, like crowds today shout at sporting events. What unforgettable excitement that moment would have meant to him and everyone else in the crowd. Yet he also could feel the chill in the air that Jesus had a mission beyond a great crowd's roaring honor. His mission, so unlike the mission of many sports stars, entertainers, or politicians who receive similar adulation today, was not to celebrate his achievements or exalt himself. He had something much greater yet to achieve, something that would not look at all like an honor, indeed something terribly dark and difficult. He imagined that had he been among the crowd and known the rest of those events of the week of Passover, the crowd's cheers would have an ominous roar to them, echoed shortly later in the crowd's calls for a murderer's release and Jesus's execution.

48 Authoritative.

Matthew 21:23; *see also* Matthew 7:29; Mark 1:22, 2:10, 11:28; Luke 4:32, 20:2; John 10:18, 14:10.

Jesus's calling also included to have his Father's authority in all things. He would not act on his own but with the right, power, and ability of his Father. Various Gospel accounts record Jesus saying that he had the authority both to judge and to forgive. The religious leaders denied that Jesus had the authority either to judge or forgive because both powers were God's alone, and they did not acknowledge Jesus to be God's Son. In another Gospel account, Jesus added that he had his Father's authority both to lay down his life and to take it up again. In that instance, Jesus was clear that the authority was not his own but that of his Father *who lived in him*. Jesus's teaching also amazed the crowds because they saw that he taught *with authority*, unlike the law teachers. Yet because the religious leaders rejected what Jesus said and, so far as they were able to do so, also ignored the miracles that he did, the religious leaders had particular problem with Jesus claiming that he had

God's authority. On one occasion very late in his public ministry by which time the religious leaders had already plotted to kill Jesus, the chief priests and elders challenged Jesus's authority in the temple courts where he was teaching. They asked what authority he had to do the things that he did. Jesus replied with a question, saying that if they answered him, then he would answer them. Jesus asked the source of John's baptism, whether from heaven or men, knowing that the religious leaders could not answer without either acknowledging Jesus as John had done so or angering the people who believed John to be a prophet. When they refused to answer, Jesus also refused to answer their question about his authority, the answer to which he had already given many times. Instead, he told them two parables that both embarrassed the religious leaders while also making clear Jesus's claim to authority. The leaders would have arrested him if they had not been afraid of the crowd. Jesus's words and actions made perfectly clear that he had God's authority as his calling.

The sense of Jesus as authoritative, as holding authority within him, is an important one on which followers can reflect. Scenes of Jesus teaching, speaking, and of course performing miracles with such convincing authority show a very significant difference between God and the rest of us. God carries his own authority, while we borrow whatever authority that we have. To speak or act authoritatively, we must have another source. We do not carry our own authority. We are only as authoritative as the quality of our source of authority. Jesus, by contrast, spoke with inherent authority. What he said was not true because it fit or resonated with other sources. What Jesus said was true because *he was and is* the source. When the source of authority speaks, people must listen. Whether or not they choose to accept the words, the words remain authoritative. Everyone may have rejected what Jesus said at some point, but his words nonetheless remained authoritative. Because it is authoritative, what Jesus said judges us, rather than our judging whether it is authoritative. The religious leaders made the gross mistake of questioning Jesus's source, when he was and is the source. Only God carries his own authority. Every other authority carries delegated power, subject to its consistency with the delegation.

Authority, he understood. He never quite knew what in his nature, whether genetic, environmental, cultural, psychological, or educated, made him so sensitive to authority. In the end, though, he decided that his sensitivity to authority was spiritual. God vests all kinds of people and institutions with delegated authority, he could see. He knew that those delegations were always limited that the people and institutions must exercise the authority consistent with God's delegation. He also knew that people and institutions often didn't do so, making them subject to correction and to loss of the delegation. Yet whether right or wrong, they remained authorities as long as so recognized, which was his special sensitivity. He never wanted to insult authority, again whether right or wrong, as long as it remained authority. His reason had to do not with the person or institution but instead with God. He never wanted to challenge God, deny God his authority. He would rather submit to what he believed was an authority's rank error than to risk denying an authoritative word or action that God had actually authorized. Who knew how God planned and acted? Who was he to judge that an authority acted without delegation from God? Even when the action was clearly wrongheaded, he felt that God might be using the action to refine something in his character or remove something from his spirit. He didn't want to make the mistake of the religious leaders. He knew that God both held authority and delegated authority. He also knew and loved that Jesus, as the Son of God, was inherently authoritative.

49 Scriptural.

Matthew 22:37; *see also* Matthew 5:17; Mark 12:10, 12:28.

While Jesus's calling as the Son of God may have seemed to give him certain liberties to say and do as he wished, on his own authority, the Gospels instead record Jesus citing and quoting the Old Testament on points with which the religious leaders tested him and tried to trap him. Jesus was scriptural in his calling and his approach to doctrine. One Gospel account from very late in Jesus's public ministry, summarized in greater detail in a following section, records Jesus using scripture to silence a group of religious leaders who did not accept resurrection. When other religious leaders who did accept resurrection saw how Jesus had defeated his first test, they too tried to trap him with a question. Once again Jesus quoted the Old Testament to silence them.

The leaders asked which was the greatest of God's commands, presumably hoping to get Jesus to diminish other commands. Yet Jesus quoted the Old Testament that they must *love the Lord your God with all your heart, soul, and mind.* Jesus then quoted them the second related commandment to *love your neighbor as yourself,* explaining that everything else depended on these commands. Jesus indeed had a way to give primacy to certain commands without undermining, and instead while supporting, other commands. Confirming that he knew the heart and not just the letter of scripture, Jesus then asked the leaders whose son was the Christ. When the leaders answered that the Christ would be Israel's King David's son, Jesus quoted them scripture that David had called the Christ *Lord* such that the Christ could not be David's son. Jesus once again silenced the leaders and, the account concludes, finally defeated all of their remaining tests, solely by relying on scripture. Jesus repeatedly quoted and cited scripture, even asking his questioners whether they *haven't read the scriptures.* Jesus was scriptural in approach to doctrinal questions.

The many scenes of Jesus citing and quoting scripture to defeat the religious leaders' tests, resolving points of contention with them, should inform followers in their reflections on Jesus. Followers may not have considered that as God's Son with all authority, Jesus could presumably have spoken out of his own authority. In the vernacular, the authoritative Jesus could in theory have *gone off script.* Jesus could have resolved points of contention with the religious leaders simply by saying that truth was as Jesus said it was, in effect authoring his own doctrine. He could in theory have given new commands disconnected from Old Testament commands, maybe even replacing those commands with his own commands. Yet Jesus did not see authoring new, original, fresh, and creative doctrine as his calling. He instead said in his Sermon on the Mount that he had not come to change the scriptures but to *fulfill* them, even that not a single smallest point of scripture would disappear until he accomplished all of it. Jesus bound himself to those scriptures, constrained his will within them, and proved himself so bound by citing those scriptures when the religious leaders tested him. Those who would use scripture to attempt to undermine Jesus's authority would see instead that Jesus was entirely scriptural in the deepest way that they had not even understood scripture.

She treasured the scriptures because she found Jesus so fully within them. For her, reading the Bible was unlike reading anything else, even clear commentary on the Bible. The text just seemed to live in some way that no other text lived. She could almost feel Jesus's life on every page of scripture, even when those pages contained no direct reference to him. One of the ways in which the text seemed to her to live was that the Bible just kept yielding to her and others more and more meaning. Reading the Bible was almost as if Jesus himself were still preaching and teaching, which she felt he may indeed have been through his Holy Spirit. She remembered the verse that the word of God was living, breathing, and active, and indeed she felt as if it were just so. She remembered too how John's Gospel called Jesus *the Word*, in her mind mysteriously mixing the person Jesus with the words of scripture that he quoted and then fulfilled. While she didn't want to be mystical about the meaning, she still felt a strange sense of other-worldliness about the way that Jesus related to the text that she read. The Bible seemed a little less like his story alone, less like a prophecy of his life and then a description of him living, and instead a little more like him presently guiding, counseling, speaking, informing, instructing, and commanding. The way in which Jesus related to scripture, and was scriptural in approach, or maybe *was scripture,* just seemed to her to be as significant as anything else that she could discern of his calling. She loved having the Bible in her hands simply because of the connection it gave her to Jesus.

50 Path.

John 14:6.

Jesus had another fundamental calling that he pursued and fulfilled closely connected to his role as Christ and Savior, indeed another attribute or image reflecting the same role. The Gospels reflect Jesus as the *way* or path to the kingdom, the only way that one has to his Father. A Gospel account records that at the Last Supper, the night of his arrest, Jesus explained to the disciples that he was leaving for his Father's house to prepare a place for the disciples, although he would come back for them. Jesus then added that the disciples knew the *way* to the place where he was going, to his Father's house. The disciple Thomas, though, said that they didn't even know where Jesus was going, so how would they then know the way? Jesus answered *I am the way* and the truth and the life, adding that *no one* comes to the Father other than through him, through the Father's Son Jesus. Jesus had given the disciples the path to his Father's house, through him. Oddly, the disciple Philip still asked Jesus to show them the Father, but Jesus replied that anyone who has seen him *has* seen the Father. He continued that he was in the Father and the Father in him, the Father doing his work by living in him. Thus Jesus had shown the disciples the way or path to the Father, and Jesus was that way. Jesus is the one and only path to the Father's kingdom of heaven.

The image of Jesus as a way or path to the Father, or more accurately *the* way or path because he is the *only* way to the Father, is a central image on which followers reflect. Jesus as the path may be followers' primary reflection when thinking of salvation. Jesus as savior implies his ability to save, his capacity to offer others entry into the Father's kingdom. Jesus as *the way* instructs even more directly, more concretely and succinctly how one proceeds toward salvation. Yes, Jesus *can* save, but also yes, Jesus is *the way* to the kingdom. One does not first recognize that Jesus can offer kingdom citizenship and then go try to find the right gift, correct formula, or magic words that Jesus will recognize to grant one's request for entry. No, one instead takes the holy image, redemptive work, and resurrected life of Jesus for kingdom entry and citizenship. Jesus is in that sense not merely Savior but also the way to salvation. The image of Jesus as path is thus significant in its own manner, even when one already considers Jesus to be the Savior, capable of offering salvation from death and entry into eternal kingdom life. That Jesus also explained that he was the only way to the Father reassures followers that they have no need for any other accomplishment, resource, or knowledge to gain the kingdom. Jesus offers it in himself as sole way and path.

He appreciated so much this attribute that Jesus was not only Savior but also *the path* to salvation. How much different he felt that the faith would have been if Jesus was indeed Savior but not also the path to salvation. If Jesus saved, but then he also had to gain some rank, perform some service, provide some gift, or know some secret code to induce Jesus to save him, then he knew that he was going to be in big trouble. He was absolutely sure that he didn't have the rank, hadn't performed the service, couldn't provide the gift, and didn't know the secret code, if any or all of those things were necessary. He never felt like royalty, never felt like he had done much of anything worthy, knew that he didn't have any great gifts to offer, and had no idea of ancient Hebrew, Greek, or Aramaic so as to have a clue about any entry code. He would have been out of the kingdom race, off the kingdom journey, out of kingdom running if any of those things had been necessary to induce the Savior Jesus to let him in with others whom he knew had all of those wondrous things and probably many more. No, he liked Jesus not only as Savior but also as *path*. He could see Jesus, he could follow Jesus, and he knew that he could gain kingdom entry simply by holding fast to the only path that, or actually *whom*, he knew.

51 Vine.

John 15:1.

While Jesus described himself as the path to salvation, the Gospels also record Jesus describing himself as *the vine* to whom the disciples must remain connected for the life with which Jesus would supply them and the fruit that they would then produce. Jesus not only saves but also vitalizes for productive work. Jesus instructed the disciples about many things at the Last Supper, especially as John's Gospel records in a long series of accounts. One of those accounts reports Jesus describing himself to the disciples as the *true vine* with his Father as the *gardener*. His gardener Father would indeed cut off branches that bear no fruit while pruning fruit-bearing branches to make them even more fruitful, Jesus continued. Jesus then made himself clearer that the disciples must remain him and he in them if the disciples were to bear any fruit. They would die otherwise, picked up and thrown into the fire like discarded branches. Jesus repeated *I am the vine* with the disciples *the branches*. If the disciples remained in Jesus, then they would bear much fruit to his Father's glory and proving themselves Jesus's disciples, while apart from Jesus the disciples would do nothing at all, Jesus concluded. Jesus is the vine and his followers the vine's branches.

The image of Jesus as the vine should be especially powerful for followers who have some appreciation for the cultivation of fruit of any kind but particularly the cultivation of grapes and for wine production, although the image may be nearly so powerful for any who reflect on it earnestly. Walking through virtually any orchard or vineyard in harvest season gives one the picture of sweet, delicious, nourishing, natural abundance. While owners certainly tend orchards and vineyards to promote their growth, just as Jesus's teaching indicates that the Father tends to the shaping and pruning of disciples, when the good harvest comes, it can come in such ripeness and plenty as to seem to have come straight from the hand of God. In giving his disciples the vine image, Jesus surely intended to convey an image of abundance that his followers when staying connected to him would bear so much fruit that those who saw it would know them to be Jesus's disciples and would glorify the Father. Jesus is not merely about salvation, although salvation would certainly be enough. Jesus is also about his followers producing rich harvests, so rich that their fruits make people think of Jesus and his Father. Think of something so special that someone has done that it made you think of Jesus, that it even glorified God in heaven. Jesus wants his followers to produce those things. Followers should want to do so also. Imagine how special it would be to do things that make people think of God and his Son. The only way to do so is to stay connected to the vine, meaning Jesus.

She understood what Jesus meant about staying connected to the vine. She had walked through luscious vineyards and orchards, picking delicious ripe fruit as if a gift of God. She fully appreciated the image of producing such special works that people credited God. Yet she had no sense that she had any capacity to do so, indeed was instead embarrassed at the pretense. She certainly wouldn't claim that any of her modest works were the actual work of God. Still, she did have the full sense of Jesus's capacity of using his followers for good works. She had seen followers do much good and had heard or read of followers doing much more good. She also knew that she wanted to stay connected closely to Jesus, even wanted to have the Father's pruning as painful as it might be, in order that she bear the Father and Son their due and capable fruit. She wondered again what that fruit might be, looking back through her life at what might have been God's good works borne out of her because of her connection with Jesus. While she thought that she might count some, indeed possibly many, godly fruits in her life, she quickly stopped the thought again. Jesus had not said to count one's fruit. He had only said to stay connected and produce it so that *others* may see it. So she prayed again to the Father that he would conceal her fruit from her while producing much in her and through her for others to notice, giving only the Father due glory.

52 Glorifying.

John 17:4.

At the root of Jesus's calling in each of the above respects is his role to glorify his Father. Everything that the Gospels record Jesus doing he did to glorify his Father, as a Gospel account of the Last Supper records Jesus explaining to the disciples. Jesus had already spoken long at the Last Supper. His betrayer Judas had already left, and Jesus had already washed his disciples' feet in demonstration of the service that they were to give to all and one another. The account then records Jesus looking to heaven to pray directly and vocally to his Father. Jesus first acknowledged that his time had come. Jesus then asked his Father that the Father glorify the Son *in order that* the Son may glorify the Father. Jesus wasn't calling for honor and attention for his own satisfaction but that he could glorify the Father. Still speaking aloud to his Father, Jesus added that the Father had granted the Son all authority to give eternal life, meaning to know both Son and Father as the only true God, to all those whom the Father had given to the Son. Jesus ended his prayer by telling the Father that by completing the work that the Father gave him, he, the Son, had brought the Father glory, now needing the Father only to return to the Son the glory that the Son had with the Father before the world's beginning. Jesus glorified the Father as his calling.

The image of Jesus both seeking the Father's glory throughout his ministry and then asking that the Father glorify him for the Father's greater glory should be a central one on which followers reflect. Jesus's prayer in the account summarized immediately above teaches followers that the Father's glory is the central purpose. Followers must understand and embrace that bringing glory to God is the follower's mission just as it was Jesus's mission. What, then, glorifies God? What does it mean to glorify anyone or anything? The concept of glory is a familiar secular concept in the sense of a military general or political leader earning the people's adulation. Glory connotes grandeur or magnificence, qualities that others both promote by exalting the glorified person or entity and also observe in its evident splendor. To glorify is to praise and otherwise treat in a way that increases the standing of the person or object, such as in secular settings to venerate or even lionize. The spiritual meaning of *glorifying* goes further to deify and worship. Followers know that God created humans to do exactly that, to worship God as sole deity, just as Jesus acted to exalt his Father. Just as worship comes in many forms, glorifying God also comes in many forms, as Jesus's pursuit of his calling through ministry and miracles perfectly illustrated. Jesus's calling was to glorify the Father even as the Father glorified him, just as a follower's calling is to glorify the Father through simultaneous exaltation of the Son. Contemplating Jesus's worship of God should be a follower's central inspiration.

She held in awe the thought not just of God's glory, which of course would be wondrous and fearsome all at once, but also that she might in some way contribute to that glory. The thought frankly made little sense to her. What could *she* possibly do that would glorify God to whose magnificence the whole creation already attested? Yet there stood Jesus, also fully human, saying that his role on earth had been exactly that same role, to glorify his Father. Of course, she knew that Jesus had done miracle after miracle, which once again put far beyond her the sense that she, too, might glorify God as Jesus so clearly did. On the other hand, Jesus had done many other things, smaller things even though profound and special things, that must also have glorified his Father. While she couldn't picture herself performing any miracles, she *could* picture herself doing some of those smaller but still-special things that Jesus did, like welcoming little children, guiding and protecting a vulnerable woman, teaching, and even feeding the hungry, if only by purchasing, preparing, and sharing food and not by miraculously multiplying bread. As she thought about what Jesus might have meant by *glorifying* his Father, she realized that glory, honor, praise, and worship might be just as much the product of small things as of large things, as much the product of ordinary and common service as of miracles. After all, she had seen in Jesus's teaching that heaven's economy had a strange way of valuing the small contributions over the large ones when one gave all that one had. She decided that she was going to think more about glorifying God in everything. She was going to think more about Jesus's calling to both glorify and receive glory.

⁵³ Commissioner.

Matthew 28:19; *see also* Mark 16:15.

While Jesus glorified the Father in all he did, he did so while commissioning the disciples to do likewise. Jesus's role included to commission his followers with his authority to make disciples of others. The Gospels record that after his burial and resurrection, Jesus told the disciples to meet him on a mountain in Galilee. One account records that when Jesus appeared there, the disciples worshiped him, even though some doubted. The account continues that Jesus then *came to them* to say that with all authority on heaven and earth, he was sending the disciples out to make *disciples of all nations,* what followers know today as the Great Commission. They were to baptize others in the name not only of the Father and Son but also the Holy Spirit. Jesus continued that the disciples were also to teach others to obey his commands. Jesus also wanted the disciples to know that he would be with them at all times right up until the *very end of the age.* These words were the last that the disciples together heard directly from the resurrected and visible Jesus before he ascended again into heaven. Another account records that Jesus wanted the disciples to *preach his good news* to all creation. Those who accepted his good news he would save to eternal life, protect against sin, and empower to heal, while those who rejected it he would condemn. In his final role on earth, Jesus commissioned disciples.

The image of Jesus commissioning the disciples holds particular significance for followers. Jesus was not a so-called *one-man act*, not a one-off charismatic performer. His role instead included to grant to others the authority that he held to baptize persons into the faith and make disciples of them, instituting and promoting faith fellowship within the church. Put simply, Jesus shared his role. His followers are to *be like him* in his role of making other disciples. Far from having their newfound faith isolate them into protected sect, followers thus become key and active parts of this supremely significant world-historical movement. Every follower shares an institutional role. We not only belong to the greatest movement ever, the work on earth of Father and Son creators, but are the church's active force, empowered and guided by the Holy Spirit. Jesus commissioning the disciples isn't merely some technical investiture of church authority over sacraments. Jesus's commissioner role invites followers into core kingdom work, which is to see the kingdom stretch to its greatest reaches that all would obey, all would flourish, and all would glorify God even as they move forward the great work. Everyone has some degree of wanting to belong while wanting to be significant. Jesus's act as commissioner gives everyone that chance, indeed equal chance to take his authority out of which to make new disciples.

He had for some time felt some real hesitation about his disciple's role to *make other disciples*. Part of the reason was that he had never felt any confidence that he could convince anyone to do much of anything. Jesus seemed to him to have given an even taller order when he commissioned the disciples to make disciples *of all nations*. He felt particularly ill-equipped to tell anyone of another culture and nation to obey Jesus's commands, even though he recognized that Jesus himself, and the eleven disciples whom he commissioned, had been of another nation. He knew that following Jesus was not a cultural or national pursuit but a choice that transcended culture and nationality, bringing all people together around the King of all kings. He also saw Jesus teaching just as much as preaching and knew that even in the Great Commission Jesus had told the disciples to *teach* others to obey his commands, not to coerce or manipulate them into anything. Indeed teaching was exactly where he felt that he could carry out Jesus's commission. Others who, like him, may also have been without great confidence had nonetheless taught him long, patiently, and graciously. He had nothing but deep appreciation for those many who had taken the time to share instruction with him. Others had even baptized him, for which he was also deeply grateful. So he sensed that he could carry out his own commission, with whatever effectiveness entirely up not to his own confidence but instead to the movement and work of the Holy Spirit. Yet the thing that he knew most was that he wanted to be a part of this great and eternal work. He was finally and fully part of something *big*.

4

His Ministry

Leader. Matthew 4:19. *Preacher.* Matthew 4:17. *Teacher.* Luke 4:15. *Unschooled.* John 7:14. *Surprising.* John 3:7. *Worshiper.* Luke 4:16. *Warrior.* Luke 4:30. *Participant.* Luke 5:29. *Knowing.* Luke 5:17. *Signifier.* John 1:42. *Harvester.* Mark 2:23. *Appointer.* Mark 3:14. *Convener.* Matthew 5:1. *Dispatcher.* Matthew 11:4. *Resting.* Matthew 11:28. *Intercessor.* Luke 11:1. *Partaker.* Matthew 9:10. *Expositor.* John 6:26. *Counteractive.* John 6:41. *Liberator.* Matthew 15:14. *Allegorical.* Matthew 16:11. *Egalitarian.* Luke 9:48. *Inclusive.* Mark 9:39. *Childlike.* Matthew 18:3. *Pursuer.* Matthew 18:12. *Forgiving.* Matthew 18:22. *Divider.* John 7:43. *Defender.* John 8:7. *Verified.* Luke 10:25. *Calming.* Luke 10:41. *Persistent.* Luke 11:8. *Ready.* Luke 12:35. *Shrewd.* Luke 16:9. *Savior.* Luke 19:9. *Serving.* John 13:15. *Friend.* John 15:14. *Restorer.* John 21:15.

Given the extraordinary nature of his prophetic calling, salvation mission, awful crucifixion, and spectacular resurrection, that Jesus also had an extended, three-year public ministry might be surprising were it not that his ministry was so dynamic, memorable, miraculous, exquisite, and effective. Couldn't Jesus have skipped the ministry part and still been just as successful in his mission? Yet followers often seem to draw as much or more from the scenes, images, and events of Christ's ministry as followers do from his unprecedented heralding, calling, sacrifice, resurrection, and revelation. Christ's ministry includes so many poignant lessons, rich parables, and profound encounters that followers would do especially well to recall and rely on them frequently. To elide the events of Christ's ministry would be to lose an enormous resource in navigating a day or life, in preserving and promoting the faithful relationship with Christ on which followers so much depend. We do well not to ignore Christ's calling, crucifixion, and resurrection because we find our life in Christ's salvation. But we also learn much, draw deeply, and wisely rely on the scenes, images, and events of Christ's ministry. Confirm the following images of Christ as powerful resources in deepening Christ relationship.

54 Leader.

Matthew 4:19; *see also* Isaiah 9:2; Matthew 9:9; Luke 5:27.

Following Jesus's water-and-Spirit baptism and triumphant wilderness testing, and then his Spirit-powered return to Galilee, the Gospels next record Jesus recruiting his first disciples. In a scene that followers tend to know quite well, Jesus recruited his first disciples, the fishermen Simon Peter and his brother Andrew, as Jesus walked by the Sea of Galilee. The brief but powerful account makes it appear as though Jesus as yet had no followers, at least no disciples or entourage. He was simply walking by the lake, and apparently not on a city or village grand promenade but in a humble working district for fishermen. The account clearly makes it appear that Jesus just came upon Simon Peter and Andrew casting their nets, almost incidentally or casually, although given Peter's central role in the following three-year drama, one can hardly think that happenstance had anything to do with their predestined encounter. In any case, *Come, follow me,* was Jesus's direct invitation, to which Jesus added that Simon Peter and Andrew were to become *fishers of men.* They were no longer to fish for a lake catch but to recruit additional disciples of Jesus. Significantly, the account has Simon Peter and Andrew joining Jesus *at once.* Jesus then promptly saw two other fishermen brothers, James and John, in their boat preparing nets to fish with their father. Once again, Jesus's call to James and John caused them immediately to leave their boat, nets, and father to join Jesus. Jesus would later invite other disciples including Matthew whom he simply called out of a tax-collector's booth, saying again, *Follow me.* While many would join Jesus in his wandering preaching and teaching, Jesus specifically chose, called and recruited disciples.

The image of Jesus recruiting his first disciples resonates with followers, particularly active and devoted followers for whom the scene may make them recall their own path to fellowship in Christ. Jesus does not yet seem to have been well known in the region when he called the pair of brothers Simon Peter and Andrew, and James and John, as his first disciples. The account gives no indication that any of the brothers knew or recognized Jesus. They appear from the stark account to have simply dropped their nets and followed him the moment they heard his invitation. Some followers might have the same sense of having dropped everything to follow Christ, figuratively if not literally, although many others may instead have found their way to Christ incrementally. The account may indeed at first reading seem unduly stark in that respect of depicting the brothers as dropping everything to join Jesus immediately. Yet that another Gospel account says that Jesus returned to Galilee *in the power of the Spirit* may help explain his invitation's powerful effect, as a prior section addresses. The same account records that *everyone* praised him as he began to teach in the region. In the Spirit's power, he must have had powerful attraction, demonstrated so clearly in having mature men suddenly abandon their careers at his simple call. The point of the image, though, is that Jesus called them. Jesus wants allies in his cause to save persons in order to glorify the Father.

Once he began to think about it, he realized that one of the things that he liked most about his called and chosen faith was its inclusive character. The world seemed to him indifferent as to his participation, membership, cause, and inclusion, as if it could either take him or leave him. That indifference, he realized, was the scariest part of modern and post-modern culture, trying day to day to deal with its existential nihilism, with its strong tendency to declare everything and anything ultimately meaningless. Sometimes, the world even seemed to say clearly that the universe would be better off without him. Yet Jesus had wanted Peter, James, and John, and the other disciples. Jesus had commissioned them to recruit and want others. Jesus had admonished the disciples not to drive away children or reject others who used his name in good works. Jesus had recruited twelve disciples and then seventy-two disciples, sending them out to make more disciples. And so from these images and other things that Jesus and his followers said, he concluded that Jesus wanted *him,* too. Because Jesus wanted him, the church wanted him and not just him but everyone else who would accept Jesus. As he discerned the value of membership, of *being wanted*, he also realized the gross error of those who, in rejecting Christ, would especially scoff at followers' frequent evangelizing, inviting, and recruiting to inclusion and membership. The very invitation that he most valued because it gave him cause to live was the very thing that most offended those who rejected the invitation. Ah, a calling was indeed an extraordinary thing. Jesus received his call and then came calling.

55 **Preacher.**

Matthew 4:17.

Matthew's Gospel clearly records Jesus preaching from the time of his baptism and first return to Galilee. The account states that Jesus *began* to preach, making clear that Jesus, unlike his cousin John, had not been preaching until after his baptism and return to Galilee. The account gives no specific cause for Jesus beginning to preach, although John's powerful preaching at the Jordan River, his witness to Jesus as the coming Messiah, and then the Spirit's descent on Jesus together seem to be the obvious triggering events. Hugely important things had happened at the Jordan River, so important that one would think that Jesus's conduct must change. From the silence of the Gospel record, Jesus had to the point of his baptism apparently been leading a quiet sort of Nazarene's backwater life, without public notice since his temple-courts encounters nearly two decades earlier. Now, filled with the Spirit's power, Jesus must do something. What he first did was to preach. No longer the private Nazarene son of Joseph and Mary, he would now be a preacher. The account also states that Jesus preached not only *from that time*, referring to his first return to Galilee, but also from that time *on*, suggesting that Jesus continued to preach, by inference from subsequent accounts, for the three-year duration of his ministry. Appreciate the image: Jesus was a preacher. The account also tells the reader exactly what Jesus was preaching from that time on, which was to *repent,* and not just because he, the Messiah, said to do so but specifically because *the kingdom of heaven is near.* Jesus had a message, and from the time of his return to Galilee following his baptism, he was sharing that message as a preacher. Those who encountered the Spirit-powered Jesus were going to hear his message.

The image of Jesus preaching should be a confirming one for followers, particularly those who feel the occasional sting of complaint against Christian preaching. The thought of *preaching* has a connotation peculiar to Christian witness, suggesting evangelizing or proselytizing toward the hearer's conversion to the point of view of the Christian witness. To *preach* also carries a more-general meaning of tireless support for a condition or cause. Those who do not follow Christ also preach but do so with different messages and toward their hearer's different conversions. Those non-Christian witnesses would maintain that they do not in fact preach toward any conversion at all, instead carrying a message of simply to live and let live. They may even profess tolerance of all views other than those of the evangelizing preacher, communicating to some degree that things would be fine everywhere if the voice of the Christian witness would only fall silent. And so the tension goes, the preacher wanting the message heard, while the hearer accepts or rejects the message and, when rejecting, rejecting also the preacher and preaching, such that the witnesses themselves debate the proper nature and true value of preaching. Christ, though, left followers with an image of his prompt and consistent preaching, although preaching of a specific sort inviting the hearer to see the kingdom's nearness. When God is suddenly near in the person and Spirit of Christ, and God's kingdom is thus all around us, who wouldn't want to let the world know? If the preacher were to remain silent, then the stones would cry out.

He had driven through the fast-food outlet for a soda on the long commute home so regularly that he was on a first-name basis with some of the window attendants. On one late-night commute, so quiet and late that rushing through the line was completely unnecessary, he paused to make polite small-talk with one of those familiar attendants, one who had a peculiarly melodious name that he found especially easy to remember. His pause gave the window attendant a moment to ask what he did for a living dressed as formally as he usually did. Out of surprise at the question more than anything else, he demurred, asking instead that the attendant guess. *A preacher,* she answered, and not with any hint of denigration but with the excitement of one who followed the King, as he had long assumed that she did from her patience, persistence, and unusual kindness in the difficult job. He smiled broadly out of the sudden satisfaction at having had his vocation mistaken for preaching. Still smiling, he answered that he was only a preacher *of a sort* but that he was quite glad to be thought of as Christ's witness. She smiled back and nodded appreciatively as she handed over the receipt. Christ's witness indeed lived even in the late nights at the drive-up window of that interstate fast-food outlet. And maybe, he thought, she was not at all mistaken. Maybe his vocation was preaching, just as preaching is or should be the vocation of every witness to the glory of Christ. Angels will visit in human guise when one least expects, he thought that he recalled the Bible as saying. Who knows, he smiled again to himself, but that God had sent an angel as a fast-food window attendant to deliver a message regarding true vocation? Curiously, he never saw the window attendant again.

56 Teacher.

Luke 4:15; *see also* Matthew 4:23, 9:35.

The Gospels make plain Jesus's frequent role as teacher, not just from the many individual accounts of his teaching but also in explicit statements that he taught. Indeed, before saying anything else about Jesus's ministry other than that he returned to Galilee in the Spirit's power, Luke's Gospel mentions first and foremost that Jesus taught. The Gospels record Jesus teaching in many outdoor places including on open mount and plain, and from a boat along the lakeshore. Yet the three times that the Gospels mention Jesus's teaching generally rather than in specific event, they each say that Jesus taught *in their synagogues.*

Teaching in the Jewish synagogues may have been natural in one respect that the Israelites had designed and constructed them for public gatherings. The Israelites may well have had no ready alternative for public teaching such as in a Greek gymnasium or Roman forum. On the other hand, the synagogue was also the place of God's worship and prayer. Far from some outsider or religious rebel, in teaching in the synagogues, Jesus was assuming an insider's place and prominence. He was not attacking the figurative citadel walls but taking rightful position of authority inside the houses of God. The accounts also make clear that Jesus taught in synagogues *throughout the region*. He was a traveling teacher, one who may not have made a specific synagogue his pastorate or teaching home. The biblical record appears that he taught everywhere without respect to the specific synagogue forum, one account even saying that he went through *all the towns and villages* teaching in the synagogues. Jesus was not just a preacher but also a traveling teacher.

The image of Jesus teaching in synagogues throughout the region should encourage followers in their earnest study of God's word. The moment that the follower hesitates in that study, the image of Jesus teaching and teaching should encourage resumed studies. Jesus plainly cared deeply that his followers would know, understand, and appreciate God's revealed mind, the thought, construct, and principle through which he governs the world. The indicated frequency and geographic scope of his teaching should confirm for the skeptic that Jesus wants followers educated, aware, thoughtful, and able in recalling and applying God's word. The image of Jesus teaching should alone provoke study. Think often of the rich timelessness of sitting in an ancient synagogue listening to Jesus open the scriptures' mysteries. See the sunlight slanting through the door and windows, feel the hard ground softened only slightly by the dull robe pulled underneath one's seat, and taste the dry, dusty air carrying Jesus's warm voice through the hushed synagogue. Imagine his breath releasing the Spirit onto each stilled listener. Then realize that we continue to hear his voice both in the Bible's red letters and the Spirit speaking in the stillness of our souls. Pursue and accept Jesus's teaching because he meant teaching to be central to his ministry. Then teach others, doing as he taught.

She had an appetite for learning about God's word that she could not explain other than to trace it to Christ himself. She realized one day that she probably had a greater desire to learn about what the Bible said, particularly as it related to Christ, than desire for any other routine activity, not that studying God's word was really routine. Instead, her studies were somehow fresh, like she was reading, hearing, and understanding things for the first time. She was not a voracious learner, she knew. She cared little for knowing the trivial information to which others seemed to her to attach far too much importance. She didn't have a great appetite to know everything and anything, not the common data and details that some others seemed somehow to know. Instead, she had only a great appetite to know God's word. And even here, she had no particular desire to know the historical, literary, archaeological, and other details that some especially well-versed teachers knew so well. She appreciated those details as they informed her about the meaning, inspiration, and revelation of God's word, but at the same time she wasn't especially committed to remembering them. She instead almost felt the opposite that every effort she made to recall a *fact about* the Bible or the settings in which its events and teachings took place was a slight detour that might cause her to overlook or forget a *revelation of* God's word. She fully appreciated knowledgeable teachers and the important context that their details could bring, but she needed revelations, not facts. She needed to hear and see Jesus teaching, just as he so often taught.

57 Unschooled.

John 7:14.

While Jesus was plainly an enthralling and profound teacher whose instruction gathered crowds throughout the region, the Gospels also record that Jesus was *unschooled* in that teaching. People knew that he had not studied in the schools and manner that other religious teachers, particularly the well-known and formally recognized scholars, had studied. An account late in Jesus's public ministry emphasized the point. Jesus's brothers, still not understanding who their brother was, had told Jesus that if he wanted to be famous, then he should be teaching in Judea where the famous scholars taught, not his home region of Galilee, especially during the great festival when crowds thronged Jerusalem. Jesus initially resisted in part because the Jews lay in wait to kill him. But halfway through the festival, Jesus finally went up to Jerusalem's temple courts to teach. As usual, his teaching amazed his hearers. And as usual, their response was to wonder *how he got such learning* when he had not even studied. Jesus explained that he had no need of studying because his teaching *was not his own* but instead came from the Father who sent him. Jesus then elaborated. Anyone doing God's will would learn that his teaching came from God. His purpose was not to gain his own honor but to work for the honor of the Father who sent him, which was why he was able to speak truth. Jesus ended his response by implying that they should not trouble themselves over whether he was schooled because their great leader Moses had given them the law, and yet they had not kept it. Schooling had meant nothing to them in the past, so why should it mean anything with Jesus.

The image of the unschooled Jesus schooling the schooled Jews provides an important insight for the follower who reflects on it. Schooling, while critical for learning the world's ways, has only a little to do with learning the ways of God. Schooling cannot impart fully God's deep truths, which is instead the role of the Holy Spirit. Schools are fundamentally human institutions, dependent on human initiative, role, structure, and will. Schools will thus inevitably produce teachers who teach human design and thought, and who honor themselves and their own teaching. In the above event, Jesus acknowledged openly what the Jews' question about his schooling only implied, which is that the source of a teaching is as important as or more important than its direct content. Who should care precisely what one thinks of what another says if God is the source of the talk? The source carries the significance. If God authored a message that only a donkey carried, then one should listen just as much if not more. Jesus was brilliant as a teacher and could have taught for his own honor. If he had done so, then he would have gained great honor. Yet his purpose was not to promote himself or his own thought. His purpose was to carry his Father's message. The Son had come to speak as unschooled because he had no wish that any school would influence the content of his Father's message. Followers, consider carefully the source of teaching, while ensuring that you listen carefully when God is the source, no matter who carries the message. Remember that Jesus himself was unschooled.

While schooled himself, he had learned not to trust everything that comes from the schooled. He had learned to examine the source, and not just the academy or publishing house, or the party or ideology, but the deep source. He had learned to seek the things of God rather than of man. He appreciated the work of scholars but wanted little or nothing of giving honor or deference to schools of thought no less than to certain teachers or scholars. The unschooled Jesus was of course his model. Yet he also felt a kinship to the highly schooled Nicodemus who had visited Jesus at night to inquire of and learn from the one Master. Like Nicodemus, he studied Jesus in the nights, and in the small spaces and dark corners of his days, until the Master's teaching suffused and gave great light to his thought. The more that he drew from the Master, the less that he saw in the teaching of highly honored men. He still read what others read to, as they say, *stay current*, but he read with a different eye and ear than he had previously read when he had not known the Master. His eye and ear led him quickly to whether the writer wrote from the one great source or instead without source and for the writer's own honor. When he discovered a writing from the one great source, he treasured and reread it. When he encountered the many other writings each from their own little sources, he scanned them quickly and set them aside, hoping that their authors would someday find the one great source.

58 Surprising.

John 3:7.

The Gospels record Jesus surprising his followers including the most learned who, Jesus simultaneously indicated, ought not to have been so surprised. John's Gospel gives the well-known example of the religious leader and ruler Nicodemus visiting Jesus at night, acknowledging that Jesus had indeed come from God, as his miracles attested. Although Nicodemus was a religious authority and had just given Jesus an honor that other rulers had not, Jesus was surprisingly not going to let Nicodemus control their agenda and communication. Instead, Jesus promptly replied that no one could see God's kingdom unless *born again*, a premise that stunned the learned Nicodemus, one whom spiritual truths should not have been able to stun. Surely *birth again* was impossible, Nicodemus replied. Jesus then had to explain about birth in God's Spirit. Yet Jesus also admonished Nicodemus that Jesus's teaching *should not have surprised* him. Jesus then explained that just as the wind is unpredictable as to its source and direction, so those born of the Spirit would also be so. Nicodemus was still incredulous, so Jesus admonished him again that Nicodemus should as Israel's teacher know better, indeed should accept Jesus's testimony. Jesus explained that if his speaking of earthly things had confused Nicodemus, then how could Nicodemus learn of heavenly things? Only the Son of Man had been to heaven, and now, Jesus added, he must be *lifted up* that all who believed would have eternal life. Jesus concluded his surprising discourse to Nicodemus with his best-known revelation that *God so loved the world that he gave his one and only son, that whoever believes in him shall not perish but have eternal life*. Jesus had great capacity to surprise.

The image of Jesus confusing the religious official Nicodemus, who Jesus simultaneously said should have known better, reminds followers of how Jesus constantly challenged and surprised. As already indicated in a section above, Jesus was to some persons inscrutable in his teaching. He may also have been to a degree impenetrable or unknowable, which of course would be true that the divine has qualities that humans cannot fully know, only those qualities that the divine chooses to reveal. Jesus was also in a sense freshly and positively unpredictable, not that he was at all arbitrary, capricious, unreliable, or whimsical in the way that other religions depict lesser gods. To the contrary, what Jesus did and said made perfect sense when his hearers had time to consider his words and actions *in retrospect*. Yet those who did not have the benefit of hindsight as they encountered Jesus often found what he said or did to be unexpected, surprising, creative, original, and unique. No one spoke quite like Jesus spoke, and no one moved, acted, healed, taught, and served quite like he did. Jesus's capacity to surprise may indeed have been just as he explained to Nicodemus that persons born of the Spirit are to a degree, and only in the most positive sense, unpredictable in their origin and course, moving like the wind, fresh and without apparent origin, just as God is without origin. The Spirit must have room to act as the Father wills it, and who knows the mind of God other than the Son and Spirit?

Followers have much to treasure in contemplating that attribute having to do with Jesus's propensity to surprise.

He absolutely loved Jesus's freshness, his originality and uniqueness. He had discovered on deepest reflection that Jesus had this extraordinary *uncreated* quality as if he came from no place, had no origin, spoke and acted against no standard other than his own. As much as he studied Jesus to discern his divine principles and guides, he always felt that Jesus's standard was at the same time a standard that followers could not fully discern, even if Jesus revealed plenty of that standard on which followers could duly rely. He knew well the literally hundreds of things that Jesus said to do and not to do. Yet he also felt as if Jesus could at any moment come up with dozens of other things equally reliable and consistent, and still also somehow original and profound. Jesus's teachings felt at once complete and incomplete, complete in the sense that they supplied everything needed to survive and thrive, but still incomplete in the sense that those teachings could always have so much more to them. Jesus could reveal and reveal and reveal without exhausting revelation. He did not feel as though he was conjecturing unsoundly in so concluding because he had the Gospel record on which to rely. In that record, Jesus never seemed to repeat platitudes. Everything that he said seemed to be fresh, original to its specific circumstance. He so badly wanted to have Jesus's freshness on which to draw himself and share with others. He wanted everything every day to be new, as he imagined that everything every day had been new in the company of Jesus during his public ministry. And then, when he turned again to the account of Jesus instructing the learned Nicodemus, he realized fully for the first time that with the Spirit, everything was indeed new, with every day in some sense inhabited by the divine and therefore uncreated, original, and surprising. He hoped then to rise each morning looking for that surprise, sensing moment to moment the Spirit's fresh presence.

59 Worshiper.

Luke 4:16.

The Gospels give clear clues that Jesus worshiped in the local synagogues. An early Gospel account records that Jesus went into the synagogue when he returned to his boyhood home of Nazareth from his baptism and wilderness fasting and testing. The account continues by recording that Jesus had a *custom* of entering the local synagogue. The specific account recording his customary synagogue attendance further suggests that other members, indeed the full synagogue community, were in attendance on that occasion of Jesus's return. The event appears to have been the community's routine gathering for ceremonial reading and worship, other than for the fact of Jesus's return and the extraordinary words that he spoke on that occasion. Because the passage speaks of Jesus's customary attendance in connection with a specific instance of what was likely the usual ceremonial reading and worship, readers can draw an inference, one hopes reliable to the text's intention, that Jesus regularly attended synagogue reading and worship services. His customary synagogue visit was likely not a private time for solitary reflection given that this instance, which the text connects to his custom of synagogue visits, involved a gathering for reading. Throughout his Nazarene boyhood and well into the prime of his adult life, Jesus likely worshiped and read or heard readings in the synagogue with other worshipers, all in regular attendance.

The image of Jesus worshiping in local synagogue powerfully reinforces for the follower the value of participating in a local Christian community in celebratory worship and scripture reading. The image of Jesus regularly attending synagogue services is simply an enormous witness to communal worship. One might easily and readily conclude on the point that if God's own Son did it, then followers should do it, too. Jesus himself did not say so on the one early occasion described immediately above. When he read and spoke on that extraordinary occasion, as described immediately below, he spoke about a different subject outside of worship attendance. Readers should not miss the prelude point to his revelatory reading, though, that Jesus was likely a regular worship-and-reading attendee. Communal worship may at times today seem ordinary, either for the frequent or infrequent attendee. Regular practice can become ritual, ritual practice can become rote or habit, and habitual readings or other repetitive communicative acts, even when ostensibly worshipful, can lose their celebratory meaning. Yet that God's own Son worshiped his Father among other worshipers in regular attendance should make any thinking worship participant today think again. Nothing that the Son did in celebration of the Father could ever be meaningless or ordinary. The pew may be hard, the sanctuary cold or hot, and the celebrants less than victoriously energetic, but when the follower sits, kneels, prays, or sings in worship, and sits or stands for the reading of God's word, the follower does as Jesus did, from which the follower should draw the deepest inspiration. Jesus worshiped his Father much as followers today worship Father and Son.

She hadn't thought of Jesus worshiping before she came across the brief passage of text that Jesus's custom was to be in the synagogue. She realized that she should have thought of it earlier. If as a boy Jesus had called the temple *his Father's house*, then why wouldn't he spend time in the local synagogue as he grew and worked in Nazareth? Jesus would have been at home in the synagogue, at home in the place that the local community made for dwelling with God. The synagogue would have been *his* home, the place where he most felt the devotion of local worshipers and where he could also most clearly, naturally, and publicly express his own Son relationship with and devotion to his Father. She mused at what it must have been like for local worshipers to see Jesus in the synagogue, particularly after he had that day in the synagogue declared his own fulfillment of the prophecies, and afterward as crowds began to follow him. Like the disciples, the crowds must have been slowly realizing what Jesus meant when he spoke, sometimes openly but more often circumspectly, about who he was, God's own image and Son. Did some in those crowds follow him into the synagogue to watch him commune with his Father, the Son even while in worship still the image of the Father? She imagined herself sitting across the small room from him, stealing glances at him to see his posture and demeanor, maybe to see his lips moving in prayers, maybe even to hear him read and pray, revealing so directly God's own mind and Spirit. As she meditated on her images of Jesus in the synagogue, the Spirit seemed to say to her that the worshipers sitting around and across from her in church, praying and reading, revealing the mind and Spirit of God, were also the images of Jesus and that she needed to see them that way.

60 Warrior.

Luke 4:30.

The account of Jesus announcing in Nazareth's synagogue his extraordinary role as scripture's fulfillment does not end in the people's celebration, as one might have expected and thought, but in the people rising up as one to condemn and kill Jesus. He was in his own hometown where, in making his extraordinary synagogue announcement, one might have expected him to have earned the people's indulgence and tolerance even if not their acceptance and respect. One might have thought that a neighbor of Jesus who was in the synagogue, or maybe a doctor or teacher or mentor of Jesus, would have at least excused his announcement, maybe assumed that he was mistaken, fevered, or misunderstood. Yet the account makes perfectly clear that the people who heard Jesus's synagogue announcement were *furious* with him, and not just some of the people but *all* the people. The account also makes clear that they were ready to act on their fury with deadly intent. Getting up from their synagogue seats, they first drove Jesus out of Nazareth. They then specifically took him to a cliff outside of town *in order to throw him* down the cliff, presumably to his death. Here, though, the account takes another turn as astonishing as the first. At the cliff, Jesus simply *walked right through* the crowd on his way out of town. Jesus was no push over. Just as the soldiers who came to arrest Jesus the night of his trial would at first fall back when coming upon Jesus, Jesus held a warrior's stance and power. The warrior Jesus would have voluntarily to relinquish himself if anyone was to take him by force.

The image of Jesus walking right through the murderous crowd as if it was no longer there can be an astonishing image for followers to contemplate, one from which followers should also draw great strength. The astonishment lies in the mysterious power that Jesus must have suddenly exhibited. The account makes clear that the crowd first *drove* Jesus to the edge of a cliff, indicating that the crowd at least for a time had control. The account also leaves no doubt that the crowd intended to throw Jesus over that cliff, surely to his demise. A lone figure does not ordinarily prevail against a murderous mob that has already succeeded in setting up the victim's demise. Jesus, though, clearly held some extraordinary power beyond that which any ordinary person would possess. He also clearly held the authority to choose just when to exercise that power. One moment, he remained subject to the driving crowd. The next moment, he decided to walk straight through and away from it, not subject any longer to its murderous designs. Jesus plainly held sovereignty, a freedom from violence that he could choose to exercise or not exercise at his own will. Followers should appreciate and, to the degree that the Spirit desires and allows it, appropriate that warrior's power.

As he mulled the event of Jesus's near murder by the angry mob, he kept wondering what power had enabled Jesus simply to walk away. He also wondered what access that he might have to that same power. What destructive situations was Jesus right then enabling him to walk straight through? How was the Spirit guiding him away from the edge of the cliff? Could he in fact simply turn and walk away from committed enemies and situations in which he seemed trapped? As he kept pondering Jesus's strange power, he began to realize how God had in fact guided him away from cliff after cliff just as Jesus had walked away. Things had looked so bleak so many times, whether at his hand or the hands of others, that he could hardly count them. Yet time after time, he had through God's mercy and grace walked on through intractable challenge after intractable challenge. He had stumbled many times but never fallen over the cliff. The power that Jesus held was the same miracle force of protective authority with which God ruled the world, sovereign in every respect as to when to extend or withdraw that authority. Cliffs, he realized, had their function. His own unruliness and the equal unruliness of others needed disclosure, if God's mercy was to work its corrective and healing power. He needed the march to cliff's edge as much as he needed God's power to avert the final disaster. He just needed to turn consistently to God's redemptive plan, indeed to God's redemption Son, for the path through the crowd. He needed Jesus's warrior Spirit, the flint face of resolve to defeat impending disaster after disaster.

61 **Participant.**

Luke 5:29; *see also* Luke 7:36.

The Gospels record Jesus participating in meals, indeed in banquets, with those whom the religious leaders regarded as unfit social and religious outsiders and outcasts. Jesus moved in and about the crowds, staying and eating with the common people in the working class, rather than keeping to himself or residing among the powerful religious elites. On one of those occasions among the people, recorded in Luke's Gospel, the disciple Levi also known as Matthew held a banquet at his house to honor Jesus. The account makes clear that a crowd of tax collectors and other guests ate with Jesus and his host Levi. The tax collectors would have been Jews who nonetheless served the occupying Romans—not favored but rather scorned and even hated company. In any case, the tax collectors and other guests must not have been individuals whom the religious leaders respected because the account records the leaders complaining that Jesus and his disciples ate with *sinners*. Jesus replied that his doing so was exactly the point. He admonished the religious leaders that he had come as doctor to the sick rather than the healthy and to call the sinner rather than the righteous. But the religious leaders complained again that while others fasted and prayed often, Jesus's disciples simply went on eating and drinking. Jesus then told the religious leaders three brief parables the first of which confirmed that the sinners with whom he ate and drank so regularly should indeed rejoice in his presence. They could fast later when he was gone. Jesus brought something new and better.

Followers should take heart from the image of Jesus eating and drinking with tax collectors and other sinners. Jesus did many things that showed how often and intimately he interacted with every member of the community as a complete and natural participant in the everyday things of life. Jesus does not represent a remote, distant, arbitrary, or capricious god. He is instead the incarnate Son and living embodiment of an intimate and loving God who cares about those whom powerful rulers and strict teachers do not care, who knows and meets both the smallest needs and largest concerns in ordinary lives. Followers do not forget that Jesus grew up as an ordinary member of the community, not yet known for startling miracles, miraculous healing, inspired teaching, and raising the dead. Jesus participated in life. He was accessible. The needful could find him, reach him, and know him as *one of us*. He was not a cloistered academic, fusty philosopher, or cosseted priest. Jesus was instead authentic with his actions practical, position accessible, and life participatory, organic, and real. His ministry was *bring me your tired and poor* rather than the religious leaders' *not my problem*. Jesus participated, shared, celebrated, grieved, and cared. Imagine Jesus accepting your invitation to eat and drink with your friends and acquaintances at a banquet held in your own house. Gods don't ordinarily deign to dine with common folk, but Jesus, ever the participant, clearly did, from which followers should draw great encouragement.

She simply loved the human quality of Jesus. She wasn't a philosopher. Great truths didn't particularly impress her. People impressed her, and not impressive people but ordinary people, the more down-to-earth the better. She could see a person's high-and-mighty airs from a mile away, holding themselves at arm's length from the commoners. She knew when people were looking over and past her for someone more important with whom to speak, and like anyone, she didn't like it when it happened. Like anyone, she wanted others to engage with her, communicate with her, and relate to her. As she thought of it, she found it a little odd at first that when thinking of Jesus, she never, ever got the feeling that he was looking past her. Of all individuals, Jesus would have the greatest cause to give her short shrift, with everything else he had to do and accomplish. Yet he never did look past her. Everything that she had learned about him and his actions reassured her that he gave her his full attention whenever she needed it. He had no agenda greater than caring for her and each other person who reached out to him. His salvation mission guaranteed his deepest participation in her life no matter how inconsequential her life might seem to others, particularly to the high and mighty. She knew that he would greet her, look her in the eye, listen to her, speak to her, touch her, heal her, guide her, dine with her, and provide for her, just as he did the same for all others who looked to him. Very few people made her feel like they wished to participate in life with her to anything like the degree to which Jesus made her feel his participation. She had indeed found a savior.

62 **Signifier.**

John 1:42.

The Gospels record Jesus naming, identifying, and signifying persons, things, and events. One very-well-known example involved Jesus's first meeting of Andrew's brother Simon whom Jesus would name Cephas or, translated, Peter. The account tells us that a certain man named John had two sons Andrew and Simon. This Andrew was one of two who had heard John the Baptist declare Jesus the Messiah at his baptism and had followed Jesus away from the Jordan River, apparently desiring and intending to become Jesus's disciple. The account tells us that Andrew also promptly went to find his brother Simon to tell him that they had found the Messiah, whom they also called the Christ. Andrew would have been so excited at the Messiah's extraordinary discovery that he very likely had to tell someone close to him, his brother Simon, and then bring Simon to Jesus. Here is where the distinctive event occurred in which Jesus renamed Simon. The account states simply that Jesus *looked at him* telling him that although he was Simon son of John, henceforth he would be Cephas, again translated as Peter, the common meaning of which was *rock*. Simon had a new name, at one look given to him by the Lord Jesus. The scene in general and Peter's naming in particular foreshadowed a deep and complex relationship between Jesus and Peter, stretching from Peter's early witness to Jesus as the Messiah, his subsequent denial of Jesus under trial, his later restoration by the resurrected Jesus, and his great witness to the emerging Church, all very much involving the symbolic sense of a great stumbling stone, deep foundation, and immoveable rock.

The scene of Jesus naming Peter can deeply inspire and inform followers. As the Son of God, Jesus is the litmus test of all persons and things. He reveals the true condition of all persons and things, identifying who and what they are. The Son of God does so effortlessly by his presence alone. All must respond to him when he is present, and their response illuminates their nature and condition. Yet Jesus also sometimes reveals the nature and condition of others with intention by his literally naming persons and things, just as the Father named him the Son. Jesus identifies, and when he identifies he also dignifies, signifies, and ennobles. When Jesus gives a person or thing a name, that person or thing takes on a divine-like character of its own, Jesus having given its *holy* name and in so doing revealed how God views it. The person or thing itself may not change, but they suddenly have an aspiration to do so to fulfill the God-given signifier. The person or thing takes on significance in relationship to Father and Son, both identified and signified. So it was with Peter whom Jesus named. Although he would continue to fall far short of his new name, he would never be the same after Jesus gave him his name, and in due time, he would come to live up to it. So it may it also be with you. May God reveal your name to you, may you understand, appreciate, and cherish it, and may you live up to it, finding in it and in him your significance.

The thought struck him like a thunderbolt. The impression of it was so strong and clear that several years later, he would remember where it had first occurred to him, like people remember where they stood when they heard of some epochal event. His name had a hidden God meaning that he had never before known, and not just his first name or last name but rather his first, middle, and last names, each signifying precisely who he was and what he would most do. His parents, he knew, had not intended anything of the sort. Certainly, they had never told him so, and a lifetime of living with and around them had absolutely convinced him that they had no impression of the deep godly meanings that his first, middle, and last names had, as he had, thunderstruck, suddenly discovered. God had not exactly spoken his name to him, had not audibly told him the meaning, but God may just as well have done so, the meaning and impression of the meaning both being that distinct. He had never heard God and didn't expect to do so, but he had also drawn impressions from events and received periodic inspiration that, if he were just a little more bold, he might attribute to God. This occasion was among the clearest of those occasions. The god-meaning of his name certainly had an uplifting quality to it, something to which he should and in fact did aspire. Yet the meaning was also in some respects so over-the-top unattainable, as any god-name must be, that he really had no impression that he was anything fit to attain no less really to pursue it. He rarely and in very small respects may have appeared to others to have lived up to his god-name, if others had any inkling of that name's meaning, which they certainly did not. But he knew instead that he never really did live up to it and, trying as he might, would routinely not. Funny, though, he thought. The name's unattainable quality didn't really matter. The name still meant everything to him, like a beacon but shining inward.

63 Harvester.

Mark 2:23; *see also* Matthew 9:38; Luke 10:2.

If Jesus was a signifier who *named* individuals, he was also one who *claimed* people, calling them out to join him in eternal life. He did not simply identify Simon as Peter but also invited and called Peter to follow him trusting in Jesus's divinity. Jesus further called Peter and other disciples to join him in the harvest of souls, giving them the commission of inviting others into eternal life. In one instance, he sent out seventy two disciples commissioned as workers in his *harvest field*, to perform miracles that won souls. Jesus was in that respect the Lord of the Harvest, harvesting souls himself while also sending others out to reap their own, or really his own, crop of souls. He wanted as many as who were willing to join him in the kingdom of heaven for eternal glorious life. Followers thus see Jesus as the harvester. While Jesus spoke directly about such harvest, one particular scene, depicted frequently enough to be familiar to followers, may subtly illustrate Jesus as the Lord of the Harvest. The Gospels record Jesus leading his disciples through a grain field. The account gives no indication of why Jesus would walk among the grain. Yet as his disciples followed him, they began picking the grains, the disciples harvesting while following the Lord of the Harvest. The religious leaders who saw them do so on the Jews' holy day of rest challenged Jesus that they were breaking the law by working on the day of rest. Citing the example of King David eating consecrated bread, Jesus answered that God made rest for man and that the Son of Man was *Lord even of the Sabbath*. Jesus was a harvester of souls, commissioned others to harvest souls, and justified his disciples in literal harvest even on the lawful day of rest.

The image of Jesus leading his followers through the grain field is a rich one on which to meditate. One does not ordinarily walk through a grain field for any purpose other than the grain. To the contrary, the field's owner would protest that passersby should walk around rather than through the field, preserving rather than trampling or harvesting the grain. While one hesitates to draw too much from Christ leading his disciples through the grain field, the fact that he did so as suspicious religious leaders watched strengthens the inference that his subsequent lesson was deliberate, even ripe with the meaning that one naturally wants to draw from it. Christ who was the Lord of the Harvest and would commission his disciples to harvest had just led his disciples on a literal harvest of grain. Christ was healing, winning, and feeding souls even on the holy Sabbath. The religious leaders thought Jesus to be without authority to act as he did when to the contrary he was the constituted authority, fulfilling the law as the Son of God whose work and rest was to win and feed souls in harvest.

She easily imagined Jesus walking humbly and maybe pensively but also regally through the golden field of tall, ripe grain, his disciples following at close but respectful distance. The heavy heads of grain swaying in the light breeze would have bent over the stalks, inviting the disciples to pluck at them, to fill their hands and folds of their cloaks with nourishing grain. She could also see the religious leaders watching suspiciously at first and then disapprovingly from the field's edge, waiting to *tsk-tsk* at Jesus as he and his disciples emerged from the grain field. For some reason that she could not yet fully appreciate, she treasured this image of Jesus quietly leading his disciples in the midst of the ripe heads of grain. She gradually realized that the scene was inviting her into the disciples' role. She could see herself quietly following Jesus through the grain, picking at the attractive grain heads as she and the other disciples recognized his tacit approval that they should do so. She sensed in the image a much greater meaning than that they were simply preparing to satisfy their hunger with the grain. She imagined instead that the grains were like the Master's words following in his wake or maybe like the harvest of souls that the Master would soon commission them to pursue. Whatever the scene's meaning, she let it warm her like the gentle sun that she imagined had shone down on the small band that Jesus led through the gently swaying grain stalks. She walked in Jesus's train, easily and naturally doing as he invited and approved, no matter the disapproving stares of the distant religious leaders.

64 **Appointer.**

Mark 3:14; *see also* Matthew 10:1; Luke 6:13.

The Gospels record Jesus appointing disciples to carry out his mission under specific instructions. Followers are so familiar with the Gospel story, including the disciples' tribulations, that Jesus's act of appointing disciples seems both forgone and compelled. His baptism impressed some disciples to follow. He happened upon and called other disciples when walking past the fishing boats or espying a tax collector. Other disciple candidates appear unbidden to have simply started following him from among the growing crowds. At one point, though, Jesus made a point of withdrawing up a mountainside, where a parallel Gospel account details, he prayed to God all night. After having prayed alone all night, Jesus called to him up the mountainside only those disciples *whom he wanted*, the Gospel account states, adding that upon his call up the mountainside, the disciples *came to him*. After all-night prayer, Jesus wanted something special with and from certain disciples whom he thus called apart from the crowds. Those disciples heard and obeyed his call. Jesus then appointed them, giving them his specific designation as his twelve disciples. They were each thereafter *one of the twelve*. Jesus gave them each specific designation as his disciple. The record states that his appointment was first for the purpose that the disciples *remain with him*, surely to learn and draw from him but perhaps also to care for and receive care from him. Yet the disciples were also to *go out preaching* while possessing Jesus's authority to drive demons out of those whom they encountered. The event must have been an extraordinary wonder for each of the disciples that Christ the King had chosen them from out of the crowds of eager followers. Another Gospel later records that Jesus called the twelve disciples together to give them his own authority to *drive out evil spirits* and *heal every disease*. Jesus had an unmistakable role as a chooser, designator, and appointer, not only recruiting but also selecting out, entrusting, and equipping specific individuals for peculiar relationship and service.

The scene of Jesus appointing persons to be with him, tell others about him, and accept his authority to force evil out of and away from others is such a powerful image for followers. Everyone knows that Jesus appointed disciples. Indeed, followers know well the names of many and even the character of some of those disciples. Followers today duly regard each of the original twelve disciples, other than Judas, as singular champions of the faith. Yet Jesus did not travel the world seeking out the wisest, most courageous, most charismatic disciples. While he certainly chose with divine insight, particularly given his preparatory night of prayer, Jesus nonetheless chose disciples from among those persons readily at hand, at first almost as if by happenstance as he walked past the fishing boats, even if he later prayed in earnest before designating his core twelve. Maybe then in seeking disciples today, he would not have posted the position online in order to sort through the dozens or hundreds of applicants from around the region, nation, or world, for the most qualified candidates. Jesus readily appointed nearby disciples then, suggesting that he today may just as readily appoint and empower nearby candidates, those closest to him, to carry forward his continuing mission. Follow Jesus. Stay close to Jesus. Then hear his call as a disciple. Follow him up the mountainside. You might just be that special disciple candidate.

She occasionally wondered just what status she had with Jesus. Was she one of the crowd, maybe even one of the *raucous* crowd, or was she instead one of his close disciples? She knew that she was not one of the doubters and of course not one of the haters. Imagining a spectrum of discipleship, she placed herself well to the Jesus side, no question. Her question was instead just how far to that side Jesus would consider her. She wanted to be his disciple. She imagined herself among those whom Jesus would choose if he were to see her among his following crowds. Yet she wondered just why he would choose her. What, if anything, really distinguished her from his legions of other followers? She didn't want discipleship to be a competition. To the contrary, she wanted Jesus to recognize and choose her friends just as much as she wanted Jesus to recognize and choose her. She just didn't want to be left behind, left out of his inner circle. As she meditated on the question, the thought gradually occurred to her that heaven would have no inner circle. God's presence would instead light up heaven all around her and every other resident equally. You were either in or you were out, she knew, with no halfway measure. Jesus had even declined to give the closest and most trusted of his original twelve disciples a special seat in heaven. So maybe, she concluded, the important contemporaneous question of discipleship wasn't so much about inner and outer circles. She needn't wonder whether Jesus would give her special-disciple designation. He had plainly called her to know him, trust him, and carry out his word. She would do so with all her heart, creativity, and conviction, without making any show of discipleship.

†

65 Convener.

Matthew 5:1.

The Gospels repeatedly record Jesus teaching, as an above section already indicates. Jesus was a spellbinding, humorous, insightful, entertaining, challenging, and profound teacher, whether teaching individuals or to small groups or large crowds. The Sermon on the Mount, recorded in Matthew's Gospel, is Jesus's best-known and longest teaching, in which Jesus reflects his extraordinary teacher attributes. Yet in the Sermon on the Mount, Jesus first seems to have taken some measure to stage or convene the great gathering. The account begins by stating that when Jesus *saw the crowds, he went up on a mountainside and sat down.* Only once there, did Jesus begin to teach. The account and its popular depictions suggest that the mountainside venue provided an especially conducive setting for capturing and holding the large crowd's attention. From this introduction to the great Sermon on the Mount, Jesus clearly treated this one special teaching, as he also appears from other accounts to have similarly treated other special teachings, as an *assembly* or *gathering* of the faithful. He did not simply teach to incidental gatherings, although he also did that as he traveled around the region. Instead, Jesus occasionally convened crowds into something more like assemblies. He brought large crowds together into a body expecting perhaps that those within the assembled gathering would become like-minded listeners. Something in the opening of the Sermon on the Mount account, and in its length, breadth, and conclusion, suggests that Jesus had more in mind than to simply teach. He also sought to convene and convoke, as schools, colleges, and universities offer convocations to departing graduates. The chapters-long Sermon on the Mount account ends by saying that when Jesus had finished, the listening crowds *were amazed at his teaching.* Jesus had just equipped them jointly for a new journey. He had constituted a fellowship among the assembled.

The scene of Jesus gathering the faithful on the mountainside to hear his incomparable Sermon on the Mount is a resonant image. If Jesus had instead sat in seclusion to write out the same sermon for his disciples to pass down through millennia, then it may not have had the same character and effect. The fact instead that Jesus convened crowds of faithful to hear his message together is consequential. We do not journey alone but in fellowship with others. We do not only learn alone but also in groups and assemblies. We learn in and from groups, taking cues and drawing energy from the posture, demeanor, and response of other listeners. Speakers influence us, but so do listeners. The very fact of a crowd signifies something important to us, pulling us in out of curiosity and for society and emotion. We are social creatures, formed for empathy, joviality, and other communication. When a speaker then convenes that crowd, something even more significant happens. Attention sharpens, while words come into focus. A speaker can mean little until placed in front of a crowd, when suddenly the words have an impact that they would not have had when spoken to one or a few. That the Sermon on the Mount ended with the crowd *amazed* confirms the success of the assembly. Consider the character of amazement, which opens the mind and heart to new wonders. If Jesus had not convened these assemblies but only spoken as if incidentally, then even the very same words may have fallen on harder hearts, closed minds, and shuttered ears. Simply in convening the crowds, Jesus was accomplishing something important and valuable. While faith is individual and salvation sole, the follower does not follow alone.

She loved her church. What she loved about it most was that it was a body of like-minded persons having such different characters and souls. She couldn't really think of anyone in her church who was much like her, not in character, career, family composition, or life station. Nothing particularly fit her about her church in that respect. The many things that she did in her church, including teaching, serving, speaking, and leadership, she did as if traveling alone, not with a close friend or companion, even though she was friendly and companionable with all. Her church probably did fit a sort of demographic, and in some respects she recognized that she was a part of that broader demographic, but even there the demographic, whether measured by age, income, education, or other affinity, was actually quite broad. Rather than a homogenized population, her church instead seemed very much like a motley collection of curious if lovable characters. Yet as one of the most unusual of her fellow congregants, a person of foreign language and culture from literally half way round the world, once told her with a big smile of satisfaction or even joy, *we think alike*. The words of Jesus had settled richly in this odd assembly that she loved so much. She was so glad that Jesus was a convener. She valued her salvation but didn't want to live it out alone.

⁶⁶ Dispatcher.

Matthew 11:4; *see also* Matthew 10:5; Luke 7:22; John 20:21.

The Gospels record Jesus sending others back to report on the miracles that they saw Jesus perform and heard about him performing. Jesus wanted others reporting his miracles in their prophetic context. Jesus had been teaching and preaching in the Galilean towns for some time when John the Baptist's disciples came to him asking if Jesus was the Christ to come. John, who was by then languishing in Herod's prison, had sent his disciples to ask Jesus that very important question. Jesus replied that they should *go back and report* what they had heard and seen, which was that the blind were seeing, lame walking, deaf hearing, and sick cured. The dead were living again, while the poor were hearing the Gospel's good news. Jesus wanted them to tell of this good news. As John's disciples began to leave to share that good report, Jesus told the assembled crowd that John the Baptist was the messenger whom God had sent ahead of his Son Jesus to prepare the way for Jesus. Jesus continued that, while because of the message that John carried John was greater than any who had come before him, any who then entered the kingdom of heaven by receiving the heralded Jesus would be greater than John. The kingdom of heaven had long been advancing, Jesus added, but now the kingdom was open for forceful persons to take hold of it. Jesus wanted John's disciples to carry and report this long-prophesied and now-fulfilled message. Jesus also dispatched his disciples on such harvest mission. In another Gospel account, he sends his twelve disciples out to preach that the *kingdom is near* while healing the sick, raising the dead, and driving out demons. Another Gospel records that when Jesus appeared to the disciples after his resurrection, he told that just as the Father had sent him, he was sending the disciples. Jesus sent or *dispatched* his followers to promote his mission.

The scene of Jesus sending John's disciples back to report Jesus's miracles to John may give followers clues how to treat old acquaintances and relationships. We each start our spiritual journey somewhere when, in effect, Jesus dispatches us on that journey. When we learn Jesus's message, taking his good news to heart and receiving his salvation, we necessarily leave behind the old shape of former relationships. We don't necessarily leave old friends and acquaintances. Salvation does not mean isolation, although sometimes salvation will lead to the end of some old relationships and beginning of new relationships. Yet salvation has transformed us and in doing so subtly changes those old relationships that we retain. In those cases, Jesus may want us *going back* to old acquaintances and relationships, as he sent John's disciples back, carrying the new and clear message of the miracle life that attends following Jesus. The scene of Jesus sending John's disciples back to tell John clearly that they have seen and heard about Jesus's miracles should embolden us to do likewise, particularly to friends and acquaintances whom we perceive are, like John was then, in their own veritable or figurative prisons. When we do go back to report the miracle life of Jesus, Jesus may also want us sharing the good news, the prophetic context in which those miracles occur. Even as he sent John's disciples back to report the miracles to John, Jesus also taught of how Jesus fulfilled the ancient prophecies of a messiah messenger, one who would save. Tell old acquaintances of Jesus's miracle life, and give old acquaintances the lifeline and hope that you hold in Jesus's fulfilling all prophecy. And, like Jesus's own disciples, carry his healing and his salvation message to others. Jesus sends his followers to do so.

As his faith understanding grew and he participated ever more richly and fully in his newfound faith community, he had several old acquaintances with whom he knew he would need to adjust relationships. He had no less devotion to those old friends and acquaintances now than he had previously. Indeed, the opposite was truer. He wanted those old relationships to continue and prosper, and his old friends to receive new blessings. Yet he also wanted and maybe needed to share the faith reason for his new outlook, hope, excitement, satisfaction, and joy. He and his old acquaintances still faced the same challenges, just as they still shared in the old satisfactions and comforts. Jesus had nonetheless changed his perspective on just about everything. He had new reason for service, new reason to give, and new reason for confidence in outcomes. He had new people to meet, new stories to hear, and new stories to tell. Before he could move forward, though, he sensed from the Gospel account of Jesus's encounter with John's disciples that he might need to *go back* to those old friends and acquaintances with reports of the miracle life of Jesus. While he wondered how old friends and acquaintances would receive the good news, he just felt that he owed the report to them. Jesus was sending him. The miracle life of salvation, the free entry into the kingdom of heaven that Jesus offered, was not something one should hide, even from old acquaintances. He trusted the Spirit to give him just the right moment and gentle words of the good news of Jesus. Then he would be even more free and equipped to carry on Jesus's mission with new acquaintances.

67 Resting.

Matthew 11:28; *see also* Exodus 33:14; John 7:37.

The Gospels record Jesus resting while also offering others rest *in him* to relieve their burdens and remove their weariness. Among other pastoral scenes, accounts show Jesus reclining at his host's table to take food and drink, staying behind to rest at a well while his disciples go off to town, and frequently withdrawing to solitary places. Jesus plainly rested. Yet Jesus also specifically offered that others should rest *in him*. The Gospels are replete with accounts of crowds seeming to hang around Jesus without particular purpose other than to rest in his presence. In at least two instances, the crowds lingered so long and so ill-equipped around Jesus that the disciples worried that they would go hungry. Jesus obviously had not just an attraction but also the capacity to hold crowds even while at rest. Large numbers of people seemed to be at peace around Jesus who in one teaching gave the reason. In that teaching, Jesus encouraged the weary and burdened to come to him so that he could *give them rest.* He explained what the crowds must already have perceived that he was so *gentle* and *humble in heart* that their souls would rest in him. Jesus added that what he required of them, what he described as his *yoke*, was *easy* and that any burden that he placed on them was *light.* As God had promised in the Old Testament book of Exodus, Jesus's presence would accompany the follower toward the Promised Land, giving the follower rest. And as the Gospels asserted elsewhere, Jesus gives the hungry follower food and thirsty follower satisfying drink. Jesus gives rest and in doing so restores life.

The image of Jesus giving followers rest revitalizes followers who, when harried and burdened by the day's demands, should meditate on that image more often and more fruitfully. Life can be wearying. One cannot turn it off, although people certainly try with various sedatives. Events keep rushing at us at their 24-hour, seven-day-a-week pace. In doing so, events can too easily turn from opportunities to engage and share one's faith into unwelcome demands from which to seek shelter and then finally heavy burdens from which to seek relief. Where, though, do we shelter, when our shelters themselves—our hobbies, diversions, and recreations—too often seem to demand wearying attention? Jesus says simply to rest in him. One's mind wandering across Jesus's words, actions, and attributes gives one's soul a solace and rest that nothing else does with the same consistency and to the same extent. Spiritual intimacy with Jesus is true mind's rest. When Jesus offers rest, he does not mean only relief from physical exertion, although Jesus rested physically just as we also need to do. Yet the mind also exerts itself, indeed so constantly even while we are physically at rest that we require a special kind of mind rest. While the mind's attention to demands and activities can weary, we cannot simply turn off the mind. Instead, in order for the mind to rest, the mind must focus on something other than those demands and activities on which it ordinarily focuses. We speak wisely of the *refreshing thought.* No thought refreshes like thought of Jesus. The fullness of Jesus as the image and life of God is a thought that one cannot exhaust. You can think as often and deeply of Christ as you wish and never run out of thought. Thinking of Christ also does not exhaust but instead vitalizes, giving the mind its most-effective rest. Jesus gives rest.

Her mind wearied her, she supposed, just like others' minds wearied them. She could tell from her daily small talk with acquaintances and especially with friends that the train of thought that they followed was often, like her own internal dialogue, simply draining. Her mind kept running down the same over-worn paths to nothing but tiresome effect, just as she could see even more clearly in her friends' talk that their minds were often unnecessarily tiring them. What character did the mind have that made it so one-track as to push her to the point of exasperation? As she turned the thought over in her head, *thinking about thought*, she realized again that she needed periodically to focus her thoughts on those things that gave her mind rest. Fortunately, she had no doubt of what those things were on which she could concentrate, while simultaneously giving her mind its needed rest.

As odd as it had at first seemed to her, she actually found rest in concentrating on memory verses, particularly those that reminded her of Jesus. She didn't feel that she had an especially disciplined mind. Who did, as wild as the mind so often seemed? Yet she had learned that she could direct her thoughts to Bible verses. While at first she had thought that the inner recitation of verses would exhaust her and require some other refreshment, she instead gradually found that her memory work was in an important way her mind's own rest. Scripture, and again particularly those verses that drew her to Jesus, seemed to conform her mind to a sort of *actively restful* state, which she knew was a contradiction but yet just seemed to work. God had made her mind to rest in Jesus. In that thought, she found her own special rest.

68 Intercessor.

Luke 11:1; *see also* Matthew 6:9; Luke 18:1.

The Gospels record Jesus praying often, sometimes with little indication of his prayers' content but at other times intimating the nature of his prayers. Those intimations suggest that Jesus prayed for others often, interceding with God for the welfare of his disciples and followers, Jerusalem, Israel, and others. The Gospels also give accounts of Jesus teaching the disciples and others how to pray including to intercede for others as Jesus did so often. Jesus was an intercessor and taught others to intercede with God for the spiritual welfare, forgiveness, provision, and healing of others. Jesus's Sermon on the Mount famously taught the crowd to pray that the Father's will be done, his kingdom and our daily bread come, that he forgive us our debts while we forgive our debtors, and to keep us from temptation while delivering us from evil. A similar account in Luke's Gospel begins with Jesus praying alone but in view of the disciples. The account suggests that the disciples must have been observing curiously because when he finished, one disciple asked him to teach them to pray. Jesus promptly did so in much the same form as he had taught in the Sermon on the Mount. Prayer first hallows God's name, then asks provision, forgiveness, and protection, not just for the one who prays but also corporately for the family, fellowship, and community of which the one praying is a member. In this instance, though, Jesus exhorted the disciples to pray boldly on behalf of others, as if we were waking and disturbing a friend after midnight for a loaf of bread for an unexpected visitor. *Ask*, Jesus exhorted, and *seek* and *knock*, for those who do have their prayers answered. Jesus interceded with God for others often and taught that followers should do likewise. The Father, Jesus concluded, would even give his Holy Spirit to those who ask him. Another Gospel account has Jesus urging the disciples to pray always without relenting, illustrated by the parable of the persistent widow whom the judge granted relief simply because she would not give up. Jesus was the great intercessor himself and also urged his followers to pray.

The image of Jesus praying often and alone, while interceding for others and teaching others to do likewise, gives followers one of Jesus's most-specific and important models to draw from and imitate. Jesus teaches that God gives as we ask. What greater privilege might followers have than to ask and receive from the One who holds everything? That even Jesus, the Son to whom the Father gave all, would pray often, both alone and with others, in small groups and before large crowds, day and night, should give every follower full motive to do the same. Jesus taught so often and clearly on prayer that followers cannot miss its significance. Yet beyond his teaching on prayer, Jesus plainly modeled that teaching, giving followers multiple scenes and examples from which to draw inspiration for prayer. Gospel accounts show that Jesus himself prayed that God would give food, healing, discernment, protection, and even restored life to others, at so many different times and under so many different circumstances. The follower who does not pray simply does not know the Lord whom the follower follows with the familiarity that the follower should know that Lord. One cannot know the life of Jesus without knowing the praying and prayers of Jesus. Christian life is prayer life. The follower who does not pray should meditate for inspiration on the several rich scenes of Jesus praying.

He had long felt that prayer was just an area in which he was not going to be much of a spiritual warrior, indeed not much of a success and maybe a frank failure, let alone a mentor, model, or guide. He knew the admonitions to pray and was perfectly willing to obey, like any long-time and committed follower who placed faith first and gave good priority to reading and relying on God's word. He knew that the Bible said to pray, and he knew why it said to pray. Over the lengthening years of his faith, he had occasional bursts of prayer, even rich ones filled with longing, intimacy, relief, and revelation. He was of course deeply grateful for those times of divine connection, just as he was eternally grateful for the many answers God had given to his prayers. His problem, though, in not praying more often and deeply, more consistently and richly, seemed to be partly in inspiration and partly in distraction. Too often, he felt that he was making an obedience and discipline of prayer, rather than treating it the way he suspected that he ought to treat it, which would be as the spiritual equivalent of entering a rich storehouse of treasures in the presence of a most-generous host. And too often, he just didn't think enough of praying, as he gave in so readily to so many of the world's tempting distractions, things that occupied his mind but failed to feed his future and sow into his soul. Yet then he kept thinking of Jesus praying and then praying some more, both here and there, now and then, on the mountain, after midnight, in the garden, and even on the cross, for himself, for the Father, and for others. Jesus hadn't lacked the inspiration for prayer, tired, or given in to distraction. So instead solely of searching his own heart, disciplines, practices, and soul for prayer inspiration, he turned from one scene to another of Jesus praying. As he did so, he imagined himself praying right along with Jesus. After all, wasn't that what prayer was all about?

69 Partaker.

Matthew 9:10; *see also* Matthew 15:11; John 12:2.

That the Gospels record Jesus dining with social outcasts and transgressors of various stripe likely surprises those who are unfamiliar with Jesus's authentic character. Jesus had just healed a paralytic, striking such awe in the observing crowd that they praised God for having shared authority to do so. On his way from the dramatic healing, Jesus walked by a tax collector's booth where he saw Matthew sitting. Matthew, we don't know whether curious, impressed, moved, or overawed, promptly got up and followed Jesus as soon as Jesus told him to do so. The account records that Jesus then dined at Matthew's house, from which one readily suspects that Jesus and Matthew must have quickly grown familiar and even friendly with one another as they walked. Indeed, the account reflects that Matthew also invited Jesus's disciples to join them. The account's key disclosure, though, is that many tax collectors and other so-called *sinners* joined Jesus and the disciples at Matthew's house for dinner. The religious leaders took notice, asking the disciples on the side, quite likely with evident disapproval, why their master did so. Overhearing the religious leaders' condescending query, Jesus told the religious leaders to go study their scriptures saying that God *desires mercy, not sacrifice*. Jesus further explained that he had come to *heal the sick, not the healthy*, indeed to *call sinners, not the righteous*. Jesus accepted dinner in his honor among ordinary friends, not only among dignitaries and rulers. At other times, the religious leaders chastised Jesus for letting his disciples eat without the ceremonial washing. Jesus again explained that being clean in the way that God expects is not a matter of outward appearances such as by washing the hands. Rather than having to do with what food goes into the mouth with clean or unclean hands, staying pure for God has to do with what comes *out* of the mouth. Jesus did not minister by staying away from sinful people or certain foods but instead partook of food and drink without ceremony and with sinners.

The image of Jesus dining with the unsavory characters who surrounded a social-outcast tax collector reminds followers of Christ's special character so necessary to his mission. *God as partaker companion*, particularly partaker with ordinary folk including even social outcasts whose character and behavior is not exactly exemplary, seems a contradiction to all but knowledgeable followers. Those followers grasp God's plan for Christ as a savior of the sick and sinner rather than endorser of the high and mighty self-righteous. In that role, Christ must be a companion, one who dines and spends ordinary time with the unsavory character especially, if Christ is to fulfill his salvation mandate. As Jesus said, *only the sick need a doctor.* The first thing that a doctor must do is find patients who are aware of their sickness. The doctor must then get close enough to the patient to supply the necessary treatment, which may even require making frequent *house calls*. The people whom Christ reached when dining with tax collectors and their hangers-on were people who had no pretension over their low status and corrupted or corruptible condition. Jesus must have known that they were the most likely to recognize and accept their need for the Christ-doctor, as long as that doctor was one who did not stand above them or at a distance but who *ate and drank* with them. They had no need of further judgment from the self-righteous because they already knew their judgment. These admitted transgressors instead had need of recovery and freedom from the temptation and impermeable stain of their corruption. Followers who reflect on the image of Jesus as the sinner's partaker companion find Jesus nearer and more familiar and accessible.

As he reflected on the familiar scene yet again, the image of Jesus dining with sinners at the tax collector Matthew's house meant more to him than he had previously appreciated. Why did he feel such closeness to Jesus, as if Jesus was more like a *brother* than a divinity, when he knew that Jesus was utterly without the sin that he knew impermeably stained him? He was here, trapped in his corruption, while Jesus was there, in his glorious corruption-free kingdom. He knew that gulf between them as exactly the problem with any philosophy, ideology, theology, or religion. One could never truly attain to any standard's necessary perfection. One always fell short because, well, *look honestly at who we are*, he kept thinking frankly. He knew though that Jesus solved perfectly this seemingly insoluble conundrum. Holiness could approach corruption only by explicitly committing to its own purposeful destruction. Corruption usually turns perfection imperfect. But the perfect could retain its perfection while in service of relieving corruption if that perfection accepted its resurrection-anticipating demise in the course of that service. He knew that Jesus could dine with sinners, indeed could eat with *him*, as long as Jesus intended his sacrifice in sinners' redemption. He had only to go along for Jesus's ride, to hitch his future to Jesus's future in submission and appreciation. He would dine joyously with Jesus, his willing companion, knowing that Jesus partook of his corrupt company not in condescension but rather in ascension. Jesus would ascend, taking him with Jesus. They would first dine and then shine together.

70 **Expositor.**

John 6:26.

The Gospels record Jesus not only exemplifying and fulfilling the scriptures as the Son of God but also frequently expounding on the scriptures' meaning. Jesus opened the disciples' minds to the meaning of the scriptures often during his public ministry and then especially richly at the Last Supper. Shortly after his resurrection, he promptly returned to exposition, walking the road to Emmaus with two acquaintances of the disciples, to reveal to them the scriptures' meaning. Yet Jesus also expounded quite openly on the meaning of the scriptures with crowds of other people. John's Gospel provides a dramatic early example. A pursuing crowd met Jesus on the other side of the lake just after Jesus had walked on water to join the disciples out in the Sea of Galilee. Sensing that Jesus had accomplished something miraculous to get across the lake, the crowd began asking him question after question. While the crowd's practical questions did not address the scriptures directly, Jesus answered each question specifically in ways that opened the scriptures. The Son of Man, whom God had sealed with approval, would feed them eternal life, he answered. Their work was to believe in the Son of Man whom God had sent, Jesus answered again. The true bread that God gives is the Son of Man who descends from heaven, Jesus answered again. *I am the bread of life*, Jesus answered a final query, adding that whoever looks to the Son *will have eternal life*. Jesus made quite clear how he fulfilled prophesy, as the most-profound of expositors. The Gospels leave no doubt that Jesus answered a lot of questions, indeed all of the key questions.

The image of Jesus opening the meaning of the scriptures repeatedly both discretely to his own disciples and openly to crowds and even the antagonist religious leaders should strongly encourage followers. Although Jesus told many parables, Jesus was not generally a puzzler. While at times he spoke guardedly against the worst intentions of the religious leaders who sought to destroy him, and at other times he spoke indirectly as if to reveal his hearer's character and intent, for the greater part Jesus had a rather incredibly direct way about his communications. As in the above account, Jesus disclosed to large numbers of persons exactly who he was and what he was about, for anyone who was willing to listen. As clear of an expositor as Jesus was, the bigger challenge that his listeners faced was to comprehend fully just what he was saying so directly. The problem was seldom Jesus's obscurity with his communication. The problem was the communication's content. If the hearers were to believe what Jesus said, then both they and their world would never be the same again. Jesus's quite-clear explanations were simply enormously impactful, so much so that unwilling hearers could easily pretend not to comprehend. The Apostle Paul and other writers of the magnificent epistles confirmed and elaborated so much of what followers know of the scriptures as they reveal the person and work of Jesus Christ. Yet Jesus himself was the first, primary, and clearest to open the scriptures to his divine role and glory. Jesus expounded as the premier expositor.

While she never considered herself a theologian nor in any sense a scholar, nor a convincing apologist or strong on expounding doctrine, she nonetheless loved the profound truths that Jesus both revealed and embodied. Indeed that unique quality of being open and available to all while often obscure to the learned was one of the things that she loved about scriptural truths. She felt that she could see and know those truths, if not always repeat and expound them convincingly, even when the highly learned did not do so. Jesus spoke both profoundly *and plainly* to her. His explanations had a way of planting themselves in her mind and then also in her heart and soul, ringing and resonating with truth without her having to justify them by other rationales, sources, or statements. Jesus's truths were not circular or self-referential in the way that she understood that weak arguments can be but were yet complete and contained in the person of Christ. She knew that Jesus's truths judged other premises rather than other opinions and assertions judging them. They were reliable beyond anything else she knew. She trusted them so much that when she wore out her red-letter Bible, the one that put Jesus's words in red so that the reader could not miss them, she insisted on finding another one *with red letters*. She never wanted to give any other words greater primacy. Jesus was her great Expositor, the One who both fulfilled and revealed eternal truth. Thank God for Jesus.

71 Counteractive.

John 6:41.

The Gospels record Jesus contradicting the unbelieving statements and counteracting the unbelieving attitudes of others. Jesus concerned himself with mitigating and opposing wrong attitudes and actions. Although the Gospels give many examples, an especially clear example followed Jesus's revelation to the crowd, described in the above section, that he was the *bread of life* come from heaven. The crowd had apparently been listening, getting much if not all of his meaning, because the account records that they *began to grumble* about Jesus. The account makes clear that the source of their grumbling had to do with the fact that they knew Jesus as Joseph's son, of which they reminded one another as they grumbled. Those who heard Jesus call himself *bread from heaven* knew both his father and mother. Rather than ignore their grumbling and leave them to their wrong attitudes, Jesus told them directly to *stop grumbling among yourselves*. He then elaborated on what he had just explained that he was the source of eternal life, if they would only believe what he said. While the crowd's forefathers had eaten God's manna on their desert wanderings and yet died, those who ate the bread of Jesus would live forever. At the last day Jesus would *raise up* those whom the Father drew to him. Jesus repeated that he was the *bread of life* whose sustenance would enable those who accepted it to *live forever*. Jesus was giving himself for the world's life. Jesus had already once explained his nature and role yet still opposed the crowd's grumbling directly and explained his nature and role in even clearer terms to counteract and correct their wrong attitudes.

The scene of Jesus contradicting, counteracting, and correcting the crowds, particularly when they grumbled in disagreement and confusion, is an important one on which followers should reflect. How often do we go through our days grumbling, confused over our responsibilities and opportunities? More often, one suspects, than we would wish to admit. Our grumbling can be both general, as if life owed us more, and specific as to various demands, assertions, and contentions, like whether we owe a person or situation some redress. While Jesus may concern himself with both general and specific grumbling, the foregoing Gospel scene suggests that his greatest concern is with grumbling that denies his mission and offer of a path to the eternal Father. One might think that Jesus could just ignore such grumbling, letting each person take his offer or leave it. Yet because of both the personal price that he paid and the infinite value of his grand offer, Jesus would have every right and reason to contradict grumbling with the greatest clarity and fervor. *Know what gift I bring and what this gift costs my Father and me,* Jesus must respond to grumbled questions and denials, if he is himself going to reflect adequately that cost and value. Jesus cannot remain aloof from complaint as lesser deities might in other religions because Jesus is the full image of the one great Deity who involves himself with his subjects both fully and fatally for their complete redemption. A master will let the workers complain all day until they go home at night tired of their labors. But the master won't accept the same complaint from the child of his own household who will one day soon rule the household in the master's lineage and image. Reflect on Jesus countermanding the grumblers, knowing that Jesus is both the master whom we must obey and the brother who invites us into the household.

He no doubt had a grumbler's spirit, one that he didn't particularly appreciate even if that spirit was not in some other but in him. He found odd his willingness to grumble over things because he didn't respect grumbling in others. When he heard someone grumble, he would have to catch himself not to countermand the grumbler, which he knew better than to do because one never quite knows what others suffer. Yet even as little as he appreciated grumblers, his own grumbling continued as he would catch himself talking to himself about himself in ways that made it clear to himself that he was once again grumbling over this or that matter. He supposed that his grumbling was like anyone else's grumbling that whatever conditions were just then, *they shouldn't be.* As the scene of Jesus contradicting the grumblers came to mind again, he realized that the nature of grumbling was pretty much just that the grumbler refused to accept things as they were, not as if to improve things but rather to complain about things that the grumbler just felt shouldn't be. He realized then that the one area where he had firmly learned not to grumble was to do so against Jesus. He once might have done so without even thinking about it. Now, though, he had no doubt that he would not grumble that Jesus wasn't who he said he was, didn't do what the Gospels said he did, or owed him something other than what Jesus had already offered and accomplished for him. The key then, he concluded, was to translate Jesus's offer, one that he had long ago accepted, into better attitude about other things. Maybe he didn't need to grumble at all if, as he knew, he had accepted Jesus's invitation into the kingdom. After all, no subject of the kingdom had any cause to grumble, certainly not about the kingdom's King but also in fact not about any other thing.

72 Liberator.

Matthew 15:14.

Just as Jesus countermanded and counteracted the religious leaders' false teaching, so too did Jesus liberate followers from those false teachers. The Gospels record some religious leaders and teachers of the law coming out from Jerusalem to challenge and test Jesus. They began by asking why Jesus's disciples didn't follow their ceremonial rules. Rather than answer, Jesus pointed out that the leaders and teachers broke God's own command, indeed one of the Ten Commandments, to honor father and mother. Jesus exclaimed to them that they were *hypocrites* for nullifying God's commands while making others follow their own traditions. Jesus even quoted prophetic scripture against them that they honored God only with their lips but not their hearts. Their worship was vain and their teaching simply human rules, not divine law. Then Jesus called the crowd closer to further explain how the religious leaders and law teachers were teaching false doctrine against God's commands. The disciples approached to warn Jesus that he was offending the religious leaders. But Jesus just continued that his Father would undo anything that others did without him. Then Jesus concluded telling the crowd to leave the false teachers who were only *blind guides*, warning that blind men would only lead blind followers into a pit. Jesus wanted no one to follow false teachers. He instead told everyone to leave rather than follow them.

The scene of Jesus commanding the crowd to leave behind their false teachers and religious leaders who only followed their own traditions should be a constant warning to followers. So many of us are so often susceptible to the influence and control of others. Jesus wants no one under the sway of false guides. Jesus wants everyone free to approve of, accept, obey, and follow him, and thus to know God's will and enter the eternal kingdom. False philosophies and teachings bind us. We are prisoners to our own false thoughts and the undue influence of misguided others. The teaching, salvation, and life that Jesus shares set us free. Jesus urges us, indeed *commands* us, to leave those blind guides. Their influence is not always their fault alone but too often also our fault for wanting their imprisonment. Sometimes, we fear freedom, the courage that it can take, and the responsibility that goes with it. Sometimes, we do not so much fall to the sway of blind guides as seek out and prop up those guides for the false comfort that they provide us. Rather, we should listen to Jesus when he commands us to leave blind guides in order to be able to hear him, obey him, and follow him. He wants us free to do so because he gives us life while blind guides only lead us into a death trap, the trap that all knew and expected until Jesus's advent. We are free at last, Jesus having liberated us from all false teaching.

From childhood, he had dreamt of a desperate and hopeless end, an end in annihilating death. The details of the dream, which was always the same, were unimportant. The dream wasn't terrifically lurid or frightening, just a tense and absolute, monotone and monolithic hopelessness founded on seeming certainty. The dream beset him, burdened him, and imprisoned him. Because of it, he carried around a black mood that would first tame and then squelch any burgeoning hope or joy, so that he could barely feel any comfort or security, no less offer or provide it to others, or see or hear any beauty, no less create and share it with others. He brooded because of the dream. Yet somewhere at his desperate dream's edge, even as a boy, he sensed the contrary liberating will and presence of the man-God Jesus. And before long, he was old, mature, and courageous enough to grope his way to Him, blind at first, but gradually learning, hearing, feeling, and seeing. He increasingly embraced the man-God Jesus, studying him or, more accurately, studying under the influence of his granted Spirit. And the more that he ate and drank of Jesus, the more that Jesus unburdened and liberated his previously desperate spirit. When he finally knew himself to be fully free at last, he no longer dreamed the desperate dream, which turned out only to be a false teaching.

73 **Allegorical.**

Matthew 16:11; *see also* Mark 8:15.

The Gospels record Jesus not just teaching in parables, in a way that forced his hearers to decide whether to understand Jesus and sometimes stumped his hearers as to his meaning, but also speaking allegorically in a way that forced his disciples to follow his meaning. In one such instance, the disciples were crossing the lake in a boat soon after Jesus had twice fed thousands from next to nothing. Oddly, the account begins with the disciples realizing that they had forgotten to bring bread along with them on the boat. Having overheard the disciples, Jesus told them to be on guard against the *yeast* of the religious leaders. The disciples did not immediately get Jesus's meaning. Jesus's reference to yeast, an ingredient of bread, initially had the disciples saying among themselves that Jesus's quizzical reference must have been because they had forgotten bread. Again overhearing their discussion, Jesus corrected them, indeed rebuked them, first by saying that they were *of too little faith. Don't you understand?* Jesus continued, reminding them that he had just fed five thousand once and four thousand a second time, in both instances with basketsful left over. He rebuked them again over how they had failed to understand that he was *not talking about bread*. Jesus then explained that his reference to be on guard against the religious leaders' yeast was instead telling the disciples to guard against the religious leaders' *false teaching*. In Jesus's allegorical sense, yeast meant only one thing, and that thing was false teaching. Jesus certainly used allegory and must have done so with purpose.

The image of Jesus speaking allegorically can be a puzzling one for followers, just as allegories can puzzle hearers. Followers must answer a question similar to the question of why Jesus often taught in parables. Parables, a full-blown story carrying a moral meaning, are similar to allegory, a reference with a secondary allusive (and sometimes elusive) meaning. The reader saw in a section above that Jesus's parables gave hearers the option of accepting them on their face as simple and often entertaining little stories or of searching out and embracing their deeper moral meaning. Parables present a test of whether the hearer chooses to follow the speaker toward meaning that the speaker intends but the hearer may instead choose to resist. Allegory works similarly, although in the way that Jesus used it, allegory doesn't so much as present a choice as compel a decision. When Jesus spoke of the yeast of the religious leaders, he expected the disciples to follow his allegorical, not his literal, meaning. Indeed, his statement had no literal meaning, only allegorical meaning. Religious leaders do not spread literal yeast. In referring to the religious leaders' yeast, Jesus intended to compel the disciples to follow the one meaning that his statement had, which was purely an allegorical meaning. Jesus forced the disciples to communicate on his plain, which was a spiritual, transcendent, and divine plain. At times, he would have none of plain talk, such as of having forgotten bread, particularly when he could at an instant feed thousands. He wanted his disciples thinking of spiritual and transformative things that showed their trust in Jesus, not common and mundane things that ignored the presence of the bread of life, Jesus.

Like anyone, she tended to laugh when she read again of the disciples falling again for one of Jesus's little faith tests, like the time that they mistook his caution against the religious leaders' false teaching as some kind of an odd admonishment for forgetting bread. *She* would have understood Jesus, she wanted to tell herself. Yet then, she suspected that just like the disciples, she too would not have understood Jesus and would instead have taken him too literally. Indeed, she sometimes worried a little that she would have understood *less* than the disciples understood. Maybe, she even thought, she wasn't understanding things that he said even now, in full hindsight, with his mission accomplished and so clear. She picked up her Bible again and read a passage or two for reassurance. Yes, she now saw what Jesus was saying. She recognized his allusive meaning. No, she didn't think that she was any smarter or more insightful than the disciples, but she knew that she had a full record on which to rely, and not just of the grand Gospels but of the following magnificent letters that so clearly spelled out Jesus's purpose, pursuit, and accomplishment. She flipped again through those letters, pausing at favorite places as if to drink in the full confidence that the letters offered. She stopped at James's epistle, the exquisite letter written by Jesus's own brother. That letter made Jesus's meaning so crystal clear that she had decided to memorize it. Then the realization dawned on her. Jesus's allegory had indeed required her to step forward and step up, to put on her game face and big-girl pants enough to embrace deeply profound meanings. Jesus had challenged her to reach a spiritual plain for which she would never have thought herself qualified. Much as the disciples had eventually stepped up and forward at Pentecost, embracing Jesus's full meaning, she too had in her own way done so. She was no longer a foolish adherent. She was now a disciple.

74   Egalitarian.

Luke 9:48; *see also* Matthew 20:16, 23:8; Mark 9:35, 10:37, 12:43.

The Gospels record Jesus rejecting an explicit hierarchy within his disciples and instead suggesting a kind of equality, democracy, or egalitarianism among them and other followers. Parallel Gospel accounts describe the disciples as having argued among themselves as to *which of them would be the greatest.* One account places the event in Capernaum, the disciples' argument having been on the road and Jesus's following teaching in a house. The disciples were reluctant to share the nature of their argument with Jesus who even without their disclosure knew their thoughts. Having gathered the disciples for a teaching, Jesus admonished them that whoever wished to be first would need to be last in the sense of a *servant of all.* The least among them would thus be the greatest, Jesus repeated. To illustrate his point, Jesus called a little child to stand beside him, then telling the disciples that they should welcome such little children in Jesus's name if they intended to welcome Jesus. Jesus added that when they welcomed the child and thus welcomed Jesus, they also welcomed Jesus's Father. In his kingdom, the least, Jesus concluded, would indeed be greatest by serving all, while to welcome the least was to welcome the greatest. Another Gospel account records the disciples James and John asking that Jesus let them sit at his right hand and left in his glory. Once again, Jesus called the disciples together to instruct them that any who wished to rule must instead be like a servant, indeed that the one who wanted to be first must be like a slave. Jesus added that even he, the Son of Man, came to serve, not to be served. Another Gospel account has Jesus instructing his disciples not to let others call them *rabbi, father,* or *teacher* out of honor because they all had only one Master and Father, and only one Teacher in Christ. Jesus's egalitarianism extended beyond titles even to money and work. Another Gospel account records Jesus telling the parable of the workers working different hours but earning the same wage, from which Jesus summarized that in the kingdom of heaven, the first will be last and last first. Another Gospel account has Jesus saying that a poor widow who gave her very small coins had given more than the wealthy who gave large amounts. Jesus was unconcerned with rank, hierarchy, standing, and resource, instead only with relationship to God, sacrifice for others, and service to all.

The image of Jesus rejecting his disciples' attempts to establish rank and hierarchy should encourage followers. Ignore for a moment the scholarly arguments about the great or conversely limited extent of Jesus's egalitarianism, whether for instance it extended to women having leadership roles in the church. To recognize that Jesus had in some situations an outlook that many would see as quite egalitarian would not necessarily mean that Jesus regarded all in every circumstance as perfectly equivalent. Having egalitarian perspective in some situations does not prohibit having complementarian or hierarchical perspective in other situations. Yet close followers know Jesus for what in his day, indeed in any day, would be an extraordinary egalitarianism. Although of highest rank and order, Jesus reached down so far as to touch the untouchable leper and dine with the hated tax collector. He let a prostitute honor him among stunned religious leaders and let the unschooled school the schooled. Jesus protected subordinate and sinful women against dominant and righteous men. Then to make perfectly clear his kingdom's lack of rank and order, or indeed *reverse* rank and order, he gave the disciples a lesson in the least being the greatest. In an ordinary institution, Peter, James, and John would have had every right to claim privilege, given their superior sacrifice, leadership, devotion, and insight, but they would have no particular honor in Jesus's church unless they first relinquished every such privilege in order to serve all. Indeed, only a child's heart would lead them into the kingdom.

He knew rank and file. His whole life had been a matter of paying dues, gaining ground, earning respect, and earning seniority. He didn't particularly depend on superior rank, at least not too often. He certainly didn't want to make a habit of pulling rank, again at least not too often. Yet he certainly knew those who were his own superiors and also knew how to respect and treat them with a degree of deference that he afforded no others, at least not those whom everyone recognized as his subordinates. That realization of his reliance on rank was why he kept reflecting on Jesus's extraordinary egalitarianism. Jesus flipped the whole order. He realized that Jesus probably would have quite willingly offended his own boss, one of those to whom he gave such extra deference, if his own boss had given undue offense to the lowest subordinate. Jesus would have cared for the lowest just as quickly and probably much more quickly than he would have cared for the highest. As he went through his day thinking of Jesus's new order, he began to see more clearly the people with whom he interacted. They had needs and interests, indeed had dignity and honor, just as his superiors had needs, interests, dignity, and evident honor. He began to imagine everyone as his superior, or at least everyone as worthy of his time, attention, and service. He soon found that he liked himself and his day better when he could manage to keep up at least a semblance of Jesus's flipped order, the greater serving the lesser, and the lesser having greater honor. And as he did so, he found that the hard edge to his world had just grown softer.

75 Inclusive.

Mark 9:39; *see also* Luke 9:50.

In addition to showing how Jesus rejected ordinary rank among followers, the Gospels also record Jesus showing a remarkable inclusivity among those whom he would recognize as followers. Multiple accounts record the disciple John interjecting promptly after Jesus had used the little child to teach the disciples that the least would be greatest in his kingdom. Incongruous to Jesus's lesson, John then suddenly interjected that someone whom the disciples did not know had been doing miracles in Jesus's name, and so the disciples had tried to stop him. A second account has John saying that the disciples had tried to stop the man because he was *not one of us*, not, in effect, a member or insider. Jesus's teaching on kingdom rank may somehow have triggered John's question on kingdom membership, although the accounts do not make clear. In any case, Jesus admonished John *not to stop him.* Jesus then corrected John that anyone doing a miracle in Jesus's name could not at the same time say anything bad about Jesus. Miracles, John should have known, did not work that way. Jesus then added the remarkable statement that whoever did not oppose the disciples was actually *for* the disciples. To emphasize his kingdom's remarkable inclusivity, that any who did not oppose were supporters, Jesus added that anyone who did so little as give a follower a small drink in Jesus's name would have a certain reward in heaven. The kingdom would be open to all who accepted Jesus, not just to those who knew prominent others, like the disciples, who personally knew Jesus.

The image of Jesus admonishing the disciples to let an unknown man, an outsider, participate in kingdom work, indeed perform miracles in Jesus's name, should be a powerful one on which followers may reflect. How many of us have felt like outsiders, in fact been outside of the circle of apparent influence within the religious community? Followers share a rich fellowship of faith, and yet any one fellowship, no matter how prominent, influential, or well placed, does not comprise the whole faith community. In the unusually inclusive manner in which Jesus construed his kingdom, the faith extends to any who act in Jesus's name, whether or not known to other members. One need have no title or degree. One need not know the secret code or handshake. One need not even know the address of headquarters or even outpost. Wherever one finds an opportunity to act in Jesus's name, to heal, serve, teach, admonish, or encourage, one has membership in Jesus's kingdom. Outsiders who mistakenly view the church as an exclusive club do not know how readily Jesus waits to count them within his kingdom. Even the disciples made that mistake of believing that Jesus counted only those whom they, his trusted disciples, could count as familiar faces. An elder, pastor, or greeter may not know your name when you enter the church building, may not even recognize you. Yet when you follow Jesus, he counts you as much a member of God's kingdom as his most-recognized followers. His kingdom has no rank, and his kingdom welcomes as members all who serve in his name as long as not opposing him.

She could have had a complex over that membership thing, but she had long ago gotten past it. Her faith had taken her from church to church with what in retrospect appeared to be divine plan, even if at the time her movement had not seemed so. Every church of which she had become a member seemed to her to be her final destination, but God had other plans. Those remarkably rewarding plans had included friendships, service, hospitality, teaching, and learning, and then of course worship, joyful and constant worship. At each of her few new stops, she had faced that membership question. Some fellowships had made membership deliberately unimportant, while others had made formal membership significant. She knew that each had their reasons, and she for the most part respected those reasons. Indeed at most stops, she dutifully attended new members' classes and made the requisite public commitments. She just found that she cared less and less for whether a certain local body recognized her as a member because she knew that *Jesus accepted her as member*. Whatever work she did, whether or not connected to a local faith fellowship, she did in his name, which she believed from his words and actions were enough for *his* fellowship. She valued local church community, but she valued *his* fellowship even more, to the point of concerning herself little with local membership. If the Spirit led her to work in this vineyard or that vineyard for a time, then work she would, always in Jesus's name, whether known to others or not.

76 **Childlike.**

Matthew 18:3; *see also* Matthew 19:14; Mark 9:33; Luke 9:46.

The Gospels also elicit an attribute that either Jesus possessed to some degree himself or at a minimum expected his disciples to exhibit, which is to be *childlike*. As already referenced once above, parallel accounts record that late in Jesus's public ministry, Jesus used a little child to demonstrate that whoever wanted to be great in the kingdom of heaven would need to be, like a little child, least among those here, particularly in the willingness to serve all including the least. Yet one of those parallel accounts records Jesus saying something a little different and a little more. In Matthew's account of the event, Jesus says that the disciples will never even enter the kingdom unless they *change to be like little children*. Yes, as a section above recounts, Jesus also said that whoever remains as humble as a little child will be the kingdom's greatest. But beyond kingdom rank, earned through humility, kingdom *entry* alone requires being childlike. One does not enter the kingdom without becoming like a little child. Jesus extended the instruction with a warning against causing a child to sin, the result of which would be a punitive drowning. Better, Jesus concluded, to cut off one's own hand or feet, or put out one's own eye, than to have hand, foot, or eye cause sin, leading to eternal damnation in hell. Jesus also welcomed the little children whom parents brought to him for Jesus to place his hands on them in prayer, telling his disciples who questioned the practice that the *kingdom belongs to such as these*. Jesus wanted his disciples to be childlike, presumably in some special way that Jesus may also have been childlike.

The scene of Jesus telling the disciples that they must *become like little children* if they were to enter the kingdom of heaven must stop many followers short. Followers may naturally tend to make the pursuit of Jesus a head thing, raising intellectual, doctrinal, and theological questions of assent. One must first acknowledge one's inescapable corruption and sin, then rely not merely on personal reform but instead fully on Jesus's redemptive sacrifice, while also discerning resurrection's truth. Given the extraordinariness of this divine sequential solution to human fate, how can one not seek at least some solace in formulaic faith? Yet then Jesus tells followers that they must become like little children, whom one doubts would make much of such formulas. As significant as the doctrines are, have you ever heard a child define *substitutionary sacrifice, redemption,* or *resurrection*? One doubts that even the most-wise Jesus would have had such thoughts in mind when embracing his Father's will for his only-He-could-do-it mission. Wouldn't Jesus instead have had in his heart a child's utter devotion to his one-and-only and ever-glorious father? What Jesus meant when he said that entering the kingdom required childlike attitude was not, one suspects, a child's impulsivity or irresponsibility. Rather, he must have had in mind something of how he, the Son of God, regarded his own Father. Imagine then to learn from this scene that he likely regards his own Father as a *little* child, perhaps a *very* little child, would regard its own father, which must be with a mixture of complete confidence, warm love, deep awe, and above all utter procreator reverence. Followers do well to reflect on childlike entry into the kingdom of heaven.

She had a huge soft spot in her heart for children maybe because they seemed to have a huge soft spot in their hearts for her and other adults whom they trusted. Children were cute and funny, sure, but also endearing and maybe above all vulnerable. She wanted so badly to protect the children whom parents entrusted to her care even if briefly.

She wanted so badly to equip those children for the things that they would encounter in life, both the challenges and the opportunities. She wanted so badly to guide the children away from the bad things and toward the good things. She wanted their lives to be just the right mixture of hard and easy things, of challenging and rewarding things, things that both shaped them and encouraged them. Above all, she wanted them to know the One before whom she was also childlike, whose protection, equipping, provision, challenge, healing, guiding, and comforting *she* needed. As she thought of Jesus inviting the little children to come to him while warning the disciples and others not to cause the little children to sin, she thought too of Jesus himself as childlike, trusting his Father for everything as she also trusted him. She even imagined Jesus as her brother, maybe even her *baby* brother, as he would one day have been such a baby entrusted not just to his mother Mary but to other women, perhaps even young women and girls, for his care. Oh, how baby Jesus must have looked then to his parents, to Joseph and Mary, and even to a neighbor girl maybe much like herself. She vowed again to care for the children entrusted to her, turning them ever so gently the only way that she knew to be fit for a child, to Jesus.

77 Pursuer.

Matthew 18:12; *see also* Luke 15:6.

Even as Jesus spoke to the disciples of the childlike love of Jesus, so evocative of Jesus's childlike love of the Father, and that followers would need to exhibit that kind of love to enter the Father's kingdom, Jesus also spoke of his willingness to pursue those followers when they wandered off lost. Children may indeed wander, and Jesus wanted his disciples to know that when they did, he would pursue them. Parallel Gospels record the event. Jesus first reminds the disciples not to look down on little children whose angels always see the Father's face in heaven. Jesus then caught the disciples' attention with *what do you think?* He then posed the question whether a flock owner who saw one sheep wander off would stay with the flock or go look for the lone lost sheep. Jesus left the answer—that the owner would go find the lost sheep—unstated as too obvious. Instead, Jesus asserted that the owner would be happier for the one sheep that he found than for the nine-nine that never wandered off. In case the disciples missed Jesus's meaning, Jesus then stated plainly that his Father, indeed *the disciples'* Father in heaven, was unwilling to lose *any* of his little ones. Jesus sees himself pursuing the wandering and lost, and wanted his disciples to see him that way.

Few images may be more satisfying to followers than that which Jesus paints of himself searching for the wandering and lost. That Jesus uses the image of a flock owner looking for a single lost sheep is even more precious. Imagine a sheep owner searching the crevices and ravines of a mountainside for a single desperately lost sheep that wandered dangerously from the precious flock that the owner tended on the mountain pasture. Lost sheep die, and they die quickly, sometimes from heat, cold, thirst, or hunger but most of all from thieves and predators. When Jesus says that God pursues the lost even over valuing the found and saved, he describes a life-or-death situation. God could be ambivalent about human life, certainly about the life or death of a single miserly soul. Lesser gods are indifferent. This one great God, though, cares for every soul, we may not even know why, except that we know that he made man in his image, indeed in the image of his Son. How could God not love his Son and by extension his Son's brothers and sisters? These are the kinds of warming thoughts that Jesus's revelation of God as the pursuer of lost lives bring. Followers may indeed reflect warmly and often on the God who pursues one more, just always one more, over the assurance of one hundred.

She kept an old framed image, always near her on her wall, of Jesus crowned with thorns, reaching down into a sheer mountain crevice to grasp a lost sheep, vulture circling overhead. The image caught her eye often, every time also tugging at her heart. Whenever she paused to reflect more deeply on the grasping God reaching down into the wild crevice, she ended up in tears. She knew the source of her tears, which was that she had once been lost when Jesus came grasping desperately after her, when *she* was that *just one more* whom Jesus so badly wanted over the many whom he already had. She also knew that she cried easily over the image of the just-one-more God because she had friends and family members who had been lost, whom Jesus had somehow also grabbed out of desperate crevices because he was a just-one-more God. She knew too that she cried easily over the image of the agile and muscular crowned-thorn Jesus grasping deep into the broken crevice for that one last lost sheep while vulture circled overhead because she had friends and family members who *still* were lost. She never seemed to tire of examining that very old framed image on her wall and suspected that she never would tire of it, until of course she had seen it for the last time and was instead facing the living, breathing, agile, muscular, pursuing, striving, and reaching down deeply just-one-more Jesus.

78 Forgiving.

Matthew 18:22.

The Gospels of course record Jesus forgiving the offenses and sins of others. Jesus was certainly forgiving, his mission being one of salvation from sin. He could be nothing less than forgiving. On one occasion, Jesus explained to his disciples the extent to which they, too, must then forgive. Jesus began with the example of brother sinning against brother. The offended brother should show the sinning brother his fault but only do so privately. Only if that private attempt didn't work should the offended brother involve one or two others in the reform effort, and only then finally the church to reinforce an unheeded message. Only when all else fails in reforming the offending brother should the offended brother treat the intractable offender as a pagan. A private message heard and accepted best brings forgiveness. Peter, though, wanted to hear more of what Jesus truly expected of the disciples on the difficult question of forgiveness. He asked Jesus what he should do if a brother sinned against him not once but seven times. Jesus replied that Peter should forgive not just seven times but seventy-seven times. To make certain that Peter and the other disciples appreciated the lesson, Jesus told a parable of a debtor who owed the king a huge debt for which the king prepared to sell the debtor's wife and children. The king relented when the debtor begged forgiveness, only to see the forgiven debtor go out contrarily demanding that others pay *him* back, ignoring or promptly forgetting the king's gracious forgiveness. When the king found out that the forgiven debtor was throwing others in prison to recover debts, he warned the forgiven debtor that he should have forgiven others as the king forgave him. The king then jailed the forgiven debtor for torture. Jesus ended saying that his heavenly Father would treat the disciples the same way if they did not forgive their offending brother. Jesus was forgiving and expected others to forgive.

The image of Jesus warning the disciples to forgive others as God had forgiven them sternly warns followers, one of those scenes on which followers hesitate to dwell but must adequately reflect. Jesus could not have been any clearer to the disciples. Jesus forgives, and so too must Jesus's followers forgive, not stingily but generously. The direct and even dramatic way in which Jesus describes his forgiveness imperative must impress every follower with his deadly seriousness. True, Jesus introduces the difficult lesson of forgiveness with an instruction to take grievances first privately then if necessary publicly to an offending brother before treating the recalcitrant brother as one would treat a pagan. Yet that introduction only barely leavens Jesus's warning that one must forgive because God has forgiven. None should act like the forgiven debtor who jailed his own debtors even though the king had forgiven *him*. God has forgiven every one of us. Hence, every one of us owes forgiveness. Jesus of course had more credibility than anyone else would ever have in so firmly warning followers to forgive, and not just because he had the Spirit's wisdom and the stature, honor, and integrity of God. Jesus paid everything that God should forgive us. What claim have we to withhold forgiveness from him who paid everything?

He heard Jesus so clearly on this subject of forgiveness and saw so clearly what Jesus had done that God should forgive *him* that he searched and searched for anyone whom *he* should forgive. If he read one admonition most clearly more than any of the rest, that admonition was that he should forgive or else God might not forgive him. Every day, he asked whom he should be forgiving whom he may not yet have done. Where had his heart hardened and against whom for what? Where was he nursing a grievance and against whom for when? Anywhere that he found himself a potential enemy, he would declare that person a winning friend. Anywhere that he found himself taking offense, he would declare that offender a counselor and confidante. He just wanted no score against anyone and would instead accept any score against him. He would apologize quickly even for things that he might not have done and yet expect no apology back for wrongs that he knew he had suffered from those to whom he apologized. He was *serious* about this forgiveness thing, *deadly* serious. The only thing that he would do occasionally, not that he had to do it quite often, was to walk quietly but firmly away from some situations and persons, indeed to stay far out of their way, when he knew or suspected that proximity would soon lead him to an unforgiving place. Better then to treat them as pagans, not as unforgiven but as beyond frequent fellowship. Let no score accumulate that one cannot forgive.

79 Divider.

John 7:43; *see also* Luke 12:51, 14:26; John 10:19.

Followers know and accept that the things that Jesus said and did divided people, including not just broader communities but also people who had committed to the same institutions, including even members of the same family. In one example, late in his public ministry when he had just addressed the crowds in the temple court during the week of Passover, the Gospels record some people as *sure* that Jesus was the Prophet and indeed the Christ. Yet at the same moment, the account records others as saying that Jesus could not be the Christ. The account specifically states that Jesus *had divided the people*. His address had produced disagreement, even strong disagreement, among members of the crowd, so strong that some wanted to *seize him* while others defended him. Indeed, the account next records that the very temple guards whom the religious leaders had sent to arrest Jesus did not do so, instead going back to the chief priests explaining their dereliction by saying that *no one ever spoke* the way that Jesus had. The religious leaders angrily called the guards *deceived* while cursing what they labeled the *mob* that had believed Jesus. In an even greater illustration of the surprisingly contentious nature of Jesus's good-news message, when the religious leaders claimed that at least *they* had remained unified against Jesus, one of their members Nicodemus promptly disagreed, saying instead that they should at least give Jesus a due hearing, for which the religious leaders admonished Nicodemus. The account ends poignantly, saying that each then *went to his own home*, unity lost, communities and institutions divided. At another time, Jesus specifically said that he did not come to bring peace on earth but division. He also said that following him would divide even families, to the point that one would hate one's family even as one hated one's own life. Jesus's message divided.

Scenes of Jesus's message dividing crowds, institutions, and even families may challenge followers but should ultimately instruct followers who reflect thoughtfully on those messages. Why would such a good-news message as Jesus's message divide? Couldn't people just listen and agree, or if not agree then at least just move on without disagreement? Yet Jesus's message did fracture and divide political, religious, and social institutions, as the above account clearly and concisely indicates. The reasons that the message did so reveal important things about both the message and Jesus's mission and intent. The above scene shows the Gospel message challenging individuals, whether unidentified crowd members or the religious leaders and their temple guards, to accept or reject it. Jesus's message on its face requires either commitment or rejection, not neutrality or unthinking assent. One must either agree or disagree because the message asks for, indeed demands, recognition. One has no prospect for remaining neutral when the message itself requires reconstruction of fundamental beliefs about how life, relationships, and societies, and even history and the natural world all work. Jesus was turning beliefs upside down just as his message still does today. It does so because his mission is a deeply personal, indeed an eternal-destiny mission. The message divides because its acceptance or rejection has consequences, and not just minimal or moderate but maximum, life-changing, life-saving consequences. When God shows up in person, one cannot simply shrug indifferently. One must either fall to one's knees obediently and worshipfully or walk away incredulous. Jesus was, in the best of ways, a divider, as many scenes on which followers can instructively reflect project.

She felt a little uncomfortable at times about the way in which Christ's message confronted and in some instances divided. At times, she wished that it wasn't so, wanting instead for everyone to go along and get along. Yet she also appreciated that life must include some fundamental opportunities and challenges, of which she long ago had faced her own. What after all would life be if one never got to confront critical truth? Why *wouldn't* life have big questions that one *must* answer and not just answer any old way but answer *correctly*? While she didn't always want to live in a *divided* world, she knew that she wanted to live in a *consequential* world, one that had differences and made differences. She wanted some things to *matter* and not just a little but in big ways, like the saying to *go big or go home*. She wanted to embrace a larger world, one that had no boundaries or at least boundaries that were far beyond her present horizon. She wanted to go places and do things where the going and doing were important. Indeed, she wanted to know things and say things where the knowing and saying were important. She didn't want to hold anything against anyone, didn't want to divide or stand against unnecessarily. Let every person believe as they will. But she knew from Jesus's message that where one stood in response mattered hugely. And while the choice wasn't hers to make, she concluded that she would have it no other way. She was in the end just fine with Jesus as a challenging divider.

80 Defender.

John 8:7.

The Gospels record Jesus defending others against condemnation, punishment, and other offense. Some outside the circle of faith may believe Jesus to be an accuser when to the contrary his mission is essentially one of defense and his character that of a defender. Jesus's defense of the woman caught in adultery is a prime and well-known example. During his last week of Passover leading to his crucifixion, Jesus had taught in the temple courts, retired for the night to the Mount of Olives, and then appeared again in the temple courts at dawn. As usual, a crowd surrounded him as he sat to teach. The religious leaders, though, used the occasion to try to trap Jesus whose teaching the day before had won yet more believers. The leaders brought before Jesus a woman whom they had caught in adultery, challenging Jesus to pronounce the death-by-stoning sentence that the Law of Moses commanded. The leaders presumably suspected that if Jesus assented, then the crowd would abandon him as judgmental and harsh, while if Jesus objected, the leaders and crowd would have cause to condemn

Jesus for disregarding the Mosaic command. Yet after bending down to write on the ground with his finger, Jesus straightened up briefly to say *let the one without sin be the first to throw a stone*, before stooping again to write on the ground. With that one statement in her defense, Jesus had successfully defended the woman. No leader could cast a stone because the law also said that all sinned. Each leader left in silence, until only Jesus and the woman were left. Jesus pointed out to the woman that none any longer condemned her, neither did he condemn her, and that she should now leave her life of sin. Jesus came not to condemn but to defend.

The hugely evocative and powerful scene of Jesus defending the woman caught in adultery should hearten every follower who finds any moment to reflect on it. While the scene has so much to teach, its central point seems incontestably to be that Jesus does not condemn but instead defends, indeed saves eternally, against condemnation. Every glance at Jesus, every momentary thought of him, should have some of this sense of Jesus as defender, protector, one who gave his life for the life of anyone who would see the necessity of his defense. Oddly, in this scene, both the religious leaders and Jesus were correct that the law condemns every one of us. The law would condemn both the woman caught in adultery and the leaders who were so ready to judge and condemn her, those who ultimately refused to do so in recognition of their own frequent offense. Jesus had not simply cited a technicality to free the woman, had not simply played a sort of defender's trick. Rather, the Father sent the Son for precisely that purpose to relieve the guilty of conviction and sentence, to redeem all from all offense. Jesus at that moment saved not only the woman but also the religious leaders who in walking away acknowledged to Jesus and the crowd their own guilt for other uncharged offense. One only hopes that at least some in the crowd and maybe also some of the leaders soon saw Jesus as ultimate redemption for all offense. One only needs the scene of Jesus defending the guilty woman against her guilty prosecutors to know Jesus as the great defender.

He had come to the conclusion, an easy one, really, that he had need for just the kind of defender whom Jesus was for the woman caught in adultery. Actually, no one had leveled a charge directly against him, at least not one that required his public defense. At the moment, he didn't need someone with legal knowledge or oratorical skill to keep him from public conviction, although who knew whether he or anyone might face such future charges, just or unjust? What he knew that he needed right now and at every other moment was relief from the perfectly sound and reasonable judgment that he held against himself that at times, probably at many times and possibly even right then, he had offended law, rule, morality, and custom. The frequency and seriousness of his offenses was not so much the question because he knew that in the grand scheme of things, one little offense would have been enough. He just knew that but for Jesus, he carried the constant and heavy weight of cosmic judgment, a weight that should crush every person who had any real sense of what judgment of God truly entailed. God held with such enormous power such an exquisite balance in the universe that even a single little offense would topple the whole structure if God himself did not deign to withhold that judgment. And why would he so deign other than for the benefit of his own Son? Every time that he thought of Jesus, he thought of the crushing weight of the universe that Jesus, the great defender and protector, withheld for him.

81 Verified.

Luke 10:25; *see also* Matthew 19:3.

Long after Satan tested Jesus in the desert at the beginning of Jesus's public ministry, Jesus continued to face tests of another kind, more like verification of his nature and mission. Satan appears to have known Jesus's identity and mission. Satan's test was thus one of Jesus's will, not of Jesus's identity and mission. Yet throughout Jesus's public ministry, the Gospels record Jesus facing questioning by those who suspected who Jesus was or claimed to be but wanted to verify their suspicion. Luke's Gospel provides an example from later in Jesus's public ministry. The account says that on that occasion, a law expert *stood up to test Jesus.* The expert's question made it clear that he knew who Jesus claimed to be because he asked what he must do to inherit eternal life. Jesus knew, though, that the expert was merely testing Jesus rather than asking Jesus a real question the answer to which the expert did not know. So Jesus questioned the expert back, asking what the Law said. Why of course, to *love the Lord your God* with all heart, soul, strength, and mind, and also one's neighbor, the expert answered. Jesus simply agreed. But the expert wanted the upper hand and so asked Jesus *who is my neighbor?* Jesus then told the story of the Good Samaritan who cared generously for an injured stranger while the religious insiders and leaders did not. Another Gospel account shows the religious leaders testing Jesus over divorce laws, while other accounts have the leaders testing him on other subjects, trying to catch him contradicting God's law. Leaders, experts, and crowds often tested Jesus, not to question his will but to prove him inconsistent or at least to confirm and verify his extraordinary claims and intentions. Jesus repeatedly verified his nature, mission, and intentions, both explicitly and implicitly, in ways made plain and in ways veiled for only those who wished to embrace him.

Scenes of Jesus responding firmly to frequent tests of his identity and intentions, each time in a manner that accounted for the will and intention of his questioner, should be reliable lessons for followers. Jesus responded differently to different questioners, discerning which asked in earnest and which asked in challenge and self-justification. Jesus had no pat answers. He always communicated consistent with the needs of the one who asked him the question, needs that ranged from gentle insights and instruction to the strongest rebukes. Every time he did so, though, Jesus verified his own identity and mission. Jesus is the model for effective communication. Followers must not relinquish their faith identity, yet they must also adjust to the intentions and needs of those whom they encounter, particularly those who question or even challenge their identity and mission. Jesus engaged everyone effectively, although some, like the law expert in the account above, received what they did not want or expect, instead what they needed. How effective is your communication? Under the Holy Spirit's guidance, followers should be able and willing to discern their questioners' motive, character, and intent, and to respond, usually subtly but at times boldly, in ways that communicate faith in Jesus, thus preserving their identity while also aiding their hearers. What have we to say other than that which, even if in widely varying form, consistently testifies to Jesus?

He had learned much about distinguishing his questioners' character and intent, although he had much more to learn. Everyone was different, he had concluded, with none really conforming to form, pattern, or stereotype. Each had their own experiences, interests, and ambitions, and each had their own personality and character. Some came gently needing gentleness back, while others came boldly needing boldness back. Some came openly with earnest questions, others furtively with hidden agendas. What they had in common was that all had need, while none had answers. He seldom purported to supply answers because the answers were not his, and those who questioned him were not really looking for his answers. What they needed was just what he needed, which was the Spirit of God to guide all to the Son who is the way and truth. While he learned how to turn deftly his questioners back to the source of all answers, he also learned about his own character and ambition for truth. He found that he could tell more often when he spoke only for himself or instead under the Spirit's influence. He found in himself one flaw after another, some that he had long known, others that were new and disappointing to his sight, but every such discovery welcome. The questions that he faced were shaping him just as his responses, he hoped, in small ways turned and guided his questioners, both searching their way until verified in Christ.

82 Calming.

Luke 10:41.

Jesus's teaching and presence could be disruptive and divisive, of course always in the best of senses. His mission demanded that those whom he encounter make choices whether to follow. Yet the Gospels also record Jesus being a calming influence, not just in the sense of restfulness but also in smoothing unwise divisions and soothing unnecessary differences. Jesus's surprising response to his gracious host Martha late in Jesus's ministry provides an example. Jesus and his disciples had stopped at Martha's home while passing through her village, accepting her food and hospitality as respite from their travels. Jesus, though, kept the rapt attention of Martha's sister Mary who sat at his feet listening, while Martha busied, distracted, and doubtless tired herself with preparations for their esteemed guest and his disciples. Martha finally came to the Lord exasperated, asking why he didn't care that Mary had left Martha to do all of the work alone. Martha demanded that Jesus tell Mary to help her. Jesus's response, in which he first twice called Martha's name as if to refocus her attention on him, revealed how earnestly he wanted peace restored in the household of his ardent believers. Jesus calmly explained that while Martha was worried and upset over many things, she really had only one need, which was what Mary had already chosen, of which Jesus would not deprive her. While the account ends there, Jesus's powerful personal address to Martha leaves one imagining nothing other than full restoration of the household's peace in unity around Jesus. At several other occasions, Jesus restrained his disciples and followers from argument or even violent action.

Scenes of Jesus calming his disciples and followers over unnecessary disputes and unifying them again after unwise divisions should guide and encourage followers. While followers' households would usually foster the Lord's serene peace and restful tranquility, the kind of domestic division that Martha's story reflected must happen with some frequency in every faith household. Every household faces strains, whether over chores and maintenance, or over health, vocation, finances, recreation, or relationship. Household members need to address duties, equities, and sensitivities but must do so in ways and at times that build rather than disrupt domestic tranquility. Time and manner of correction are both important. As Jesus's response to Martha's poor timing showed, devotional time is probably not the time for correction. When the time for correction seems appropriate, manner of correction remains important. Emotional rebukes, speaking out of offense or complaint, can unduly further strain a household's already-strained members. Martha may well have had cause to remonstrate with Mary, as the heaviness of Martha's labor suggested. Yet Jesus's correction reminds followers that right and equity are alone insufficient. Above all, followers must respect one another's worship and study of, and devotion to, Jesus. A household or other body without the Spirit has no peace. Only his Spirit's presence maintains unity and tranquility among followers. Know and draw on the calming effect of Jesus.

She had many times borne the weight of preparations just as Martha had done so, particularly, as in Martha's case, around hospitality. At times, indeed many times, she had felt the inequity that Martha felt and had wanted to complain like Martha. Most of the time she had not, sensing that although she bore an unjust proportion of preparations, the event itself had the greater claim to everyone's devotion. Do not squelch the Spirit when the Spirit is present, she had thought at many of those times. Her feet and back would ache, and she would grieve at missing the spiritual company and conversation that her family and guests enjoyed, but then she would remind herself of Mary and Martha, and most of all of Jesus. The gatherings were neither about the preparations and their satiating products, nor about the relative honor of guest and host, or labors of preparers. Whenever two or more gathered in Christ's name, his Spirit was present. God was in the preparations going on in the kitchen and pantry just as much he was in the merry conversation. And oddly, at the end of those gatherings, when she had thoroughly exhausted her energy and resources on behalf of her guests, she for days after felt the Spirit's closeness. Jesus had approached, calmed, and supported her once again in her service. His gentle and loving Spirit had satisfied her own need for his attention while unifying her household.

83 Persistent.

Luke 11:8.

While the Gospels record Jesus calming, restraining, and unifying his followers, the Gospels also record Jesus persisting, particularly in prayer, and teaching his followers his persistence. In one instance, the disciples had been nearby as Jesus prayed, the account says, *at a certain place.* Evidently, Jesus must have prayed for some time in that place under the watchful eyes of the disciples, because the account reports that when Jesus had finished, his disciples asked Jesus to teach *them* to pray. Jesus did teach them, starting with hallowing the Father's name and calling for his kingdom to come, and moving on to asking for provision, forgiveness, and protection. Yet Jesus had more to teach about the *persistence* and *frequency* with which his disciples should pray. Jesus did so first with a parable of one who late at night disturbs a friend for loaves of bread. Jesus pointed out that the friend would not relent out of friendship, for what friend makes such a request so late at night, but rather because of the requester's *boldness.* Jesus drove home the parable's point by urging the disciples to *ask, seek,* and *knock,* because everyone who does receives what they seek. Indeed, Jesus added for emphasis, everyone gives good gifts to their own children, so *how much more* would the Father give the Holy Spirit to those who ask him. Jesus persisted in prayer to his Father and wanted his disciples to do so also.

Scenes of Jesus going often and boldly to his Father for provision, for protection of those whom the Father had given him, and for generous miracles such as raising the dead, giving sight to the blind, and most of all for the gift of the Holy Spirit, should encourage every follower to do likewise. Jesus made perfectly clear that he expected his followers to make bold and persistent prayers to the Father. One suspects, indeed followers must trust and know, that no one was more bold or persistent in matters, particularly prayer, than Jesus. The life of the Spirit need not be one of denial but may instead be one of lavish request, particularly when the request is for the life and glory of the Son that the Father wishes to lavish. Jesus could have been no clearer when the disciples asked how they should pray that they should pray boldly and persistently, as Jesus must have prayed in order for the Father to have made such a glorious work out of Jesus's public ministry. The Gospels give us picture after picture of Jesus either retiring to solitude for prayer, praying, or returning from prayer. How the disciples must have marveled at Jesus's persistence in prayer when they might have thought that of all persons, Jesus, already the Son of God, would have least need of communing with the Father. Jesus instead prayed most often and taught his disciples to pray likewise. Draw deeply on the scenes of Jesus praying and teaching persistence in prayer. Let Jesus pray with you.

Probably like any follower, he wondered at times how persistent he should be in things of faith, particularly but not exclusively in prayer. Should one keep a balance to spiritual life, neatly partitioning off prayer and other spiritual disciplines so as not to interfere with an otherwise good if mundane life? He knew the value of moderation, and he even knew the mantra for moderation *in all things.* Yet he wondered whether moderation should apply to spiritual disciplines including especially prayer. Somehow, he didn't think that reserved prayer, prayer cordoned off into a safe and restricted space, was what Jesus had in mind when praying himself or teaching about prayer. Instead, he kept thinking of Jesus saying to *ask, seek,* and *knock,* while telling the parable of the bold friend honored not for friendship but boldness. How could his own prayers be bolder? Where was he not asking when he should? He began to realize that everywhere he looked, he was missing opportunities for prayer. He saw that he had in fact long cordoned off prayer to a traditional space that hardly any longer seemed lavish, and instead now looked quite cramped, in its dimensions. He realized that he may have misconceived the Father's vast dimension and intense interest, missed entirely that the Father had been waiting long, maybe even waiting impatiently to hear petition after petition. All he could think was to thank God that Jesus had been interceding persistently and extravagantly for him. And so he prayed for more of Jesus's persistent Spirit.

84 Ready.

Luke 12:35.

The Gospels reflect Jesus always at the ready, never off duty or unprepared, always able to do as his Father willed without delay. No account suggests that Jesus first needed time to dress, think, plan, and prepare for action. He always just spoke and acted as if long prepared and fully ready. His only delay was purposeful delay to ensure that the time was right to glorify his Father through his words and actions. The Gospels further record Jesus's admonition that his followers should, like him, also be ready. Jesus addressed another crowd late in his ministry, telling its members to *be dressed ready for service.* Followers should expect the Lord to return at any time, even when they least expect it, and so should be ready for his return, watching, prepared to open the door quickly when he knocks and then to serve him generously and graciously. Jesus told the crowd that he, the Son of Man, would indeed return when they least expected it. Peter asked Jesus if his message was only for the disciples or for everyone. Jesus answered in effect that the message was for all who wished to prepare to welcome the Lord's return. Those who were ready to welcome and serve Jesus would receive their just reward, while those who were not ready and who instead distracted and mistreated other followers would lose even the bare position that they once thought that they had and then suffer even greater punishment. Those who know the Lord's will must be ready and prepared, as Jesus was always ready and prepared.

The many events that the Gospels record requiring that Jesus be ready to act promptly, and his admonition that his followers should also always be prepared for prompt service, make for productive reflection. Readiness is a big part of life. Opportunities come, and opportunities go. Those who are always ready, willing, and able have so many more experiences and accomplish so much more than those who are habitually unprepared. One wonders how Jesus always seemed ready to act with just the right gesture, action or word, even in instances when the demands that the crowds made on him appeared unexpected. Jesus had the attitude of expecting the unexpected, which is just what he counsels his followers to do. When he says to *be dressed ready for service*, he means more than literal dress. Jesus instead refers to a consistent attitude or thoroughgoing character for service. When he explained that he would return at the least-expected hour, he was saying to expect the unexpected, which is simply to maintain a willingness to answer, respond, act, and serve no matter the surprise or inconvenience. Followers should always have their minds and attitudes right, and their affairs in order, to be able to respond immediately. Yet even if responding requires interrupting something else, as the unexpected hour would indicate, or seems out of place and awkward, as the unexpected hour would also indicate, one should still respond. Keep your life in an order that enables you to serve the Lord promptly and effectively. Doing so would be proper dress and proper readiness for service.

He had taken a long time to do so, but eventually he had learned what Jesus might have meant by being *dressed ready for service*. Sure, he suspected that *readiness* meant having the big things in place, including making a good confession, acknowledging Jesus's recompense, and trusting in Jesus's resurrection. Yet he also suspected that readiness required a lot of little things to be right, too, whether those things meant keeping vocational, legal, and financial things, and social relationships, in reasonable order. Responding to others when in the midst of one's own crisis is too hard. So he gradually honed the habit of staying on top of the little things, too, even as he kept the big things firmly in place. He also learned, though, that readiness for him meant an attitude of service. He had to learn to give up many little and even a few big things that were, in the grand scope, inconsequential. Being dressed ready for service meant foregoing distracting little things while refusing enticing but burdening big things. He had to have the right attitude that service took precedence over comfort, convenience, entertainment, or acquisition. Finally, he just had to be at the ready, *willing* to act rather than insubordinate, surly, or lazy. When he heard the call, he had to move rather than justify or rationalize inaction. With these attitudes and practices in place, he for the first time began to feel just a little ready, as if Jesus could indeed return at the least-expected moment, and yet he just might, just might be prepared. That return was one event that he sure didn't want to miss.

85 Shrewd.

Luke 16:9; *see also* Matthew 10:16.

To accomplish all that he did in his public ministry, Jesus must have been extraordinarily astute, judicious, and prudent, or what he called *shrewd* when teaching the disciples to be likewise. Late in his ministry, a Gospel account records Jesus teaching the disciples the parable of the shrewd manager who, expecting his termination, reduced the accounts of his master's debtors so as later to have friends and help. The master commended rather than condemned the manager for his shrewdness. Jesus told the disciples that they should be more like the shrewd manager than the *people of the light* who are unfortunately often not so shrewd. Jesus summarized the lesson by saying to use worldly wealth to gain friends, thereby also earning welcome into eternal dwellings. God cares how we use wealth when it reflects whether we value him more than we value money. The religious leaders who overheard what Jesus had been telling the disciples simply sneered, the account records, because they loved money more than God. Jesus then told them the story of the rich man who found himself in hell, pleading that the poor beggar who had languished at the rich man's own gate, now in heaven, should come quench his awful thirst, but too great of a chasm separated them. The rich man plainly should have used his wealth more wisely when he had the chance. As another Gospel account records Jesus saying elsewhere, followers should be as *shrewd as snakes* even while *innocent as doves*.

The image of Jesus acting shrewdly and teaching his disciples to do the same may somewhat jar the follower's thinking. *Shrewd* is not the first word that anyone would usually associate with Jesus or with his followers. Even Jesus indicated that others did not know *people of the light*, as Jesus called his followers, primarily for shrewdness. Yet Jesus certainly acted shrewdly, meaning judiciously, with foresight, in a street-smart sort of manner, as he moved through the short years of his public ministry. What Jesus did obviously worked, not just for himself in helping him accomplish that which his Father set before him, but also for his disciples and church. Jesus accomplished his mission not *in spite of* a *lack* of prudence but *because of* his astute and judicious action. So too have his followers been astute in their actions, the disciples included, after they received the Holy Spirit. The church was extraordinarily successful against all likelihood, doubtless because of the extraordinarily insightful words and actions of its Spirit-guided leadership. Indeed, look at some of history's more successful ministries, and one may discover much astute insight and action, even as shrewd managers under the Spirit's guidance make ministries effective today. A follower's life need not, indeed should not, be one of inept plans implemented senselessly. Jesus was shrewd and expected his followers also to be so.

He respected astute, well-thought-out, sensible plans. When he saw them, he respected even more what appeared to be incisive, adroit, keen actions. He had met many followers who also respected the shrewd, who could not only respect astute plans and effective actions but who could also make those plans and take those actions. Jesus, he could see, had an extraordinary way of getting things done. Indeed, he could see how Jesus counseled his disciples in such sensible planning and action, things like counting the cost first, knowing whether one has the resources to finish, and making sure to make friends along the way. While he trusted the Spirit even in actions that were not obvious and could carry some risk, he also believed that the Spirit not only gave him fruitful work but also guided him in shrewd ways to go about the work. He saw nothing inconsistent between being wise and intelligent on the one hand while letting the Spirit lead him on the other hand. He figured that the Spirit wanted him using his intelligence. He could also see much smarter men and women than he, putting their gifts into God's service through remarkably astute insights and plans. He also loved being part of their work, part of their organizations. In fact, he loved the church not only as a shelter for the needful but as a place to see creative, prudent, resourceful, and remarkably effective work. He had learned a great deal from the mentors whom he met and with whom he worked in church, finding them good representatives of the shrewd Spirit of Christ.

86 Savior.

Luke 19:9; *see also* Luke 23:43.

Jesus's core ministry was of course salvation. Interestingly, the Gospels record Jesus bringing salvation to a specific man and his house late in his public ministry. Jesus and his disciples passed through Jericho on the way to Jerusalem for Jesus's final time. The account records that Zacchaeus, a wealthy chief tax collector, wanted to see Jesus passing through. Jesus's fame must have been great because the account records that such crowds lined the road that Zacchaeus, a short man, could not see Jesus over the crowds. So Zacchaeus climbed a tree. When Jesus reached the tree and looked up, spying Zacchaeus, Jesus told him that he must immediately come down so that Jesus could stay at his house. When people began muttering that Jesus was now the guest of the sinner Zacchaeus, doubtless disliked or even hated as a chief tax collector, Zacchaeus announced that he was giving to the poor half of everything he owned and repaying four times anything that he had cheated from anyone. Zacchaeus's announcement prompted Jesus to tell him that *today salvation has come to this house* for *the Son of Man came to seek and save what was lost.* Jesus added that he meant salvation even for Zacchaeus who, though a sinner whose subordinate tax collectors had made him rich off of other Jews, was still a son of Abraham like other Jews. Jesus then told a parable to the people who, the account states, saw Jesus headed to Jerusalem and expected that the kingdom of God would therefore come at once. The parable had to do with putting the master's money to work while the master was gone, until the master came back. Those who did, the master, returning as a king, would reward, while those who did not, the king would punish.

Jesus's core ministry was salvation, just as Jesus in this event both announced and did. Even on the cross, Jesus would tell a dying criminal that he would that day be with Jesus in paradise, when the criminal acknowledged his own guilt, feared God, and declared Jesus's innocence.

The image of Jesus pronouncing salvation for a sinful man whom God drew to Jesus so powerfully that he climbed a tree to see Jesus, should satisfy followers who reflect on it. At different times, Jesus spoke obscurely and in generalities about his salvation mission, even while less often he spoke more specifically and clearly to the disciples. Jesus's several statements and explanations about his salvation mission certainly made that mission sufficiently clear. Yet seeing a specific example of Jesus saving, in pronouncing Zacchaeus and his household saved, and then having Jesus connect and generalize that example to illustrate his salvation mission, give his mission and intent special clarity and focus. Jesus saves. Jesus saved Zacchaeus because of Zacchaeus's aggressive, self-shaming pursuit of Jesus, his welcoming Jesus into his home, and his standing by Jesus when Jesus came under public criticism. Jesus then turned Zacchaeus's heart away from extorting excessive taxes out of the people. Thus, salvation works. One could not have much clearer of an example on which to reflect and over which to celebrate. While many may find Zacchaeus's behavior amusing and in doing so subtly take the side of the crowd, earnest reflection may have the follower identifying more closely with Zacchaeus and taking his side against the crowd. We ought to be just as eager to see Jesus, just as willing to embarrass ourselves for that sight, just as willing to welcome Jesus when others despise him for seeking the lost, and just as willing to remedy our own wrongs and change our ways. That Jesus saved Zacchaeus means that Jesus saves us.

Like many others, she thought that the story of Zacchaeus and the sycamore-fig tree was funny, even funnier because of the children's song about it. The thought of someone too short to see over a crowd amused her, and the man's climbing a tree to see over the crowd amused her even more. But somewhere in her amusement, she found something in which she could identify with Zacchaeus. She realized that God had also drawn her to Jesus. She had no doubt that if a crowd had blocked her vision of Jesus walking through her town, then she would race ahead to climb a hill or tree hoping to catch a glimpse of him. She knew that she didn't really have Zacchaeus's position or reputation among her own people. She was not the chief of anything, certainly not a chief tax collector. She wondered whether her good reputation would interfere with her willingness to act foolishly just to get a glimpse of Jesus, in the way that Zacchaeus's bad reputation clearly did not. The point that she saw was that Zacchaeus didn't care how the people felt about him, either way, for better or worse. He only cared about seeing Jesus. And when it came to defending Jesus against the people, Zacchaeus was ready to do that. Now, she could certainly identify with that. She decided that while his story could still amuse her, Zacchaeus she could also respect.

87 Serving.

John 13:15.

Gospel accounts clearly reflect Jesus as a servant Savior, servant master, and servant leader. The Gospels also have Jesus teaching his disciples to serve as he did. At the Last Supper, after Jesus's betrayer Judas had already left to prepare for Jesus's arrest, a Gospel account records that Jesus got up from the meal. He removed his outer clothing, put a towel around his waist, poured water out of a basin to wash his disciples' feet, and then dried their feet with the towel around his waist. The account records the reason that Jesus did so in that he knew that his Father had given him all power and was returning to him. Peter tried to keep Jesus from washing his feet, but Jesus insisted that unless he washed Peter's feet, too, Peter would have no part with Jesus. Returning to his place at the meal, Jesus then taught the disciples that although they rightly called Jesus both *teacher* and *Lord*, now that he had washed their feet as an example for them, they should wash one another's feet. Although he had the status and authority to rule, Jesus came to serve, and so the disciples should also serve like their Lord and Master. Jesus summarized the lesson that no servant is greater than the servant's master, nor the messenger greater than the one who sends the message. Jesus came to serve and expected his disciples to serve as he did.

The image of Jesus washing the disciples' feet is a powerful one, particularly for those who provide similar service to others or who have participated in feet-washing ceremonies. Washing another's feet requires kneeling very much below the person whose feet one washes, in a humbling position. Feet don't always smell good. Washing feet is also not especially easy, as many odd shapes as they present, and drying wet feet using a towel around one's waist is even harder than washing the feet. The entire act requires humble position and real labor. Jesus doubtless chose the demonstration for those reasons. He meant to show how humbling one's service to others should be, even and especially when one has the position and power not to have to do so. While followers may have the impression of Jesus mostly teaching and preaching, from prominent or even privileged places such as in synagogues and the temple courts, Jesus nonetheless served others continually, always healing, often protecting, constantly instructing, sometimes even feeding or in this instance washing feet. While Jesus's washing feet at the Last Supper may have been ceremonial, for instructional purpose, no one gave more than Jesus. The crowds may have formed and followed Jesus in large part because of his profound and authoritative teaching, but they also brought their sick to him knowing that he would use his time and power to heal. People followed Jesus at least in part because he was a servant to all in addition to their Savior.

He treasured the images of Jesus serving others, indeed serving all. He wanted to use his own energies, wanted to be tired at day's end, wanted to feel the strain of having deployed everything he had to each venture, initiative, or activity. Yet he didn't want to feel that he had wasted effort on useless, meaningless, frivolous things. He instead wanted to feel engaged, purposeful, in some sense significant to God, himself, and others. He didn't want to be tired for the sake of being tired, maybe like one who runs marathons for recreation would naturally feel, but for the sake of having accomplished something helpful, beneficial, and good for others' welfare. He knew where he got this purpose, which was from Jesus. Without the knowledge, model, and image of Jesus's sacrificial service, he doubted that he would have had that same sense of seeking purposeful engagement around service to others. He also doubted that he really achieved anything like what Jesus meant in the way of service. He seldom really gave up much of anything in order to serve others, didn't really feel that he washed feet, for instance. He knew others whose service was so remarkable as to inspire, true saints at service. Still, he kept thinking of those images of Jesus serving and the lessons on service that Jesus gave, drawing inspiration and reminders from them. He might not be doing the hard work of service for which others were so well fit, but each day he hoped to do his own small part. He just understood the service thing.

88 Friend.

John 15:14.

The Gospels record Jesus telling his disciples that they were his friends, just as the Gospels record Jesus acting as friend to the disciples. The Gospels show that Jesus's calling included unique roles that no other could fulfill including Messiah, Christ, King of kings, and Savior. Yet one role, that of friend, Jesus also assumed, as he expressed to the disciples in private very late in his ministry. A Gospel account records Jesus telling the disciples at the Last Supper that *you are my friends*. In saying so, Jesus added the condition that they were his friends *if* they obeyed his commands, but condition or not, the Son of Man, Messiah, and King of kings still offered them friendship and called them friends. Jesus then distinguished what he meant by *friend* from what the disciples might until then have been or might have thought that they remained, which was *servants*. Jesus explained that a servant doesn't know the master's business, while a friend knows everything about a friend. Friends keep no secrets from one another. Jesus made even clearer that he had made known to his disciples everything that he had learned from his Father, which was why he could call the disciples friends rather than servants. Jesus added that he had chosen the disciples rather than the disciples choosing him, confirming that he intended their friendship. The Gospels certainly show Jesus and the disciples forming a remarkable bond throughout Jesus's difficult years of public ministry, from which one can easily construe friendship among them. Jesus's saying at the end of that ministry that they were in fact friends confirms another one of his precious attributes.

The image of Jesus as friend should be something special for every follower. As the Savior and Son of God, with all that Jesus did and all that he is, one can easily elevate him so high as to put him too far off. Jesus did not intend that he be inaccessible or remote. When Jesus called the disciples his *friends*, he indicated something intimate, familiar, close, and personal. He rules over all authority. He is the way, truth, and life. He is beginning and end. Yet Jesus is also a disciple's *friend*. One must think then of one's *best* friend because Jesus could be no ordinary friend. Followers go through seasons of life with and without ordinary friends, even with and without best friends, or with friends only far away rather than close. Jesus remains a disciple's friend. Followers have traditional descriptions for this sense of Jesus as friend, such as to *walk and talk with Jesus*, which is what one does with a friend, with a close friend. One spends time with a friend, thinks of a friend, looks to a friend, and desires the company of a friend. One wants a friend happy especially with the friendship but even beyond the friendship in all things. One wants the best for a friend and then takes steps to provide it where able. One gives unexpected gifts to a friend, does unexpected favors, and shares unexpected kindnesses. Jesus does all of these things for followers who would hope also to do them for Jesus as friend.

She held Jesus in such awe that she treasured the image of Jesus as friend. Whenever she began feeling too far below Jesus, too far away from Jesus, too small when near Jesus, then she would reflect again on Jesus as her friend. She almost couldn't believe that Jesus had given her, had given all followers that image. She also recognized when he had shared the kindness, at the intimate and so-difficult Last Supper, and to whom he had given the image, his disciples who had followed him for so long and through such an arduous ministry. She didn't expect cheap friendship from Jesus, easy friendship. She suspected that he wasn't immediately everyone's friend, although she also remembered how quickly he embraced figures who sought him, even a few unpopular and particularly disreputable figures. She didn't get the sense that Jesus kept an exclusive club, at least, like she needed first to complete some kind of friendship boot camp. She instead felt that if she wanted Jesus's friendship *and obeyed him* as he had told the disciples that they must, then he would be her friend. She already felt that he was her friend because she already walked and talked with Jesus. He was her Lord and Master, and her Savior, but he was also her friend, one whom she knew she could call her *forever* friend.

89 Restorer.

John 21:15.

Jesus is not only a friend but a forgiving friend, a friend *to the end* even when we fall away in hard times from him. The Gospels record Jesus renewing friendship, restoring a lost disciple to the faith even after his rejection. Jesus not only saves but *restores* to salvation. Just before the resurrected Jesus's ascension, in one of the very last times that the disciples saw him before his return to the Father, Jesus appeared on the seashore after Peter, James, and John had fished fruitlessly from their boat all night. In that instance, as another section below further details, Jesus helped them make a miraculous catch of fish and then invited them to shore for a breakfast that Jesus had prepared. After breakfast, Jesus addressed Peter, the disciple who, though professing commitment to Jesus the night of his arrest, had during Jesus's trial said outside that he did not even know Jesus. Peter had wept bitterly over his abandoning Christ as such a critical hour. Now, though, on the seashore the resurrected Jesus would gently restore Peter to his good relationship and standing. Echoing Peter's three denials the night of Jesus's trial, Jesus asked Peter three times whether Peter loved him. Each time, Peter answered that he did love Jesus, although the account records that Jesus's question hurt Peter the third time that Jesus asked. Each time Peter answered, Jesus replied that Peter must *feed and care for his lambs and sheep*, in effect restoring Peter to faithful ministry. Jesus continued by prophesying that when Peter grew old, others would take him where he didn't want to go, where Peter would have to stretch out his hands, a reference to Peter's future crucifixion. Jesus then turned to walk away while saying that Peter should *follow him*. Jesus restored his friend Peter after a bitter rejection.

The image of Jesus restoring Peter should be one that comforts many followers. Few if any followers have not had the bitter experience of having in some respect failed Jesus. Most of us have in overt or covert ways overlooked, ignored, or even outright rejected Jesus in some situations. Life presents many challenges, some of which all of us fail because none of us is perfect. While Jesus wants, deserves, and commands our devotion, Jesus also forgives. More than merely forgiving, Jesus also restores. Jesus could forgive but hold us at arm's length, outside of intimate relationship. Yet Jesus did not do so with Peter. Jesus was instead incredibly sensitive, merciful, and gracious with Peter, first feeding him breakfast and then giving Peter the opportunity to express his love for Jesus repeatedly, just as many times as Peter had denied Jesus. While the restoration hurt Peter, that hurt helped Peter. That Jesus repeated his simple, gracious question a third time, one too many times for Peter's sensitivity, made Peter *commit* through his hurt, more than merely answer easily. Jesus then reassured Peter, in the only kind of reassurance that might have been effective for Peter, that Peter would now grow old in faithful service to Jesus, so much so that Peter would die as Jesus died. If Jesus restored Peter, who had rejected Jesus when Jesus might have needed him most, then no one who abandons Jesus would appear to be beyond restoration. This scene should deeply reassure followers that Jesus remains available to us in the worst of our faith failures.

He needed the scene of Peter's restoration, he knew all too well. He could remember times, fortunately few but times nonetheless, when others had suddenly raised the question of whom he followed, the issue of what Jesus meant to him. Those times had taken him by surprise, much as he imagined Peter surprised that someone would recognize him and challenge him with the same question while Jesus stood trial. He remembered giving answers that in retrospect he felt had dismissed Jesus far too quickly. Somehow, almost without thinking, he had clearly diminished his servant relationship to the Lord Jesus, even if not outright denied Jesus. He even recognized the possibility that those who had asked the question had thought that he *was* denying Jesus, even though he had not meant to do so. He had instead just mumbled something that he at the time thought would be innocuous enough not to offend his questioner or embarrass both of them. Only afterward did he realize that his questioner may have benefited from a clear statement of faith. Afterward, he had realized that he may well have missed the one opportunity to lead, love, or challenge his questioner. He also understood afterward that he probably should not have counted his own embarrassment, the social sensitivities or graces of the situation, in the equation at all. He was accountable to Christ first, not first to others in their preferences and sensitivities. Whenever he thought of his failures, over which he could easily have grown bitter and which still from time to time weighed on him, he would think of Jesus restoring Peter. Then he knew that he could still eat, talk, and walk with Jesus, even care for Jesus's followers. Jesus had restored him.

5

His Miracles

Healer. Matthew 4:23. *Rescuer.* Luke 4:35. *Facilitator.* John 5:6. *Testifier.* John 5:37. *Celebrant.* John 2:1. *Visitor.* Luke 4:38. *Willing.* Luke 5:12. *Knowing.* Luke 5:17 *Drawing.* Luke 6:19. *Astonished.* Matthew 8:10. *Compassionate.* Luke 7:13. *Astonishing.* Matthew 12:23. *Fearsome.* Luke 8:25. *Vanquisher.* Luke 8:27. *Accessible.* Luke 8:42. *Merciful.* Matthew 9:27. *Secretive.* Matthew 9:30. *Provider.* Matthew 14:19. *Testing.* John 6:6. *Terrifying.* Matthew 14:25. *Receptive.* Matthew 15:28. *Therapeutic.* Mark 8:25. *Superior.* Luke 9:40. *Dutiful.* Matthew 17:27. *Worker.* John 9:4. *Verified.* Luke 10:25. *Fruitful.* Luke 13:9. *Humble.* Luke 14:11. *Restorative.* John 11:44. *Unequivocal.* Mark 11:23.

Their curious, magical, and spectacular nature help the miracles that Jesus performed hold a special place apart from his extraordinary coming, calling, and public ministry, and the sacrifice, resurrection, and revelation that followed them. A miracle is any event so out of the natural order as to have no explanation and instead to suggest supernatural intervention. Jesus performed many miracles. As the following summaries show, some miracles he performed with the apparent purpose of convincing observers of his divine nature. Indeed, many demanded to see miracles for that very reason that they wanted

Jesus to convince them, to leave no room for their doubt. Jesus resisted such invitations, perhaps because removing all room for doubt would also remove all room for faith. He instead applied his miracles judiciously when confronted with situations in which the miracles themselves seemed to be the contentious point. He would, for instance, perform a miracle anyway when religious leaders challenged him not to on the Sabbath. Yet Jesus would not perform a miracle when Herod demanded one of him, perhaps because Jesus wanted no part of entertaining the evil ruler and needed not to sidetrack his coming crucifixion. The point of the miracles seemed only in part to be that Jesus could do them, that he held this power explained only by his divine nature. The point of the miracles also seemed to vary, sometimes to build the faith of those who witnessed them, while other times to defy the religious leaders, and still other times simply to heal, serve, save, or celebrate. Jesus was certainly not stingy with miracles but instead generous while also wise. Draw on the following scenes of Jesus performing many miracles, while recognizing that one Gospel account reports that Jesus performed many more miracles than the Gospels record.

90 Healer.

Matthew 4:23; *see also* Luke 4:38.

The Gospels provide many accounts of Jesus instantly healing those who sought him or whom others brought to him for care. Jesus appears to have healed others routinely throughout his travels, although nothing would have been routine about the miraculous healing itself. Jesus just healed others in so many places and under so many circumstances, virtually without time, place, or circumstance restriction. One early account states simply that he healed *throughout Galilee.* Followers may also not fully realize that Jesus healed every condition that people carried to him. The same early Gospel account records that Jesus healed *every disease and sickness* that he found among the people. Whatever was the source of power that people attributed to Jesus's miracle healing, that power was effective uniformly on all conditions. The same

Gospel account gives as example Jesus relieving severe pain, stopping seizures, curing the demon-possessed, and restoring the paralyzed. The accounts make perfectly clear that Jesus was able to heal not just the mildly or moderately affected but the severely diseased. Many of those whom Jesus healed were not even able on their own to reach him. Rather, others brought the disabled and paralyzed to Jesus for his healing. Jesus also healed others swiftly, indeed instantly, rather than through regimen. Another early Gospel account gives as an example that when Jesus healed Simon's mother in law of a severe fever, she immediately got up and waited on the disciples. The Gospels also make apparent Jesus's methods, at least those that one could observe. Jesus rebuked diseased conditions or laid hands on the diseased. Those who touched Jesus, even when he was unaware, also received his healing.

The many accounts of Jesus healing those who sought him or whom others brought to him for care encourage followers powerfully. Who hasn't thought often of, and often sought, Jesus's healing for one's self or others? The scenes of Jesus healing others provide abundant and encouraging witness to God's healing power. Illness pervades life. One hardly goes a day without hearing or thinking of another who faces severe disease or disability from either or both mental and physical illness. Illness, disease, and disability are so frequent, and God's love and individual concern so great, that one naturally would feel that if Jesus could do one thing to help others most, then he would heal. And so indeed he does heal, frequently and without limit as to time, place, circumstance, or condition. The Gospel accounts might not be nearly so compelling and credible if they did not record that Jesus healed as frequently, broadly, instantly, and generously as he did. Anyone who has suffered disease or disability or cares for others who have done so, which surely includes *every one of us*, can find one or more accounts in the Gospels of Jesus healing a condition like that we know and abhor. Jesus's healing others may be the greatest witness to God's love, thinking of the pain he relieved, fear he removed, and abilities that he granted or restored. Few if any things are more powerful demonstrations of care, involvement, concern, and service than to work for another's healing. When Jesus showed himself to be the great and generous healer that he was, he proved himself to be the Father's incarnate Son. Followers have so much to draw from the many Gospel accounts of Jesus healing others.

She realized one day how many of her prayers were for one kind or another of healing. She seemed to pray nearly constantly for someone's healing. She actually could have prayed just about daily for her own healing of one kind or another but rarely did so. Others, she knew, prayed for her healing, but when the subject had to do with prayer, she just had more concern for the mental and physical well-being of others than for her own. While praying for healing seemed perfectly natural and customary within her Christian fellowship, something that she and others did frequently, she also knew that Jesus shared her concern for the healing of others. Why would she even bother to pray if she didn't trust that Jesus both cared deeply about healing and also healed often and generously? She thought back to the many various injuries and conditions that she had suffered over the years, appreciating how often and fully she had healed. Her health today might not be perfect, but then again, had it ever been perfect, and moreover, hadn't she healed repeatedly? Sometimes her healing had been gradual, responding to various therapeutic regimens. Other times, though, conditions had just come on suddenly and left just as suddenly, not with any apparent connection to a therapeutic regimen. The treatments themselves often worked but just about as often didn't work and sometimes even seemed to make her condition worse, as treatment sometimes also did of friends and relatives. She supposed that prayer seemed just a little that way, too, that healing seemed to occur in response sometimes but not at other times, which she attributed to God's sovereignty that he knew better and did better in all things. What the Gospels made absolutely clear to her, though, was that Jesus healed, a character of his that she treasured and on which she would continue to rely no matter what the condition or its prognosis or outcome. Jesus healed, and she loved him even more so for it.

91 Rescuer.

Luke 4:35.

Following the account of Jesus's cliff-side defeat of the angry Nazareth crowd, the Gospel record tells the reader that Jesus traveled to another Galilean town Capernaum to teach. Jesus amazed all in the Capernaum synagogue who heard him teach that Sabbath, just as he had previously at first impressed the Nazarenes. The Capernaum account, though, records Jesus as doing much more than simply teaching. As Jesus taught, an evil spirit cried out very loudly to Jesus from within the man that the evil spirit possessed. The account makes clear that the evil spirit knew Jesus, announcing not only his name and hometown for the gathered crowd to hear but also declaring loudly that Jesus was the *Holy One of God*. The spirit also knew Jesus's plan and purpose. The account relates that the spirit disclosed loudly to the crowd that Jesus had come to destroy not just the spirit who spoke but also other demons that apparently inhabited others in or around the synagogue crowd. Jesus had a stern but simple response to this extraordinary demonic outburst, which was that the evil spirit should *be quiet* and *come out* of the possessed man. The account records that after first throwing the man down without injuring him, the evil spirit obeyed Jesus by coming out of the man. The synagogue crowd was understandably amazed that Jesus could order evil spirits that would then obey. The account continues that demons came out of not just the one man but *many people*, those demons shouting that Jesus was the *Son of God*. The remarkable account ends saying that Jesus rebuked and silenced the demons *because they knew him as the Christ*. Jesus, Son of God, delivers us of demons.

The image of Jesus delivering evil spirits out of many makes a follower pause in awe. Many today may misunderstand, mock, mistrust, or misrepresent the concept of demonic possession. No matter one's personal feeling or beliefs about evil spirits, the account indisputably indicates that spirits then possessed individuals, as indeed they still in certain respects seem to do today. Moods and mental states certainly take over our reason, sympathies, rationales, and passions. We see others act foolishly, even demonically, and surely see news of evils so horrible as to be nearly unimaginable, as if evil itself possessed and controlled the persons committing the horrible acts. We also sense the presence of that same reasonless passion attempting to influence our own thoughts, or at least we hope that we recognize it because in failing to do so, all may be lost. Sanity itself is the will and ability to resist senselessly destructive passion. How powerful, then, is the image of Jesus identifying and commanding that evil spirit directly? Think of the healing that would occur if more of us had and exercised his capability to diagnose, control, and relieve swiftly and directly the destructive mental states of others. How often have you wished that you held that power to deliver and heal another, even to deliver and heal one's self? Jesus had an extraordinary ability to deliver others instantly, setting them free to walk right paths immediately, not only after years of bitter hurt and failure through arduous counseling and therapy. That Jesus told the evil spirits to be quiet may indicate that his extraordinary ability must have confounded witnesses of his day, just as it confounds many today. Capernaum's synagogue crowd was not ready for proclamations of Jesus's divine identity, just as his deliverance of many amazed them.

She trusted Jesus's deliverance power because she had seen it in action and experienced it herself. For her, the stories of Jesus delivering persons of evil spirits were as real, straightforward, and simple as baking bread. She understood the culture's curiosity about demon possession along with its mocking judgment of Christians for their demon foolishness. She didn't like thinking about or trying to picture literal demons and distrusted her and anyone else's ability to do so with any confidence in their thoughts. Who knows what a demon looks like, how it acts, or what it really is? She also distrusted her ability to discern and label anyone as demon possessed, or if not *distrusted* it because sometimes people acted with obviously harmful irrationality, at least put a firm *check* on it so that she would not be unwisely judgmental. Yet she never for a moment doubted that frequent influences existed that caused, contributed to, and aggravated negative, even horrible mental states. Who hadn't at one time or another thought such negative thoughts that one wondered about their source? And who hadn't seen someone so mentally overwrought and distraught, and even felt such influences one's self, as to discern evil's presence? She wanted always to be able to see the demon coming, hear its subtle talk, in order that she may pray for Jesus's deliverance from it. She knew personally and had also witnessed the relief of deliverance. Salvation's incomparable salve aside, she loved Jesus for his ability to deliver freedom from that awful evil influence.

92 Facilitator.

John 5:6.

Jesus did more than simply heal the sick for the purpose and with the effect of easing pain, suffering, and illness. His healing also restored function. He facilitated recovery of abilities lost to injury or disease or never held due to congenital malformation. He did not simply take the fevered, bleeding, or leprous and remove their illness. Jesus also made the paralyzed walk, deaf hear, mute talk, and blind see. The Gospels record Jesus healing the disabled in ways that made them instantly able. John's Gospel gives an example from early in Jesus's ministry. Jesus had returned to Jerusalem at another feast time, apparently entering through the Sheep Gate where he came upon the many disabled laying by the colonnade-surrounded pool of Bethesda. The disabled included the blind, lame, and paralyzed, one of whom had lain invalid on his mat for 38 years. On learning how long the man had lain disabled, Jesus asked him if he wished to get well. The man only answered indirectly, saying that no one had helped him into the pool quickly enough when its healing powers were present. Yet the man's answer implied his belief in the possibility of healing. He did not complain that healing was unlikely or impossible but instead attributed his lack of healing to not being able to get into the healing pool quickly enough when its power was present. Jesus replied simply *get up*, and the instantly cured man picked up his mat and walked. Religious leaders chastised the man for carrying his mat on the Sabbath, but he responded that the unknown person who had healed him had told him to get up with his mat. Jesus later identified himself to the man who then disclosed Jesus's identity to those religious leaders who were already making their case against Jesus. In any event, John's account of the scene clearly states that *a great number* of disabled *used* to lie by the pool. One wonders why the disabled no longer did so by the time that John wrote the account, except that Jesus healed so many in his day that one might expect to have seen many fewer disabled. The Gospels frequently depict Jesus making the disabled suddenly able.

The image of Jesus restoring long-lost abilities to the disabled or granting them ordinary abilities that they never had should encourage every follower. Jesus as facilitator is an important inducement to relying on him, his word, and his power over relying on our own limited selves, narrow thoughts, and inadequate authority. Jesus has a way of making persons capable of doing things that they would not otherwise be able to do. He can help us see what we would otherwise not see, understand what we would without him not understand, and go where we would otherwise not go. He helps us carry burdens that without him we could not carry, surpass obstacles we would otherwise not surpass, and reach heights we would alone not reach. When Jesus heals, he shares his strength, sight, reach, and endurance, so much greater than our own. God, who first knitting one together in the womb makes all ability, certainly has the capacity to *remake* ability. Yet the ability that he creates is beyond natural ability. It is instead the ability to do as he would do, which is to love the unlovable, turn the other cheek to offense, give not merely out of plenty but out of want, see possibility where others see none, stand firm when others flee, and serve as a ruler and king rather than be served. His ability, an ability that he shares generously, is to forgive and welcome back, embrace the worthless until they become worthy through the embrace, making them able to do likewise for all who turn to him. The image of Jesus restoring ability to the disabled reminds us that he is the one great facilitator of all meaningful life, the gateway to eternal life.

He had never felt particularly able. Every time that he took stock of his abilities, he came up short. He had no gift to which he could point, none on which he could rely, none to which he felt that he could turn when caught in a pinch. He could not even hide his inability, which seemed evident to all. He was instead an open book, obviously defenseless, without means or capabilities, with nothing in particular to contribute, not one to whom others would naturally turn. And that, he gradually learned, was his one great gift, the one thing that he had received in full from his beloved Master, that all would look past him to that Master on whom he so fully relied for every little capability with which the Master blessed him. Somehow, through some generous gift of grace, the one thing that others did find and trust in him was that he knew and relied on the Master. Seeing that he had no gift, neither strength nor courage, speed, intelligence, wisdom, or wit, others then naturally and properly attributed every little thing that he managed to the Master who guided and supplied him in making those little contributions. Then, the odd thing was that because he made these little contributions so often and consistently, and so obviously out of his own weakness but also his Master's strength, others indeed turned to him as if relying on the Master's great capabilities. In this on-loan-only way, the Master had thus given him legs, strength, and sight, and just the right kind of legs, strength, and sight, doing only that which the Master desired and commanded. A follower only of the Master, and the smallest, slowest, and weakest follower at that, he somehow against all odds became a sort of disabled leader, facilitated so fully and obviously by the Master.

93 Testifier.

John 2:23; *see also* John 5:27.

The Gospels provide accounts of Jesus performing miracles for the purpose of testifying to his divine nature and salvation mission, and then having that actual effect. For example, when still early in his public ministry Jesus traveled from his home region of Galilee to Jerusalem for the Passover Feast, where he would turn over the money changers' tables and drive the livestock from the temple courts, John's Gospel adds that many people saw Jesus's miraculous signs and believed in him on account of them. Those people may in their miracle-induced belief have urged and entreated Jesus to lead them. The account continues by saying that Jesus *would not entrust himself* to them, suggesting just such a demand or invitation. The account ends by adding that Jesus instead knew what was in those people who had just come to believe in him, suggesting that they were not trustworthy. Later in the same Gospel, Jesus would explain that he would not testify about himself but instead let the miracles that God had given him to do testify that indeed the Father had sent him. Jesus continued that John the Baptist had also testified truthfully about him and his salvation role. Indeed, the Father had also testified about Jesus, he added, even though none had seen the Father or heard his voice. While they studied the scriptures about Jesus with diligence, thinking that the scriptures gave them eternal life, they refused to come to Jesus whom the scriptures said would give them that life. And so while miracles remained convincing witnesses to Jesus's divinity, without God's word and Son, they alone did not give life.

The image of Jesus performing miracles to testify to his divine nature and role carries competing meanings for his followers. On one hand, the Gospels make plain that when observed, the miracles demonstrate absolutely Jesus's supernatural authority, his divine nature and role. People saw the miracles and believed. How could one not? One's worldview would change instantly when a miracle confronted it. Our sanity requires that we incorporate and make meaning of what our senses perceive. Not to change one's opinion of a miracle worker would be to reject one's own senses, to admit that one could no longer make meaning out of the world. One might as well just be crazy. Miracles command and compel rational belief. On the other hand, many who witnessed Jesus's miracles had already rejected, or would soon reject, that the scriptures spoke about him. While the miracles had forced many momentarily to believe in him, outside of the reach and reform of God's word, those many new believers remained essentially corrupt. They could not retain the miracle-based belief without having the faith that comes from hearing, understanding, and accepting God's word. So while Jesus saw his miracles compel belief in ways that caused the new believers to solicit his trust, the Gospel account is plain that Jesus did not trust them. The Gospel account is equally plain that he did not trust them because they refused to accept what the scriptures said about him. Miracles, while testifying to divinity, are alone not enough. Far better to hear, understand, and receive God's word than to witness miracles without it.

Jesus's many miracles didn't confront so much as console him. He knew that those miracles were a big issue for others. He knew that many people, particularly those who had no affinity for Jesus, felt that accounts of the miracles were mythical fictions, exaggerated from natural events or fabricated outright for hero effect. He appreciated also that even some followers of Jesus had no particular use for the miracles. To those followers, Jesus was who he said he was, no matter the credibility or true nature of surrounding miraculous events. For a while he, too, had looked askance at the miracles, maybe not doubting them outright but just not wanting their extraordinary improbability to trouble his growing faith. He had instead soaked himself in the word of God, letting its meaning and the Spirit that it carried grow within him. First comes hearing the word of God, he thought, and only then comes full and complete faith. In time, he found himself drawing from the miracles, even to an extent exulting in them. First it was Jesus multiplying the bread, then Jesus walking on water, then Jesus raising the dead. These events no longer seemed to him at all doubtful or even so fantastical. They instead seemed probable and even natural given who he now fully appreciated that Jesus was. He recognized in the end that he had come to faith not through the miracles but through God's word. The miracles didn't have to prove Jesus's divinity and salvation plan, which God's word instead certified. The miracles were instead a comfort, balm, and ointment healing, protecting, and promoting his already-laid foundation of faith.

94 Celebrant.

John 2:1.

The Gospels also show Jesus performing miracles not specifically to testify to his divine nature and role, although the miracles inevitably had that effect, but in addition to celebrate important events of life. The Gospel account of Jesus turning water into wine is the example. Jesus had just gone to Galilee with his few brand-new disciples following his Jordan River baptism. The account has Jesus and his disciples attending a wedding in Cana with Jesus's mother on just his third day in Galilee. The wine ran out during the celebration, what would have been a significant embarrassment to the bridegroom who was responsible for its provision. In a precious scene, Jesus's mother turned to Jesus pointing out that the wine had run out, leaving unspoken the strong implications that Jesus could and would do something about it. Jesus protested lightly that *his time had not yet come.* Yet his mother, apparently knowing Jesus's heart, capability, and intention in a way that only a mother could, simply turned to the servants saying to *do what he tells you.* Jesus promptly had them fill six huge stone jars with water but then miraculously draw out fine wine to serve to the banquet master. As yet unaware of Jesus's miracle, the master called the bridegroom to complement him on saving the best wine for last. The account, all at once touching, mysterious, and joyous in its nature and import, ends with the statement that Jesus's turning water into wine to continue the wedding celebration was his first miraculous sign, the result of which was to *reveal his glory* while also causing the new disciples to put their faith in him.

While followers properly take Jesus's miracles as testifying to his divine nature and salvation role, the image of Jesus turning water into wine serves both that divinity-confirming function and a different function. The account itself ends by saying that the new disciples put their faith in Jesus because of the miracle. Miracles convince. They will always play that role. Miracles also always point to the supernatural authority of the one performing them. Indeed, the account here specifically mentions that turning water into wine *revealed Jesus's glory*. Yet in this instance, Jesus's mother appeared to have no such purpose either to convince followers that divinity was present or reveal her son's divine glory. She instead plainly asked Jesus to do something miraculous in order to rescue the bridegroom from embarrassment while allowing the wedding celebration to continue. Jesus's response that his *time had not yet come* confirms for the reader something akin to reluctance on Jesus's part to use miracles for their recruiting and revealing purposes. This miracle, then, was not primarily about revealing divine glory. Instead, Jesus's willingness to do as his mother implied in addressing the wine running out indicated Jesus's willingness to serve her purposes to rescue the bridegroom and continue the celebration. Put simply, Jesus used the miracle to celebrate. *Let the party continue*, his miracle spoke. Moreover, his filling so many as six huge jars with so much as the best wine may suggest that he further desired that the banquet celebrating the wedding be more joyous than ever. *Let the party accelerate*, the generosity of his miracle may have said. Jesus is not a stingy celebrant but a generous one. The image of Jesus performing a miracle to prolong and promote a marriage celebration gives followers fresh insight into the joy of faith.

She loved the miracle of Jesus turning water into wine maybe more than any of his other miracles. Her problem had never been one of distrusting Jesus's divinity. Miracles aside, she accepted the scriptures' magnificent testimony about Jesus's divine nature and salvation mission. Her confidence in the Gospel record did not depend on confidence in the miracles, she felt. For her, Jesus's miracles *expressed* his divinity rather than *proved* his divinity. Somehow, she had always felt it to be so. Because she had long had full confidence in Jesus's divine nature, she could regard his miracles as having other roles. Her freedom to treat the miracles as having other meanings was what made water-into-wine her favorite miracle. Every time that she thought of it, Jesus's water-into-wine miracle made her smile for joy. She loved parties and people, not sad parties with sodden or raucous people but fun gatherings of joy-filled people celebrating life and relationship. Jesus's willing water into wine seemed to her to endorse exactly that kind of celebratory fellowship in which she reveled. If Jesus would extend and amplify a wedding celebration, then she should be able to enjoy her family and friends in similar fellowship. Faith, surely a serious matter much of the time, needn't be quite so serious all of the time. She could just imagine Jesus smiling and even laughing as the wedding celebrants poured out his finest wine.

95 Visitor.

Luke 4:38; *see also* Matthew 8:14.

Jesus went to the home of Simon Peter after having delivered many attendees of evil spirits, in the synagogue at Capernaum. Simon Peter evidently lived with his mother in law. The account tells the reader that Simon Peter's mother in law was suffering a high fever and that the disciples asked Jesus to help her there. Jesus did so as he would do for so many others. The account says simply that he *bent over her* to *rebuke the fever*, and that it promptly left her. The scene is thus another powerful example of Jesus's instant healing of others, how a simple word from God's Son brings good health to the very ill. Yet the scene does not end there. Instead, the account continues that Simon Peter's mother in law *got up at once* in order to *wait on them*. Again, evidently, Simon Peter's mother in law was accustomed to waiting on her household and its guests, as she promptly did in this instance the moment that Jesus made her once again able, the moment that the high fever left her on Jesus's rebuke. The account does not say what her waiting on them entailed, although one easily imagines that it might have included comforting food and drink. While the reader does not learn the form of service, the simple account leaves the strong inference that Jesus, Simon Peter, and the other disciples remained in the home, accepting the service of Simon Peter's mother in law.

While those who read the account of Jesus's visit to Simon Peter's home likely focus on how he healed Simon Peter's mother in law of a high fever there, the account reveals something else important to followers. The image of Jesus visiting homes should be a powerful one for followers. The Son of God had no particular need of food as his forty-day fast and feeding thousands must both have proven. He likely had no need of water because he is the living water. Jesus had no need of shelter or any other good, service, kindness, or comfort that Simon Peter's mother in law may have been able to provide because *he* is the shelter and provider. As the Son of God, Christ, and Messiah, Jesus could, and by his high standing *should*, have sought and dwelled in palaces, not the homes of fishermen disciples. Those who desired his company should by his high standing have had to pass test after test, and pass through barrier after barrier, before reaching his high places. Yet here he was, in the fisherman's house, accepting the modest service of the fisherman's mother in law just recovered from a severe fever. As incredible as it may sound, imagine Jesus in your home, stooping to heal your fevered humanity in order to accept your simple service in the very plain comforts of your modest home. Then realize that those visits happened, repeatedly, during his ministry. Jesus is a visitor. He does not hide from us but instead shows up at our doorstep to see how we are, bend over us in healing service, and accept our own modest hospitality, as humble God among us.

While she thought often of Jesus's presence, as a sort of consciousness or comfort, she hadn't thought much about his actually visiting her home. Of course, he had long ago risen from burial and ascended to heaven. He no longer walked the dusty trails with his disciples, stopping at and entering humble homes to heal, comfort, and receive the modest hospitality of whoever ran the household. Jesus had sent his Spirit, though, after his ascension. And she knew the scripture to be sure to entertain hospitably in case one serves an angel unaware. She tried hard to imagine Christ or at least an angel entering her own home. Where would he sit? What would he notice? What would she serve him? The thought was almost too large to bear. It certainly changed the way that she viewed her home. Jesus's presence would anoint the home, turning it from a residence to a temple, making its hearth sacred ground. That was it, she decided. Her home should be sacred. Even in her home, she should separate the holy from the common, preserving space and room for the Holy Spirit. She imagined the Holy Spirit alighting like a dove on the back of her sofa first to look out the window at the gardens, then to turn toward her, and maybe then to alight again on her beckoning finger held at arm's length. She then imagined Jesus seated across from her in the stillness of the garden room, speaking quietly and gently but passionately, his words at once soothing, challenging, correcting, healing, uplifting, and inspiring. She felt eternal life flowing from him, suffusing the room, and carried on his words into her heart and soul. She might sit or kneel before him, or she might rise quietly to serve him something simple and comforting from her modest kitchen.

96 Willing.

Matthew 8:3; *see also* Luke 5:12.

The Gospels record a brief but fascinating scene that reveals Jesus's critical *willingness* to meet, address, engage, and care for his followers even through miracles. Jesus had just come down from a mountainside where he had gone to pray in solitude. As usual, crowds, indeed *large* crowds, promptly gathered and followed him. Despite the crowd, a man with leprosy, that contagious, dread, and disfiguring disease that bode the bearer painful ostracism and isolation, approached Jesus to kneel before him. The man's leprosy and concomitant need for healing must have been obvious because he said nothing about his condition. Instead, the man first addressed Jesus as *Lord*, accentuating the supplicant's aspect of the kneeling position that the man had already taken. This man intended to submit fully to Jesus as a servant would submit to a master. One can imagine the man hesitating even to look up at Jesus. The man then said simply that if Jesus *was willing*, then Jesus could cleanse the man of his painfully disfiguring condition. Although Jesus faced similar supplicants seeking healing or other relief during his public ministry, the Gospels record none addressing him in quite the manner that this man addressed Jesus, asking if he *was willing*. Jesus then replied in a manner that he replied to no other supplicant, as the Gospels account. Jesus first reached out and touched the man with his hand before answering directly, *I am willing*. Jesus's command to *be clean* then instantly cured the man of his leprosy. The scene ended with Jesus telling the man to show himself to the priest and make a gift offering but not to tell anyone of his healing.

The image of Jesus as a *willing* God should encourage every follower. Other religions portray their gods variously as uninvolved, reluctant, whimsical, arbitrary, or even capricious as to human affairs. The one great God, the Hebrew and Christian Jehovah, could be exactly as he chooses. He need not be frequently or even constantly engaged, deeply concerned, uniformly caring, and even intimately involved as to human affairs, which is precisely how followers know Jesus. Followers of Jesus rightly fear God, yet the fear is not the sense of foreboding that would attend submission to an impulsive and fickle god. Rather, the fear that followers of Jesus have for their God is the trepidation that anyone feels for the other-worldly, for those immediate and hugely consequential things that are so real and present and yet so beyond understanding that one can barely comprehend them no less than grasp and explain. The fear is of a God who can give and take life, or change the course of a life or even of history, effortlessly, with certainty, and in an instant. The fear is of a power so vast, reign so magnificent, history so ancient, and knowledge so high that human power, reign, history, and knowledge seem as inconsequential as an anthill. This God, though, this fearsome and awesome God, nonetheless *wills* that we receive his love, care, concern, and healing. We simply need to acknowledge who he is and the power that he holds, while placing ourselves in right relationship to him, which is servant relationship. Jesus *willed* the man's instant healing, simply because the man sought out Jesus, kneeled, and asked.

He fairly often had the true sense of God's other-worldly magnificence, that character of God that made him both shudder in a strange fear at how ageless and vast that character must be and yet want so badly at the same time to look on that magnificence. He tried each day to at least briefly consider God's vastness, height, and splendor. He supposed that he did so because he wanted to honor God for who God truly was, not as a pocket god but as the spectacularly dimensioned and aged universe's one-big-bang creator, but also because he wanted his world imbued with God's splendor. He didn't want to miss a day without sensing that divine dimension begetting his own world's wonders. Yet he realized that he also had a nearly constant sense of God accompanying him or at least observing him. And the observation from God that he sensed wasn't simply God's awareness but instead an *involved* sort of awareness, indeed more like God *caring*. God not only cared but *acted* in care, he knew. He had seen so much grace, forgiveness, blessing, and healing. He had seen such wonders, protection, and providence. He knew, too, that God's willing involvement, *intimate* involvement in human affairs, had everything to do with Jesus, even if the wonders of Jesus he could hardly fully know and would instead be exploring for eternity. Jesus just had this *will* to be involved in human lives, relationships, and matters. Maybe that willingness was because although Jesus was fully divine, his Father's Son, Jesus was also after all *fully human*. Why would a fully human God not care enough to be involved with his sons and daughters, brothers and sisters? That God was *willing* simply meant the world to him.

97 Knowing.

Luke 5:17; *see also* Matthew 9:4, 12:25; Luke 9:47.

Gospel accounts of Jesus's actions make clear that Jesus knew the thoughts of those with whom he interacted nearly in the sense of a seer or mind reader, as God is omniscient. Luke's Gospel gives the reader an example. One day Jesus taught in someone's home a crowd that had gathered both from the nearby Galilean villages and distant parts of Judea. Religious leaders had even come all the way from Jerusalem to sit around Jesus as he taught. The account records that although the Lord's power was with Jesus to heal the sick, the crowd gathered around Jesus prevented some men from delivering a paralytic to Jesus for healing. So they lowered the man to Jesus through an opening that they made in the roof tiles. Jesus was so impressed at the men's active faith that he first forgave the paralytic and then healed the paralytic with the dramatic command to *get up and walk*. Yet the detail in the account makes clear that Jesus healed the paralytic specifically to show the religious leaders that their silently disapproving thoughts were wrong. The religious leaders were thinking that only God, not this man Jesus, could forgive sins. The account also expressly records that *Jesus knew what they were thinking*. Evidently, no one had said anything in disapproval. Jesus had instead known their minds. The account further expressly records Jesus asking the religious leaders why they were silently thinking these disapproving and false things, when to the contrary Jesus, as the Son of Man, had God's authority to forgive the paralytic's sins. The paralytic man stood up, gathered the mat on which he had lain, and left praising God. This and other Gospel accounts clearly record that Jesus knew the thoughts of those around him.

The dramatic scene of Jesus knowing the thoughts of the religious leaders while healing a paralytic to demonstrate to them that their thoughts were wrong should be a powerful incentive to followers. The incentive is to appreciate the power and purpose of God's omniscience. God is not a spy. He does not listen to our thoughts to catch us in wrongs in order to judge and condemn us. Rather, his omniscience should inform and guide us. His clairvoyance is a gift, not a curse. When one realizes that God hears one's thoughts *and acts accordingly to correct them*, the realization awakens one to a world of witness. Every event becomes a potential corrective. The boundary between prayer and simple unguided reflection dissolves. Every thought, not only a thought directed to God, becomes a prayer in the sense that every thought communicates to God. If God hears one's thoughts and responds with corrective demonstrations, then each thought becomes a request to God for guidance and direction. The thinker's communication may be sensitive or insensitive. The thinker may be aware or unaware that God listens. Yet it hardly matters whether one knows or remembers that God listens. Jesus's reading of the religious leaders' thoughts and his healing of the paralytic to correct them suggests that God may listen and act accordingly whether or not one recognizes the omniscience. Think of it: every thought a prayer. Thank God that he knows our thoughts.

One of the things that he appreciated most about God was his omniscience. The thought that God knew his thoughts gave him a very good reason not only to think right thoughts but to never feel a complete sense of isolation. He had only gradually come upon the discipline of thinking of God thinking of his thoughts. He couldn't remember when he had first begun to think of his thoughts as God might think of his thoughts. It had been a long time ago, maybe even when he was quite young. He just knew that for as long as he could remember, he had the strong sense of sharing his thoughts with God, not intentionally as in prayer, although sometimes that, too, but whether or not intentionally. That sense of God following his thoughts guided, constrained, and inspired him, no doubt. Oh, he certainly had times when he was not conscious, or was at least *less* conscious, of God following his thoughts. Yet even when he was most angry, or judgmental, or bitter, or selfish, or just plain distorted, broken, or corrupt, which was surely often enough, he still had the sense of God watching him, hearing his thoughts, and moreover *sharing his impression of those thoughts*. His appreciation for God's omniscience was not only in that God knew his thoughts but that God cared about his thoughts, judged his thoughts, and wanted him thinking right thoughts. Now, *how powerful is that,* he thought? God not only willed and participated but also guided and corrected one's constant thought.

98 Drawing.

John 11:15.

As a prior section indicates, after Jesus's baptism with the Spirit in the Jordan River, Jesus exhibited a power that caused people to hear and speak well of him. Until his baptism, Jesus had been a mostly unknown Galilean carpenter, even if his mother had long been storing up the many private indications of his prophetic stature. After his baptism, people began to hear of Jesus and, when they heard, to believe and report good things of Jesus because of the power with which the Spirit imbued him. As another prior section indicates, Jesus's public ministry then included his healing through the Spirit's power all who came to him. He was a healer in addition to a teacher and preacher. People who received his healing words and touch regained their good health or gained normal capacities that they had never had. Yet Jesus's Spirit-imbued power had another miraculous quality to it in its extraordinary attraction. Luke's Gospel records that when Jesus came down the mountainside after praying all night and then calling his twelve disciples, he met on the plain a large crowd from all over the area all the way to the distant coast. The large crowd had come both to hear Jesus speak and for Jesus to heal their many diseases. Heal them, he did, as he routinely did for the crowds on other occasions. But the account of this one occasion also made clear that the people who crowded in on Jesus were all trying to touch him *because power was coming from him*. The crowd could tell that the power emanating from Jesus was healing all, even those whom evil spirits were troubling. Jesus's Spirit-imbued power was drawing crowds, a spectacular witness to the miracle presence of the divine.

The miracle image of Jesus emanating such healing power that it drew crowds to him should inspire every follower. The Gospel account does not suggest that the power was evident to the eye in anything other than the healing that it induced in those whom it touched on this and many other occasions, not like the disciples Peter, James, and John later witnessed Jesus's transfiguration into a shining figure. Jesus might not have looked any different on this occasion when power was coming out of him because the account says nothing specific about any change in his appearance. Yet the power was so evident in its healing and freeing effect that it was drawing crowds to Jesus. What is this power with which the Spirit imbued Jesus? Followers would make a mistake to see that power as anything independent of God, as if God would set something loose that others could wield and control contrary to his will. The Father baptized the Son with the Spirit because the Son pleased the Father in knowing and following his perfect will. Followers might then better understand the power as God's will, whether that will be for healing, provision, walking on water, or resurrection. Creation behaves as God desires. Miracles are only extraordinary to us, not to the One who desires and performs them. We do not see the world as he formed it because we have no such capacity. We only see so much of it as he equips us to see and reveals to us, not its undiscovered workings but only the things we have so far discerned. Jesus's drawing power is in that sense more like God's revealing more of himself than we ordinarily see, not something unusual to God but only unusual to us because we rarely see it. If we were to see all of the world as God sees and formed it, then everything would be miracles emanating solely from the will of God rather than the illusions that our limited senses and minds construct of an uncreated, probabilistic, and wholly natural world.

The one thing that he could consistently draw from God's miracle power, as Jesus so often evidenced it, was that he had no explanation for it other than God himself. The Spirit's transformative effect had no natural explanation, which was entirely the point of miracles. They were miracles because they had no natural explanation. He could not explain the miracles by any cause other than God's desire to reveal them. They were sui generis, unoriginated, unique, and without cause other than that God willed them. He also grew in his confidence that God revealed them for that purpose of drawing attention to his power. *You should know me*, the miracles said to him, and nothing more, not that he should somehow change his outlook about anything in the apparent world other than that God created, ordered, and controlled it as God desired. *See me and nothing else in these events*, the miracles said to him about God Almighty. While for years he had looked for more in the miracles than their source in God, he came gradually to appreciate the miracles alone for that revelation of their author. The miracles were not in human purpose, posture, purity, or incantation. They were not in the perfect prayer or the perfect intention, and were not for the perfectly deserving. They simply said *look to me as and for everything*, and for that reason he loved them as he loved their author. He wanted no god other than the miracle God whom Jesus embodied. The miracles, in his case less observed than reported, had served their purpose. He looked to this miracle-making God not because of the miracles but in the miracles. He did not need the miracles as evidence but rejoiced in the miracles as credit to God's numinous glory, proving that his universe had a shape and capacity befitting his unbounded love and power.

99 Astonished.

Matthew 8:10; *see also* Matthew 9:8; Luke 7:9.

The Gospels record a surprising attitude and attribute of Jesus, one that fewer followers may recognize but all should appreciate, in his capacity to let faith surprise and even astonish him as he performed his healing miracles. Just as Jesus entered his familiar Capernaum once again, a soldier asked him for help healing the soldier's paralyzed servant. Jesus promptly replied that he would go to the soldier's house to heal the suffering servant. Jesus's instant willingness must have triggered in the soldier some pang of regret, for the soldier replied that he *did not deserve* Jesus's presence in his home. Instead, the soldier suggested that Jesus's simply *saying the word* would heal the servant because Jesus's healing order would be like the orders the soldier's servants carried out under the soldier's own authority. The Gospel account then records the remarkable reaction of Jesus that the soldier's words *astonished* Jesus. A parallel account states that the soldier's response *amazed* Jesus. Explaining his astonishment, Jesus declared that he had not seen from anyone in Israel such faith as the soldier had just exhibited. Jesus then gave an impromptu lesson building on the soldier's surprising faith, one that implied that many who thought that they were pleasing to God were not quite so. Jesus then turned again to the faithful soldier, saying that he should return to his home because Jesus would do just as the soldier had believed that he would do. And indeed, the account ends saying that the servant received his healing at precisely that hour. The soldier's faith preceded and presaged Jesus's miracle, even while astonishing Jesus.

The image of a soldier's faith astonishing Jesus even while Jesus acceded to the soldier's request and performed the miracle healing maybe shouldn't be so surprising. At other times, Jesus showed that he knew the minds of those with whom he was speaking. His astonishment at the soldier's faith might suggest that Jesus did not already know the soldier's mind, which would indeed surprise a follower, given Jesus's consistent insight into the character of all with whom he came into contact. On the other hand, Jesus may well have exhibited astonishment not because he had misread the situation or soldier but instead to call attention to the following teaching moment. Jesus's astonishment highlighted and illustrated his statement and brief homily that followed. The citizenry of Israel had so few of real faith and so many religious figures claiming hierarchy on the basis of false faith that Jesus wanted all to understand that true faith of the soldier's kind was indeed so rare as to astonish. Faith should not have been rare among God's chosen people but had somehow succumbed among the showy religiosity of the ruling elders and many burdensome rules of the temple teachers. Jesus had once again turned upside down the religious order, placing a soldier's simple belief in Jesus's ability to heal and the soldier's profound insight into Jesus's authority at the pinnacle over the shows, rules, and hierarchies of the religious order. Followers should want a simple and profound faith that astonishes others, not the self-righteousness of religious rules and orders.

She supposed that she had seen astonishing faith on only a few occasions, but she knew that she had indeed seen it. She couldn't easily recall more than a couple of examples, but she knew that it was out there somewhere among God's people. She could just barely recall those couple of instances when someone in a difficult situation had expressed such a firm stance of faith so readily and confidently that the moment had taken her aback. She remembered thinking briefly that the person might have been delusional, overcome with the stress and grief of the situation. Yet she had managed to force herself then to agree that the person had simply exhibited appropriate faith, indeed astonishing faith. Jesus would heal, or Jesus would find a way forward, the person had indicated simply and confidently, when she suspected that most persons would have fallen apart, wailed, and given up hope. To others, that faith might look like foolishness or what others would call being *in denial*. She had seen denial, too. But on those couple of occasions, the Spirit had seemed to tell her that she had instead just seen authentic faith, astonishing faith. What grieved her was that she didn't yet feel that she consistently exhibited such astonishing faith, indeed if she ever really did. She wanted to astonish her Lord with her faith in his power, authority, care, and goodness. She wanted him to smile, even to laugh, at the audacity of her faith in him. Lord, her prayer became, give me *astonishing faith*, the kind of faith that truly glorifies you. Jesus, she knew, deserved nothing less.

100 Compassionate.

Luke 7:13; *see also* Matthew 9:36, 14:14, 15:32; Luke 17:13.

The Gospels also record Jesus performing miracles because of his compassion for those whom he encountered. At one point well into his three-year public ministry, Jesus approached the gate of a town known as Nain. His disciples and a large crowd followed him as he walked along, as was usual at this point in his ministry. Just then, though, at the town's gate, they met another large crowd carrying the coffin of a widow's son out of the town. The account clearly states that when Jesus saw the grieving widow, his *heart went out to her*. To relate and later record that observation, the disciples must have seen Jesus's countenance change upon encountering the grieving widow and recognizing that she had lost her only son. One can then easily imagine and indeed nearly hear the compassionate Jesus telling the widow, *don't cry*, just as the account continues. Further moved by the widow's grief, Jesus walked up to touch the coffin containing her dead son, stopping those in the crowd who carried it. Jesus then commanded, *Young man, I say to you, get up!* The account relates that on Jesus's command, the dead man promptly sat up and *began to talk*, both living and fully cognizant. Jesus then presented the living son back to his awe-struck mother while the whole crowd praised God, declaring Jesus a great prophet among them while adding that God had come to help his people. Word spread throughout the countryside that Jesus could raise the dead. Notably, when he first did so, he would do so out of compassion for the grief of a widowed mother. As the Gospels record in another place, Jesus had compassion on the crowds because they were *harassed and helpless*, indeed like *sheep without a shepherd*. On another occasion, the Gospels record that when Jesus came upon a large crowd, his compassion for them led him to heal their sick. Another Gospel account records ten men with leprosy calling for Jesus to have pity on them, meaning empathy for them, in accord with which Jesus healed the ten. Compassion moved Jesus.

The scene of Jesus raising the widow's son should arrest the first-time reader's attention while reminding the long-time follower of Jesus's incomparable power. Jesus not only healed the sick but raised the dead. Physicians heal, even if for the most part gradually rather than instantly like Jesus and with medical methods rather than Jesus's straightforward command. Yet physicians do not raise the dead. The dead remain dead no matter the marvels of medicine. Only Jesus raises the dead. Jesus would raise others in addition to the widow's son, while God would soon resurrect Jesus. The other notable aspect of Jesus's raising the widow's son, though, is what clearly moved Jesus to do so. The account is unmistakable in relating that Jesus did so *out of compassion* for the dead man's grieving mother, a widow who had already lost her husband and now, out of all natural order, had also lost her son. Having no husband or son to care for her would have been cause not only for the widow's grief but for real concern for future welfare. And so compassion, indeed his specific knowledge of the widow's very difficult circumstances, moved Jesus. Followers know God as compassionate. Jesus again revealed and perfectly illustrated that critically important quality of God's compassion. Lord knows, in this broken world, we need a compassionate God, one who not only empathizes deeply and cares for our welfare but who also then *acts* directly, effectively, and in miracle fashion out of that concern.

As she meditated on Jesus's compassion for the widow's son, she realized that she not only wanted to *show* compassion as Jesus had done but also that she wanted to understand and reflect the posture that *draws* compassion from so loving of a God. Why precisely did Jesus favor the widow in raising her son? As she reflected on the event, she realized that proximity to Jesus may be one such condition for the compassion of God. God can doubtless be compassionate at any distance, but Jesus first showed compassion to the widow because he encountered her. She felt that she needed proximity to Jesus, to be close to Jesus, to receive God's compassion more often and freely. Then, she didn't want to be a whiner or complainer, but she did want to be honest and open with God in her needs and grief. She knew that she was deeply needy, as everyone is. She also had matters over which she grieved, as everyone does. She hoped and believed that she could share that grief openly and frankly with God. When the time came to share intimately with God in prayer, she decided that she had no need of putting on a happy face. She trusted that God was compassionate. Jesus's raising the widow's son proved to her that she could share her greatest challenges, those insurmountable endpoints that seem to offer no relief, with God who could out of his compassion share miracles. The miracles might take many forms, but whatever form they took, they would reflect the love and compassion of God.

101 Astonishing.

Matthew 12:23; *see also* Luke 8:56.

Just as an above section shows that Jesus had the capacity for the faith of followers to astonish him, the Gospels also record Jesus performing miracles that astonished those who brought the sick, possessed, and disabled to Jesus for healing. In one such account, the people had brought a demon-possessed man who was both unable to see and unable to speak, to see what Jesus would be able to do with such significant disabilities. Helping a woman recover from a fever or a man to walk would be one level of miracle, but granting new sight and speech would be quite another. When Jesus promptly did exactly that, giving the formerly blind and mute man both sight and speech, all who were watching reacted in astonishment. The news that Jesus could heal miraculously was true, indeed wondrously true. The next reaction of those whom Jesus's miracle astonished may reveal why Jesus performed the miracle, not for its magic-like effect of wonder but for the testimony that it gave to Jesus's divinity. In this account, the astonished people promptly asked whether Jesus could be that special *Son of David* whom the Israelites had long awaited. Yet the jealous religious leaders also noticed how Jesus's astonishing miracle turned the observers' hearts and minds toward Jesus's divinity. The account records the religious leaders promptly rebuking the crowd's *could-this-be* query that had reflected their burgeoning belief that Jesus was God's divine Son. The religious leaders scoffed instead that Jesus performed miracles, even healing miracles, under the devil's evil power rather than out of God's supernatural goodness and holy divinity. While the crowd reacted with astonishment and belief, the religious leaders were neither impressed nor believing.

Scenes of Jesus's miracles producing astonishment and wonder among people who trusted him enough to bring him their sick are evocative encouragement for faithful followers. Jesus brought, inhabited, and offers a world of wonder for the faithful. Everyone faces the same choice to live either in a hard, fixed, mechanistic, probabilistic, and solely material world void of creator and creativity or instead to recognize, approach, and embrace in astonished awe a world filled with God's creative wonders. By following God in faith, disciples choose astonishment as much as astonishment happens to them. The religious leaders who rebuked the seeing-is-believing crowd saw or could have seen the same miracles that the crowd saw. Yet their cramped rigidity, hardness of their hearts, and falsely limited capacity of their views, kept them from doing so. Skeptics question miracles because they do not open their minds and follow their senses enough to see God's miracles occurring all around them. Many of those who saw believed, but Jesus said that those who did not see and yet also believed would exhibit even greater faith and experience similar wonders. Seeing may be believing, but *hearing* can engender sound belief, too, particularly when we hear and accept the very good news of the Word of God, the one who healed miraculously. God offers the same wonders to all of us. Contemplating and then trusting the record of Jesus giving sight and speech brings the follower more than mere hope and instead something more like joyful confidence. Wonder of wonders then that this astonishing miracle-worker Jesus would also give followers eternal life.

He had finally come to accepting the important proposition that miracles are not the measure of God, of whether the Father exists and gave life and miraculous power to his beloved Son, but instead measure us. He had realized that like every other point of faith, the question *do you believe in miracles* is not a question of whether miracles actually occur and exist. Miracles are not a test of God in the way that leaders tried to goad Jesus into performing miracles to prove his powers and divinity. Instead, miracles test man, he could finally see from the Gospel accounts and from his Spirit-guided discernment. Miracles simply measure one's openness to wondrous experience, he had concluded rather simply and directly. He knew, like everyone else knows, that the Gospels and so much of human history are replete with reports and records of miracles, just as he knew that God had filled his own life with them. He had come to the point of recognizing that he would have to deny his own senses and so much of the Gospel record and history in order *not* to believe in miracles. Fortunately, he was not so willful, not so obstinate as to reject such evidence, particularly when the conclusion that he would then draw in the veracity of reports and experiences of miracles filled his world with astonishment and wonder. If such acceptance had turned things inside out, making him unable to function responsibly in the world, then he would have considered rejecting miracles. Yet in this instance, accepting the evidence of miracles did the opposite, making him far more able to sustain and enjoy a life of blessing others while receiving even richer blessing. From that point on, he welcomed every encounter he had with the accounts of Jesus's miracles, even reflecting with increasing joy on each account as it once again came to his attention. Do you *really* believe in miracles? How could one not do so, he smiled and answered again to himself.

102 Fearsome.

Luke 8:25; *see also* Mark 5:1; Luke 8:37.

The Gospels record Jesus performing miracles in ways that not only astonished observers but also *struck fear* in them, including even in his own disciples who knew him most closely. Jesus could be fearsome. Luke's Gospel records one such instance when Jesus invited the disciples to sail across the Sea of Galilee, what Jesus referred to as *going over to the other side of the lake*. The disciples dutifully got into a boat with Jesus and set sail. At this point, the account first takes a curious turn, recording that Jesus fell asleep, and then a dangerous turn, recording that a squall swamped the boat, placing them in *great danger*. Jesus, though, appears to have remained asleep in the swamped boat because the account records the disciples going to wake Jesus with cries of *Master, Master, we're going to drown!* In response, Jesus did something that the disciples must not have expected. He simply got up and *rebuked the wind and raging waters*, promptly causing the squall to subside while also calming the raging waters. The account next records the disciples turning to one another *in fear and amazement* that even the winds and water obeyed him, and asking *Who is this?* Jesus just asked them where their faith had been. The account ends with the group sailing on to their destination in the region of the Gerasenes on the Sea of Galilee's eastern shore, where Jesus would perform another astonishing miracle, this one of healing a violent demoniac. Once again, in that subsequent miracle, the reaction of those who saw observed it was to *fear* Jesus so much as to ask him to leave the region. From these two consecutive miracles and other accounts, followers know that Jesus had the capacity, and his actions sometimes had the strong and immediate effect, of striking fear even in his most-devout and appreciative followers.

The image of Jesus striking fear in his disciples for having calmed a raging storm and boat-swamping waters is an important one for followers in more than one respect. Certainly, the event bears reflection for the extraordinary fact that Jesus controlled not just illnesses, disabilities, and demon spirits but that he also controlled nature at instant command. The event shows a side of Jesus's capacity and authority nearly like no other. Yes, he made water into wine, multiplied bread and fish, and performed other miracles affecting supernaturally other natural conditions. Yet from the disciples' reaction in stunned fear and amazement, Jesus's calming the raging storm and lake must have felt like a miracle of much greater proportion. That the disciples reacted saying *Who is this?* as if they *didn't even know* Jesus, confirms the surprising new dimension of Jesus's miracle. He had shocked the disciples into realizing that they did not even know the man, or the authority and power of the man, with whom they had been living. Interestingly, the account does not show Jesus giving a reason for the sail across the lake, leaving open the possibility that the reason at least in part was the sail itself rather than its destination. Preachers have accordingly made good use of the image of the disciples getting into the boat and setting sail with Jesus, an action that has its own rich allegory of joining the church on a journey of faith. Beyond such allegory, the journey's point may well also have included to show this fearsome dimension of Jesus. Followers should appreciate that Jesus is fearsome, not at all in arbitrary and capricious sense but in the utter magnificence and unlimited scope and power of his authority. Perhaps followers need to fear Jesus, in fear's rare positive and respectful sense, just as much as they need to love and obey him.

Strange as it seemed, he actually felt that he wanted, needed, and could reasonably embrace Jesus's other-worldly character, nearly as much as or maybe even more than he embraced Jesus's love, mercy, care, kindness, healing touch, and intimacy. While he recognized that others might need more of Jesus's intimacy and less of his fearsomeness, he actually felt more than a little the opposite. He couldn't entirely figure out why he wanted and needed his God to be a fearsome God, but he knew that he did need it. The images of Jesus calming the raging storm and, later at his crucifixion, of the sky going dark at mid-day and of the ground breaking open, reminded him of the Old Testament God whose sudden, almost absurdly majestic, and always-definitive acts, like parting a sea or striking down hundreds of thousands, elicited such abject fear, shock, and awe. God should be capable of striking fear, or maybe more to the point, humans should be capable of awe before God. He had actually felt that awe-related fear or fear-related awe probably only a few times before, although he thoroughly understood it both intellectually and emotionally. Each time, the sense of it had opened him to new possibilities and dimensions that he knew he needed to acknowledge if he was truly to know and respect God. That Jesus also so clearly possessed that fear-striking capability was equally important to him because it confirmed Jesus's full divinity. Jesus was no lesser version of the Father, no mere prophet or little god. Like looking through a strange portal into a different dimension, the more that he reflected on Jesus's calming the raging water, the more that he knew that he followed the one vast Creator, the ultimately incomprehensible God, even when incarnate in Jesus's image.

103 Vanquisher.

Luke 8:27; *see also* Matthew 8:16.

As the prior section intimates, right after calming the raging waters, Jesus performed another fear-striking miracle of relieving a violent demoniac of his possession and restoring his sanity. While this subsequent miracle had the same effect as the prior one of overcoming observers with fear, the miracle itself showed Jesus's capacity to vanquish violent, barbarous, and destructive spirits, moods, temperaments, or conditions. The Gospel account records that a demon-possessed man met Jesus when the boat with Jesus and the disciples reached the Gerasenes shore. The account describes the man as having for a long time lived outdoors and naked among the shore's tombs. Indeed, it relates that the area's residents had previously chained the man hand and foot, and kept him closely guarded, until his violent propensities had broken the chains and driven him into solitude among the tombs along the shore. Yet instead of attacking Jesus and the disciples as the man would presumably have done to others, the man fell at Jesus's feet shouting *Jesus, Son of the Most High God*, not to torture him. Extraordinarily, the man, or the demoniac presence within him, recognized Jesus exactly as who he was and instantly submitted, preparing for vanquishing, indeed begging that Jesus not order the demoniac horde *into the abyss*. When Jesus asked the man his name and the demoniac horde within him replied *legion*, the account states that Jesus *gave the horde permission* to enter a nearby herd of pigs that then rushed down the shore into the lake to their drowning. The report of those who had tended the pigs attracted the area's residents who, when they saw the demoniac now dressed and seated peacefully at Jesus's feet, let fear overcome them, despite explanations that Jesus had simply healed the man. Jesus complied with the frightened throng's demand to leave but not before telling the healed man, who had wanted to leave with Jesus, to instead go home and tell everyone the great healing that God had done for him. Other similar accounts, such as in Matthew's Gospel, record Jesus vanquishing spirits and healing the sick with a word, fulfilling Isaiah's prophecy that he would *take up our infirmities* and *carry our disease*.

The image of Jesus banishing demoniac presence from a violent, destitute, and isolated man can be a powerful scene on which followers may beneficially reflect. Jesus was not merely a counselor or therapist in his miracle vanquishing of barbarous dispositions and temperaments.

Counsel and therapy can be extraordinarily helpful to the prompt easing of mental, emotional, and spiritual distress, and to the gradual improvement of their underlying causes, conditions, dispositions, and temperaments. Yet Jesus's capacity to improve mental and spiritual health reached far beyond easing or improvement, and far beyond simple distress, to the point of instant and complete relief of the most destructive of conditions, even violently demoniac conditions. Jesus *vanquished* viciously disabling conditions. Some readers may mistake the ancient context and reference to demon spirits as suggesting the absence of credible cause and effect, as if people today do not suffer from similar conditions, and if they do, that demon possession would be an inapposite characterization. Others might equate Jesus's ridding the demoniac of disabling spirits, as he also empowered his disciples to do, with a ritual akin to a modern-day exorcism, even though the Bible says nothing of any such ritual which may have been unknown in that day. None though would disagree that violent and other grossly unstable dispositions isolate, disable, and imprison far too many individuals today. And from the above account, none should doubt that Jesus could just as instantly, completely, and beneficially heal the condition of those cruelly disabled and fiercely dangerous individuals today. Followers know Jesus as capable of utterly and at once cleansing individuals of all unsavory spirit and condition. Jesus defeats and destroys evils.

Some experience with the deeply mentally disturbed and dangerous, indeed the rankly criminal, had taught her the threat and ferocity of persons possessed by readily apparent evil. If she had not had those experiences, then news stories alone would have forced her to the same conclusion. Anyone who does not recognize the extent to which evil can lead persons to the most horrifically destructive wrongs just has not been paying attention, she knew. She didn't like to think of such deep evil and so studiously avoided the news. Yet when experience or news of evil forced itself in on her consciousness again, as it far too often did these days, she learned to turn again to the image of Jesus healing the demoniac man. Two things about that story reassured her, one of course that Jesus had instantly and completely healed the man. Yet the other conclusion that she drew from the scene had to do with the reality and depravity of unmitigated evil. The news and her experience of evil somehow demanded evil's recognition. The scene of the demoniac man satisfied that demand. The world includes despicable horrors, but as the scene starkly proved, horrors over which Jesus can rule utterly and as he wishes. She kept thinking not just of how the demoniac spirits had instantly recognized and submitted to Jesus's lordship but also how they had spoken to Jesus of not returning to the abyss. Just as heaven is real, so too is the abyss, the scene reminded her. In the end, the scene gave her context for making some sense of what would otherwise seem like utterly senseless violence. Jesus did as he pleased to free people of horrors and banish violence. With each confrontation of evil, she would pray again, *Oh come, Lord Jesus.*

[104] **Responding.**

Luke 8:41; *see also* Matthew 9:25; Mark 5:42.

The Gospels record Jesus responding with miracles to the pleading of those who sought him out in faith for healing. In one Gospel account, a crowd had just welcomed Jesus's return when the local synagogue's ruler fell pleading at Jesus's feet with a remarkable request. The ruler throwing himself prostrate at Jesus's feet might have startled the crowd, although the account gives no indication. Jesus did not ordinarily get such treatment from the religious leaders. The ruler's request, to come to his house to heal his dying twelve-year-old only daughter, revealed his desperate need for a miracle from Jesus. Jesus responded to the ruler's request not with words but action, promptly heading for the ruler's house. A crowd delayed Jesus on the way, during the course of which Jesus supplied another miracle described in the next section. The delay may have contributed to the next event, though, when a person came from the ruler's house with the news that the ruler's daughter had died and so *not to bother* Jesus any further. But Jesus told the ruler that rather than fear, the ruler should instead *just believe* that Jesus would heal her, which would mean bringing her back from death. People at the ruler's house laughed derisively at Jesus when he told them to stop wailing over the child's death because he would wake her. Yet wake her, or more accurately *bring her back to life*, Jesus did, with the command to *get up*. She promptly rose, Jesus even saying to give the risen child something to eat. The event of course astonished and enormously relieved the child's parents whom Jesus nonetheless told not to tell anyone. Jesus can and does respond promptly and earnestly to requests made with such faith as the ruler exhibited.

The scene of Jesus responding so promptly and earnestly to what at the time seemed to some observers to be an utterly improbable and even pointless request should embolden and fortify followers. Jesus didn't question or test the prostrate ruler. Jesus simply immediately got going to do as the ruler requested. God is not an indifferent divinity. God engages his power and presence in fruitful, indeed life-restoring and life-giving activity. Jesus must have done precisely as the Father willed in immediately making his way toward the ruler's house to heal his dying daughter. The account manages in small ways to communicate the ruler's abject distress and great pain over the daughter's impending death. That the dying girl's mother is also a small part of the account makes the account even more compelling. These parents faced the worst possible event that can befall a parent, and yet instead of despairing, they sought and trusted Jesus even against the scoffing of non-believing mourners. God responds to faith, and he sometimes does so through instant miraculous restoration and healing. Every follower should trust, as the ruler and his wife trusted, that Jesus can and does respond, and not only respond modestly but instead act miraculously including giving life in apparently hopeless situations. Disciples follow a God who does more than simply empathize but also responds actively and effectively, indeed miraculously. Notice in the Gospel accounts how Jesus repeatedly responds. Then reflect hearteningly on those instances in order that you also may exhibit deep faith engendering miraculous action.

Although each day's many small and few large demands often wearied and distracted him, he nonetheless carried energy, activity, and direction through most of his days. Only rarely did he feel that he really fell down from that positive forward direction. Even then, he did so only briefly. He sometimes wondered why he kept moving so resolutely forward, as so many others whom he knew also did so. He wondered even more why others who faced far greater challenges also did so. Why bother? The answer that made the most sense to him was that God cared deeply about how he conducted himself including the faith that he showed in staying engaged in life and its service activities. The key, though, was in his recognizing Jesus as the model for that forward motion. He realized how much Jesus's public ministry meant to him both as a model and also for the hope that Jesus's actions engendered.

Jesus's three-year public ministry was a veritable blaze of exquisitely timed and super-effectively engaged action. He saw Jesus repeatedly responding to situations and stimuli, always for the deepest benefit of those who requested or encountered, and confronted or received, his action. He gradually even felt that he wasn't so much maintaining his own forward motion out of recognition of and respect for Jesus's action as he was instead carrying Jesus's own momentum forward, not that he felt at all worthy of doing so and instead feeling that he more often delayed and interfered with the Master's great workings. The point was that Jesus responded and acted, and that somehow by pure grace he was sharing or participating in, but surely benefitting from, Jesus's action. He surely wanted it to be that way because he suspected that he had little or no other reason for the constant motion. God made all the difference, and Jesus made that difference so plainly evident.

105 Accessible.

Luke 8:42; *see also* Matthew 14:36; Mark 5:27, 6:56; Luke 15:1.

The Gospels repeatedly display Jesus's accessibility, the constant way in which he made himself available for frequent contact with those who had little or no access to other powers, institutions, programs, and resources. The account of the woman healed by touching Jesus's cloak is a prime example. Crowds nearly crushed Jesus as he was on his way to heal the ruler's dying daughter, ultimately to raise the ruler's dead daughter. A woman among the throng had suffered from a bleeding condition for more than a decade. The woman's decade-long suffering might suggest that she had no access to whatever healing arts and sciences were available to the more-powerful members of society in that day, although the account also says that *no one could heal her.* Yet here she encountered the incomparable Lord among throngs of Jesus's other admirers and observers. No entourage shielded, isolated, or protected him. Anyone could approach Jesus to the point that the account makes clear, as just referenced, that the crowds *almost crushed him.* The woman accordingly walked up behind Jesus, not to confront or embrace Jesus but barely to touch the edge of his cloak, presumably in faith that she might heal in doing so. Indeed, her bare hidden touch of the edge of Jesus's cloak immediately stopped her bleeding and healed her condition. Sensing that *power had gone out from him*, Jesus wanted to know who had been its beneficiary. After everyone else pressing in around Jesus denied it, the woman finally fell trembling at Jesus's feet in confession, also explaining her long suffering and instant healing. Although her trembling might have anticipated Jesus's rebuke, Jesus instead told her simply that to *go in peace* because her faith had healed her. Other Gospel accounts record people begging Jesus to let them touch the edge of his cloak and that his power healed all that did so. Another Gospel account says that sinners all gathered around Jesus to the point that the religious leaders and law experts muttered against him.

The image of Jesus so constantly pressed by crowds and in at least one instance having his power heal one particular woman who virtually snuck up behind him to touch his clothing, should encourage every follower that Jesus makes himself accessible. Consider the lengths to which leaders, even religious leaders, go today, or their protectors and handlers go for them, to keep them safe, secure, and available for service even if only or primarily to the rich, powerful, and famous. Those who want access and have the political, financial, or social capital to acquire it can readily do so, whether the service they seek is entrepreneurial, medical, charitable, or otherwise. Audiences are available, at least if you know the right people or have the means to get the attention of the right people. Jesus, though, simply walked daily, weekly, month by month, and for his three years of public ministry, among the throngs who wanted and needed his attention. One would be wrong to assume that he did so only because he and other leaders had no alternative to granting such access. To the contrary, plenty of other Gospel accounts show how effectively the day's political, military, and religious leaders and authorities kept themselves from those same throngs, by keeping to their compounds, garrisons, temples, and palaces, while moving about only on horseback, in litters, or surrounded by entourages and guards, and only in certain favored districts. Jesus eschewed those favored districts and households except when his ministry called on him to confront their residents. Then he would promptly return to the common streets, towns, villages, fields, shores, and byways where the crowds could daily gather and press in on him. His constant presence and ready availability must have enormously reassured the common people whose days he brightened, illnesses he healed, and needs he provided. If a daughter fell ill, son died, or woman bled, then someone need only find Jesus among the crowds along the way from town to town and common household to common household. How few leaders have ever displayed the same accessibility, which by far most leaders would assume unwise in the extreme if not impossible? The scene of a desperate woman sneaking up behind Jesus to draw miraculous healing power from a touch to his cloak's edge, and Jesus's refusal to rebuke her for assuming such access, should convince every follower of Jesus's availability.

She once in a while wondered whether Jesus was really *hers* as much as she wanted to believe it. Given that he was the one incomparable Son of God in all his magnificence and splendor, his availability and closeness to her seemed to her at times to be a powerful contradiction. He sat on God's throne, ready to judge the nations. Could he also hear her prayers and heal her soul? Could he really walk and talk with her even when she had no specific need of his miraculous powers? Then she would recall the account of the woman sneaking up behind Jesus to touch the edge of his cloak. The account always made her smile, maybe because she felt that her own approaches to Jesus were like sneaking up on him from behind. She suspected that if she had lived in that day and, walking the dusty way, had encountered a crowd thronging Jesus, she would not have walked right up to him, trying to gain his attention. Oh, she would have followed him, no doubt. Yet she felt more so that she would have done just what the bleeding woman had done, which was to quietly move around behind to get as close as possible to Jesus, she hoped even to touch the edge of his cloak as the bleeding woman had done, if not the strap of his sandal. Yes, that was it. She would find a moment to kneel behind him to touch his sandal in case he turned around suddenly to see who or what touched him. If he had done so, then she was sure that she would have felt just as the bleeding woman apparently felt, which was that she was not worthy. She would want nearly to be hiding and to admit that she had been the one to touch his sandal only if no other did so. She also knew from the account of the bleeding woman that Jesus would not rebuke her for her proximity, even for her touch. He would instead speak gently to her just as he had spoken gently and reassuringly to the no-longer-bleeding woman, in confirmation of the miracle even of a hidden touch.

[106] Merciful.

Matthew 9:27; *see also* Matthew 15:22, 20:31; Mark 10:47; Luke 18:38.

The Gospels record Jesus more than once performing the miracle of restoring sight to blind beggars when the blind beggars asked for Jesus's *mercy*. In the first such account, two blind men followed Jesus along the road demanding loudly that Jesus *have mercy on them*. The blind men addressed Jesus as *Son of David*. Jesus did not at first respond, instead just going indoors, but the blind men followed Jesus in. So Jesus asked them whether they believed that Jesus was able to *do this*, evidently referring to restoring their sight, even though the blind men had only so far asked for mercy, not sight. When the blind men replied affirmatively in faith that Jesus was able, Jesus touched their eyes *according to their faith*, following which they could instantly see. The same Gospel again records two blind men loudly demanding that Jesus, Son of David, *have mercy on them*, this time as Jesus and a crowd walked by the two men who sat by the side of the road to Jericho. The crowd's rebuke for the two blind men to be quiet only made them shout for mercy more loudly. Here, Jesus stopped and asked them expressly what they wanted him to do, to which they answered that they wanted their sight. The account ends with Jesus touching their eyes *in compassion*, instantly restoring their sight. Another Gospel gives a third account of another blind man, identified as Bartimaeus, shouting to Jesus for mercy, this time along the road leaving Jericho. Again, the crowd rebuked the blind man, only causing him to shout louder. Stopping while telling the crowd to call the blind man, Jesus then on the man's request instantly restored his sight, this man then following Jesus. Another very similar account has substantially the same events occurring on the way into Jericho. The accounts do not elaborate on why blind beggars required mercy, nor do they record Jesus explaining the connection between his miracle and mercy. Yet the accounts strongly suggest that Jesus performs miracles out of mercy.

Other than its suggestion that Jesus is indeed merciful, the image of Jesus more than once performing the specific miracle of restoring sight at a blind person's request for mercy may seem a curious one to followers. Followers know Jesus to be extraordinarily merciful, indeed ultimately merciful. If mercy means forgoing just punishment in favor of substitute remedy, then Jesus is certainly the most merciful ever. Jesus punishes none without prior full offer of a mercy for which his sacrifice is itself the substitute remedy. Jesus is above all merciful. Followers should attend closely to any scene or image that evokes Jesus's mercy. Yet these particular scenes of blind beggars shouting for Jesus's mercy are curious for not revealing the beggars' peculiar need for mercy over their obvious need for healing in the form of restored sight. Many had come to Jesus for healing. Very few of them, indeed only the blind beggars, shouted for mercy, even in the face of strong rebuke to *be quiet.* Why would blind beggars need mercy more than the sighted sick and otherwise disabled? Indeed, what does mercy have to do with miracle healing? The scenes' reflective value for followers may be exactly that lesson that persons, whether or not possessing sight, deserve nothing from the utter magnanimity of Jesus. Anyone who asked for healing should ask first for mercy because none deserve Jesus's favor, and all instead merit only condemnation. Only in Jesus's own refusal to punish as deserved can the requester find justification for demanding miracle healing. The blind beggars had it exactly right. We should all be crying out for God's mercy while searching for sight of Jesus.

Blindness both frightened and fascinated her, as she suspected that it did others. Its frightening sense was obvious to her. Living in darkness must make the world seem full of awful risk. Living blind after having had sight must seem like a horrible deprivation. Yet blindness also fascinated her for reasons that were a good bit less obvious. Did, as she sometimes heard, blindness really open interior worlds rather than simply close exterior ones? Did blindness sharpen other senses including the ability to read others' energy, intentions, and spirits? She wished sometimes that she had the sensitivity of the blind, although she never really wished for blindness, which instead continued to sound like horrible risk and depredation. While she concluded that no one other than the blind can really know what blindness is really like, she nonetheless drew one strong lesson from the Gospel stories of the blind beggars crying out for Jesus's mercy. That lesson was that Jesus holds a profound mercy for us, an attribute on which every one of us depends, even if only the blind fully perceive our need for it. She decided to consider herself blind when it came to seeing her own need for mercy, committing instead to cry out like the blind for Jesus's miracle-healing mercy.

[107] Secretive.

Matthew 9:30; *see also* Matthew 8:4; Mark 1:44, 7:24; Luke 5:14; John 6:15, 7:4.

The Gospels record Jesus warning and instructing those for whom he performed miracles, not to tell anyone. In one such instance involving Jesus's restoring sight to two blind men, the Gospel account records that Jesus *warned them sternly* against disclosing the miracle. Indeed in that instance, Jesus's warning was explicitly to *see that no one knows* about the miracle. Equally oddly, or even more so, both recipients of those sight-restoring miracles promptly disobeyed Jesus's stern warning. The account records that they instead made a point of spreading the miracle news *all over the region*. In other accounts, the Gospels record Jesus as saying simply *don't tell anyone* what he had done, without such a stern warning. In those other instances, though, Jesus combined the commitment to confidentiality with the important exception that the beneficiary should go show the miracle to the priest, while there offering the gifts or sacrifices that Moses had long ago commanded. In similar situations where he sought not to be publicly involved in a matter, whether to turn water into wine or to attend a Jerusalem festival, Jesus had added the enigmatic explanation that his *time* or *hour* had *not yet come*. While the circumstances of each such event and the words and instructions that Jesus gave thus differ in certain respects, the Gospel record is quite clear that Jesus meant to control or influence to some degree public knowledge about his action, location, authority, or intention. John's Gospel records Jesus's brothers telling Jesus to quit hiding in secret in Galilee and instead go to Judea so that the Jews there could see his many miracles, although Jesus knew instead that the Jews there lay in wait to kill him. Another Gospel account indicates that Jesus withdrew to a mountain in solitude lest the people came to make him their leader by force. Another Gospel account records Jesus entering a house wanting no one to know it but that he simply *could not keep his presence a secret*. Jesus with some frequency acted secretly or surreptitiously, desiring that only a few, primarily the beneficiary of his miraculous authority, know of his intervention.

The several scenes of Jesus performing astonishing miracles but then telling the recipients not to tell anyone may puzzle followers. Jesus came with a salvation mission that would require widespread knowledge of his capacity, divinity, and divine purpose. Why would he ever have wished to act in secret, especially when performing healing miracles? Jesus's cryptic *my time has not yet come* certainly gives strong hints that he intended to control or influence the public unfolding of his ministry. Maybe public knowledge, or indeed notice of the religious and political leaders, of too many of Jesus's miracles too early would have meant too early of an arrest, conviction, and crucifixion. His roughly three-year public ministry was already remarkably short to have accomplished its history-altering purpose so spectacularly, which it might not have done had it been any shorter. On the other hand, Jesus may simply have wanted to keep some miracles between him and the beneficiary. Indeed, many such beneficiaries may have followed Jesus's warning and instruction, keeping confidential their miracle healing. We would very likely be wrong to assume that the Gospels record anything more than a small fraction of Jesus's miracles. How many more miracles must Jesus have performed about which we never heard because the beneficiaries followed rather than ignored his instruction? The point may simply be that followers need not know everything, or indeed much of *anything*, as to Jesus's justifications or rationales. Simply accept that Jesus often preferred to act secretly, clandestinely, or surreptitiously. Rejoice that we share a Savior Lord who often preferred that none other than the beneficiaries know of his great miracles.

He had no desire to hide any of the wonders with which Jesus blessed him, things that at least seemed to *him* like wonders, even if others might not have thought them so wondrous. He was perfectly willing to testify to Jesus's glory. He felt that the Lord healed, protected, and otherwise blessed him far beyond anything he had ever deserved. Yet he often felt as if the Lord did not necessarily want him giving all of those testimonies. Instead, he often felt as if his consistent quiet attribution of all good to the Good Shepherd satisfied the will of the Lord. Indeed, he sometimes felt as if the Lord preferred that he *not* share certain blessings. People knew to whom he attributed all good things. Further testimonies could in those instances sound more like he was calling attention to *himself* rather than to the Lord, as if to communicate the opposite of what he intended that he somehow deserved and thus received such blessings. No, he thought, better to be demure about some testimonies. Better to listen to the Lord's will even as to sharing *or not sharing* the good things that the Lord did for him and with him, in him and around him. Miracles abounded, not just for him but for everyone following the Lord's will. He liked to listen to testimonies just as much as he liked to give them. Let others also discover and share word of the Lord's miracle life, he concluded. He wouldn't hide that life, but he wanted also to leave enough space for the testimony of others.

108 Provider.

Matthew 14:19; *see also* Matthew 15:29; Mark 6:30, 8:1; Luke 9:10; John 6:1, 21:6.

The Gospels of course record Jesus performing the well-known miracles of feeding five thousand men plus women and children who accompanied them and, later, four thousand more, proving that Jesus was a spectacular provider. In the first account, appearing in all four Gospels, Jesus had taught the crowd in a remote location, away from homes and villages where crowd members might have stored or purchased food. When the day grew late, the disciples interrupted Jesus, urging him to send the crowd members away to buy food. Jesus replied that the crowd had no need to leave and instead urged the *disciples* to give them something to eat. Presumably incredulous, the disciples answered that they had only five loaves and two fish, plainly not enough to feed the crowd of thousands. John's Gospel identifies the disciple Andrew, Peter's brother, as the one who says that *a nearby boy* has five *small* barley loaves and two *small* fish. Jesus simply asked for the loaves and fish, while directing the crowd members to sit. He then looked to heaven, gave thanks, and broke the loaves, handing them to the disciples who gave out the pieces to the sitting people, all of whom ate to their satisfaction, leaving twelve baskets filled with leftover pieces. Jesus then sent the disciples away while he dismissed the crowd. The later account of Jesus feeding four thousand men plus women and children who accompanied them proceeds similarly, although with seven rather than five loaves, a few small fish, and seven baskets left over. Jesus could do more than teach, preach, and heal. He could also provide.

The two scenes of Jesus feeding thousands from meager supplies should supply followers with endless satisfaction on reflection. These bread-and-fish multiplying, feeding-thousands miracles have a quality distinct from Jesus's healing miracles and even from the miracle in which he calmed the storm. Even though Jesus's instant healing and instant storm-calming were utterly miraculous, bodies do heal naturally, just as storms calm naturally. In those instances, Jesus accelerated natural processes, even while one recognizes that some of the many whom he healed, particularly the blind and lame, not to mention the dead, would not have recovered. Yet to take a processed food supply like bread and simply *multiply* it exponentially is utterly wondrous, without precedent, and so far beyond the natural as to be a miracle in its own category or class. Preachers readily reveal its deeper communion meaning, foreshadowing the body of Christ broken for us, the followers of Christ fed by his flesh while cleansed by his redeeming blood. While followers can indeed draw on the feeding miracles' deeper communion meaning, followers find simple joy in the miracle itself, in Jesus just handing out bread to sustain and satisfy his followers. Are you *hungry*, in the very most natural sense of that state, not only in the word's figurative spiritual meaning? Then Jesus can also satisfy that natural hunger if and when he wishes. Bread can simply usher forth from his hands, as from a skilled and well-supplied baker's oven. Followers understand the spiritual path and peace that Jesus brings, but they should also understand and appreciate the literal and natural life that Jesus, who is the very author of life, offers. Reflecting frequently on Jesus providing literal food, not just spiritual satisfaction, deepens and strengthens one's faith.

She absolutely loved the feeding miracles. She had seen several portrayals of those miracles and relished every one of them. She loved the feeding-thousands miracles both for their simplicity and their familiarity. They were simple in the sense that Jesus instantly made very much out of very little for very evident purpose benefiting thousands. The feeding miracles were familiar because from her household, neighborhood, church, and community duties she was intimately acquainted with what obtaining and preparing food actually required. She even felt, always with a little bit of humor, that she would have been one of those disciples asking Jesus what, when, and where were the people going to *eat?* Yet the feeding miracles were also special to her because they were spectacularly generous. She knew how generous the miracles were because she had been a part of feeding small crowds, at home gatherings, church events, wedding or graduation receptions, and soup kitchens. She knew the purchasing, preparation, and labor that feeding dozens took. She could hardly imagine the supplies and work that feeding hundreds no less *thousands* took. And yet Jesus did exactly that out of next to no supplies, with no more preparation or labor than breaking the bread. She could even laugh to herself at each recall of the feeding miracles that of all the power that she would wish for herself from Jesus, she would choose the power to feed others. Imagine: no more grocery store, kitchen, or preparation! She only wondered if she'd still have to clean up.

[109] **Testing.**

John 6:6; *see also* Matthew 26:75.

The Gospels record Jesus testing his disciples to reveal their faith or lack of faith around his ability and willingness to perform miracles. Jesus clearly did so in the account in John's Gospel in which Jesus feeds the crowd from just five small loaves and two small fish, with twelve basketfuls left over. The account begins with a *great crowd* following Jesus as he crossed the Sea of Galilee, the crowd pursuing him because he had healed so many persons so miraculously. Jesus withdrew with the disciples up a mountainside, but the crowd again pursued. The account relates that when Jesus saw the great crowd coming, he knew what he was going to do, which was to feed the crowd in place. His decision may have had something to do with a preceding reference that the Passover Feast was near. In any case, rather than simply begin with his miracle of feeding the great crowd, Jesus first turned to his disciple Philip, the account expressly states, *only to test him.* Jesus asked Philip where they should buy bread for the great crowd. Philip answered incredulously that buying bread would take eight months' wages just to get enough so that each could have but one bite. The disciple Andrew, though, pointed out the boy who held the five loaves and two fish from which Jesus would indeed feed the great crowd. Although Andrew may have shown some faith in pointing out the boy and his foodstuff, Andrew nonetheless asked *but how far would the food go* with so many to feed. Jesus then completed the miracle as related in the prior section, withdrawing to a solitary mountainside afterward so that the people would not make him king by force. The account makes clear that Jesus tested the disciples' faith about his ability and willingness to perform miracles, even though the account does not say precisely why Jesus decided to test his disciples.

The image of Jesus testing Philip and to a degree also Andrew can be a helpful one on which followers may productively reflect. In a way, everything is a test. Every question, every decision, every path taken tests one's faith, but particularly when the circumstances directly involve a question of the capability and intention of Jesus. Philip likely had little clue that Jesus intended as a test his question about where to buy bread. The circumstance of a great crowd that had already pursued Jesus across a lake now rushing up a mountainside toward Jesus, and Jesus asking Philip where to buy the crowd bread, might well have given Philip little reason to suspect that Jesus's question was a test. Yet we credibly have only one response to anything that Jesus puts to us, which response is whatever is in the Good Lord's will. Even though Jesus often sought refuge from crowds, he taught, preached, and miraculously healed when they found him. Philip may not have suspected a test, but given Jesus's character and mission, Philip's incredulous response was clearly not one of faith. One never has cause for incredulity, at least not in the form of doubting disbelief, around Jesus. God can certainly provide bread for a great crowd, just as he provided abundant manna for the many long-wandering Israelites. Philip's response that whatever quantity of bread that they somehow managed to buy, even with so much as eight months of wages, would only give each person a single bite, hardly reflected Jesus's extraordinarily generous character. Jesus miraculously turned several huge jars of water into the very best wine, not a thimble full for each wedding celebrant. Although the account does not say why Jesus chose to test his disciples, his having done so provided a stunning lesson not just for Philip and Andrew but for all subsequent readers.

This business of Jesus testing his disciples with challenges and questions intrigued him. He could see the teaching and corrective value of Jesus's practice from the account of Philip failing Jesus's test. Philip certainly must have learned from Jesus's question and subsequent miraculous actions. He knew, too, that the account of Jesus testing Philip was reminding him to be ready for tests and to pass them. He almost liked tests, except that he knew how painful tests could be. He liked tests because he realized that one doesn't change so much from succeeding as from failing. Failure instructs, while success puffs up, he had long felt. Yet failing was always at least a little painful, and Jesus would be the last one before whom he would want to fail. Philip's test made him think of Peter's much greater failure when Peter denied Christ the night of his trial. He imagined just how crushing Peter's failure must have been to him, indeed just as the account revealed that Peter wept bitterly over it. But he also remembered how gently and persistently the resurrected Jesus restored Peter. He thought, too, of how majestically the restored Peter then represented Christ, with such courage and at such peril. Maybe failing *faith* tests, not just other tests, was an essential part of a successful faith journey, he decided. Jesus knew his heart, he had no doubt. Jesus knew where he lacked confidence, commitment, and courage. Indeed, Jesus likely knew in advance that Philip would not respond in faith, which may have been why Jesus decided to test him, to reveal and correct his lack of faith. He decided in the end to keep thinking about Jesus testing his faith. Maybe if he reflected on the failure of Philip and Peter his own failures would be fewer and less painful, he just hoped. But if Jesus wanted to test him to reveal his lack of faith, then Lord, please do so, he concluded.

110 Terrifying.

Matthew 14:25.

The Gospels record Jesus walking on water, as another of his best-known miracles. The account, though, makes clear that Jesus's doing so *terrified* the disciples who observed it. Jesus had just finished a long teaching, fed the crowd of well over five thousand, and then dismissed that crowd. Readers get the impression that Jesus must have exhausted himself because he then sent his disciples on ahead across the lake in a boat. Jesus remained behind by himself, walking up a mountainside in solitude to pray. Darkness fell with Jesus still alone in prayer. The disciples had struggled to navigate the boat well off from land because wind and buffeting waves were against them. The account records that very late at night, as the disciples continued to struggle with the boat well out from shore, Jesus *walked out to them on the water.* The account continues that although the disciples saw Jesus walking on the water, his miracle so terrified them that they assumed instead that they saw only a ghost. Jesus had to tell them to *take courage* and *not to be afraid*, indeed to reassure them that they indeed saw *him*. Still stunned at the miracle, Peter replied that *if* the image was indeed Jesus, then he should call Peter to him on the water, which Jesus promptly did. Peter climbed out of the boat and, like Jesus, walked on water until the wind once again stoked his fear, causing him to begin to sink and cry out for Jesus's help. Jesus promptly reached out his hand to catch Peter, asking Peter why he had doubted. The wind died as the two then climbed into the boat. The stunning event ended with the disciples worshiping Jesus while confirming that he was truly the Son of God.

The Gospel account that Jesus *walked out to the disciples on the water* must be among the most arresting historical passages ever written. It forces readers to a full stop. With each rereading, one still thinks briefly that the eyes or mind must have been mistaken. No one has ever simply walked out on water, nonetheless well out into an inland sea against buffeting waves. Yet as often as one rereads the page, the miracle stands confirmed. Jesus, indeed also Peter at Jesus's behest, walked on water. No wonder, then, that Jesus's water-walking miracle terrified the disciples. The miracle rips open what suddenly seems like only a veneer of humanity to show Jesus as so much more than only human. Jesus actually does things that utterly defy natural laws and that others, even followers, can barely imagine. Although the image of Jesus walking on the water properly terrified the disciples, it also very quickly led to their worship of Jesus. As many miracles as Jesus performed around the disciples, few scenes actually record them worshiping Jesus as God. The scene of Jesus walking on water and of the impression that it left on the disciples should likewise encourage every follower to worship Jesus as the Son of God. When you need the tonic against doubt, think of Jesus walking on water. Let its full-miracle force strip away all doubt or pretension that Jesus was merely a profound teacher and prophet. Jesus was God incarnate. Strange indeed that something as utterly improbable as walking on water should so effectively confirm it.

This walking-on-water thing held endless fascination for him of a kind that he worked to keep healthy. He knew that many others, particularly but not exclusively those who *didn't* follow Jesus, mocked the improbability of water-walking. He understood that Jesus's walking on water served as a sort of litmus test for many persons, as if to say that if one would believe *that*, then one would believe *anything*. Yet for him, one miracle was pretty equally as improbable as the next, when one got right down to it. And he was long past *not* believing any of them. So Jesus's walking on water was for him not a question of trust, confidence, or belief. Instead, the water-walking miracle raised important questions of *response*, just as it had for the boat's stunned disciples. He fully appreciated that, after the disciples' initial terror including their need to confirm that they indeed saw what they saw and who they saw, their response had been *worship*. Their worship response was indeed what fascinated him most about the miracle. He wondered again how he would have responded if he had seen Jesus walking on water, concluding again, as he had every other time that he gave the miracle deep reflection, that he would have worshiped Jesus as God. Jesus's water-walking miracle thus became for him a sort of well of worship to which he could turn again and again for inspiration as to the proper response to his Lord. *Give me a water-walking Lord*, he thought again with a deep smile. Now *that* was true divinity worth worshiping.

111 Receptive.

Matthew 15:28; *see also* Mark 7:29.

While Jesus could be terrifying in his miracles, the Gospels also record individuals of great faith persisting with Jesus, even standing up to Jesus, to the point that Jesus would answer their miracle request. Jesus was receptive of persistent and bold requests. The account of the Canaanite woman coming to Jesus begging for a miracle healing of her daughter is a memorable example. The woman came crying out to Jesus to have mercy on her and to heal her daughter who suffered badly from demon possession. When Jesus ignored her, the woman's cries became so loud and persistent that the disciples told Jesus to send her away. The disciples' request was apparently the moment that Jesus had awaited because he replied instead that the Father had sent him for just such *lost sheep*. At those welcoming words, the woman knelt in front of Jesus but still repeating her strong demand to help her. Jesus at first replied instead with a sort of test, saying that a parent should not give to dogs their children's bread. Here, the woman said one of those things to which the Spirit must have guided her. Instead of taking offense at Jesus's apparent rebuff that she might not be worthy for Jesus's help, she acknowledged the temerity of her request, saying only that dogs, too, eat crumbs from their master's table. The woman's persistence, boldness, and humility confirmed for Jesus what he then declared that she had shown such *great faith* that he was granting her request for her daughter's miracle healing. The account ends saying that the daughter's healing occurred at that very moment. Jesus was receptive to bold, persistent, and humble faith.

The scenes of Jesus putting up with pleading from faithful followers and even rewarding their boldly persistent requests encourages followers that they may pursue Jesus without trepidation. Boldness and persistence do not irritate Jesus. Jesus reacts negatively to *lack* of faith, not to its humble and consistent expression. Only those who approach Jesus and respond to Jesus in challenge, mockery, and disbelief need fear his reproach. By contrast, Jesus is so generous in response to faith that no follower need have any concern that they ask too much too often or too boldly. Jesus listens. He doesn't respond immediately when an immediate response would weaken the supplicant's persistence and faith. Jesus must have known that the woman whose daughter needed healing also needed to persist in her faith-grounded requests. Jesus surely had a reason for delaying his response until the disciples showed their lack of patience while the woman showed the depth of her faith. Jesus is patient with petitioners when their petition reflects humble faith. Another of God's miracle attributes is that he receives rather than rejects petitions. He wants us to ask and, as evidence, patiently endures even our most awkward and bold requests in faith. While the disciples responded in exasperation as any of us would respond to an awkwardly bold petitioner's requests, Jesus did the opposite, showing his patient receptiveness.

She realized one day that she needed a God who was willing to hear her requests. She thought now and then of how patient she had to be with her family members and how patient they had to be with her. Maybe God was like that, she thought. He accepted her as family because she carried the redemption and image of his Son. She was a sister to Christ and thus a child of God. As the most-loving Father, God would be patient with her, more patient than she or her family members had ever been. A big part of that patience was that God listened receptively to her many requests. That attribute of *wanting to hear* was one way that she had learned to judge other philosophies, systems, and putative gods. Did they want to engage her, want to hear her, and want to reward her tenacity and audaciousness? She found that few or none did. The world was pretty uncaring, while her God cared more deeply than any other one could. God's kingdom rewards petition because God desires to supply. God's kingdom rewards requests made in faith because faith glorifies God. She loved that attribute of the kingdom into which she daily entered in that it heard her requests. She knew that she had *agency* in the kingdom. She mattered, which was a big part of life. God was authoring and vitalizing her life daily because he heard her requests. If what she needed and wanted made no difference, then why would her life matter? She knew that she only needed to exhibit faith in God, hear and obey God especially as God loved his Son, for God to answer her requests, giving her life the meaning for which he had created it.

112 Therapeutic.

Mark 8:25.

The Gospels record Jesus healing many instantly in miracle full recovery. Yet among Jesus's many miracle healings, followers know that the Gospels record at least one that may reveal something different of Jesus or our relationship to him. Jesus and his disciples had just come to Bethsaida when some people brought him a blind man, begging Jesus to heal him. The Gospels of course record many people asking Jesus for healing. Many times the accounts suggest something more than a simple request and often something more like pleading. In this instance, the account clearly records the people as *begging* that Jesus would heal the blind man. Unlike other accounts in which parents brought their sick children or adult children their sick parents, this account leaves the reader to guess at why the people so badly wanted this blind man healed. Maybe he had been influential, kind, generous, or an employer, or maybe his blindness had come on suddenly, scaring the people. Nonetheless, Jesus did not instantly restore the man's sight. Instead, he first *took him by the hand* and then *led him outside the village*. Jesus then *spit on his eyes* and *put his hands on him*. Still the blind man did not see when Jesus asked, answering only that he saw people *looking like walking trees*. Again, Jesus *put his hands on the man's eyes*. Only then did the blind man's eyes open fully with his correct sight restored. His healing had not been instant but progressive, unlike the many other miracles that the Gospels record. The account ends with Jesus sending him home but telling him not to go into the village.

The image of Jesus leading a blind man through a series of steps as the man slowly regained his sight in this therapeutic, remedial, and progressive fashion is an unusual one for followers on which to reflect. Jesus healed so many persons of so many different conditions, in each instance appearing to do so instantly. Some of Jesus's other miracle healings may instead have been like this one, with Jesus applying specific therapies as the condition improved, although the accounts do not so indicate. One other Gospel account records Jesus applying mud to the eyes of a blind man, although that account does not record delay in the therapy restoring sight. That blind man's recovery appears not to have required repetition of the therapy. Followers might reasonably assume that Jesus could have simply said the word, and both blind men would have found their sight restored. The accounts give no indication that these particular blind men had unusual conditions, ones that required a therapeutic regimen rather than merely the Good Lord's word. One thus suspects that Jesus used these methods to benefit those who observed the healing rather than those who received it whom Jesus could just as well have healed with a word. Jesus restores instantly but may rehabilitate progressively. One who finds faith in Jesus can expect both instant recovery and progressive strengthening. One who follows Jesus may also submit in faith to therapeutic regimen, just as one who follows Jesus may also offer his therapeutic regimen to others. Some conditions heal instantly, while others warrant treatment and time.

Even though he wanted instant relief, instant healing, and wasn't getting it, he could still feel Jesus's therapeutic effect. Yes, he felt some frustration over not having his good health and spirits promptly restored. Yet he also felt some benefit from having some delay. First, he was finding the will to be patient, and in his patience he was finding a health and resource for which he knew he would have future need. Second, he was finding that he needed to exhibit greater faith, a faith that he also knew he would need more of later. Jesus formed faith with instant miracle, but he also formed faith with miracles delayed. Third, the delay in healing required him to look more closely for Jesus, to draw nearer to Jesus in deeper faith. When the gifts are always there, one has less need of looking for the giver. He found that he was looking for Jesus, pursuing Jesus for the healing that his condition required. That pursuit, he recognized, had its own value that may have been greater than the healing that would follow. And finally, within the delay as he endured his broken condition, he realized that his condition was less important than he had thought. Conditions are only circumstances, when he knew that circumstances had far less consequence than relationships, particularly relationship to Jesus. God, give me what you will and I will accept it, he thought, but be sure to give me Jesus. He decided that he would rather have Jesus dwell over him in his recovery, maybe take him by the hand to lead him to another place, burnish him with his miracle touch, and speak to him about his restored ability. Better a good visit with the doctor than one swift magic pill.

113 Superior.

Luke 9:40; *see also* Mark 9:28.

While the Gospels record Jesus empowering his disciples to heal others miraculously much as he healed at his own word and touch, the Gospels also record Jesus exercising superior miracle-healing powers. Jesus remained more able and more effective in fashion superior to the disciples whose prayers also healed miraculously. Jesus's healing a man's demon-possessed son right after Jesus had come down the mountain from his transfiguration provides a clear example. The Gospel account records that when the usual large crowd met Jesus and the three disciples on their return from the mountain, a man stepped out of the crowd calling Jesus *teacher* and asking that Jesus heal his only child of the spirit that so badly and frequently convulsed him. The man described how that although the convulsions were destroying his son, Jesus's disciples had been unable to rid the boy of the convulsions even when the man had begged them to do so. Jesus replied that the problem was their *unbelieving and perverse generation*, indeed so perverse that he wondered how long he would remain putting up with them. When Jesus then called for the man's son, the approaching son fell to the ground in yet another convulsion. Jesus simply rebuked the spirit, instantly healing the boy whom Jesus then gave back to his amazed father. A parallel account in another Gospel records the disciples asking why they were unable to cast out the demon, to which Jesus replied that such a demon could *only come out by prayer*, implying that the disciples had not prayed or had not prayed with the faith required of them. Jesus could do what the disciples were unable to do even when he had given the disciples his healing authority.

Gospel scenes of Jesus doing miracles that his disciples could not do, even though Jesus had empowered the disciples with miracle-healing authority, remind followers of Jesus's satisfying superiority. Jesus lived and traveled with the disciples in some respects as a brother, even calling his followers his mother, sisters, and brothers. Jesus also gave his healing authority to his disciples who, the Gospels tell the reader, performed many miracles like those that Jesus performed. The disciples' miracle-healing ability suggest at least some manner of equality among Jesus and his followers. Jesus said that his followers would do work, even wonders, like Jesus did, if not greater. Yet when the Gospels also confront the reader with his followers' *inability* to do as Jesus did, the reader's reaction is not surprise or sorrow. That Jesus retains superior authority should instead comfort and reassure followers. Following a god only equal to ourselves would certainly be possible. Indeed, many and maybe most persons do follow only equal gods, particularly when they reject the one great God and instead follow only theories, philosophies, or themselves. Followers of Jesus embrace something special when they embrace a superior God. Who after all wants to live in a world void of authority? Only by embracing a superior God does a follower confirm what accurate observation otherwise makes quite evident, which is that we inhabit a world in which we are not quite the world's equal and certainly not superior.

She sometimes considered the thought odd, given her natural independence, but in the end she always easily concluded not only that God was far greater than she but also that *she needed it that way*. Oh, like anyone, she would occasionally get on her figurative *high horse*, as her grandmother had used to call it, thinking that she was equal to the high and mighty. She never quite realized when she was doing so, or she would have promptly stopped. Yet she knew that superiority was in her nature just like it was in anyone else's nature. And she knew that she could see superiority and arrogance in others before she could see it in herself. Thankfully, though, she found Jesus's obvious and welcome superiority to be the best check on her natural but unwelcome tendency toward superiority, a tendency that in the end always hurt those around her before hurting her worse. She knew that she needed to have authority in her life, something or indeed some*one* to whom to turn before whom she was subordinate. The natural human spirit without a ruler is a loose and destructive spirit, she had often seen and resolutely learned. She wanted no part of her own superiority and thus kept herself firmly in check with Jesus.

114 Dutiful.

Matthew 17:27; *see also* Matthew 22:21, 23:3; Luke 17:1.

Even while Jesus was clearly superior to all with whom he interacted, whether friend or foe, leader or follower, the Gospels nonetheless record Jesus complying with specific duty, even miraculously so. Leading to one of the stranger miracles that the Gospels record, Jesus and the disciples had just arrived at Capernaum when tax collectors asked Peter whether Jesus would pay the two-coin temple tax. Peter, evidently aware of Jesus's dutiful nature as to matters of temple order, or maybe just fearful of the potential harsh consequences of a negative reply, answered that Jesus would indeed pay the tax. Jesus must have known of Peter's exchange with the tax collectors, whether from first-hand observation or otherwise, because the account next reports that when Peter entered the house of their visit, Jesus promptly queried Peter over the tax question. Jesus asked

Peter whether authorities taxed their own children or the children of others. *Others*, Peter answered predictably. Jesus replied that indeed, authorities exempt their own children from such obligations. Jesus, being the Son of God, who is the ultimate authority, was certainly exempt from taxation. One would not tax the Son of God, just as one would not tax God, who is the source of all authority, not just government or religious authority. Yet Jesus then made a surprising exception followed by an even more-surprising miracle. Jesus first told Peter that they should *not offend* the tax collectors. They would pay the temple tax after all. Jesus then told Peter to go fishing because he would find the necessary coin, having the exact value of the temple tax for both Jesus and Peter, in the mouth of the first fish that Peter caught. *Give it to them* for the tax, Jesus instructed dutifully. In another Gospel account, the religious leaders brought some government officials to trap Jesus, asking him whether the people should pay Roman taxes. Jesus had them look on the coin with Caesar's portrait and told them to give to Caesar what is Caesar's but to God what is God's. In another Gospel account, Jesus tells the crowds and his disciples that they must obey the religious leaders even though they should not do as those leaders did. Jesus was dutiful.

The image of Jesus wanting to comply with the temple tax so as not to offend the tax collectors, and working a miracle to do so, presents both a curious and guiding reflection for followers. The scene's guiding value is relatively clear. Jesus was at times extraordinarily considerate, particularly when his being so ensured the greatest reception of his good-news message. If he and Peter offended the decent men whose collections, though sometimes misused, were to maintain God's temple, then the offense might dissuade the men from listening to and following Jesus. As Jesus said in a different context in Luke's Gospel, offenses will come, but woe to the one through whom they come. One ought not to place obstacles in front of a brother if those obstacles will cause the brother's faith to stumble. Although paying *any* tax is probably prudent, that this particular tax was a *temple* rather than government tax may also bear on Jesus's dutifulness. Why would he not contribute to the maintenance of what the Jews regarded as his Father's house? The curious part of the scene, though, has to do with Jesus choosing a miracle to confirm the instruction and, at that, such an unusual miracle. Judas the Gospels report to have carried the money that the disciples used to sustain their travels. Why not simply ask Judas for the tax money? Jesus may simply have wished to impart a degree of wonder, or instead he may have wished to confirm again that he held *all* authority, even over natural conditions. Jesus would thus make a fish depart from its school, seize Peter's hook, and give up a specific coin that it somehow carried. Although duly dutiful, Jesus was yet the Master of all creation.

Of all Jesus's miracles, indeed of all Jesus's actions, the one in which he most delighted was the event of Peter catching a fish having just the exact coin to pay the temple tax. He first loved the event's context that here the God of all creation would have a disciple reach into a fish's mouth for a coin to reassure some tax collectors that his Son was worthy of due consideration. Yes, Jesus would pay the tax with a coin from a fish's mouth just so as not to cause a couple of tax collectors to stumble. This one event endeared Jesus to him for Jesus's considerateness quite unlike any other event that the Gospels recorded. Yet he most loved the event because of the way in which Jesus must have used it to amuse or delight Peter, the tax collectors, and any others who might have witnessed or heard about it. God didn't always need to make mountains smoke and skies thunder. God could just as well plant a coin in a fish's mouth and then call it to the hook of a lifelong fisherman who still then may have felt that he only masqueraded as a disciple. He wasn't absolutely sure whether Jesus intended the event to delight, but then again, he thought, *how could it not?* While to some the wonder of a coin in a fish's mouth might suggest something more akin to magic or even charlatanry, he felt exactly the opposite that the miracle made Jesus so much more authentic and believable. Imagine, he thought, of anyone having such miracle powers. If someone who was both truly divine and yet also truly human did in fact have those powers, then wouldn't they *just once* have a little fun with it, especially if that fun was so endearingly instructive?

115 Worker.

John 9:4.

The Gospels record Jesus as a *worker* of miracles, not just one who *did* miracles but one who *worked at* miracles, who saw miracle healing as his divine vocation. Jesus didn't come to perform miracles, instead having a salvation mission, but while in public ministry he worked at miracles as a service, talent, and calling. Jesus spoke about this quality and aptitude during his final week of Passover when restoring sight to a blind man. His disciples had asked Jesus who had sinned to cause the man's blindness. Jesus corrected them that no one had sinned but that the man was born blind in order that his healing would display *the work of God*. Jesus emphasized that Jesus and his followers *must do the work* of the Father who sent him before night came when no one could work, Jesus clarifying that he was the light of the world. Jesus healed this blind man by putting on his eyes mud made from Jesus's saliva and sending him to the pool to wash. When everyone saw the formerly blind beggar able to see, they demanded to know the source of his healing, whom he revealed to be Jesus. The miracle divided the people. The religious leaders condemned the work for having been on the Sabbath, denying that a Sabbath-breaker would have come from God and even denying the miracle, even though the man's parents confirmed it. The blind man defended Jesus to the point that the religious leaders threw him out. When he heard what the leaders had done to the man, Jesus went and found the man specifically to encourage and confirm the man's faith, thus completing his healing work.

The many images of Jesus healing all who came to him confirm for the follower that earnest service encouraging a healing faith is a follower's legitimate vocation. Scenes of Jesus's nearly constant healing work should leave no doubt about the centrality of vocation to Jesus's mission. When in the above scene of one of those healing miracles Jesus said specifically that followers are to do the *work* of the Father, he confirmed faith-generating service to the sick and disabled as vital vocation. Jesus wants followers at work, just as he said that the Father wanted him at work, although followers know that he pursues the work to form and confirm faith, as in the above scene. Where he found no faith, he performed no service. Followers who tire of service should take model and heart from the scenes of Jesus's service, which suggest that he finds it acceptable to *work* at such service. Vocation can include a faith calling. While we work for food and shelter, the meaning of work goes beyond basic or lavish provision, well beyond security and accumulation. Work can glorify God, indeed work should glorify God. Those who receive our service should see the glad and earnest manner in which we share it, discerning then that it comes from a heart filled with Jesus. Seeing Jesus work at miracles should be enough to encourage followers to work with fruitful faith. A follower who does so might even see a miracle.

She didn't want to make work out of a ministry. She wanted everything that she did to be from her heart and very evidently filled with the love of Jesus. She felt that showing Jesus's love would be the only way that her service would be effective in the way that she most wanted it to be effective, which was to build others' faith. If she worked without the joy of Jesus, then how could she communicate the love of Jesus? Sometimes, though, the physical and even mental and emotional labor of ministry felt like work rather than the joy of Jesus. At those times, she would get down on herself, wondering what was wrong with her that she couldn't always work with the lightness and happiness that she felt should accompany her faithful service. She would worry that her service, though effective in its material sense of satisfying some natural need, would not carry with it the message of faith. She wanted her work to point to Jesus, but often she wondered whether it really did so. She knew from many Bible scenes that Jesus worked diligently at healing service. He healed so many that his work must at times have been tiring. Indeed, those scenes often showed him retiring to solitude, suggesting that he needed rest to restore his capacity for service. So in her times when faithful service seemed too much like work without Jesus, she tried to find quiet times of solitude when she could restore her relationship with Jesus. As long as she felt close enough to Jesus, she knew that her service in his name would be effective, even when it seemed a lot like plain old work.

116 Fruitful.

Luke 13:9; *see also* Matthew 21:19; John 15:8.

Jesus's miracles displayed so many of his extraordinary attributes, those characteristics that followers would do well to exhibit as the Spirit fills them. Another one of those miracle-sustaining attributes that Jesus consistently exhibited Jesus himself described as *fruitfulness*. Gospel accounts display Jesus as constantly fruitful in his work, meaning that his actions produced beneficial results. One never sees Jesus going through motions that have no positive effect. When he acted, people and their attitudes and abilities changed in prompt and positive reaction, not just marginally but miraculously. In witness to Jesus's constant fruitfulness, the abundance that his actions produced, the Gospels record that Jesus once confronted a crowd whose members told him about some Galileans whom the ruler Pilate had killed, presumably for some transgression. Jesus warned them that they were no different than the Galileans. They too would perish if they did not change promptly in ways that showed their own right living. Jesus then told a parable to illustrate the point that those members of the crowd who had pointed to the Galileans' punishment also needed to turn away from their corruption. In the parable, the owner of a vineyard planted a fig tree expecting the tree to produce fruit. Year after year, the tree produced nothing until the owner told the vineyard's manager to cut it down. The manager, though, pleaded with the owner to give the tree just one more year while the manager gave it special tending and only then have it cut down if it still bore no fruit. As if to confirm Jesus's point, the same Gospel next records Jesus instantly healing a woman who had been crippled for eighteen years, simply by placing his hands on her and telling her that she was now free. Another Gospel account has Jesus causing a tree to wither immediately when it bore him no fruit. Another Gospel account records Jesus telling his disciples that they would show themselves to be his disciples and would glorify his Father if they bore much fruit. Jesus was extraordinarily fruitful in his work and expected his followers also to be so.

The image of Jesus and his followers as bearing abundant fruit is a powerful inducement for followers to hold to their commitment to Jesus. No one wants to live an unproductive, wasteful life, with the feeling of just taking up space. The peril of feeling unhelpful, barren, or sterile is real for those who have no life in Christ, who lack the Spirit to guide and vitalize their work. God creates good works for us to do in advance and in abundance. Followers accomplish those good works when they remain close to Christ, listening to the Spirit, calling on the Father, drawing abundance not from their own strength but from the Spirit's strength. When we are unproductive, Jesus intercedes with the Father for us, asking that the Father give us another year to bear his fruit. The Spirit then tends us, breaking up our ground, watering our roots, and giving us the light to bear the good fruit for which the Father created us. While Jesus brought about such abundant miracles that our producing anything like the same degree of abundance would seem impossible, Jesus wants us to remain connected to him so that we do produce our harvest of good works. You may be, indeed very likely are, the only one who can do that for which he created, positioned, and equipped you to do. You are his miracle, now commissioned to produce his abundant good fruit.

She loved being a part of abundance. She seldom felt like she brought a whole lot about in a day. Who does? We all go through so many motions, she thought, and for what? What do we have to show for a day's labor? Yet at times, she saw special things coming about, things to which she had indeed made her fair contribution, where she had done her part. Those things of course tended to have to do with people and their progress in capacity, faith, and hope. She might have helped a grade-schooler learn to read as part of a program that turned out to be pretty special in its impact. She might have helped a single parent get back on her feet after a financial or relationship issue and, along with many others also helping, eventually seen the parent and children prosper. She might have contributed home-made quilts to a program that gave dozens of quilts to women battling cancer, many of them later hardy survivors. She might have helped plan a church dinner for the community or served at a soup kitchen and pantry ministry. She could also look back on her family and household to see a certain kind of abundant life, life in witness to the power and blessing of Christ. Then she remembered picking apples, peaches, and pears in a splendid orchard, great fruit in abundance. She could just gain the sense that her life in Christ was like being in that wonderful orchard.

[117] Humble.

Luke 14:11; *see also* Mark 12:38.

The Gospels accounts consistently reflect Jesus's humility even when doing miracle after miracle. One never sees him pursuing or accepting his own honor, or seeking credit or notice, for any miracles. One instead sees Jesus often telling those whom he healed not to tell anyone what he had just done for them. The Gospels also record one occasion when Jesus performed a miracle and then promptly instructed *in being humble* the religious leaders and law experts who witnessed it. On that occasion, Jesus was dining in a prominent religious leader's house when he healed a man who suffered swelling. Jesus knew that the leaders and experts disapproved his having performed the miracle on the Sabbath, but they remained silent. Jesus noticed, though, that guests coming to the host's table were picking the seats of honor nearest the host. Jesus told them that they would do better to take the humble seats and, if the host wished, let the host honor them with a better seat. Otherwise, the host might humiliate them by moving them out of a place of honor. Jesus then gave the rule that God humbles those who raise themselves up while exalting those who remain humble. Jesus then extended the lesson to say that one should throw banquets not to honor one's family, friends, or rich neighbors who would repay in kind but instead to honor the poor, crippled, and blind who could not repay. God would then reward you, Jesus added. Jesus then gave one more example of a man throwing a great banquet for honored guests who were all too busy to come. So the man invited in the poor, blind, and crippled, and anyone else who would come, while the invited guests who had not come received their just punishment. Another Gospel account has Jesus warning a large crowd to watch out for the religious leaders who walk around in flowing robes and who take the most important seats, all for their own honor and attention. Jesus was extraordinarily humble and encouraged others to be so also.

Scenes of Jesus performing wondrous miracle after wondrous miracle but then telling the beneficiaries not to tell anyone, and teaching others to likewise be humble, should guide and encourage his followers. What a great gift followers have in such an extraordinarily humble Son of God who out of anyone could have claimed honor. Jesus's remarkable humility, then, must have had a reason and source. Jesus's role was to show others his Father, to point others to the Father, to glorify and honor the Father rather than to call attention to the Son. If Jesus had done miracles for his own honor, to his own credit, then he would have been diminishing the attention that he wished to lavish on his Father, just as the Father wished to lavish attention on the Son. Love's nature is to desire and promote the honor and welfare not of one's self but instead of the other. Jesus loved his Father completely, ultimately giving himself to the Father in sacrifice, accepting the most ignominious demise solely to honor the wishes of the Father, which were ultimately to honor the Son above all others. Love is the root of humility, so that when one sees perfect love, one also sees complete humility. Jesus was so selfless because he was his Father incarnate, love in human form. Although Jesus had great honor readily available to him and could have led schools, factions, parties, and even armies, Jesus would be nothing other than humble in pursuit of his Father's honor. He also wanted us humble in his pursuit and pursuit of his Father.

He understood humility as a characteristic and wanted to be humble but found that humility as a practice could prove elusive. The odd thing about humility was that it seemed to recede the further one pursued it. Indeed, that direct pursuit seemed to be the problem. He began to realize that if one wanted humility, then one may already have lost the struggle for it. Those who want to be humble, or at least to appear humble, may at times attempt to do so for their own benefit rather than for others' benefit, he realized even from time to time from his own actions. He remembered Jesus even saying not to go around looking all sorrowful and downtrodden just for show. If you are fasting, then just fast without letting everyone know it. He saw in this way and other ways that the point of humility is not humility itself but rather love, service, kindness, and promoting the honor and welfare of others. He wanted then just to love, serve, and show kindness, without thinking so much of how it appeared or did not appear to others. He wanted his left hand doing things that his right hand did not know, as he recalled Jesus putting it another time. So he kept listening to the Spirit for guidance, hoping that the Spirit would continue to show him the small or large things that he might be doing for show rather than for love and service. He wanted any honor to be Jesus's honor, just as Jesus wanted to honor his Father.

118 Restorative.

John 11:44; *see also* John 12:9, 12:17.

While Jesus raised several dead back to life during his ministry, followers often think first and foremost of his raising of Lazarus four days after Lazarus's death. The Gospel account reports that Jesus loved Lazarus and his sister Martha, and also knew his other sister Mary, who had poured perfume over Jesus and wiped his feet with her hair.

Lazarus, though, was sick, yet Jesus deliberately delayed in coming to Lazarus's aid until days after Lazarus's death, in order that Jesus's next action would glorify God. The disciples expected also to die with Lazarus because they knew that the religious leaders were plotting against Jesus there. Martha met Jesus on his way, telling Jesus that he had come too late to save Lazarus. Jesus told Martha that *he is the resurrection* and life, and that those who believe in Jesus would live even though dying, even as Martha acknowledged Jesus as Christ, the Son of God. Mary then greeted Jesus, weeping over her brother's death, moving Jesus so deeply that he also wept. Yet at Lazarus's tomb, Jesus ordered the stone rolled away, even though Martha cautioned him that Lazarus's body, four days dead, would have a bad odor. Jesus reminded Martha to believe. He then thanked his Father that his Father heard him, saying that he did so only for those who stood near that they, too, may believe that the Father had sent him. He then called in a loud voice to Lazarus, who walked out in his grave clothes, Jesus saying to take off his grave clothes to let him go free. Many of the Jews who had come from Jerusalem to be with Mary in her grief then believed in Jesus, which only accelerated the religious leaders' murderous plot against him. Another account adds that later, people would come out from Jerusalem to the house of Mary, Martha, and Lazarus not just to see Jesus when he was there but also to see Lazarus whom Jesus had restored to life.

Each of the several scenes of Jesus raising the dead stops the reader in awe, yet the scene of Jesus bringing back the four-days-dead Lazarus simply stuns to incomprehensibility those who give it deep thought. Medical marvels occasionally revive someone who has briefly stopped breathing and even whose heart may also have briefly stopped. No medical marvel has ever accomplished anything like bringing someone back to life days later after natural processes have so long stopped that the body has decayed. Jesus obviously controls natural order to a far greater degree than, one might think, like influencing the weather. He can *restore life, revive life, and create life anew*, out of long dead matter. Indeed his miracle of raising Lazarus leads one to conclude that Jesus is incapable of nothing. He can instead do anything that would be his Father's will to accomplish. His Father would, of course, bring Jesus back to life in similar miracle except that the Father brought Jesus into some form of resurrected body that gave Jesus more than merely natural life. Jesus here instead only appears to have restored Lazarus's natural life rather than given him supernatural life in transformed body.

Followers should remember and reflect every day that *Jesus restores life*, indeed *restores dead life*. Stand in constant awe and celebration of the incomparable power and authority of the King. Jesus gives life.

As he kept thinking about it, he realized how important Jesus's raising of Lazarus was to him in his way of thinking about Jesus. He actually didn't often give the miracle much thought, which may have been because of its extreme nature. How could one give raising a four-day-dead body frequent thought and still maintain a semblance of normalcy going about one's day in the world? Yet that giving-up-normalcy was eventually exactly what attracted him to Jesus's raising-Lazarus miracle. Maybe Jesus didn't want him living normally. Maybe Jesus wanted him to live differently because of Jesus's raising-Lazarus miracle, indeed to live anticipating his own resurrected life. That message seemed to be one inescapable demand of the miracle that if Jesus showed it possible for Lazarus then Jesus showed it possible for anyone. He remembered the tenets of the faith, yes confession of sin, yes acceptance of Jesus as redemption, but yes also recognition of the reality of Jesus's resurrection *and one's own resurrected life*. Jesus had challenged Martha not only to say that Jesus was the Son of God but to say that she believed that her brother would live again. And then her brother did live again, which again seemed to him to be the event's message that he must embrace resurrected life. He was going to need to keep reflecting on the risen Lazarus, even as he reflected on the risen Christ and his own resurrected life.

[119] **Unequivocal.**

Mark 11:23; *see also* Matthew 21:19.

The Gospels record an unusual miracle that Jesus did that at the same time revealed another important attribute that Jesus possessed and expected his disciples to share. In what he believed, did, and said, Jesus was unequivocal, unquestionable, without doubt, sure, and absolutely confident. As indicated briefly in a section just above, the Gospels record that when Jesus and the disciples were moving into Jerusalem during the day and retiring outside of Jerusalem for the night during Jesus's final week of Passover, Jesus cursed a fig tree for not bearing him the fruit that he desired. In that account, the tree immediately withered in miracle response to Jesus's curse. Another account records Peter noticing the withered tree the next morning as they entered the city. When Peter exclaimed to Jesus in surprise at the miracle that the tree had withered in response to Jesus's curse, Jesus replied that Peter should *have faith in God*. Jesus then emphasized that when the disciples prayed for things, they *must not doubt* but instead believe that God will answer their request, in which case their prayer request will come about. Unequivocal belief, belief with no doubt, impresses God in prayer, not hesitating, uncertain, doubt-filled prayers. Jesus illustrated that if the disciples prayed with faith in the outcome, then they could even tell a mountain to throw itself in the sea and have it come about. Indeed, Jesus added that as they pray, they should *believe that they have already received it*, in which event the request will be theirs. Those who pray in anticipation of sure answer must be equally sure to forgive anyone against whom they hold something, so that the Father will forgive them their own sins, Jesus concluded. Jesus was unequivocal in his confidence in prayer and expected his disciples also to be so.

The image of an unequivocal, completely confident Jesus should impress followers in ways that they may not always fully realize and thus on which they could further reflect. The world has few things in which to be completely confident. Very few things are reliable. Fashions, philosophies, strategies, and commitments all come and go. What is sure today is tomorrow uncertain. One finds hard having any great confidence in anything. Jesus, though, reflects certainty about his Father's commitments, character, and attributes, and thus also his own. Jesus just never waffled on anything. Jesus may at times have briefly withheld clarity or limited disclosures as to his intent and meaning. He left some situations ambiguous. Yet Jesus's occasional ambiguity had nothing to do with doubt, nothing to do with any uncertainty. Jesus always knew what he was about. He exhibited complete confidence in what he knew to be true of his Father's will and character. One sometimes hears that leadership must above all things be clear and certain, even when wrong, indeed especially when wrong. But Jesus's certainty wasn't of the fallible type. He was instead unerring. His confidence wasn't misplaced, wasn't ignorance, but was instead fully informed. Jesus counseled the disciples to be just as certain, not in their own judgments but when relying on God. Prayer is above all relying on

God. One who relies on God has no cause to doubt. One can doubt about anything other than prayer.

She believed in prayer's efficacy. Prayer worked. Her confidence in prayer wasn't due entirely or even mostly to having seen it work. She was pretty sure that she had only seen the positive outcome of a fairly small percentage of her prayers. Yes, she had seen evidence of remarkable healing, amazing blessing, and remarkable turns of heart, in answer to prayer. She had enough evidence, some of it extraordinary enough to be miraculous, to believe that prayer worked based on evidence. Yet she also felt that God didn't want her believing only on the evidence. He seemed to say much the opposite that she should believe primarily or solely on *faith*, which she took to mean *belief without evidence*. She also suspected that God had answered many of her prayers, for things like the comfort, forgiveness, provision, peace, and security of others, without her ever seeing direct evidence of those answers. How could she see evidence of whether God answered most of her prayers, when most of her prayers were for things that one could not see? As she reflected again on Jesus telling his disciples that they must be certain in prayer, and thought again of how certain Jesus had always seemed to be, she was satisfied that she could indeed pursue prayer in just the manner that Jesus instructed, with complete confidence. She loved having an unequivocal God and confident Savior. She wouldn't have had it any other way.

6

His Sacrifice

Denouncing. Matthew 11:20. ***Refusing.*** Matthew 12:38. ***Offending.*** Matthew 13:57. ***Persecuted.*** John 5:16. ***Refugee.*** Matthew 8:20. ***Prophetic.*** Luke 9:44. ***Resolute.*** Luke 9:51. ***Watchful.*** John 7:21. ***Threatened.*** John 10:31. ***Besieged.*** John 11:53. ***Guarded.*** Luke 12:1. ***Condemned.*** John 11:50. ***Weeping.*** Luke 19:41. ***Troubled.*** John 12:27. ***Hated.*** Mark 13:13. ***Betrayed.*** Matthew 26:14. ***Broken.*** Matthew 26:26. ***Poured.*** Matthew 26:28. ***Abandoned.*** Matthew 26:31. ***Arrested.*** Matthew 26:50. ***Tried.*** Matthew 26:57. ***Convicted.*** Matthew 26:66. ***Sentenced.*** Matthew 27:11. ***Appealed.*** Luke 23:6. ***Scourged.*** Mark 15:15. ***Burdened.*** Luke 23:6. ***Crucified.*** Matthew 27:35. ***Separated.*** Matthew 27:45. ***Mourned.*** Luke 23:48. ***Pierced.*** John 19:34. ***Buried.*** Mark 15:43.

    The scenes and images of Jesus's sacrifice compel, challenge, and inspire followers in various ways. Gospel readers often treasure the stories of Jesus's coming and may thrall to the accounts of his call. The many scenes of Jesus's ministry surely encourage and guide believers, while records of his miracles testify to and confirm belief. Yet the detailed accounts of Jesus's sacrifice serve their own special or, perhaps better put, critical-but-awful function for the follower. Sacrifice of anything can make one uncomfortable, human sacrifice far more so. Yet sacrifice of the Son of God bounds beyond all proportion to the point of incomprehensible horror, except that God himself planned it for exquisite purpose. The several descending scenes of Jesus's awful sacrifice, which followers know from scripture reading and imagine from many graphic depictions, utterly fulfill the crucifixion's twin terrible and tremendous dimensions. Jesus's arrest, trials, sentence, scourging, parading, and crucifixion so thoroughly capture and consume the imagination that many followers must look deliberately away from them much of the time lest they cloud the mind and despair the soul of all hope for the very bright dawn that quickly followed. While guarding the soul, though, followers must not look entirely away from the crucifixion. Indeed, followers should instead look frequently to Christ's cross, only in the way that his uplifting Spirit informs and intends it. Followers have just as much or more to draw from Jesus's sacrifice as they do from his glorious mission's other dimensions. Consider the following scenes and images of Jesus's sacrifice and how you might contemplate them more often and fruitfully.

120 Denouncing.

Matthew 11:20; *see also* Matthew 23:13; Luke 11:45; John 7:7.

Jesus did not receive his calling in order solely to love, care for, and bless those who chose to follow him, ignoring those who did not so choose. As an above section indicates, Jesus also had the calling to serve as a judge, his Father having entrusted judgment to him. In connection with that judge's role, the Gospels record Jesus denouncing cities, religious leaders, and others in the strongest of language for not having accepted the good-news message and turned away from sin and toward him. In one of several similar examples, Matthew's Gospel records that Jesus *denounced* the cities in which he had performed most of his miracles because their residents did not repent. Jesus was not simply giving advice, counsel, or even mild rebukes. Instead, the account quotes Jesus as pronouncing *woe* on those cities, with special emphasis. Indeed, Jesus added that if he had performed the same miracles in other cities, then they long ago would have turned away from their sins. He further explained that when judgment day came, those other cities whose residents had turned from their sins would find their judgment much more bearable than the judgment against the cities that had failed to repent. Jesus even singled out Capernaum, the center of his own public ministry, for denouncement, saying that God would send it to the depths because it had ignored miracles that would have saved even the notorious Sodom, which would also find judgment day more bearable. Jesus's denunciations were so strong that one of the religious leaders, an expert in the law, cautioned Jesus that he was insulting them also, to which Jesus promptly denounced those very law experts for how they burdened followers with unbearable loads. Late in his public ministry, Jesus would even tell his brothers in Galilee that he could not travel to Judea, where the Jews lay in wait to kill him, because the Jews hated him for testifying that what they did was evil. Matthew's Gospel records Jesus calling the religious leaders *blind men, blind guides,* and even *blind fools, snakes,* and *brood of vipers*. Jesus's calling clearly included speaking truth publicly in great candor about those who rejected his message, even to the point of denouncing them in the strongest of contrasts and terms.

The image of Jesus denouncing regions, cities, groups, leaders, and individuals can be an uncomfortable one for followers who embrace the positive side of Christ's salvation mission. Like his calling to judge, Jesus's calling to *denounce* those who did not heed his message reflects the harder but nonetheless *necessary* negative side of his salvation message. Salvation for some means no salvation for others. Salvation implies saving *from* something, indeed something very difficult, hard or impossible to bear, terribly burdensome, and bad. God cannot countenance sin in his presence, and yet sin-filled we are, and thus needful of Jesus's sacrifice and redemption. In that very clear sense, Jesus's denouncing cities and their residents is not at all a negative or unnecessary attribute but instead reflects his complete concern for every unrepentant resident. Coddling does one no good, especially when aimed to shelter one from ultimate demise. The worst leader is the one who refuses to tell the truth to a wayward and failing follower, whether that leader is an employer, counselor, or guide. If any message bears candor, then that message is the Gospel message. Good news based on a personal choice must come with the alternative bad news for those who choose alternatively. Thank God that he called Jesus to judge and then denounce cities and their residents. Only in denunciation do we stand a repentant soul's chance. Followers properly embrace Jesus's denunciations as powerful images on which to reflect.

Nothing caused her to search her soul quite like Jesus's denunciations did. She encountered them so frequently in her Bible reading that she really could not avoid them if she had wished to do so. Jesus simply had a strong streak of denouncing that he fulfilled with the same fullness that he fulfilled other, gentler aspects of his calling. She loved the forgiving side of Jesus and his miraculous healing, revealing teaching, sacrificial love, and Spirit's intimate presence. Yet here he was again, denouncing regions, cities, and people who didn't listen to him closely enough to change their ways. The utterly condemning tenor of Jesus's denunciations nearly made her cringe, recoil, or cower, which she gradually accepted was their point. She had times, just as anyone had times, when she needed to pull back on her impulses, to control her emotions and desires. She knew that she thought too much of herself too often and on occasion not enough of others. She didn't feel that her life was accordingly filled with rank sin. Indeed she instead felt that taking Jesus's life and lessons to heart had over time cleaned up her life to an extent that she had not previously imagined either warranted or possible. But again, that turning, which she could also call *repentance*, was precisely the point. Because she had not previously recognized how much she needed to change to rid her life of sin, until she received more of Jesus's guiding Spirit who showed her what she needed to reform and gave her the strength to do it, she accepted now that she had more sin from which to turn, more things for the Spirit to show her. She felt a little as if Jesus's denunciations were not only for those who did not accept and follow him. They were for her, too, in those still-corrupt parts of her that she had not yet given over to him for reform. Maybe Jesus's denunciation attribute wasn't such a cringe-worthy thing after all but instead another very important call.

121 **Refusing.**

Matthew 12:38; *see also* Matthew 13:58, 16:1.

Even as the Gospels record Jesus performing astonishing miracles, they also record Jesus *refusing* to perform miracles. Jesus's response whether to perform a miracle or not to do so was far from arbitrary but instead clearly depended on the faith or other motive of the persons making the request. Matthew's Gospel gives an example. Jesus had just restored sight and speech to a blind and mute man whom the believing crowd had brought to him for healing. The crowd began rightly to infer that Jesus might be the long-awaited Christ, exhibiting just the kind of faith and belief that Jesus would reward with miracle healing. Yet when the religious leaders instead rebuked the crowd, saying that Jesus healed from Satan's power rather than God's divinity, Jesus responded by correcting the religious leaders with an explanation and lesson. The religious leaders, though, were having none of it. Those leaders and their teachers, calling Jesus a *teacher* in what was likely a form of sarcasm or mockery, ignored his teaching and the miracle that preceded it, instead demanding that they wanted to see a *miraculous sign* from Jesus. Rather than perform on cue as the leaders and their teachers requested, Jesus gave them a sharp rebuke, telling them that their wicked and adulterous generation would see no such miracle. They would instead see only the sign of Jonah, Jesus continued, explaining that he, the Son of Man, would like Jonah spend three days in the earth's heart, referring to his death following his crucifixion. Those like the religious leaders who had already seen miracles and not repented and believed would see no more miracles, only the crucified and resurrected Christ. The request of the religious leaders that Jesus perform a miracle and Jesus's refusal together further identified Jesus as a threat to the religious hierarchy, accelerating the frightening march to his sacrifice.

The image of Jesus refusing to perform miracles makes an important point for followers to contemplate. Jesus is not a performer. He acts not to engender faith but to reward it. Those who have seen miracle after miracle and not believed will receive no more, not at least if their purpose is to test and even mock the miracle maker. Life is a miracle. God forgives repeatedly and blesses continuously. Those who ignore their need for repentance and forgiveness, and who accept his blessing without asking for it and thanking him, indeed without acknowledging that he exists no less that he came in the person of Christ, have no standing to demand another miracle. God knows how we respond to blessing and hardship, to miracle and refusal of miracle. If another miracle would have saved the religious leaders, then likely

Jesus would have so performed. Yet they had already seen miracle after miracle. Jesus's refusal to do another one showed no lack of mercy and grace but instead showed what those leaders had already demonstrated, which was that no number of miracles would open their hearts and minds. Jesus knew the path of his march toward the cross, one that would place him in the hands of those religious leaders. Jesus had no will contrary to his Father's will. Jesus would not delay the divide that had already begun with the religious leaders. His path God had long ago determined. Jesus really had only one course, which was to refuse the religious leaders yet more miracles on demand as evidence of his divinity. Jesus would perform many more miracles in response to the faith of those who continued to throng to him, but he would not perform for those who showed no faith and instead already harbored the murderous designs that would end with Jesus on the cross.

He had no desire to test God for miracles. Oh, he prayed often for miraculous healing, protection, relief, and restoration. He just didn't pray waiting to see whether God would answer the prayer as proof that God answered. Sometimes, he wondered briefly whether he should pray in that fashion, which would be to pray waiting for an affirmative answer to build his faith. Yet he would quickly reject that sort of nonbeliever's prayer, which seemed to contradict everything that he knew from Jesus and the epistles about prayer in faith. Indeed, he didn't so much have *faith in prayer*, which seemed to have too little to do with God, making God more like a dispenser and prayer more like a method. Instead, he tried to practice *prayer in faith*, believing solely in God's power and desire to answer affirmatively rather than in the value of the practice of prayer itself. While he felt that he had plenty of scripture to support his approach to God in faithful prayer rather than prayer for a faithful god, Jesus's rebuke of the miracle-seekers was really what kept him trusting in God. He didn't want to be one of those praying for a miracle for the miracle's sake, meaning largely or solely to increase his faith. He wanted his faith to precede the miracle, to be large *before* the miracle rather than *because of* the miracle. The scenes of Jesus refusing miracles to those who came to test him convinced him that Jesus wanted it that way.

122 Offending.

Matthew 13:57; *see also* Luke 11:42; Mark 6:4.

Much like the Gospels record Jesus refusing to perform miracles for the religious leaders who came to test him and who would before long seek his crucifixion, the Gospels also record Jesus offending the religious leaders. Luke's Gospel, for instance, shares an account in which Jesus pronounces one woe after another on first the religious leaders and then the law experts until he had thoroughly affronted both groups. In addition to offending the religious leaders, Jesus offended others who did not see him as the Messiah he was. Matthew's Gospel relates one such account. Jesus had preached and taught throughout the region when he returned to his hometown, where he resumed teaching in the synagogue just as he had done elsewhere. His teaching must have been just as profound and powerful as it had been elsewhere because the amazed people asked where Jesus had gotten such wisdom and miraculous power. The problem was that the townsfolk remembered Jesus as son of the carpenter Joseph and his wife Mary. They apparently also reckoned Jesus just as they did Jesus's four brothers James, Joseph, Simon, and Judas, and all of Jesus's sisters. They could not see Jesus as the long-presaged Son of Man because they thought they knew him otherwise, as another ordinary one of them. So rather than recognize the divine source of Jesus's words and power, as faithful followers would come to do, the townsfolk instead *took offense* at Jesus's teaching. Knowing their lack of faith, Jesus quoted the proverb to them that a hometown gives its prophet no honor. The account ends saying that because of their lack of faith, Jesus did few miracles there.

The image of Jesus offending religious leaders, folks in his hometown, and others throughout the region, requires clear scrutiny from followers who know Jesus as a Lord of mercy, gentleness, love, and grace. Despite the numerous accounts in which hearers took offense at Jesus's teaching and denunciations, one suspects that Jesus did not *intend* to offend. Certainly, he had no desire to spite, demean, or destroy, no hardness of heart or innate insensitivity of the kind that attends others who speak offendingly. Yet one also readily infers from the above events and other accounts that Jesus did not alter his words and mission in order to *avoid* offense. Jesus spoke in candor. He told truth, even when truth offended and divided. Jesus could instead have softened or withheld truth, concealed his insight, and tempered his power, in order to curry favor with his hometown acquaintances or the religious leaders. He could have been diplomatic in his approach, teaching, and comments, and in doing so built popular and elite support that would have slowed or even diverted his march to the cross. Yet saving his own life was not Jesus's mission, nor his Father's will. Jesus would speak bluntly even when it cost him comfort, favor, security, and ultimately his life. The scenes of Jesus speaking hard truths to hard hearts and hearers are critical ones for followers who have chosen instead to listen to, accept, and obey Jesus. Those scenes hearten those followers who like Jesus himself have gone against the tide of local or leadership sentiment. The Gospel message need not be a popular message among leaders or neighbors as long as the message is true. Like Jesus, followers do not seek offense and instead may take some pains to avoid it. They do not, though, avoid the truth to avoid the short-term pain or popular shame that sometimes goes with it. Jesus was perfectly comfortable with the truth even when the truth made others uncomfortable. The scenes of his resolute character embolden and fortify followers who face similar rejection.

She recognized that to some extent, she didn't face much opposition for following and loving Jesus. Indeed, she tried to make her choices and keep her paths pretty much that way. She didn't want to travel frequently in circles where people disrespected Jesus and disliked or disrespected his followers. She didn't want to give offense or take offense. Offense was hard both for her and for others to whom she gave it, even though she hoped and believed that those latter occasions where she gave others offense were rare. She both wanted others to like her and wanted to like others. For the most part, she wanted to get along and go along, and to be an encourager, except that she had just this one problem that she would not do so if it meant denying Jesus. In that one area of her faith in Christ, she had prepared herself to offend occasionally, even without intending to be offensive. She wanted her witness to Christ to be a loving witness. She wanted to listen more than preach, to care and serve more than judge, instruct, and direct. Yet when the time came to speak truth about Jesus, she really didn't mind so much that she might just give offense. She took no satisfaction in doing so, surely, but she took no comfort in avoiding offense, if her conscience would tell her later that she might have misled an explorer down a fatal path. Any offense that she temporarily gave would be well worth the witness that meant a soul's salvation later. She could even recall a few occasions of her own when she had wanted to take offense at a straight-speaking message but had instead had the humility to accept it as truth. She kept thinking of Jesus offending even to the point of his judgment and death. She would speak softly and gently, but she would tell the truth about Jesus.

123 **Persecuted.**

John 5:16; *see also* Matthew 26:3.

When describing the many deep sacrifices that Jesus made, the Gospels first record the persecution that Jesus faced from the start of his public ministry. John's Gospel states that even early in Jesus's ministry, the Jews persecuted Jesus particularly because he healed others and accomplished other miracles on the Sabbath. When the Jews admonished Jesus not to break the Sabbath, Jesus would anger them even further by saying that he worked on the Sabbath because *his Father* also did so. John's Gospel records that because Jesus called God his own Father, making him God's equal, the Jews tried *all the harder* to kill Jesus. Thus Jesus's persecution was not merely inconvenience, rejection, or condemnation but also plots, plans, and efforts to murder him. Jesus would explain to them that his divine abilities, which all could see, were from the Father without whom he could do nothing. Whatever he saw his Father do, he would also do, the Father making him able because the Father loved him. Jesus also predicted to the religious leaders who persecuted him that the Father would show them even greater things through him, things like raising the dead to life. His explanations had no effect other than to further anger the religious leaders who continued and advanced their persecution. The Gospels make perfectly clear to the reader multiple scenes of Jesus's persecution. He was constantly on the move, warned by the disciples of the death threats and deadly plots against him, and aware of the mortal danger of his public appearances. The image that followers should have of Jesus's public ministry is not of a bucolic walk in the park or triumphant open campaign but more one of swift strategic strikes under constant surveillance intended to achieve his violent demise. The world was not yet Jesus's home. He instead led an insurrection.

The image of Jesus moving nearly furtively about the countryside under constant surveillance and frequent persecution, as he attempted to complete his public ministry, should further inform followers of the extraordinarily disruptive nature of Jesus's salvation mission. Even though the scriptures foretold it, and redemption through God's own sacrifice would be wondrous in the grand scheme of things, God's plan nonetheless would not serve the religious leaders' personal, political, and corporate interests. Appreciate that religious liberty, the freedom that faith in the Lord Christ brings, does not serve those who benefit from various enslavements. Jesus's persecution should surprise no one. The enslaved world in which we live must oppose the one who brings the greatest of all liberties, which is the promise of eternal life for following a faultless Lord to a heavenly destiny. Followers of course know the natural end of Jesus's persecution in his crucifixion. Persecution must precede destruction. The religious leaders had gradually to work themselves into bringing about Jesus's natural demise, although followers know that Jesus died on the cross only because the Father willed it and Jesus allowed it in ultimate plan of redemption. The many scenes of Jesus's persecution remind us not of enslavement, violence, and death, but of eternal freedom and ultimate liberty.

She wanted to think of the peace-loving and gentle side of Jesus, to meditate on his walks through the grain fields and flower-covered hills with his disciples as if she walked with them. When she thought of Jesus, she wanted to think of sun, breeze, warmth, and perfect security. She did not want to think of his persecution. She did not want to think of his having to slip away through crowds to save his own life until later when he would give his life to those same murderous leaders. She did not want to think of his having no safe place to lay his head at night, of what the Gospels made seem like his constant wanderings to keep just beyond the deadly designs of the religious leaders. These two contrasting images of his perfect peace with his perfidious persecution kept clashing in her meditations. She could not resolve on one without hearing the hint of the other. Just as she relaxed most deeply into his serenity, she would hear warning of his persecution. Just as she basked in the warmth of his greeting smile, she would imagine him beckoning her away to safety. As she thought more of this unsatisfactory tension between all that Jesus held and promised, and all that he and his followers suffered in persecution, she looked forward all the more to his promised end to suffering and persecution. She knew that the war was over even though the last battle not yet won.

¹²⁴ Refugee.

Matthew 8:20; *see also* Luke 9:58, 13:31; John 7:1.

Even though Jesus would ultimately consent to his arrest, conviction, sentence, and crucifixion as necessary to God's plan for human redemption, the Gospels record Jesus staying on the move, even furtively, at times in order to escape persecution until his time had arrived and at other times simply for brief respite from the pressing crowds. In one instance, Matthew's Gospel records Jesus seeing the crowd gather around him and promptly give the disciples orders to take him by boat to the other side of the Sea of Galilee. The account indicates that a teacher of the law replied that he would nonetheless follow Jesus everywhere. The account gives no clear reason for Jesus's flight from the crowd except that Jesus had just spent the evening healing many sick and demon-possessed, and could well have been weary. Confirming what the late evening crowd, sea-crossing flight, and law teacher's pursuit together had just indicated, Jesus replied that even animals have places to hide and rest, while *the Son of Man has no place to lay his head.* Luke's Gospel records Jesus saying the same thing at a later date as he approached Jerusalem for the final time. In another account, this one in Luke's Gospel, religious leaders visit Jesus to tell him to flee somewhere else because the region's ruler intended to kill him. Jesus answered the religious leaders by committing to continuing his healing mission while also foreshadowing his Jerusalem death. Jesus would keep on the move until he accomplished his mission. Another account, this one in John's Gospel, records that near his final and fateful trip to Jerusalem, Jesus had to travel around Galilee outside of Judea because the Jews there lay in wait to catch and kill him. Recall also that Mary and Joseph had fled to Egypt with the baby Jesus after his birth to escape his murder. Jesus even then needed refuge, as he would again during his public ministry.

The image of Jesus as a weary traveler, an itinerant wanderer, and even a refugee from murderous persecution is a frightening but important on which followers should reflect. Followers of Christ are not fully at home in the present world. Just as Satan pursued Christ, the world's defeated but still-present evil remains today at utter odds with Christ's followers who thus find too little respite and rest. Followers are in that sense like spiritual refugees when in the shelter and within the protection of Christ against that evil. Jesus's resolute but nonetheless circumspect response to evil's threat models the apt response of committed followers. Frequent effective and sometimes even furtive movement in mission pursuit is both reasonable and responsible. Followers pursue the mission in motion so as not to be evil's easy target. Followers can also face constant, wearying, and even unreasonable demands for sharing Jesus's healing and teaching Spirit. Just as Jesus crossed the sea or climbed mountainsides at night to find relief and respite, so too should followers find occasion for sheltering wherever they might find that rest. Relief may not come in one's own neighborhood, house, or bed, just as Jesus found no fixed place to shelter and rest, but God will provide relief as long as the follower continues the holy mission. Scenes of Jesus's constant movement, occasional flight, and itinerant travel should reassure followers that they have not lost all peace in such challenges.

He wondered whether something was wrong that he so often felt harried, burdened even by reasonable demands, and in some sense at risk or under threat. He would occasionally just stop to try to shake off the threatening mood or sensation. Did he lack faith? Had he missed the joy and security that Jesus offers? Having had a taste of Jesus's promised kingdom, he would wonder why he didn't yet have more of its satisfaction. Then he would remember Jesus's own seeming restlessness, Jesus's constant motion in the face of demands from the crowds and threats from the religious and political leaders. Hah! Jesus had even been a refugee when very young because of the murderous designs that pursued him. During his mature public ministry, Jesus had hardly been able to find a place to rest his weary head. He recalled how Jesus had even said so, acknowledging that he didn't even have the modest shelter that mere animals had and instead faced death threats. Yet Jesus had not been complaining, and of course not doubting, when he admitted his precarious physical circumstances. He had instead simply pointed out the impossible tension of the perfectly righteous One living in a land still filled with evil. And Jesus had simultaneously confirmed and recommitted to his healing and salvation mission. Reflecting on Jesus's hazardous and wearying circumstances, and Jesus's resolute response, he considered again whether he had something wrong in each day feeling such risk and restlessness, until he concluded that the time was for only spare rest. God would supply the relief, rest, and respite that he needed, he decided. He would stop worrying about why he so often felt so pressed. If Jesus felt the challenge of each day, then he could certainly feel challenges, even though his own circumstance seemed so much less at risk. He indeed had the security of an accomplished and complete Savior.

125 Prophetic.

Luke 9:44; *see also* Matthew 17:22, 20:17.

The Gospels frequently record Jesus foreshadowing his arrest, conviction, and sentence at the hands of the religious leaders. Jesus not only knew his mission but expressed a clear prophetic sense of how that mission would unfold. While the Gospels share several such accounts of Jesus sharing prophecies of his coming sacrifice at the hands of the religious leaders, one account from Luke's Gospel is especially concise and clear. Jesus had just come down the mountain from his transfiguration, where at the mountain's bottom he met and healed a very troubled boy whom a demon spirit had long and destructively convulsed. Amazed at Jesus's miracle healing, the crowd had properly marveled at God's greatness. Yet the account records that even as the crowd still marveled at what Jesus had just done for the boy, Jesus turned away from the crowd toward his disciples, telling them to listen carefully. Introducing what he would later repeat with much greater clarity at the Last Supper, Jesus told the disciples that someone was about to betray him, the Son of Man, into the religious leaders' hands. Although the meaning of Jesus's statement in retrospect would certainly seem clear enough, the account instead records that the disciples *did not understand* what Jesus meant. Indeed, the account records that something *hid* the statement's meaning from them so that *they did not grasp it*. The brief account ends saying that the disciples were too afraid to ask Jesus what his prophecy meant. Another account from Matthew's Gospel records Jesus telling the disciples about the same time that while men would kill him, God would on the third day bring him back to life. The account describes the disciples as *filled with grief* at the prophecy. Another later account from the same Gospel records Jesus telling the disciples that when they next went up to Jerusalem, someone would betray Jesus into the hands of the chief priests and law teachers who would condemn him, turning him over to the Romans for flogging and crucifixion, but that he would then rise to life in three days. Jesus prophesied with greater and greater clarity, even if what he so accurately predicted was so awful that the disciples feared to grasp it.

Scenes of Jesus prophesying his betrayal, arrest, conviction, and sentence at the religious leaders' hands should in their own way fortify followers' faith. Yes, Jesus's prophecies of his coming demise were dark and awful but, as followers well know, still absolutely necessary to his resurrection. Followers can, though, draw more from Jesus's prophetic statements. His prophecies confirm not only that he knew and accepted his terrible and yet magnificent mission but also that he wanted his followers to know and accept it, too. Jesus's salvation mission did not befall him, as if God plucked him out of a pool of candidates for a horribly difficult but ultimately triumphant role. Rather, God instead constituted the Trinity and shared Jesus to reunify God with humankind, to bring into existence something impossibly grander than things would have been without humankind's awful fall and magnificent resurrection. If Jesus had not known, accepted, *and prophesied* his central role in this greatest-possible drama, then its unfolding would have lost its critical prophetic element. Things that just happen without foretelling seem just that way, as if they had no plan or order. When instead God reveals his plan and then carries it out *just as foretold*, the plan takes on its obviously divine dimension. Jesus gave followers including the disciples a great gift when he prophesied what the ancient scriptures had also long foretold. Like the disciples, but with hindsight's far-greater vision, reflect in fear and foreboding on the magnificence of God's most-terrible and difficult plan for his only Son whose whole being depended on that plan's completion.

She found that every year, she both feared and looked forward to the Lenten season. She feared it of course because of the thought of the frightening trial, savage scourging, and horrible crucifixion that Jesus endured, so perfectly unfit for her glorious King of kings. Lent in general, and then the week leading up to Resurrection Day, just had a darkness to them that she could not, and didn't want to, shake. Yet she also felt that the wonder of Resurrection Day itself, the celebration of the greatest evidence of her own coming resurrection, would not be nearly the same without that prefatory darkness. Over time, she had found that she needed the foreshadowing nearly as much as she needed the relief of resurrection. What, after all, would Jesus's resurrection have been if only from a natural, rather than a human-engineered, demise? She knew that redemption needed sacrifice as much as sacrifice meant redemption. Her knowledge of her need for the dark events of that week of Passover didn't make those events any less dark. She saw nothing relieving in anything that Jesus had so wrongly suffered. But she knew that the wrongheadedness of Jesus's horrible suffering was exactly what her own soul needed for God to use Jesus's sacrifice as her redemption. She was in the end glad that Jesus had known, embraced, and even spoken of his coming sacrifice, although she suspected that just like the disciples, she would not have understood his prophecies because of their terrible darkness. In some cases, forewarned is not forearmed. She hoped that both Jesus's death and his resurrection would always spring upon her as if in shocking surprise, even though she found enduring reassurance in their prophecy.

126 Resolute.

Luke 9:51.

As Jesus headed toward Jerusalem and his arrest, conviction, and sentence, the Gospels record Jesus exhibiting another important attribute on which followers may reflect. Luke's Gospel reports that Jesus set out for Jerusalem as the time for God to take him up to heaven approached. Jesus knew that he must be in Jerusalem for events to unfold according to plan. The account, though, inserts that Jesus set out *resolutely*. The reader had already by then seen that Jesus would not let his disciples stand in his way, as much as they would have preferred that Jesus not suffer to the point of death as he had prophesied. Jesus, the account then states, started forward toward that sacrificial death with a determined attitude. The account continues with an example of the obstacles that Jesus would face on his way toward completing his mission. When Jesus sent messengers ahead to ready things for him, the Samaritan village to which they went rejected Jesus. Two disciples James and John asked Jesus if they should *call fire down from heaven* to destroy the village, but the account records that Jesus rebuked them. They turned instead to another village. The account then confirms again both the obstacles that Jesus would face and his urgency in moving past them. As they headed toward the other village, Jesus shared that while even animals had resting places, he would find none. A man then offered to follow Jesus after burying his dead father, but Jesus told him to *let the dead bury the dead* while the man instead proclaimed God's kingdom. Another man offered to follow Jesus after telling his family goodbye, but Jesus told him that one cannot *look back* while serving God's kingdom. In these ways, Jesus showed how resolute he would be in approaching even the most horribly difficult part of his mission.

Scenes of Jesus setting out resolutely toward the hardest part of his mission should encourage followers. Although followers still die today witnessing to Jesus Christ in gruesome drownings and beheadings, and even with reports of their crucifixion, most followers do not expect to face anything like the kind of torture, agony, and deadly persecution that Jesus endured. On the other hand, most followers will find times, and for some frequent times, when they must exhibit a stronger sense of commitment to the faith. Those times might be among family members, friends, neighbors, or co-workers who do not know, understand, appreciate, or respect the faith, and thus who do not understand, appreciate, or respect the faith follower. Or those times may be when poor health, bad finances, job loss, destructive relationships, or other negative circumstances test and challenge one's faith. Everyone has times when they question whether they can endure. Followers, though, should know that whether *they* can endure is not the genuine question. For followers, the point is that *Jesus* endured. A weak follower looks not to the follower's weakness but to Jesus's strength. A tempted follower looks not to the follower's temptation but to Jesus's resolute turning forward and away. Every follower must also know and appreciate not just how certain Jesus remained of his commitment but that Jesus faced questions over his commitment. Jesus, in other words, recognized and expressed that he had a choice, even while he expressed that his choice was to remain resolute. Look to Jesus's resoluteness for strength on your own path.

Being a major-league waffler himself, he loved the contrary sense of surety that Jesus carried on his march to Jerusalem. Although he wasn't a procrastinator (instead, he executed things as quickly as possible in general), when faced with matters of large concern he rarely had any sense of confidence that he knew the right direction forward. He *wished* he could be resolute like Jesus, but he just seldom felt that he knew what to be resolute *about.* By contrast, Jesus knew exactly when, where, and how to be resolute, and also how to express it, as the Gospel accounts of his march toward the cross plainly attested. In the end, that *Jesus* knew, even if he didn't know, may be precisely the point, he decided. One thing about which he could be confident was that Jesus knew his path, while a second thing that he learned to appreciate was that nothing would deter Jesus. If Jesus could face the most horrible obstacles, indeed more than *face* them, rather see them as *necessary steps*, then just maybe he also could be just a little more resolute. What that meant to him was a little less whining, grumbling, and waffling. Step up because Jesus stepped up, he thought. He might not have much courage for unpleasant but necessary things, even things of deep faith, but at least he could recognize Jesus's courage. He respected, valued, and trusted so deeply having a resolute Lord, hoping that it helped make him at least a little more resolute.

127 **Watchful.**

John 7:21.

While Gospel accounts suggest a tightening circle of religious leaders preparing to silence Jesus by his betrayal and murder, the Gospels also record Jesus's awareness and watchfulness of their threat. Unlike some victims of violence, Jesus was not oblivious but instead vigilant. One instance quite late in his public ministry illustrates that Jesus was so well aware and vigilant that some thought him paranoid, even though others were as equally aware as Jesus of the religious leaders' murderous intent toward Jesus. In that one instance, Jesus had asked the Jews whom he had been teaching and chastising in the Jerusalem temple courts why *they were trying to kill him.* The Jews answered only that he must be demon-possessed because *who is trying to kill you?* Jesus knew better. He first pointed out again how they were breaking God's law in their own religious practices. He urged them to make better judgments. Jesus's additional lesson and chastisement must have reminded some people in the crowd of how Jesus was indeed quite unpopular with the religious leaders because those people started asking *isn't this the man whom they are trying to kill?* Those people even asked how Jesus was getting away with speaking so publicly against the religious leaders, meaning that maybe now the leaders even believed him. Their only problem with accepting Jesus as the Christ was that they knew him. Jesus cried out in answer that although indeed they did know him, he had not spoken on his own but for the one who sent him, whom the crowd did not know. The crowd must again have quickly gotten the point of Jesus's chastisement because they tried to seize him. Once again, though, the vigilant Jesus, whose *time had not yet come*, slipped away without anyone laying a hand on him.

The image of Jesus as wary, circumspect, and even mistrustful can be a helpful one for followers on which to reflect. While paranoia is problematic, vigilance can be a virtue. Because Jesus's time had not yet come, he needed to remain aware and circumspect lest he stumble into a trap out of which he could not extricate himself to finish his mission. Paranoia, meaning distrust disproportionate to the threat, can destroy both mission and character. No one should be seeing friends for enemies. We should each try to see circumstances as much as we can as they are. Yet to disregard a discoverable threat is to fall prey to the predator too early. Avoid what you can avoid, when you lose little or nothing of your mission or character in the avoidance. Enemies can be powerful, more powerful than those whom they intend to vanquish. While God is on the follower's side, God does not always direct the follower to throw caution to the wind in order promptly to confront every discernible enemy. Jesus himself at another time counseled to count the cost of battles to avoid defeat and ensure victory. Still, as Jesus's own mission showed, the time may come when the follower must confront a threat directly, maybe even momentarily succumb to it in order later to override and defeat it. Jesus would soon submit to the enemy when his time had fully come, but until then, he would remain watchful, circumspect, aware, and vigilant.

She didn't like battles and generally tried to avoid them but also knew that some were harder than others to avoid. As a rule, she remained wary of engaging perceived threats or enemies directly. Better, she felt, to scope and skirt the threat, while husbanding her strength for more-important matters. She knew the social and emotional, indeed *spiritual*, cost of battles. Sometimes, she just wasn't up for it, while other times she just felt that engaging the enemy would distract her from other, more-worthwhile humanitarian missions. What she needed, then, was the kind of awareness, circumspection, and vigilance that Jesus had shown throughout his public ministry but especially as the time for his arrest, conviction, and crucifixion neared. Her need wasn't always so much to identify people as enemies. She very much preferred not to do so. Few persons were so cantankerous and belligerent that she needed to avoid them entirely. Rather, she discerned the enemy more to be a hidden presence, maybe more like something or someone inhabiting situations and persons, notably including herself, specifically to undermine faith and destroy faithful initiative and action. She could sense that dark and distracting presence more at some times than at others, more in some situations than in others, but she was generally aware of its enticements to battle. And so she just made sure each day that *she* rather than someone or something else picked the times and places for those battles, just as Jesus had moved circumspectly, even furtively, until his time had come. She drew often and sometimes heavily on the image of the vigilant Jesus.

128 **Threatened.**

John 10:31.

Even before his arrest, trial, and conviction, the Gospels record Jesus facing deadly threat and challenging those threats with extraordinary courage. In one such instance, late in his ministry, Jesus had just addressed a crowd that had gathered around him as he walked through the temple area. Members of the crowd, the account identifying as Jews, had demanded that he tell them directly whether he was the Christ. Jesus answered that he had told them already and the miracles had shown them, without them believing. He said that only his sheep know his voice and follow him to eternal life. Jesus then repeated that he and the Father *are one*. At that statement, just about as plain a revelation as Jesus could make it, the crowd picked up stones with which to kill Jesus. Jesus challenged them to say for which of the many miracles from the Father that he had done they would stone him? The Jews answered that they were going to stone him instead for the blasphemy of claiming that he, Jesus, a mere man, was God. Jesus answered back that their own Law called them *gods*, and so what was so wrong with the one whom the Father sent as his *very own* calling himself God's Son? Jesus told them to go ahead and disbelieve him if he didn't do his Father's work but to believe him if he did do that work, for the Father was in him and he in the Father. The crowd again tried to seize Jesus who instead slipped away. Murderous crowds clearly threatened Jesus who showed great courage in revealing their error and badly mistaken intent.

Scenes of Jesus facing down murderous crowds should give heart to followers challenged by adversary or circumstance. While saved life is blessed life, followers can nonetheless certainly feel beset upon, challenged, opposed, and rejected. Followers do even face physical and other coercive threats. That Jesus, the miracle-making Son of God, faced such hateful opposition in itself may seem extraordinary until one realizes the broken nature of the world in which we live and the evil force that darkens it. Yet Jesus showed in the many settings in which he faced not just general opposition but specific murderous intent that he always controlled the situation. He chose whether to face and oppose, or avoid and retreat from, the threat. Jesus's response to threats suggests that while one should not underestimate the nature and power of the threat, making avoidance in retreat a more-than-plausible option, one simultaneously has will and authority to oppose threats. Prompt flight is not always the first and only option. Scenes of Jesus facing hostile crowds tend first to show him clarifying the opposition's grounds. Why did they act as they did? His role, and maybe also a follower's role, when facing a threat remained to witness to the Gospel mission. Doing so often required Jesus to draw out of and display to the crowd the error in their actions, in effect showing that he fulfilled most legitimately the very scriptures that they purported to defend in their hostile action. Jesus then often retreated, mission accomplished.

Looking to Jesus

Reflect on Jesus's response to threats, perhaps to consider clarifying threats to the ones making them before avoiding them.

He often had to judge the motives of those whose actions he had to evaluate, sometimes challenge, often direct or guide, and other times avoid. He kept thinking of Jesus, sometimes moving furtively to avoid confronting hostile crowds or scheming religious leaders, while other times standing firm to draw out his adversaries' understanding and intent. Motive mattered to Jesus. Stance and belief mattered. And so he wanted to know the motive, stance, and belief of those whose actions he of necessity had to judge. He wanted to hear them, question them, and test them. He wanted to see if they were friend or foe, or more to the point, if they knew the truth and cared about it or did not know truth or knew but didn't care. In those instances where he did not know the stance of those whose actions and intentions he had to evaluate, he would draw close to test and question. In those other instances where he knew an adversary's stance but didn't know their intentions, he would stand at a respectful distance, demonstrating his own stance and resolve while judging their intentions. Where he knew both an adversary's stance and intention, he would decide quickly whether to engage or disengage, depending on whether his adversary showed a willingness to hedge and waiver, or whether his adversary had superior resources and numbers. Like Jesus always did, he wanted to make a right judgment of whether his time for battle had come. He had little confidence that he regularly made right judgments, but he nonetheless drew on Jesus's example for the threats that Jesus regularly faced.

129 **Besieged.**

Luke 11:53; *see also* Luke 20:20.

An above section indicates how frequently and deeply Jesus offended the religious leaders and law experts, not of course for the purpose of offense but because they would not recognize who he was. To speak the truth, Jesus had to denounce their views and, because his denouncements undermined their positions as leaders and experts, in doing so offend them. The Gospels report that the eventual result of those frequent deep offenses was that the religious leaders *besieged* Jesus with efforts to undermine his teaching and catch him in blasphemy for which they could condemn him. On one such occasion, a religious leader had invited Jesus in to eat with them. Jesus's host immediately noticed, though, that Jesus did not observe the traditional ceremonial washing before the meal. In response, Jesus promptly began pronouncing one woe after another on the religious leaders, first for making a show of being clean on the outside when inside they were full of sin and then for a series of other showy yet hypocritical actions. Jesus's condemnations were so many and so strong that one of the law experts who was present cautioned Jesus that he was insulting not only the religious leaders but also the law experts. So Jesus promptly turned to condemning the law experts for burdening people down with loads that they could hardly carry while killing God's prophets. The law experts had hidden the key to knowledge so that no one could enter, Jesus concluded. The account ends by stating that Jesus's denouncements accelerated the plots of the leaders and law experts against him, after which they began to *besiege* him with efforts to foil, catch, and condemn him. Another Gospel account records that the religious leaders even sent spies to pose as honest persons but hoping to catch Jesus in something that he said so as to turn him over to the authorities.

The image of Jesus besieged by the religious leaders and law experts, and their spies, may affect followers in a different and deeper manner than their growing mutual offenses and the leaders' preliminary threats. In some figurative sense, the skies darken considerably when religious leaders besiege any figure but especially such a profoundly good figure as Jesus. If the religious leaders had somehow represented the scriptures truly and fairly, and been free of their own self-interested corruption, greed, and other sin, then why would any figure who spoke other things, whether that figure had been the Messiah Jesus or instead a false prophet, have been any threat to them? The world contains many false prophets, idolatrous beliefs, corrupt systems, and other false things. Few of those false things sincerely threaten truth. Israel had survived well over a millennium among such things, indeed as a veritable prisoner right then of Rome, with the ruling Caesar as false of a god and Rome's power as oppressive of a force as most others Israel had faced. Truth proves true not by destroying evil but by standing in contrast to it. That the religious leaders besieged Jesus to catch and condemn him reflects not a legitimate contest of over truth, in the nature of an important and possibly great debate, but an act of evil over good. One suffers even a foolish speaker gladly lest the fool communicate a truth. Evil, on the other hand, will destroy even the one who speaks only truth. Followers do well to recognize evil's errant hand in besieging Christ.

He shuddered at the darkly dangerous things, the things that spoke so clearly and violently of unmitigated evil. The scary thing about evil, he felt, was that it could be in such surprising places, at times only lurking beneath the surface but soon seen to be clearly there. He knew that some just didn't believe in evil, which he felt was a convenience or comfort that he simply could not afford. To see the reality and depth of evil, one had only to look at its circling, tightening, gradually besieging movement around Jesus. How could anyone have wished harm to Jesus, he who was then and always will have been the most glorious person ever to walk the earth? How could any group lay in wait for and besiege such a profoundly wise and enormously charismatic man who did nothing more than teach, feed, and heal thousands? If Jesus had not been the Messiah, then would the religious leaders have simply let him alone, as one of their number advocated? He hardly wondered that Jesus so fiercely opposed the religious leaders, seeing in retrospect the depth of their insidiousness. He wondered, though, what to make of a besieged Lord, the gentle Good Shepherd so ruthlessly pursued. He decided that as beautiful as God had made the world, and as certain as Jesus had prevailed over the evil in it, evil still lurked. Lord Jesus, deliver followers from evil.

130 Guarded.

Luke 12:1; *see also* Luke 12:15.

The Gospels record Jesus being guarded in his manner and counseling the disciples to be on their guards as well against the murderous intent of the religious leaders and other rulers and authorities. Late in his public ministry, when the Gospel account says that *many thousands* had gathered around him, Jesus spoke not to the crowd but privately to the disciples. He warned the disciples to *be on your guard* particularly against the religious leaders. The leaders would find out everything, even secrets that the disciples whispered in inner rooms, Jesus continued. Although the religious leaders were out to kill them, Jesus did not want the disciples afraid of the leaders who after all could only kill the body. Better to fear the evil one who unlike the religious leaders can cast one into hell, Jesus counseled. Yet God would protect them against the evil one, Jesus added, even counting the hairs on their head and valuing them far more than the little sparrows whom God also values. When the religious leaders prosecuted and tried them before synagogues and rulers, Jesus just wanted the disciples not to give in but instead to keep acknowledging him. If they did so, then Jesus would acknowledge the disciples before God's angels. When they faced arrest, trial, and conviction, they should not worry how to defend themselves because the Holy Spirit would give them what to say, Jesus concluded. In those perilous times, Jesus guarded what he said and did, and wanted the disciples to do so also. He also counseled to be on guard against greed and other evil.

Scenes of Jesus speaking guardedly to his disciples while warning them to be *on their guards* against the deadly intent of their adversaries make sobering images for followers to digest. Faith commitments, especially following Jesus, can still, or once again, prove fatal in many parts of the world, where guarding one's disclosures is absolutely essential to one's own survival and even the survival of one's family and friends. Following Jesus liberates the soul and spirit, a liberty that many rulers and factions oppose. One gets the sense, though, that even when the threats that one faces are not deadly threats but instead only threats to one's faith, Jesus would at times have a follower act guardedly. With those who would complain, undermine, and gossip against a person of faith, a follower should probably not speak openly of faithful plans and actions. Followers have times when they should keep their plans among themselves, when disclosure would rally the opposition and frustrate implementation. On the other hand, as Jesus clearly indicates in the scene summarized above, one should not fear when adversaries confront and accuse the follower. Fear is an ineffective witness. When accusers confront a follower, others observe who just might respect the follower and potentially have the follower's actions influence the observer. Even when the accusations are made in secret, though, God watches, waiting for the witness while ready to protect the soul.

She wasn't guarded with many, but she was guarded with a few. She had once wondered whether she should ever be secretive about her faith and her faithful plans and actions. Then, she had thought that witness at all times to everyone was most appropriate. Yet as she had studied and reflected on the actions of Jesus and his counsel to his disciples, she had realized how often he had spoken and acted in relative secret, keeping his thoughts and instructions among his disciples. While he was often readily accessible to the throngs of people who pursued and followed him, Jesus still very much seemed to pick and choose his times and places for public pronouncements. She realized, too, that she had sometimes made disclosures unwisely, only to see her disclosures come back to haunt and frustrate her. She could still remember several instances when she had wished that she had never said anything, not to hide her commitment to Jesus about which just about everyone knew, but so that she could proceed with good works without the resistance of others. Others sometimes seemed to plot and plan against her, which she found crazy because she felt that all she was trying to do was the good works that God gave her. She just found that she had times when keeping her plans to herself and a few others was better than advertising those plans widely. Better to be on her guard a little bit, just as Jesus counseled.

131 **Condemned.**

John 11:50; *see also* Luke 19:47.

The Gospels record the moment when the religious leaders effectively condemned Jesus who then because of their plots on his life withdrew to a region near the desert. Jesus lived for a time *condemned*. The religious leaders had long opposed Jesus who had already faced many threats, some of them deadly. Yet after Jesus raised Lazarus, and many Jews from Jerusalem believed in him because of the extraordinary miracle, other Jews went to the religious leaders warning them of Jesus's growing popularity even in Jerusalem. So the religious leaders met to determine what to do because of Jesus's many miracles, their losing opposition to him, and the likelihood that soon everyone would believe in Jesus. The religious leaders believed that the occupying Romans would remove them if they no longer held sway over the people. So the chief priest spoke up, saying that Jesus should die so that the nation did not perish. The chief priest did not realize his statement's prophetic nature that Jesus would indeed die *and rise* for salvation not just of Israel but for all of God's children. The account continues that *from that day on* the leaders *plotted to take his life,* including giving orders to report any sight of Jesus so that they could have him arrested. The account ends saying that because of the chief priest's condemnation, about which Jesus must have heard, Jesus no longer moved openly among the Jews but instead withdrew to a region near the desert. Another account reports that although the leaders plotted Jesus's death, they were unable to bring it about because the crowds *hung on his words*. Jesus knew that he was condemned, even as he continued teaching and preaching.

The image of Jesus as condemned challenges followers in reflection. Yes, Jesus had to die to fulfill prophesy and further salvation's plan. Yet the thought of Jesus as living under a literal death sentence is just one of those desperate tensions that makes the Gospel record so compelling. The Gospel is not about philosophical truths but about life and death, indeed, about life, death, *and life*. Remarkably, Jesus's condemnation wasn't only about governmental, political, social, military, or even religious intrigue, as so many so often die. Jesus's condemnation had all of those dimensions to it *but also one more*, a *prophetic* dimension, meaning one that God had long ordained and that would finally and fully confirm the course of all history. Humans have condemned many millions to die, even tens of millions just in the last century, but only Jesus stood condemned prophetically to save humankind. One does nothing less than look into the great chasm of history when reflecting on Jesus's life after the chief priest condemned Jesus and before Jesus's crucifixion. Imagine Jesus withdrawing with his disciples to near the desert region as he also looked into that chasm formed of his condemnation at the bottom of which was his coming crucifixion. Then just begin to appreciate more fully what this God-man Jesus did.

He tried now and then in some sense to see the horror, the sheer dread, of someone dying because of what he did, or maybe to put the thought a little more precisely, dying because of what he *needed* now that he had done as he did. He really didn't want to think about it much, the part about someone, especially *Jesus*, dying for him. The thought was just too difficult, especially considering how special Jesus was. Yet he really had little choice other than to consider it. The only other option was to just expect to die one's self, indeed worse, to die and then end up in perpetual torment. His problem wasn't so much the perpetual torment part of it, although he certainly wanted to avoid that end if he could, or again to be more accurate, now that he *knew* that he could avoid it. He was more than ready to admit his need for a way out of this *life* thing that did not end where he knew it would otherwise end. He was also more than ready to acknowledge Jesus's satisfying that need for a better end, a *much* better end. Rather, his problem was making Jesus's death *personal to him*. To do that, to admit that Jesus died *for him,* and not just for everyone else in a way that let him sort of tag along, meant that he had to think of Jesus's condemnation as something due *him* rather than Jesus, that if *he* had been different, then Jesus need not have stood condemned. He *had* to look at Jesus's condemnation, reflect on Jesus's condemnation, think about Jesus walking around condemned, and while thinking about it, think that *he was the cause* for Jesus's condemnation, not some political or religious order, not some leader's or ruler's fear, but instead *him*, that the perfect man had died for him. He was now just beginning to see the significance of thinking of Jesus condemned.

132 **Weeping.**

Luke 19:41; *see also* Luke 13:34; Matthew 23:39.

Jesus reacted emotionally to the Jews' great loss in rejecting him as its Savior, even weeping over that loss as he prophesied of it. The Gospels record that as Jesus approached Jerusalem for the last time and saw the city, *he wept over it* in lament at what its people were losing. *If you had only known what would bring you peace*, he said of Jerusalem, speaking both of its residents' lost opportunity to turn to him for salvation and of its coming military destruction after revolt. Jesus then prophesied Jerusalem's destruction, which in fact occurred not long after it had rejected and crucified its spiritual Savior. Jerusalem's conquerors would destroy man, woman, and child, while leaving no stone standing, *because Jerusalem had not recognized God coming to it,* Jesus concluded on that occasion. Jesus had similarly grieved for Jerusalem early in his ministry. As he taught in the villages and towns, Jesus had said that he must press on to Jerusalem where *prophets must die.* Jesus sorrowed deeply in that he wished to gather Jerusalem's children as a hen shelters its chicks but knew instead that Jerusalem would kill him just as it had stoned other prophets whom God had sent to it. Another Gospel records Jesus repeating the same lament during his final week of Passover in Jerusalem. Jesus would weep at other times, at Lazarus's death and in the Garden of Gethsemane the night of his arrest. Jesus felt and exhibited deep emotion to the point of weeping over the people's great loss.

The image of Jesus weeping must be one on which followers reflect deeply enough to recognize the weeping's cause and what it shows of God's character, of the character of the Son of God who would weep over lost souls. Jesus weeps for having lost as few as one person. He desires intensely, emotionally, humanly, and humanely that no one should die. To Jesus, no one should perish apart from him and his glorious Father, but all should instead have eternal life. Jesus sorrowed and wept because he wanted to gather *all* of Jerusalem's residents, *all* of his children like a hen gathers its chicks, and yet many would not have him do so. As hard as Jesus tried, as often as he taught, as many miracles as he performed, as deeply as he reached into the ravine for that one last lost sheep, Jesus would not win all because some would choose their own end. Some would choose their own path, when no path leads to the Father except that the path go through the Son whom the Father appointed for that purpose. God does not weep at righteous judgment, at sticking to salvation's plan, but instead weeps at losing souls. Yes, God knows whom he will win and whom he will lose, but each one still has a choice. Followers should treasure that they have a soft-hearted God who weeps over the loss of a single soul, even grieving over the loss of a city that would kill his own Son.

She wanted to get very close to this wonderful God who wept over lost souls. She, too, wanted to weep, had wept, at the thought of losing family or friends who could have joined her in eternity, even though she had no clear knowledge of whom God would welcome or whom God must leave. That the universe has as its creator a God whose emotions run so deep as to weep at the loss of human life, affinity, companionship, and honor meant everything to her. The world could never be a cold and heartless place with such a God as its creator, sustainer, and continual benefactor. Anytime that she heard anyone attributing anything hard-hearted, rigid, or judgmental to God, she wanted to show them God weeping over lost souls. She wanted them to see that the hard-heartedness was not in God but rather in the lost souls who refused to accept God's extreme love. When they didn't see, and when they rejected God's standing offer of salvation through his Son, she wept with God, even as she entreated God to draw them even nearer that they might finally turn enough to see his weeping face. She felt that just one look at his weeping face would change them forever, make them pursuers of God. Then she would remember that the world had already seen Jesus weep and yet had still rejected him. She would never understand how anyone would reject the weeping God, God with a heart so big and emotions so deep that he would part for a time even with his own Son to bring other sons and daughters back to him like a hen bringing back her little chicks.

133 **Troubled.**

John 12:27.

Much as Jesus wept at the loss of Jerusalem, the Gospels also record Jesus emotionally burdened or *troubled* by the very near approach of his crucifixion death, just as the fast-unfolding events late in the week of Passover would deeply trouble the disciples and other followers of Jesus. Some Greeks who were visiting for the feast asked the disciples if they could see Jesus. When Jesus heard of their request, he replied to the disciples that the *hour had come* for the Son of Man's death and glorification. The kernel must die and fall if it is to produce many seeds, Jesus continued, adding that one must hate life in the world to keep life eternally. Jesus then said that although his heart was *troubled* at his coming death, he would not ask his Father to save him because he had come for that very reason to die for the Father's glory. Just then, the Father answered from heaven that he had glorified and would glorify his name. Some in the attending crowd had thought that an angel spoke, while others heard only thunder. Jesus answered only that God was about to judge the world, driving out its prince while lifting Jesus up in crucifixion to draw everyone to him. Jesus told the inquiring crowd that they should trust the light that was leaving them, in order to become sons of light. Jesus had much more to say to the crowd explaining how he was the light who spoke only what the Father told him, but he then left and hid to await his final hour.

The image of Jesus speaking to his disciples and the crowd of how he was emotionally burdened or *troubled* at his coming sacrifice, indeed at his coming crucifixion, helps to further humanize Jesus. Crucifixion bespeaks a horror beyond words, one that anyone finds difficult to contemplate no less than to anticipate. That Jesus revealed his emotional stress over his coming crucifixion confirms how fully human Jesus was. If crucifixion had not troubled Jesus, weighed him down, maybe even appalled him, and clearly made him share his burden with those around him, then followers might find less reason to recognize Jesus's full humanity. In a frightening sense, Jesus had to be fully human for crucifixion to be redemptive. If Jesus was something other than fully human, such as someone instead only divine, then crucifixion may not have held its shame, pain, and horror, and thus not have redeemed sin. Crucifixion without humanity wouldn't redeem because it would not pay for human sin. Jesus had to be both human *and* divine, both able to suffer the agony of crucifixion while also be the divine Son of God, for God's plan for human redemption to work. As awful as it was, that Jesus's impending death, such difficult death, troubled and soon agonized Jesus, was necessary evidence of an extraordinary divine plan.

He had gone back and forth on what he thought of Jesus facing crucifixion. On one hand, he wondered how anyone could face such an awful death without losing all sense of rationality never mind hope. That Jesus retained all sense, indeed remained his profoundly thoughtful, insightful, and foresight-filled self even while knowing that he was on the way to the cross was simply further proof of Jesus's astonishing quality, moreover of his divine character. Yet that was just the oddity that on the other hand, he realized that Jesus was the Son of God and knew that he would rise and return to the Father after crucifixion. Did Jesus's absolute confidence in his resurrection relieve in any sense what Jesus faced? He kept wondering whether knowing that one will live again makes dying any easier, especially when one anticipates dying an extremely difficult death. He decided that because Jesus was fully human, even if also fully divine, that Jesus must have faced his death like anyone today who also trusts in resurrection. Jesus was, in a sense, the first to die knowing that God would bring him back to life in resurrected body, as followers of Jesus today know that they will live again. He read and re-read the accounts of Jesus making his way to the crucifixion, seeing in Jesus's approach that tense mixture of absolute faith in the Father's love with the complete sense of loss that death must bring. Maybe, he decided, death must remain the portal that it always was, even for those who rely fully on Jesus for like resurrection, as the ultimate test of faith. One could not show the faith necessary for resurrection without showing the faith necessary to face death. In any event, because facing his hour troubled Jesus, he concluded that the Father must find it acceptable to show a considerable degree of emotional stress over one's earthly demise. Death might not be easy even when one has resurrection assured.

134 Hated.

Mark 13:13; *see also* Matthew 10:22, 24:9; Luke 6:22, 21:17; John 7:7, 15:23.

The Gospels record Jesus acknowledging that the world hated him. He gave as the reason that he testified that the world's works are evil, although Jesus also cited the prophecy that others would hate him *without reason*. Jesus also acknowledged that others would hate his disciples because they followed him. One Gospel account records Jesus telling the disciples Peter, James, John, and Andrew privately that *all men* would hate them because of Jesus. The account records the event during Jesus's final week in Jerusalem, while they sat on the Mount of Olives where they could see the temple. Jesus warned that brothers would betray one another to death, while children would do the same to their own parents. Jesus reassured the disciples, though, that those disciples who stood firm to the end he would indeed save, after they had preached the Gospel to all nations. Another Gospel account records Jesus saying the same thing much earlier in his ministry, when he sent the twelve disciples out to preach the Gospel. All would hate them. Yet their persecution, he then explained, would simply drive them from one place to another carrying his message. If possible, Jesus is even direr in his parallel prophecy in another Gospel account where he added that others would hand over the disciples for persecution to death, with all nations hating them because of Jesus. Persecution would drive many away from the faith, causing them even to hate and betray one another, although the ones who stood firm Jesus would still save. Indeed, Jesus said in other accounts that although everyone would hate his followers because of him, he would bless those whom others hate and reject as evil because of him.

The image of Jesus as a hated figure, indeed so disliked that others would also hate those who followed him, can confound followers, even as they take Jesus's prophecy as a stern warning. The confounding nature of Jesus's prophecy that all would hate him and his followers is that he gave no such cause. Yes, he criticized the views of others with great candor. Yet he did so without advocating any violence, indeed quite the opposite, while rejecting invitations to call down thunder, take up sword, or lead military action against others. More so, beyond simply eschewing violence against others, Jesus positively counseled moral action, dutiful observance, and sacrificial service. Moreover, beyond those positive actions, Jesus also healed everyone whom others brought to him in miraculous fashion. The world had every reason to embrace rather than hate Jesus, again confounding his followers. Still, the world right up to today has indeed hated Jesus much and done every manner of harm to his followers, fulfilling Jesus's prophecy. Followers have every reason to take Jesus at his word with respect to this warning, not just figuratively, philosophically, politically, or spiritually, but literally. Others seethe at Jesus and his followers with a hatred as real as it is puzzling. Apparently, no one, especially those who hold power, likes even peaceful insights that evoke honest condemnation.

Much as she believed would be true with just about everyone, she didn't like being disliked and would prefer that everyone at least put up with her. She had once also felt that way about her faith in Jesus. Then, she had wanted others to like her because she followed Jesus and had hoped that they would not dislike her for doing so. Yet over time, while she still wanted to be liked just as much as ever, she cared far less whether others liked her because she followed Jesus. Oh, she wanted others to follow Jesus and showed her best service to those whom she felt it might help in doing so. She positively wanted to *love people to Jesus*, as she understood the expression. But on the other hand, she knew by now that others would not always love her for her faith or even for her service. And she was ready to not care at all about their opinions if they specifically rejected her because she loved Jesus. She didn't want others to hate or harm her, even though she knew Jesus had prophesied others would hate and harm his followers. She nonetheless recognized that hate and harm were certainly possible in such a crazy world. She simply counted her blessings that she lived in a time and place where her faith in Jesus did not at the moment expose her to risk and ridicule. She also prayed that if and when it did, that she would be among that number who remained standing by Jesus. She certainly expected to be so.

135 Betrayed.

Matthew 26:14; *see also* Mark 14:10; Luke 22:3; John 13:26.

The Gospels record Jesus betrayed by one of his own disciples. Betrayal was a surprising, disappointing, but nonetheless integral part of Jesus's mission and experience. One Gospel account records that during Jesus's final days in Jerusalem, Judas Iscariot, who was indeed one of Jesus's twelve original disciples, left the group for a secret visit to the chief priests, offering to hand Jesus over to them. The account reports that when Judas asked for money in return for his betrayal, the priests counted out thirty silver coins for him. Judas then watched for the next opportunity to lead guards to Jesus's arrest, which occurred late at night in the Garden of Gethsemane. Another account states specifically that while the chief priests were looking to rid themselves of Jesus, Satan entered into Judas to meet the priests and officers of the temple guard to plan Jesus's betrayal. That account adds that Judas's offer delighted the priests, so that Judas then watched for when no crowd would be around to betray Jesus. Another Gospel account records Jesus telling his disciples at the Last Supper that one of them must betray him to fulfill prophecy. Peter encouraged John to ask Jesus which one of them, to which Jesus replied the one, Judas, to whom Jesus would give his bread. The account ends saying that Satan entered Judas as he took the bread and then slipped away when Jesus told him to go quickly. Jesus's betrayal led quickly to his arrest. Other accounts tell the reader that Judas later hanged himself after casting the coins back into the temple, his corpse then rotting in a field the priests purchased with those coins.

The image of Jesus as betrayed can certainly be a difficult one on which followers would reflect but is nonetheless so significant a part of Jesus's mission and experience as to warrant that reflection. Betrayal of course begins with confidence. One cannot betray unless one is first an insider, one of the inner circle or group. Betrayal comes from within, not from without. Someone had to betray Jesus because of the Old Testament prophecy that one who shared Jesus's bread would turn against him. Yet Jesus's betrayal did more than fulfill prophecy. Judas betraying Jesus for coins that soon so smit his conscience that he cast them away and committed suicide creates a heartbreaking record. How many followers have found themselves briefly denying if not also betraying Jesus? While one can easily despise Judas for his betraying Jesus, closer reflection makes one hesitate at any simple condemnation of one who had walked so closely with Jesus for so long, Judas's evident love of money notwithstanding. Satan has his wiles, and may God protect every follower from them. Judas will not have been the only one to love money more than his Lord. Sensitive reflection over Judas's motive and temptation may thus in some sense inoculate, harden, toughen, or protect the follower against like error, against subtly turning away from Jesus for any other seeming benefit or cause, of which none exist. But for the grace and protection of God, more would go the way of Judas, betraying for silver the Son of God. Stand firm, believers.

While he could easily have done so, given the awful betrayal that Judas committed, he actually had little stomach for despising Judas. While indeed the Gospel record seemed too clear that Judas had literally sold away Christ's life, he nonetheless felt that he needed better to understand Judas's character and motives. The Gospels did not include Judas's story simply to give him someone to condemn to make himself feel superior, he was pretty sure, even if knowing right from wrong, and recognizing how wrong betrayal was, would be a valuable enough lesson. No, he felt like the Holy Spirit instead wanted him to construe a warning from Judas's actions, to search his own soul and actions for like betrayal. Oh, neither he nor anyone else could betray Jesus in quite the same way, with anything like the same historical, prophetic, and spiritual significance. But anyone could still for a time follow Jesus, draw close to Jesus and to others who followed him, gaining their trust, only later to turn away, and in turning, to damage the faith and confidence of those others. Jesus's mission was not at stake, but the commitment and faith of others was still certainly at stake, he knew. He decided that he didn't want to be one who for his own short-term financial or other benefit traded on the church's mission. With the Spirit's help, he would keep Judas's story in mind, letting it guard his conscience and actions.

¹³⁶ Broken.

Matthew 26:26; *see also* Luke 22:19.

The Gospels record Jesus's body broken, not Jesus or his will or mission but his body, while also recording Jesus explaining in close communion with his disciples that it must be so. In Jesus's final day in Jerusalem, the day of the Passover feast, the Gospels record that the disciples asked Jesus where he would like them to prepare the feast. Jesus answered that they would find a man in Jerusalem who would let them use his house if they simply told him that Jesus's hour was near. Jesus spoke much to his disciples at the feast that evening, but at one point while they were eating, Jesus thanked God, broke the bread that he held, and told his disciples to take the bread and eat it. In doing so, he explained that *this bread is my body*. Another Gospel account records Jesus saying *this is my body given for you* and to break bread *in remembrance of me*. Jesus would let others break his body, as he had just broken bread, so that his disciples could have his life, Christ's body in exchange for them. After his arrest and conviction, Roman guards would indeed break Jesus's body first in terrible scourging and agonizing cross-bearing, and finally in crucifixion. Jesus's earthly body, the body that Mary had borne him, would no longer hold his life. At the religious leaders' demand and urging, the Roman prefect Pontius Pilate, and on his order the Roman guards, would break Jesus's body. Jesus let them break his body for his followers. And so followers celebrate communion eating the bread as Jesus's body broken for us.

The communion image of Jesus breaking bread, while prophesying the breaking of his body in sacrifice to save us, is the follower's central image, a scene on which every follower at some time must meaningfully reflect. That God would break his own Son to redeem all others made in his image is the most moving of mysteries while also the greatest, most loving and generous of all possible acts. The broken body of Christ is human history's hinge, after the fall that shut the kingdom's door, the second great turning point that opened paradise's door once again. The smallest of gestures, a man tearing bread apart while dining with friends, represents the great opening through which all persons may now pass to join the Son of Man in the glory of his Father's heaven. Yet that smallest of gestures also represents the greatest of sacrifices. Many do not understand why God's Son would have to die, all those who do not know God and instead only know their own lesser imagination for him. From the broken world in which they live, they surmise someone or something at least somewhat stained, twisted, distorted, and broken, and thus corrupt, just like us. They do not know the purity of God, his holiness, and how in that respect he is so far above us. God though found the one possible way in which to reach so far down to us, which was by sharing with us his Son in his own person and image, and then did with that Son the one and only thing that could reunite God with us, which was to let his Son's body break in our redemption. Followers now have endless communion through the Son's broken body.

She sought depiction after depiction, whether moving, still, or text, of the broken Christ. Although his crucifixion duly horrified and appalled her, and she certainly had no wish for it and no dark or unhealthy fascination with his death, she nonetheless felt as if her spirit could never have enough of that image. The only thing that she could make of her spiritual hunger for his broken-body bread was, she discerned, just what he had intended. She had no communion with God, no nearness, no hope nor connection, other than through that bread, other than through that broken Son. She had to bear his broken image, take up the slain lamb as if carried across her shoulders, to even think of approaching her beloved Father. She had only one hope for his kingdom, which was hope in the closest communion with his glorious Son Christ. While she treasured every sound image of him, every accurate depiction that author or artist could conjure of her beloved Jesus, she still held most tightly to that one image of the broken body of Christ. She loved Jesus whole but loved him even more the way that the Father had given him to her, which was broken.

137 **Poured.**

Matthew 26:28; *see also* Luke 22:20; John 19:34.

Just as the Gospels record Jesus's body broken for followers, so too do the Gospels record Jesus's blood poured out to cleanse followers of sin. At the same event described in the above section, at the Last Supper as Jesus spoke intimately to the disciples of his imminent departure, breaking bread with them that they would do so later in remembrance of him, Jesus also had them drink. Jesus first took the cup, thanked God, and then told them each to drink from it, calling it his *blood of the covenant* and that the Father would pour it out for many to forgive their sins. Jesus concluded by saying that he would not drink the vine's fruit again until he drank it with the disciples in his Father's kingdom. The account ends reporting that they sang a hymn before heading out to the Mount of Olives. A parallel account records Jesus calling the cup the *new covenant in his blood.* The Father's promise would be that Jesus's blood would be forgiveness for his followers. Where animal sacrifice had not sufficed, the Son's blood would. The slain Lamb's blood would fit them once again for God's kingdom. Jesus would die on the cross, a soldier piercing his side that his blood would run out over us.

The simple image of Jesus sharing a cup of wine with his disciples, like Jesus breaking and sharing bread, is both the holy representation of Jesus's sacrifice and also communion with him and with the Father. The Son's sacrifice, his broken body, would not alone be enough but must join with cleansing blood to be effective in his salvation mission. That Jesus died would be significant but not sufficient if his blood, that part of him that represented his life, were not covering our own sin image. When the Father looks at us, he must see his Son's life, not our lives. He must see his Son's holiness and perfection, not our ungodliness and corruption. For God to pass us over and not give us our fit judgment and fatal sentence, he must see the blood of the Lamb on our doorpost, the sign that a follower lives here. Jesus had to pass his life to us so that we could receive it and hold it up to the Father in defense. Jesus did so not just by dying but then through giving us his blood as our life, transfusing us with his perfection. The Old Testament law had the

Israelites pour out on the ground the blood of the sacrificed animal because the animal's life was in the blood, and we are not to ingest the life of the animal. The New Testament grace, the new covenant, is not that we pour out Jesus's blood on the ground but that we take it in, ingesting it as our own life. In pouring out his blood for us, Jesus gave us the new covenant, one of God's grace, law now joined to grace.

He was a bit leery about blood, he supposed as most people were. He felt that sensitivity or skittishness to be natural. When one saw blood, one saw a life essential. When one saw bleeding, one saw life escaping because too much bleeding means no more living. Blood was indeed life. His natural aversion to blood was why the images of Jesus bleeding, of blood everywhere first at his crown of thorns, then at his scourging, and finally at his crucifixion, even of the soldier piercing his side with blood running out, were hard ones on which to reflect. He couldn't really even fathom *drinking* Jesus's blood, as in effect Jesus had instructed at the Last Supper. Because of that aversion about blood, mixed with his critical need for communion, he had to force himself to come to terms with bleeding-Jesus images. He couldn't simply look on them with revolt, although at the same time he wanted to retain that sense of being appalled at Jesus's death. He never wanted Jesus's death to seem too familiar, as if rote or trite. It should horrify. Yet he had to somehow get beyond the horror to the meaning. He figured that God did not intend simplify to horrify with Christ's death. God wanted him drawing from the image, realizing something vastly important from the image. He needed Jesus's blood. He needed God to pass over him rather than condemn him. He needed Jesus's *life*. In those needs, he began to find how he should look on those horrible bleeding-Jesus images. Not everything that we need is pretty. Not everything that we need is familiar, rote, or trite.

¹³⁸ Abandoned.

Matthew 26:31; *see also* Matthew 26:56, 26:74; Mark 14:30, 14:50, 14:72; Luke 22:34, 22:60; John 13:38, 18:27.

Even as Jesus instructed the disciples in his love and sacrifice for them, and communion with them, Jesus also prophesied contrarily that the disciples would abandon him. He would face trial and conviction alone. Right after Jesus introduced the bread and wine of communion to the disciples at the Last Supper, at what must have been the disciples' greatest moment of intimacy with their Lord and Savior, the Gospels record Jesus telling the disciples that all of them will *fall away*. Significantly, Jesus added that they would abandon him not for other things but rather *because of him*, as Old Testament prophecy had predicted. Their abandonment was imminent, Jesus continued, that very night. Peter protested that he would follow Jesus even if no others did, but Jesus replied that Peter would indeed *disown* Jesus that very night before the rooster crowed for dawn. Peter and the other disciples protested again that they would follow him. They then retired to the Garden of Gethsemane on the Mount of Olives for the night, where Jesus asked Peter, James, and John to accompany him while he prayed in sorrow and trouble over his impending death. Three times, though, Jesus had to rouse the disciples from sleep as he prayed in torment, right up until his arrest. That night, all the disciples did abandon Jesus after his arrest, as one account records, with one young follower fleeing naked when the crowd seized him by the garment. That night, Peter even denied that he knew Jesus while Peter warmed himself by a fire with the guards, with Jesus nearby on trial before the religious leaders. Jesus faced trial and all that followed it abandoned, without his disciples' support.

Scenes of the disciples abandoning Jesus, and Jesus facing trial, conviction, sentencing, torture, and capital punishment alone, weigh heavily on the heart for followers. Followers can nonetheless reflect on those scenes in many helpful ways, two of which are prominent. First, the scenes invite followers to ask how they might have behaved if they had been in Peter's position, indeed how they would behave today if facing a choice whether to deny Jesus and live or affirm Jesus and die. Followers do still face those choices today. While many would like to think that they would be brave, braver than Peter, the Gospel scenes suggest otherwise that many followers put to such tests might do as all of the disciples did. One hopes instead that one might do as Stephen did, witnessing to Christ under the Spirit even as the religious leaders stoned him. A second prominent question that the scenes of Jesus's abandonment encourage followers to ask is why Jesus had to face conviction and sentence abandoned. Yes, prophecy foretold it so, but the prophecy and its fulfillment likely also carried deeper meaning. Christ may have had to face punishment abandoned, alone, for his sacrifice to be effective. If some such as Peter had held fast to Christ through Christ's trial, then they may not in some way have had full benefit of his conviction and punishment, and they may not have had his full restoration, as Peter soon did. After all, the Father too must have turned away from the Son, darkening the skies, for the Son to finish his work of redemption. As heartrending as Jesus's abandonment was, it somehow perfected the awfulness of his sacrifice and thus the effectiveness of his redemption and glory of his resurrection.

She pained deeply at the thought of Peter abandoning Jesus, particularly at the glance that Jesus gave Peter just after Peter had done so, and then over Peter weeping bitterly. Much of her pain was over the loneliness and loss that Jesus must have felt when abandoned at his neediest hour. Yet she could also feel so much of the fear, pain, confusion, and shame that Peter must have felt, although Peter would have felt those things so much more acutely. She knew that she felt such strong sympathetic impulse for Peter because she could see herself doing as Peter did. She certainly didn't want it to be so. She was glad to have the image of Stephen holding fast to Christ through Stephen's own deadly trial, as counterweight to Peter's disowning Jesus. Stephen, of course, had the Spirit and, with the benefit of hindsight, full confidence in the completed resurrection, just as she also had. So maybe she would be like Stephen rather than Peter. Yet she hurt for Peter, hurt with Peter. Her hurt made so poignant Jesus's later restoration of Peter by the shore, an account that she could hardly read without weeping. Once again, she felt about that account that she, like Peter, would need Jesus's restoration. She kept these counter-balancing scenes, Peter disowning Christ and then Christ restoring Peter, in mind fairly often as she went about her days but particularly whenever she faced some form of faith challenge, which fortunately, wasn't often. God protect me from any temptation to abandon your Son, she prayed.

139 Arrested.

Matthew 26:50; *see also* Mark 14:46; Luke 22:47; John 18:12.

To face trial, conviction, and sentence, Jesus must first have faced arrest, that moment when officials took him into custody in order to begin the formal process that would lead to his end. The Gospels record Jesus's arrest as soon as Jesus ended his prayers in the Garden of Gethsemane with the three disciples sleeping when they should have been watching. The accounts record Jesus as rousing the sleeping disciples with the call that his betrayer Judas had come. One account records that Judas had brought a large crowd carrying swords and clubs, dispatched from the chief priests and elders. Another account identifies the crowd as a detachment of soldiers and some officials from the chief priests and religious leaders. To be sure that the crowd took the right man, Judas had arranged to kiss Jesus as a signal. The accounts report that rather than resist his arrest, Jesus simply called Judas *friend* while bidding him to do as he came to do. One account has the crowd *drawing back and falling down* when Jesus identified himself, the crowd's reaction suggesting Jesus's unconcealable command and authority. When one of the disciples, identified in one account as Peter, struck the high priest's servant with a sword, cutting off his ear, Jesus told the disciple to put his sword away and then healed the servant's ear while telling the disciples that he could right then have called down legions of angels to protect him. Yet Christ added that he would not do so because his end must fulfill the scriptures. He did chastise the crowd, though, that he was leading no rebellion and had instead taught openly in the temple courts when they could have arrested him.

The unfortunate image of Jesus suffering arrest, while utterly incongruous to his divine command and authority, is nonetheless one that followers should not overlook in their meditations on Jesus. The Son of God had to the point of his arrest suffered only ineffectual challenges to his command and authority. Although Jesus had acted dutifully in many respects, until his arrest he had not yet accepted coerced submission to his divine rule, his lordship and kingship. The moment of his arrest is thus significant as marking the point of his turning, the point at which he said that although he had legions available at his defense, he would instead accept arrest, trial, conviction, and sentence as his integral to his mission. In a sense, Jesus had to that point been primarily *speaking* of his sacrificial mission, when now at arrest he had for the first time actually *acted* in sacrifice of his command toward completion of that gruesome though necessary sacrificial aspect of his mission. While arrest was only a prelude to other proceedings that may seem more significant, arrest itself is also significant, an event having its own consequences, restraining and staining the suspect. After arrest, Jesus was no longer free but instead under the force and control of others, even if in Jesus's unusual case consensual because of his available legions. Jesus stood arrested, a turning point of huge significance.

Jesus's arrest was one of the many scenes of Jesus in which he took peculiar interest. The fact that the crowd had drawn back and fallen down when Jesus acknowledged that *I am he* seemed quite unusual, so much so as to draw special attention. Jesus had done nothing more than identify himself, had not drawn a sword or raised a club, and had not called on his disciples or legions of angels for defense. Yet the crowd had drawn back and fallen down for some reason that the account did not explain. Even during his arrest, Jesus had clearly remained in complete control of the situation. Arrests are often not pretty, and this one in a remote garden late at night had the makings of something ugly, with a crowd having swords and clubs coming head to head with a band of a dozen some of whom also had arms. Yet again, there stood Jesus, openly identifying himself, telling his disciples to put away arms, chastising the crowd, and even healing the one crowd member whom one of his disciples had injured. The more that he thought about the scene, and contrasted it with how scenes like this one ordinarily go, the more clearly that he could see the regal King of kings submitting to that which he had no reason to submit other than his one great salvation mission. He found the garden-arrest scene to be nearly as important and compelling as any other scene, a true turning point in his own journey to salvation.

140 Tried.

Matthew 26:57; *see also* John 18:24.

Following his arrest, Jesus faced trial. The assembly of religious leaders tried Jesus on charges of breaking the Jews' laws that they applied, interpreted, and administered. The Gospels record that the soldiers and officials who arrested Jesus late at night took him to the high priest who had assembled the elders and law teachers, one account saying after they first took Jesus to the high priest's father-in-law. Jesus was to face trial in the middle of the night. This night court was in itself an extraordinary aberration in procedure to avoid public notice, when fair procedure would have required the opposite public disclosure and accountability. Yet the accounts record explicitly that the assembly and chief priests were not looking to give Jesus a fair trial but were instead looking for *false evidence* with which to convict him in order that they could have him put to death. The assembly had already determined the outcome. The accounts further reflect that they did not find any evidence, whether or not false, with which to convict Jesus, even though many false witnesses came forward. The most that the assembly heard was that Jesus had said that he would destroy and rebuild the temple in three days. Frustrated in his designs, the high priest finally addressed Jesus directly, asking why he wouldn't answer. When Jesus still gave no answer, the high priest charged Jesus to say if he was the Christ, to which Jesus replied that indeed he was, adding that they would all see the Son of Man sitting at God's right hand and coming on heaven's clouds. The accounts record nothing more of the trial's evidence.

The image of Jesus facing trial, and an entirely unfair trial at that, represents another important characteristic of the risen Lord on which followers can reflect. Men tried Jesus but were unable to convict him *even with false evidence.* Jesus's trial revealed him to be without fault but the men who tried him to be corrupt beyond compare. The religious leaders who tried Jesus at night, without public scrutiny, without representation, with a predetermined outcome, and with nothing but false witnesses, violated every convention of what a fair trial should mean. They even required Jesus to in effect incriminate himself, violating due process's last bastion, although he was of course in his own words perfectly blameless. In outcome, the religious assembly did not try Jesus at all, for only the complete perfidy of its members, without any sense of due procedure, was on display. The putative trial that they gave the Son of Man could not in fact have tried him because men do not judge God. When men attempt to do so, they only judge and convict themselves. God judges men. The Son of God could not have had a fair trial, even if his accusers had intended it. Jesus spoke only one thing at his trial, and what he spoke was a simple but profound truth. He said that he was, and he in fact is, the Christ. Jesus stood trial and prevailed utterly in the test. Men found nothing of guilt in Jesus.

He kept marveling at the so-called trial that the religious assembly had purported to give Jesus. He had heard of such courts before, not really courts but corrupt places to condemn one's enemies and accomplish one's unlawful agenda with a false veneer of public respectability. People indeed twist their affairs, he surmised, believing also that they always have and always will until the return of Jesus. Every human institution has its faults, including both modern and ancient courts. Nonetheless, the accounts of Jesus's trial still surprised and depressed him at their complete lack of fair procedure. He kept thinking of the darkness surrounding that hastily assembled night court, convened for no purpose other than to convict. The only thing even approaching public scrutiny had been a few people outside, including the disciple Peter, warming themselves by a fire. Then only false witnesses testified, presumably bribed or induced by threat. And when none gave the evidence with which to convict, the high priest had demanded that Jesus incriminate himself, which Jesus did not. Even though Jesus spoke, he only spoke truth. He decided that men have no business judging God, and when they try to do so, things never go well. He had seen that kind of putting-God-on-trial many times, although not in a law court. Judging God is not man's business, he discerned and decided. It hadn't gone well for the assembly in judging Jesus, and wouldn't go well for anyone else.

141 Convicted.

Matthew 26:65; *see also* Matthew 27:1.

Trials must conclude with outcomes, usually verdicts of guilt or acquittal. The foregone conclusion of Jesus's trial was that the assembly convicted him. Jesus stood convicted. The Gospel accounts record that despite only false witnesses testifying against Jesus, and further despite that they presented no evidence on which to convict him, the assembly reached its verdict against him. When Jesus answered the high priest's direct demand that Jesus say whether he was the Christ, answered that indeed he was and that they would all see the Son of Man coming on the clouds of heaven, the high priest tore his clothes. As he did so, the high priest exclaimed that Jesus had spoken blasphemy and that the assembly had no need of any more witnesses, all of whom had in any case been ineffectual. The high priest charged the assembly members that they had heard the blasphemy, asking them only what they then thought. The assembly members gave the answer that Jesus was *worthy of death*, a conviction that was at once both false, for Jesus had spoken only truth, not blasphemy, but at the same time fitting in that Jesus had indeed come to die for human sin. Jesus was *worthy* of his extraordinary sacrificial role, yes worthy *of death*, but only in the sense of the divine plan in which he played the central role. The accounts end saying that at his conviction, the assembly members spit in his face, struck him with blows, and slapped him in the face while mocking his claim to be Christ. They then delivered him bound to the Roman governor. Jesus stood convicted, his conviction both perfectly perfidious and yet also perfect to his appointed and assumed role.

The image of Jesus standing convicted before Israel's great assembly may not be a rich one on which followers often reflect but still carries important meaning for those who do contemplate it. Conviction comes in two forms, one as a judgment imposed from without, whether a true judgment or false, and the other as a frank recognition of one's role, determined from within. The first form of conviction from without was in Jesus's case a false judgment, a biased and self-interested judgment of men against a blameless figure who in no sense deserved to die. The second form of conviction determined from within was in Jesus's case exactly right that his essential next act would be to die in human redemption as the Father had intended and the Son fully accepted. As the scriptures suggest, few are quite as willing and righteous as to die for a friend, but none other than Jesus as willing and righteous as to die for everyone and anyone. Jesus had an extraordinary form of worthiness, indeed so worthy as to be willing to carry out the unprecedented will of his Father to suffer self-sacrifice for the benefit of others. Conviction in that sense can be an enormously positive achievement, the clearing away of all doubt as to Jesus's unique and history-changing role, not simply the negative judgment that the assembly intended. Jesus convicted might just be something essential on which to reflect.

She didn't like the thought of the verdict against Jesus, this hugely loving and entirely blameless God-man judged worthy of death by this charade of a court. Why must heroes always die, she wondered? She thought of the popular depiction of heroes wrongly condemned by their adversaries, then doing one last heroic but self-sacrificial act to save the nation, save the world, or save the universe. Maybe that depiction of saving self-sacrifice was exactly the point of Jesus's conviction, though, she thought. As wrong and despicable as his conviction was, in Jesus's case conviction to die was exactly his stand-in role. Jesus, she realized, was not really in the dock that night. If he was simply standing in for the guilt of others, then *she* was in the dock that night, *she* was the one charged, as were all others except Jesus. His conviction was really *her* necessary conviction, the finding out and determination of her own guilt. If the assembly had let Jesus off on the charges, then she too would have gone without conviction and hence without his redemption, whether or not he had later died in sacrifice. The evil one is a false accuser, falsely accusing and convicting Jesus. Yet the evil one is an effective tempter, successfully having tempted her and all others other than Jesus. Humankind needed to face its judgment, and face its judgment it did late that very night. The assembly's judgment could not have been correct as to Jesus, but it was perfectly sound as to her and anyone else other than Jesus. Convict it did, and convict it needed to, she decided, even though Jesus was blameless.

142 Sentenced.

Matthew 27:11; *see also* John 19:12.

As mentioned briefly in the prior section, the Gospels record that once the chief priests and elders had convicted Jesus, they led him bound to the Roman governor Pilate for sentencing. Jesus was not just convicted and punished but also, in between, *sentenced*, a significant event and attribute of Jesus on which followers may separately reflect. The accounts record that Jesus gave no reply to the accusations of the chief priests and elders when standing before the governor who sentenced him. Yet when the governor asked Jesus directly whether he was the Jews' king, Jesus answered that indeed he was. Jesus nonetheless amazed the governor by not answering any other accusation, even when the governor encouraged Jesus to do so and knew that the religious leaders had convicted Jesus out of envy. With no reply from Jesus other than that he was the Jews' king, in effect acknowledging the conviction of the elders and priests, even if in no sense the conviction's justice or merit, the governor turned to sentencing Jesus. Sentencing would in the usual case have been brief and easy. Here, though, the governor needed to comply with a custom of the Passover feast to release a prisoner whom the crowd chose. The governor seemed both surprised and disappointed that the crowd, at the religious leaders' inducement, chose releasing a murderer over releasing Jesus, disappointed because the governor's wife warned the governor to have nothing to do with Jesus whom a dream had shown her was innocent. A parallel account records that the governor tried repeatedly to release Jesus, announcing that he found no basis to affirm the religious leaders' conviction. When the leaders replied that Jesus had claimed to be the Son of God, the alarmed governor redoubled his efforts to set Jesus free, even plying Jesus with questions. Yet when the crowd rose to an uproar to convince the governor to crucify Jesus, the governor ended the sentencing by proclaiming his own innocence of Jesus's blood, adding prophetically that Jesus's blood would be on the crowd's head. Releasing the murderer instead, the governor sentenced Jesus to flogging and crucifixion.

The image of Jesus standing for sentence before the Roman governor Pilate is a significant one for followers' reflection. Punishment does not follow conviction but instead awaits sentencing. Sentencing is its own event, with its own implications for the one sentenced. That the governor sentenced Jesus not as guilty but as *innocent*, while simultaneously releasing a *guilty* notorious murderer, gives a follower the perfect scene on which to reflect for Jesus's redemptive work. Sentencing often involves elaborate presentations of mitigating evidence on the convicted person's behalf as to why the judge should lessen the punishment. That Jesus remained silent, in plain effect *willing* that he should *die* by the cruelest means available, again provides followers the perfect scene for Jesus's redemptive work. That the governor explicitly agreed to the sentence that the crowd demanded only on the condition that Jesus's blood *be on their heads* gives further illustration of the point of Jesus's death to cleanse sinners, even if the governor did not intend his statement to be prophetic and likely meant it instead to indicate the governor's own putative innocence in the whole matter. By matching reason, rationale, and wrong to punishment, sentencing signifies much more than conviction. For the first time, in this scene of Jesus's sentencing, followers had the full illustration of Jesus's salvation mission, which Jesus now had only to complete. Reflect deeply on Jesus's sentencing to embrace more fully and firmly your salvation.

He studied the scene of Jesus's sentencing again, and again, and again. Every time he read and thought of Jesus standing before Pilate, of Pilate's wife, of the murderer Barabbas, and of the crowd's demands, he discovered something new in the scene. The Spirit kept him focused on that scene, drawing connections in his mind that he had not noticed. The scene had initially angered him as he thought of the sneering Pilate, killer Barabbas, corrupt leaders, and murderous crowd. Yet the more that he contemplated the scene, the less righteous indignation that he felt. While he still regretted the horrible scene of Jesus's sentencing, regretted that humans could treat this perfect man so despicably, his emotions slowly changed to regret for his *own* sin rather than for the corruption of the murderous leaders, convict, and crowd. His weeping, while still in some part for the dying Son of God, began to receive its fuel from recognizing his own guilt rather than the recklessness and depravity of others. After all, Christ had died and risen long ago. He could be as sorry as he wished over the governor's assent, but that event happened long ago. He needed to focus instead on who *he* was, what *he* had done, who *he* needed as savior, and his own responsibility for the awful judgment and sentence that Christ so willingly accepted. In Jesus's sentencing, God had given him the perfect scene on which to reflect. Rather than stand above the scene in judgment against the governor, leaders, convict, and crowd, he learned to put himself in the role of the notorious convict, doubtless delighted to be free and yet also forever transformed by the knowledge that a perfectly innocent man had just died for him, indeed for me.

143 Appealed.

Luke 23:6.

Jesus had an appeal of sorts in the extensive but swift procedure that led inevitably to his crucifixion. Appeal is thus another attribute of Jesus's experience on which followers may reflect. Another of the Gospel accounts of Jesus's sentencing records that in the midst of that procedure, the Roman governor discovered that Jesus was from Galilee rather than Jerusalem, when the religious leaders accused Jesus of stirring up people throughout that region. Galilee was then under the rule of Herod Antipas, son of Herod the Great who had ruled at Jesus's birth but had died shortly after ordering the execution of Bethlehem's infants. Herod Antipas happened to be in Jerusalem at the time of the Passover feast. So on discerning that the Galilean Jesus was technically under Herod's jurisdiction, the governor sent Jesus to Herod to make his own judgment of Jesus's conviction. The account indicates that Herod was greatly pleased to see Jesus because he hoped to see one of the miracles about which he had heard Jesus perform. Jesus, though, gave no answer to any of Herod's many questions, nor to any of the vehement accusations of the chief priests and elders. Having no answer and seeing no entertaining miracle from Jesus, Herod ridiculed and mocked him, as did Herod's soldiers before putting an elegant robe on Jesus to return him to the Roman governor. The account ends saying that the event made friends of Herod and the governor who had long been enemies.

The image of Jesus having had an appeal, and having had the appeal rejected with such ridicule and scorn, adds to the follower's reflection on the character and attributes of Jesus as revealed in the complex but brief and brutal procedure leading to his crucifixion. Appeal, like notice of the charge and hearing of evidence in trial, is one of those marks of due process, of that which civil society rightly regards as fundamental to fairness. Law is both procedural and substantive, though. All due procedure means nothing when the participants controlling the procedure are themselves corrupt. Hell, as others have said, will have all the procedure one could wish for but none of the relief. The governor referring Jesus to Herod for review ostensibly gave Jesus what law and fundamental rights would require. Yet the participants' depravity meant that Jesus would merely suffer greater injury from appeal rather than receive greater protection. Jesus had an appeal, but all that the appeal revealed was ever-greater human depravity. No matter where or to whom one looks in the complex and complete procedure of Jesus's arrest, trial, conviction, sentence, appeal, and punishment, one finds no justice and instead only evident wickedness and wantonness, whether among sacred or secular leaders or followers, in this ostensibly righteous region of a putatively great world empire. Through it all, Jesus remained for the most part silent, letting humans reveal their utter wickedness in the very process for which he would pay all in that wickedness's redemption.

He found again in Herod's review of Jesus's conviction such awfulness, such hopelessness in human ways and wiles, indeed even in thoughtful, well-designed, complex human processes, protocols, and procedures. He knew process from a career of ensuring its proper administration. Yet from that same career, he knew that process without decent judges, jurors, prosecutors, and administrators means nothing. Worse than nothing, such process carried out by corrupt leaders and citizens is a charade and mockery, a mechanism crushing the hope, faith, and will of anyone decent who enters it. Law without morality, law without the righteousness of God in the hearts of its instituters, is the devil's playground. Still, he knew that the scene of Jesus standing on appeal before Herod, his soldiers, and the religious leaders, all of whom would further cruelly attack and mock Jesus, was not about them so much as it was once again about Jesus. While his tormentors tried to belittle him, they instead only further convicted themselves, further revealed their utter evil, while further *elevating* Jesus. A king may appear regal in front of admiring legions. The King, our Savior Messiah, the Son of God, may have appeared most majestic in this one last scene in which he stood silent, beaten, bloodied, condemned, without defender, and yet still in resolute pursuit of his redemptive end. In contemplating the appellate scene, he could only think again and again, *glory to the King at his highest.*

144 Scourged.

Mark 15:15; *see also* Matthew 27:26; John 19:1.

As just indicated, the Gospels record that on affirming the religious leaders' conviction, the Roman governor Pilate ordered Jesus flogged, as some translations state it, or *scourged*, as other translations state it, before his crucifixion. Research indicates that Roman scourging was not a light punishment with rod or stick meant to straighten the sufferer onto the right path. Rather, depending on the intent of the soldier executing the punishment, leather lashes embedded with lead and chips of bone, applied repeatedly across the prisoner tied to a post, exposed muscle, organs, and bone. Recovery was little prospect, certainly not if the soldier didn't desire it. Yet when the soldiers had completed Jesus's scourging, they were not done. The account records that they gathered around him, stripped him of his clothes, put a scarlet robe on him, and put a painful crown of thorns on his head. Putting a staff in his right hand, they then mocked him as the Jews' king, spitting on him and striking with his staff repeatedly on his thorn-crowned head. Their brutal mockery complete, they replaced the robe with his clothes before leading him away to crucify him.

The image of Jesus scourged, stripped and flogged challenges the follower to reflect on the scene's meaning. Followers should make no mistake: scourging was the cruelest, most hideous form of torture, very likely to result in the most painful possible death. Summary execution was possible then, as it is possible and accomplished now. Rights judged fundamental in civil society today would prohibit torturing prisoners with punishment like Jesus's scourging before execution. What then could the scene of Jesus's scourging possibly add for the follower's reflection? Why must we follow a *scourged* Lord rather than simply an executed, crucified Lord? While the scene's meanings may be various or obscure, one good possibility is that the punishment must match the depth of the wrong. God accepts his Son's sacrifice in redemption for *every* sin. By giving his Son in redemption, God gave *all*, just as God had to give all for the redemption to be complete and therefore effective. Any reduction in the punishment might reduce and thus eliminate the full effect of the redemption. The world needed to see both the depth of the sin, in that men would torture and crucify the one perfectly innocent man, but also the height of the redemption, in that God would accept his Son's torture and crucifixion. One thing from the scene is certain that in his Son's scourging before crucifixion God could have given nothing more than he gave.

She had not at first understood what Jesus endured just before he endured the unendurable event of his crucifixion. She had read of Jesus's flogging, each time thinking of the many times that she had read or heard of others suffering whipping, flogging, or lashing. It must have been painful, she thought, but then, he was about to die by crucifixion, which must have been so many times worse. Then she learned more about the kind of scourging that the Romans inflicted, the lead-tipped lashes, the ripping of the flesh and exposing of bone, and the nearly certain death that would quickly follow. She thought only briefly of the new, more-accurate image she then had of Jesus's scourging. Her new understanding quickly drove home the scene's point. Jesus died the ugliest, most-painful possible way that one could die, she finally and fully realized. Jesus, her beloved Jesus, this exquisite God-man who healed so generously and lived so gorgeously, died brutally without the least shred of comfort, solace, or humanity, doing so for her. She had long known the latter part that he had died for her. Now, for the first time, she had a sound and unshakeable, if appalling, view of what *dying* had actually meant. No, she would never again take lightly that phrase *dying for her*, even though crucifixion had long for her carried its own powerfully appalling image. Jesus suffered in a way that no one but Jesus could have endured, she now knew. And for this suffering, if possible she now loved him so much more.

145 **Burdened.**

Luke 23:26; *see also* Matthew 27:32; Mark 15:21; John 19:17.

Followers have another difficult but important scene on which to reflect, once again revealing more of the glorious Christ, in the soldiers' transport of Jesus to the place of his crucifixion. One of the four parallel Gospel accounts records that Jesus carried his own cross from the place of his flogging in Jerusalem's military headquarters out to where the soldiers would crucify him at the place of the Skull also known as Golgotha. Other accounts indicate that the soldiers responsible for carrying out Jesus's crucifixion seized and forced Simon of Cyrene to carry Jesus's cross for him, suggesting to some that Jesus at some point in the awful procession was no longer physically able to complete the impossibly arduous task but to others that he consented. One account indicates that Simon had simply been passing by when conscripted for his terrible yet enormously compassionate duty. Another account identifies the cross-bearing Simon as the father of Alexander and Rufus, possibly suggesting that those two children accompanied Simon on his conscripted duty. Jesus bore his cross, but so did Simon. One account indicates that many followed Jesus in procession, the women mourning and wailing. Remarkably, Jesus turned to tell them not to weep for him but instead for themselves and their children for the terrifying times to come. Jesus quoted scripture in doing so. Accounts of the procession end with the soldiers offering Jesus a sedative mixture to drink just before his crucifixion. He refused. Jesus had borne his cross and would now endure his crucifixion.

The image of Jesus bearing, meaning physically dragging, his cross toward crucifixion, so far as he must have been able or consented to do so, and then sharing his cross burden with the conscripted father visiting Jerusalem, carries its own important meaning for followers who reflect on it. The agony of dragging one's own cross, presumably a heavy apparatus, to the place of one's own crucifixion after an all-night ordeal, brutal scourging, and other beatings and ridicule, is practically unimaginable. The event stands as further indication of the brutality of Jesus's punishment. Yet the scene's allegorical meaning also stands out. Jesus spoke about bearing one's cross, saying also that the burden he asks us to bear is light. Jesus bore the heavy burden of our sin, leaving in contrast an airy light cross for us to bear. God does not demand scourging and crucifixion from us, his Son having already paid our punishment's price. That Jesus shared the burden with another may suggest to followers that we bear only Jesus's cross, the commitment to reliance on Jesus's completed work, rather than the many crosses, none of them redemptive, that the world would have us suffer. As wrenching as the scene is in the agony and anticipation that it depicts, followers may still draw from it deep meaning as to the character of Christ in his magnificent mission.

The *light cross* was one of his favorite constructs on which to reflect for all of the meaning that it divulged from the tension of its image. Crucifixion's cross is by no means a light tool or light emotional, psychic, or spiritual burden, he knew. A literal cross would have been heavy to bear, not light. Carrying one's cross to one's own crucifixion would have been an intolerable mental and spiritual burden, he fully and quite soberly understood. Those facts were why he so deeply appreciated the image and construct of Jesus having already borne the cross that he, not Jesus, deserved. Then, because Jesus had taken his *heavy* cross rather than Jesus's cross, he could carry the *light* cross or burden of Jesus. Jesus had no guilt and so had no cross of his own. Jesus should have borne no burden. While he understood these meanings and much appreciated that he had a very light burden now to carry, he valued them even more because of the debt that they demonstrated he owed to

Jesus. A light burden is one thing. A light burden *in consequence of another's heavy burden* is quite another thing. The scene of Jesus painfully dragging his cross, not Jesus's cross but *his* cross, didn't just lighten the cross that Jesus asked him to bear but also deepened to the greatest possible depth the degree to which he appreciated how much he owed Jesus. He could never quite hear the simple though profound phrase that Jesus had *given his life* for him without also thinking of just what that giving had meant for Jesus, to whom he now owed all.

146 Crucified.

Matthew 27:35; *see also* Mark 15:24; Luke 23:39; John 19:17.

The Gospels record Jesus's long-prophesied crucifixion, in enough difficult detail to give followers substantial ground for deep reflection. The soldiers crucified Jesus at the place of Skull, on the cross that he and Simon had borne there. Meaning to mock Jesus but doing so in unintentional confirmation of his true identity, the soldiers placed the sign above Jesus's head *King of the Jews*. The Roman governor had ordered the sign written in three languages so that all could read it. The religious leaders objected that Jesus was not their king, but the governor ruled having written *what I have written*. Hideous in itself, crucifixion further subjects the slow-dying victim to observers' scorn. The Gospels record that passersby hurled insults at Jesus, mocking him, again in unintended prophecy, for having claimed to be the Son of God who would destroy and rebuild the temple in three days. The temple to which Jesus had referred, his own person, would indeed rise again in three days. The religious leaders, also present at the crucifixion, likewise heaped scorn on the dying Son of God. The soldiers had crucified two criminals, one to either side of Jesus, who also heaped insults on Jesus. One account, though, indicates that one of the two criminals chastised the other that they were properly condemned, while Jesus was innocent, and that both should fear God. As an earlier section already recounted, Jesus replied that the confessing criminal would that day be with Jesus in paradise. As they stood guard, the soldiers gambled for Jesus's clothing by casting lots, fulfilling yet another prophecy.

These events framed the all-at-once enormously significant, profane, and poignant scene of Jesus crucified.

The image of Jesus crucified is of course central to every followers' reflections on the experience, work, and mission of Christ. Ironic for what the Romans intended as an instrument of the most shameful death, the cross is Christianity's central salvation symbol, reminding the follower of all that Christ suffered while also reminding the follower of all that Christ achieved. Ancient prophecies of healing snakes on sticks, pierced hands and feet, and death on a tree had shown that the Messiah would die pierced and lifted up. Crucifixion's cross fulfilled those prophecies. A follower can duly reflect on the cross, the cross, all about the cross. Still, the crucifixion scene itself carries its own contemplative value beyond the cross's profound and inexhaustible image. Christ rises above the scene triumphant, in full glory, not in the world's manner of celebrating triumphs and glorifying heroes but in perfectly willing witness to his Father's own will. Sacrificial love in service of all humankind rose above the very venomous cruelty that love's death and death's love fully redeemed. Only a dying criminal, the lowest of the low, sees the scene as all should and so instantly receives the full reward, *paradise*, for doing so. The scene's every image, every word, every horrible prophetic turn, drips with the cleansing blood of the glorious Son of Man dying on history's hinge, his great redemption. Reflect on, oh follower, for in this scene lies your own redemption.

She had so many images in her mind's eye of the crucifixion scene that she sometimes didn't know which one of them on which to reflect, to which to grasp as she once again mulled the crucifixion. She realized that some of her images were apocryphal, the product of books or films rather than the scriptures to which she so closely adhered. She tried to sort real from fictional, tried to keep them straight, wondering at the same time what license the Holy Spirit would give her to see in the Gospels' stark descriptions the full humanity and divinity of the event itself. She could picture the religious leaders' condemnatory expressions, the soldiers' callous boredom, the criminals' pain, and the disgust and superiority of the passersby who hurled insults at her dying Lord. She could imagine the dust of the hill, the darkening sky, the wood of the cross beams, and the running and coagulating blood everywhere, even its revolting smell. The one thing that she always hesitated to picture, though, was her Lord himself. Every time she tried to look on him, particularly at his face, she failed. She could only get so far in conjuring his image before emotion, deep, welling, tearful emotion, would stop her. One thought of his potential gaze, of how his eyes must have expressed all that he in those dying moments must have wished, willed, and felt, would completely arrest her. Her world, whatever attention or action it required or demanded of her right then, would simply stop. She had nothing left to do but commune with her Lord, holding onto him so tight as if he was right then carrying her aloft to the Father. She knew that resurrection didn't work exactly that way but just couldn't shake the image that in those last moments, Jesus was carrying her spirit, everyone's spirit, all who would just momentarily embrace him. And so she would just hold on tight to his breast, to his waist, to his knees, to his feet, clutching at whatever she could of him that she would be wherever he was right then, borne aloft on her cross.

147 Separated.

Matthew 27:45; *see also* Mark 15:33; Luke 23:44; John 19:30.

An event occurred during Jesus's crucifixion to which the Gospels only indirectly refer but that nonetheless constitutes a significant experience and characteristic of Jesus. Jesus's taking on the world's sin in crucifixion *separated* Jesus from his Father. Momentarily, the Son of God lived apart from the Father. The Gospels record that from noon on the day of Jesus's crucifixion until three in the afternoon *darkness came over all the land*. At that three o'clock hour, one imagines the darkest moment, the accounts record Jesus crying out *my God, my God*, asking why his Father had forsaken him. One onlooker, among others who thought that Jesus had called the prophet Elijah, ran for a stick with which to lift a wine-vinegar-soaked sponge to Jesus to drink. One account confirms that Jesus had asked for and took that drink. The other onlookers then said to leave Jesus alone to see if Elijah indeed came, as they had assumed Jesus intended. Jesus finally cried out again in a loud voice, as one account records saying *Father, into your hands I commit my spirit*, and as the accounts further state, gave up his spirit with his last breath. One account adds Jesus saying *it is finished,* or in some translations *accomplished*, as he bowed his head with his last breath. Accounts describe the temple's tall, thick curtain tearing completely apart at that moment, revealing its inner sanctum, symbolic of the union of God and humankind following atonement. One account records the earth shaking, rocks splitting, and tombs breaking open, out of which many holy people came back to life. The accounts of Jesus's separation from his Father end with the centurion posted to observe Jesus's extraordinary death pronouncing that surely Jesus had been a righteous man and the Son of God.

The image of Jesus separated from his Father in crucifixion, confirmed by Jesus acknowledging himself forsaken, and as the mid-day darkness also symbolized, should serve followers for deep reflection. Odd as it may seem to we who are so captive in these natural bodies, Jesus's greatest agony, greatest loss, greatest fear would not have been his body's demise but rather separation from his Father. As awful as Jesus's scourging, beating, and crucifixion all were, the Gospels record nothing of any complaint from him until he reached the point that the Father withdrew his presence in noon-hour darkness, as the Father must have withdrawn when the Son momentarily assumed the world's sin. Then, and only then, did Jesus cry out to his Father in loss. We think the ripping lashes of the scourge to have been the Son's pain, or the rough nails through his sensitive hands and feet. But no, the Son's greatest pain was losing his Father, descending into an isolation from his beloved One that he had never before felt. Followers should not only see the crucifixion as Jesus's physical punishment for their sins, not primarily see what Jesus suffered as natural pain, natural demise, natural death, but instead as spiritual separation and death. Those who together had conceived and formed the universe had torn themselves apart in a cataclysm and calamity greater than any other even possible. All beauty and order, all law and justice, all good and right, indeed all life, should have ended at that momentary separation but for the Father's once-in-history, never-to-be-repeated redemptive plan. These are the sorts of profound things on which followers might reflect in Jesus's separation from his Father.

He could sense from the darkened mid-day sky, tearing of the huge curtain, the earthquake splitting rocks and opening tombs, and holy dead walking, that separation of Father and Son had turned something wild loose in creation. Whether that wildness was in the Father's anger, tears, or joy, he didn't know. Of all things, he found that he couldn't really imagine just how the Father must have felt in seeing his Son achieve the great challenge and plan that the Father had set forth, that plan that required that the Son leave the Father. Fathers would usually feel a mix of pride and accomplishment mixed with sorrow and loss when an adult child ventures boldly forth. Yet he fully appreciated that no father and son had ever had the fiercely loving, endlessly creative, and eternally enduring relationship that Jesus had with his Father up until that moment of their separation. So again, he could only imagine from the spectacular events at that momentous moment that the Father for a moment let something go free in creation that he had never before freed and might never free in quite the same way again. He imagined that what the Father had momentarily let go, not impetuously but ferociously, that which shook the earth, split rocks, and raised the dead, was something of himself, of that fierce love that had bound Father so perfectly to Son. He imagined that while the Father could have restrained himself as he so often did, the moment instead called for the Father to show his wild love for the Son and for all whom he and the Son had made in their image. He also imagined himself walking out of the broken tombs, between the split rocks, past the torn curtain, and toward the Son's arms awaiting resurrection.

148 **Mourned.**

Luke23:48; *see also* Mark 15:40; John 19:25.

While passersby, the religious leaders, and the criminals crucified with Jesus all mocked or hurled insults at Jesus on the cross, the Gospels record that some who had followed Jesus from Galilee to Jerusalem also stood nearby, presumably in shock and mourning. These followers included Jesus's mother Mary and her sister, the disciple John, Mary Magdalene, Salome, and another Mary. The latter women had followed and cared for Jesus during his public ministry. One account records that many other women who had come up to Jerusalem with Jesus were also at the crucifixion scene, standing at a distance watching. The Gospels say little about how these followers reacted, although one can imagine in horror, fear, and grief. One account records that Jesus noticed his mother Mary, telling her that his disciple John was now her son and John that Jesus's mother Mary was now John's mother. The account further records that John thereafter took in Mary to care for her, as

Jesus clearly intended. Another account records that those who had gathered to witness the crucifixion beat their breasts as they left, clearly indicating deep distress as they mourned Jesus's death. Jesus was thus not entirely alone at his demise but witnessed his mother and likely others in mourning.

The image of Jesus mourned over his death has significance for followers who reflect on it. Every follower has to some degree contemplated Jesus's crucifixion. Although its salvation purpose is today fully evident, the purpose of Jesus's death then had not yet registered with those followers who actually observed Jesus dying on the cross. Some and perhaps all had heard Jesus teach and preach about his death, but nothing about the scene or its aftermath suggests that those followers who actually observed Jesus's crucifixion experienced anything less than shock and deep grief. As just indicated above, one account records their beating of breasts, which constituted a public showing of extreme sorrow or sometimes, though not likely so much here, anger. Jesus must have witnessed some of their grief because in his last individual communication he instructed his disciple John in the care of his mother, whose extreme distress at the crucifixion of her son one can only barely imagine. Followers contemplating Jesus's crucifixion today thus have a model or image through which to interpret their own mourning. One can mourn Christ's death even while fully appreciating his victory and our victory in the salvation that it accomplished. No one needs to rejoice in crucifixion. All can mourn, as Jesus saw his mother, disciple, and other followers mourn, even while drawing closely to Jesus to accept his spectacular beneficence.

Jesus's crucifixion still shocked her. As many times as she had read about it, seen portrayals of it, and thought about it, the image of Jesus nailed to a cross and lifted up on it still wrenched her heart, causing her to mourn. She knew intellectually of its necessity and of course fully appreciated its personal benefit to her in salvation, but it still troubled her deeply. For a while, she had wondered whether something was wrong with her and whether she should instead in some sense rejoice over the cross. Yet as she thought about the scene of Mary, the disciples, and the other women and followers standing nearby or at a distance, watching Jesus die and then beating their breasts as they left, she too grieved with them. At other times, she would rejoice at her risen Lord, but she wanted also to be able to grieve at her dying Lord, grieve with the followers who had witnessed it. No, she decided, nothing was wrong with her that she felt such deep sorrow over the crucifixion. Even though she had hindsight's benefit and knew to a certainty of Jesus's subsequent rising, she could still feel at least a little as the followers then must have felt, at least in order that she more-fully appreciate the Lord's rising.

[149] **Pierced.**

John 19:34.

The Gospels record Jesus pierced, the significance of which the account and its interpretation together reveal. Accounts of Jesus's death on the cross indicate that the religious leaders didn't want the bodies of Jesus and the two criminals crucified with him left overnight on the crosses into the upcoming special Sabbath. The bloody bodies would have desecrated the Sabbath, this one following the Passover feast and doubtless drawing larger crowds. So at the religious leaders' request, the Roman governor approved that the soldiers break the legs of the crucified men, which would have hastened their death through suffocation. The soldiers first broke the legs of the criminals to Jesus's left and right. Jesus, though, had already died, when they came next to do the same to him. Instead of breaking Jesus's legs, a soldier pierced Jesus's side with the soldier's spear. The account, in the Gospel of the disciple John whom accounts confirm stood nearby with Jesus's mother, records that blood and water poured out of the wound in Jesus's side. John makes the point of testifying that he saw that the soldiers did not break Jesus's legs and also saw the pierced wound and poured-out blood, fulfilling prophecies as to both. Jesus died pierced, his blood pouring out.

The image of Jesus *pierced* carries special meaning for the follower's reflection. While odd to the modern ear, the word *pierced* is one that many followers closely associate with Jesus's crucifixion. They do so in part because of the extraordinary ancient prophecies both that the world would look on the pierced Messiah and that they would pierce the Messiah's hands and feet. Jesus fulfilled every prophecy in birth, life, and death. Yet followers also know that as the sacrificial Lamb of God,

Jesus's blood plays a special role in cleansing the follower of sin. Jesus's death culminated the sacrificial system. Many animals had died in bloody ceremony as the people of Israel brought sacrifices for their sin. When the soldier pierced Jesus's side and his blood poured out, God had both made and accepted a sacrifice that would supersede and end all other sacrifice. God had judged that to accomplish that end of a superseding sacrifice, the pierced Jesus would bleed. Followers know the image as one of having been *cleansed by the blood of the Lamb*. Piercing thus carries a broader meaning of having suffered critically not needlessly or for the sake of suffering but to save and rescue another, as in *Jesus pierced for us*. In sacrificial love's terms, Jesus could do no better than to be pierced for all.

He had long had a strong image of the pierced Jesus. He seldom really even thought of Jesus without seeing in his image his scarred hands and feet. He remembered that Jesus had shown his pierced hands and side to doubting Thomas after Jesus's resurrection. He imagined that when he met Jesus, Jesus would have the scarred hands, feet, and side. While the thought of anything scarring his glorious Savior was incongruous, he had always still felt that it must be so. Jesus's scars, he supposed, would be like the battle scars that a soldier wears proudly, except that he knew that Jesus had far greater reason than pride to exhibit his piercing scars. He supposed that in his deep and thorough, or better yet *complete*, reliance on Jesus's redemptive work, he might just need those scars as evidence of Jesus's sacrifice. He thought, too, of the slain-looking Lamb taking the throne of God. From these scenes and images, he drew that God was fine with a slain-looking Lamb or pierce-scarred Jesus. Jesus had borne those wounds for him. Jesus had no need of hiding them, and he had no desire that Jesus would do so. While he withered at the thought of anyone harming his Savior, he nonetheless felt that when he met Jesus, he might look especially at his scarred hands, side, and feet in full and constant reminder of just what his Lord had accomplished for him and what that accomplishment had cost.

150 Buried.

Mark 15:43; *see also* Luke 23:52; John 19:38.

The final event, scene, or image of Jesus's sacrifice involved his burial. Consider Jesus buried. The Gospels record a remarkable event that two of the religious leaders took steps to see that Jesus received a proper burial. One was Nicodemus who had much earlier visited Jesus at night. The other was Joseph of Arimathea whom an account records secretly followed Jesus, secretly because he feared what the other religious leaders would do to him for following Jesus in pursuit of the kingdom of God. Another account identifies Joseph as a *good and upright man* who had refused consent to Jesus's conviction. Joseph first asked the Roman governor for Jesus's body. Joseph's request was bold in part because night was approaching and in part because of the suspicion that such an early request might have engendered. Indeed, one account records that the Roman governor first summoned the centurion to ensure that Jesus had in fact already died. The governor granted Joseph's request only after receiving the centurion's confirmation, thus allowing Joseph to retrieve Jesus's body from the cross. If Joseph had not acted so boldly, one supposes that Jesus's body might not have had a timely traditional burial, especially insofar as it was the day before the Sabbath when none would have done the preparation work. Nicodemus then brought a large quantity of myrrh and aloe to apply as he and Joseph wrapped the body with linen strips that Joseph had bought. A garden at the site of the crucifixion held a new tomb in which no body had yet laid. Joseph and Nicodemus laid Jesus's body in that tomb, Joseph rolling a big stone against the tomb's entrance. Mary Magdalene and another Mary, mother of Joseph, watched where the men laid Jesus's body. One account records that the next day, the chief priests asked the Roman governor to post a guard and seal the tomb so that the disciples could not steal the body to claim that Jesus had indeed risen after three days as he had proclaimed he would. Thus ends the scene of Jesus, now buried.

The tender scene of Jesus's swift and sure burial leaves a sad but strong and final image of sacrifice on which followers may reflect. Jesus died, no doubt. The centurion charged with ensuring it, and whose career and probably also life depended on it, confirmed it. Two religious leaders, secret followers each, prepared the body and placed it in the tomb behind a stone rolled across the tomb's entrance. The scene has an unmistakable finality to it. Jesus must die, and die he did, as his burial confirmed. One supposes that he could have morphed from living to crucified to risen, as passersby to the crucifixion cruelly mocked that any authentic Son of God should do. Yet anything less than centurion-certified death and a full burial might leave open the possibility that his punishment was incomplete and thus our redemption ineffective. The Father would instead leave us with a heartbreaking scene and image of his Son's utter death, certain death, certified-and-buried death. As reflective followers, we can nearly place ourselves in the role that the secret followers Nicodemus and Joseph undertook, imagining Christ's lifeless body in our hands as we coat it with the myrrh mixture and wrap it in linen to lie dark in the virgin tomb. One would not so reflect out of morbidity but instead for the simple truth that Christ died, as dead as any other body prepared for burial and then buried. And he died *for us*.

She had heard the phrase so many times that once in a while, especially when said too quickly, lightly, or tritely, *Christ died for us* momentarily seemed to lose its meaning. On the few occasions when she realized that she was losing something huge and essential in that phrase's meaning, she had one image that always set her aright, not the image of the cross but the image of Christ's burial. Strictly, she supposed, the cross was only *killing* Christ, while the painful scene of Christ's burial fully reflected that Christ *died* for us. In some ways, as aching as the burial images were, she often preferred them for reflection over the wrenching scenes around the cross. Although she suspected that they might have had to rush the body's preparation given the late hour and approaching Sabbath, she imagined Nicodemus and Joseph being especially reverent in handling Jesus's body. She also wondered with some excitement whether they suspected anything yet to come, although she imagined not. She often thought, too, of the women who watched the men work at the body's preparation and watched them lay the body to rest in the tomb. She imagined herself one of those women, even as she reflected on the scene. Something told her that she would have been one of those women watching the burial, one of those women who had followed and cared for Jesus right up to the cross. Something further told her that she might have been one of those women returning to the empty tomb, seeing there only a familiar-looking gardener who just might call her name.

7

His Resurrection

Living. Matthew 22:32. ***Transient.*** John 7:33. ***Conferrer.*** John 7:38. ***Glorified.*** John 17:5. ***Announced.*** Matthew 28:2. ***Appearing.*** Matthew 28:9. ***Disguised.*** John 20:14. ***Doubted.*** John 20:25. ***Rebuking.*** Mark 16:14. ***Greeting.*** Matthew 28:9. ***Conversing.*** Matthew 28:18. ***Opposed.*** Matthew 28:12. ***Physical.*** Luke 24:39. ***Identifiable.*** Luke 24:39. ***Functional.*** Luke 24:40. ***Ascended.*** Luke 24:51.

Jesus's resurrection marked a new stage in his life, just as it marked a new stage in the lives of every other living being. That anyone would rise after death meant something entirely new. That this extraordinary God-man would rise after death precisely as he prophesied meant so much more, indeed everything. Jesus's prime purpose within the Trinity was to reflect the Father's love not just for the Son but for all humankind through this astonishingly unique, exorbitantly obedient, and fully redemptive sacrifice, all purpose for which the Trinity would lose were it not also for the resurrection that followed. One could have nothing other than that pristine morning's momentary recognition of Jesus's resurrection on which to dwell, about which to think for every remaining moment of the rest of one's life, and one would still have more to witness, more to think, more to appreciate. Jesus's resurrection also revealed new attributes of the Godhead, as this part attempts in small ways to suggest if not adequately document. Just as followers may reflect with good motive and effect on the other stages of Jesus's life, so too may followers find rich relationship with Jesus when contemplating his resurrection. And why not? What, or more precisely *who*, would Jesus be without his resurrection as the once-again living Son of God? Reflect frequently and deeply on Jesus's resurrection, and you in no part will have regretted it.

151 Living.

Matthew 22:32; *see also* Acts 1:3.

As a preliminary to reflecting on Jesus's actual resurrection, first consider that the Gospels clearly record Jesus expressing his confidence in resurrection and also his teaching about resurrection from the scriptures. Jesus knew that God had life within him and that he, too, as the Son of God, was also the living author of life who could not die without resurrection. Very shortly before his arrest, late in his final week in Jerusalem, Jesus faced questioning from a sect of religious leaders who spoke against resurrection. They asked Jesus how could a widow who by law had married brothers seven successive times as each died childless possibly meet those seven husbands in heaven when resurrected. Jesus turned the leaders back to the scriptures, saying that they knew neither the scriptures nor God's power. Those whom God resurrects do not marry because they will be *like angels in heaven*, Jesus explained, apparently confirming marriage as solely an earthly institution. Yet more so, Jesus continued, the scriptures showed that well after Abraham, Isaac, and Jacob had died, God had said that he is their God, *I am the God of Abraham, Isaac, and Jacob*. How, Jesus asked, could God be their God if they were not living, when everyone knows that God is over not the dead but the living? The account reports that Jesus's explanation astonished the crowds hearing it. Jesus had shown that the religious leaders who did not accept resurrection didn't even know their own scriptures. Jesus had proven them wrong using God's own words. The living God must be God over the living. As the Son of the living God, Jesus knew that his resurrection was certain. The account ends with Jesus using other scriptures to refute other religious leaders who tested him with questions. Jesus would live again, as to which the book of Acts records that he *gave many convincing proofs*.

The scene of Jesus teaching the religious leaders and crowds about resurrection shortly before his own death and resurrection should give encouragement to followers who reflect on it. Those who contemplate Jesus's resurrection may mistakenly do so as if it is an act, deed, event, or condition in some sense independent of God, something that he could either do or not do for his followers, unrelated to his character. Yet as Jesus suggested in the account summarized above, God, who lived before creation and is the creator of life and God of the living, plainly has life within him. He cannot deny his own character as God of the living. The scriptures also describe Jesus, the Son of God with the Father in him, as the *author* of life. The living Son of God, as the author of life and with life in him, cannot die without resurrection and yet still be who he is. He holds life not as we do by gift of God but instead inherently because he *is* God. In the above account, Jesus revealed that God's character as God of the living induces him to resurrect his followers. If he did not do so, then he would be denying himself, contradicting his own character. God could not be Abraham's God if Abraham were dead. Jesus would live because he must be the living God, while Abraham, Isaac, Jacob, and followers of Jesus would also live because Jesus is God of the living. Jesus is life. Jesus is living.

Reflecting on Jesus's explanation of resurrection caused him to realize that he had been thinking about God wrong and probably also been thinking the wrong way about life. He had long known the obvious that life comes and goes from natural beings. We hold life only for a time, as other things live only for a time. He had thought of life only in this way as transient, temporary, passing from here to gone. Yet he had also thought of God as only living in this same sense, when he now realized that God could not live or *have* life in the same way that he *gives* life. To give others life, he realized that God must instead in some sense *hold life within him* or have life inherently, or in some like way *be* life. Maybe, he thought, God *is* life in somewhat the same way that the Bible says that God *is* love. God does not merely love but *is* love, and so God does not merely live but *is* life. To live, then, is to be connected in some way to God, to have the life of God in one. One lives only in relation to God. He knew that Jesus had restored several persons to life during his public ministry, and so evidently Jesus could *give* life. He figured that Jesus must therefore in some sense *hold* life or *be* life. God did not merely live as we live but instead creates or authors and then sustains life. If one then takes the life of Jesus as a follower of Jesus, then with Jesus's life within one, resurrection follows. He wasn't sure that he had the thought right, but he knew that he needed to think differently both about God living and also about the nature of life, particularly when it comes to resurrection.

152 **Transient.**

John 7:33; *see also* John 13:36.

As another preliminary to reflection on Jesus's resurrection, consider next that resurrection first implies the impermanence or transience of Jesus's time on earth in public ministry. That Jesus was here only for a time before returning to his heavenly kingdom must have prime significance for followers. As he concluded his public ministry, Jesus knew and expressed that his presence was transient, temporary, or impermanent. The Gospels record Jesus teaching in the temple courts in the middle of his final fateful week of Passover in Jerusalem. His teaching on this late occasion impressed the crowds just as it usually did, indeed so much so that the account records that many in the crowd *put their faith in Jesus*. Having seen some of what Jesus did, they simply wondered whether any other Christ would do more miracles. When the religious leaders perceived the crowd's burgeoning faith, they felt the need to take prompt action to arrest Jesus. Yet Jesus told the temple guards sent to arrest him that he would be with them *only for a short time* before he left for the one who sent him. Then they would search fruitlessly for Jesus because they could not go where he had gone. The Jews who heard him wondered where Jesus meant to go where the guards and others could not find him. Maybe he would follow the other diaspora Jews to teach among the Greeks, they even speculated. The Jews kept wondering aloud what Jesus meant about leaving for a place where they would not be able to go to find him. Another Gospel account records Peter asking at the Last Supper to follow Jesus to the place that Jesus had just explained again that he was going. Jesus replied that although they could not go with him now, they would indeed join him there later. Jesus was here only for a short time, as are we, each transient and impermanent on our way to eternal destination.

The scene of Jesus coaching the Jews that he was among them only for a short time and would soon leave for another place where they could not go or find him should remind followers of Jesus's kingdom home. As much as we naturally treat our present world as home, Jesus made clear that the world in which we live was not his permanent home, suggesting that it is also not our permanent home. Jesus admitted a transience to his earthly ministry, again maybe in the way that we should admit an impermanence or transience. The world engages us but does not hold us. We live here with only one foot planted, the other foot leading us heavenward toward our permanent home. Jesus felt and expressed his transient presence on earth, letting it lend both perspective and urgency to his actions. Nothing that he did here was to be final, concrete, and permanent but instead all to invite and reflect what he would do eternally in his kingdom. So, too, nothing that followers do here is final and permanent but all to point the follower heavenward into company with Jesus. We do not build solidly if all we build is here. We build here instead with an eye toward how what we will build here reflects our heavenly eternity. Transience is a critical quality of the follower's sound view, when followers reflect accurately on Jesus's own transitory earthly presence.

She recognized that her heavenly attraction, her leaning forward toward her eternal destination, had grown significantly. That attraction had barely been a part of her early experiences, although even then she sensed that her life here was only transitory. Over the years, though, she thought more often and more deeply of the kingdom of heaven toward which Jesus had pointed her, where he himself had gone. As she thought more often and deeply about heaven, she realized more fully and more-fully embraced that heaven was her ultimate destination. She first had to learn more about the kingdom before the Spirit could develop in her a stronger sense that the kingdom was her destination. Gradually, she gained more understanding of the richness, activity, liberty, and joy of the kingdom, and of the Christ-like identity and resurrected body that she would retain in it. She knew that she could know only small parts of her future eternal residence. God revealed only what would lead her gently forward to it, without causing her to abandon important work here. She suspected that if she knew too much of the kingdom that she would promptly quit her work here. Yet she treasured the glimpses that the Spirit gave her, glimpses that caused her to redouble and deepen her current eternal service. While the sense of life's transience had for a time puzzled and even burdened her, of late she had embraced it, letting it imbue her life with rich urgency. She was on her way to Jesus but all in good time with plenty yet to accomplish.

153 Conferrer.

John 7:38; *see also* Luke 24:49; John 14:16, 15:26, 16:7, 20:22; Acts 1:4, 2:1.

Followers know that Jesus's limited public ministry would not only end in Jesus's resurrection but that his ascension would make room for the coming of the Holy Spirit. Jesus, by leaving, would confer the Spirit in his stead. The Gospels record Jesus publicly announcing that the Spirit would come, when he addressed the crowd at the last and greatest day of the festival Feast just before his arrest, conviction, and crucifixion. Jesus stood in Jerusalem's temple courts saying in a loud voice that all who thirst should come to him for drink. Jesus added that the scriptures themselves said that those who believed in him would find *streams of living water* flowing from within them. The Gospel account then states expressly that what Jesus meant was that believers would soon receive *the Spirit*. The account further explains that God had not yet given the Spirit because the Father had not yet glorified Jesus. Jesus's crucifixion and resurrection were necessary for the Spirit to come. Some in the crowd reacted to Jesus's pronouncement saying that he was the Prophet while others added that he was indeed the Christ. At the Last Supper the night of his arrest, Jesus repeated that if the disciples did as he commanded, then he would ask the Father to give the disciples the *Counselor,* the *Holy Spirit,* to be with them forever to remind them of Jesus's words and teach them all things. The Spirit would live with them and be in them. Jesus explained to the disciples that he had to leave them in order to send them the Counselor who would not come unless Jesus left. Jesus through his glorification would confer on his followers the precious Holy Spirit. Even after his resurrection, Jesus repeated to the disciples in the upper room that he was going to send them what his Father promised such that they should remain in the city until the Father had clothed them with *power from on high*. Another account records that Jesus *breathed on them*, saying to *receive the Holy Spirit*. The book of Acts confirms that Jesus told them to wait in Jerusalem for a few more days until God baptized them with the Holy Spirit. The disciples and the women who followed Jesus, including also his mother Mary and his brothers, prayed constantly together until on the day of Pentecost the Holy Spirit descended in a roar like the wind, tongues of fire resting on each of them. Jesus came to confer the Holy Spirit.

The scenes of Jesus announcing before his crucifixion that the Spirit was soon to comfort, vitalize, and guide his followers, and then breathing on the disciples after his resurrection while telling them to receive the Spirit, conferring the Spirit on them, should be special encouragement to every follower. We do not have Jesus's physical presence as the disciples had his presence. While we have the Gospel record of his words and actions, Jesus's voice and presence cannot move us directly. God instead used Jesus's glorification and return to his kingdom to send the Holy Spirit to do those things that Jesus would have done if he were still present in physical person. In essence, Jesus is present in the person of the Holy Spirit, just as the Father was present in the person of Jesus. Followers who appreciate the incomparable gift of the Spirit within these nuanced mysteries must also appreciate Jesus's role in conferring the Spirit. We can infer from what Jesus told the crowd at the great Feast of the week of Passover that we would have no Spirit if not for Jesus's crucifixion, resurrection, and glorification. Jesus came as a conferrer not only of wisdom, and not at all of scholarly degrees, but of the precious Holy Spirit who guides us in all divine things. Followers do well to reflect on Jesus as the conferrer of the incomparable Holy Spirit, without whom followers would be bereft, still in mourning from loss of Jesus to the crucifixion and resurrection. God must have known that Jesus's magnificent ministry would leave followers desperate for the return of his presence and so granted fully equal gift in the person of the Holy Spirit.

Jesus breathing on the disciples while telling them that the Spirit was theirs was one of his favorite Gospel scenes. Surprisingly, although he would have marveled unimaginably at having walked with the physical Jesus, he nonetheless had no hard time trusting that the Spirit was his and that he was the Spirit's in full recompense of Jesus's absence. God had indeed granted a great gift in this ephemeral though wholly trustworthy, reliable, and welcome guide. He knew that the Spirit moved like the wind, without revealing its origin or destination, and so moved his people like the wind, reliably even if unpredictably. He loved exactly that unpredictable-but-reliable quality of the Spirit whom Jesus had so generously conferred on the disciples and by extension on him. Because of the Spirit's presence, he found that he could trust without necessarily knowing, rest without necessary place, and act without necessary plan. The Spirit knew, comforted, and planned, as long as he let the Spirit guide him. The Spirit gave him the words to speak and the acts to complete. The Spirit nudged him, making him restless just when he should move and act. The Spirit also restrained him, making him delay and rest just when he should wait. The Spirit also showed him Jesus in ever greater dimension and glory, giving him ever more reason to love and obey him. Jesus and the Spirit were indeed one in the Father, one conferring the other, one pointing to the other, all in one. He reflected again and again on this wondrous mystery just as Jesus had expressed it.

154 Glorified.

John 17:5; *see also* Mark 16:19.

As a section in the part above on Jesus's calling addresses, the Gospels record Jesus expressing as his core calling that he had come to *glorify* the Father. Yet at the same time that Jesus acknowledged his role in glorifying the Father, Jesus also expressed that he had another role in *receiving* the Father's glory. As previously described in that section above on Jesus's calling to glorify God, Jesus had been teaching the disciples at the Last Supper just before his arrest. He had then turned toward heaven to address his Father directly, saying that indeed the Son's role was to glorify the Father in all that the Son did. At the same moment, though, Jesus asked that the Father glorify the Son, true with the purpose that the Son would then glorify the Father, but yet with the clear request that the Son receive glory. Jesus came not just to glorify the Father but to receive the Father's glory. Indeed, in that same prayer to the Father that Jesus made aloud at the Last Supper for the disciples to hear, remember, recite, and share with others, Jesus said that he had already held glory with the Father *from before the world's beginning*. Jesus was glorified in heaven while also coming to first give glory on earth to the Father and then receive glory again from the Father. Jesus prayed aloud that the Father glorify Jesus in the Father's presence, in effect restoring Jesus's prior glory. The Father would soon raise the Son in glory to appear in resurrected body before the disciples and their companions, and then before hundreds. Gospel accounts end with Jesus's ascension into heaven to *sit at the right hand* of the Father, Jesus glorified.

Followers should reflect often on the image of Jesus glorified, of the Father answering Jesus's prayer and restoring Jesus to his side in resurrection, insofar as the image confirms a follower's future in eternal life. Salvation is not simply redemption *from* sin but also *to* eternal life. Jesus's resurrection and body transformed in glory assure followers of like life together, as Jesus told the thief on the cross, with him in paradise. The image, in other words, has something personal in it for followers, which is confidence in Jesus's resurrection and thus also in eternal life. Yet when Jesus spoke of his glorification that he would also glorify the Father, he was not directly addressing a follower's belief and salvation. He was instead speaking of something essential between Son and Father. Why is glory at God's heart? For followers, the answer is enough that God wills it so. God desires and commands the worship of his followers, indeed of all creatures. One also sees evidence, though, of God's design that he made humankind far better fit to pursue God's glory than to seek its own. Working consistently for God's glory rather than one's own ensures a life fit for its own design. Place praising and honoring the life of Christ in the center of your own life, and then just watch and take pleasure as your own blessings grow. Pursue a life of service in Christ, and the glorified God will shower blessings on you. Jesus glorified is a follower's central image for frequent reflection.

The concept of God's glory enthralled her. She had found from her first embrace of it that it freed something within her. She only later began to discover that what it freed most was her own unhealthy, inward-turning pursuit in worship of self. She didn't feel that she was particularly prideful or narcissistic. Everyone, she knew, is self-involved, and she also accepted that she was blind to her own self-involvement, especially when she remembered Christ having said something about the blind seeing and those who claiming sight being blind. Yet she also had long had a strong and healthy aversion to pride, arrogance, and self-worship in herself and others. She had just needed to figure out better how to avoid what was such a natural inclination to all. Somehow, she felt constituted to need *something* to worship, and so hence her enthrallment with God's glory. She had a built-in desire to build up, praise, honor, and exalt, to exult in and look up very high to someone or something. She had no doubt that her desire was for God. That she could glorify Christ in God's image gave her exactly that for which God had made her. Unlike the worship of anything else such as pleasure, productivity, material goods, or even nature, music, or art, she could worship Christ without damaging or damning herself, indeed while doing precisely the opposite. Her worship of Christ was the source of constant personal blessing, even though she did not seek directly to bless herself. God had made her to glorify his Son, and she very plainly and simply loved doing so. Of every blessing in her life, no one and nothing could take away her worship of Christ.

155 **Announced.**

Matthew 28:2; *see also* Mark 16:6; Luke 24:1; John 19:55.

Consider now Jesus's actual resurrection, the moment of his rising from the dead or, more precisely, the moment that his followers first heard and then saw that Jesus had indeed risen. The Gospels record that after Joseph and Nicodemus prepared Jesus's body for burial and Joseph laid it in the tomb, the Galilean women who had watched went home to prepare spices and perfumes with which to further treat and honor the body. Accounts record, though, that they would have to wait out the Sabbath obedient to the command before returning. The women did so right at dawn the day after the Sabbath. One account records that Mary Magdalene went while the sky was still dark. At dawn, accompanied by violent earthquake, the Lord's angel descended to the tomb, rolled back what one account calls the *very large* stone, and, improbably, sat on it, as another account records *on the right side*. The account describes the angel as appearing like lightning with brilliant white clothes, so startling that the tomb's guards shook until frozen as if dead. Knowing that the women had come to attend to Jesus's body, the angel first reassured the alarmed women not to be afraid. The angel then announced that Jesus was not in the tomb because *he had risen* just as he had said. The angel invited the women to see the empty tomb as evidence. The angel then directed the trembling and bewildered women to tell the disciples quickly that Jesus had risen and was on the way to Galilee where they would see him. The account ends saying that the women hurried dutifully away, both afraid and yet full of joy, to tell the disciples. Another account records not one but two gleaming figures announcing to the women that Jesus had risen, reminding them of his prophecy that he would do so. Another account states that Mary Magdalene was the first of the women to tell the disciples, corroborated by another account recording that Mary told Peter and John. One of the accounts records that two disciples who met Jesus on the road to Emmaus also returned to announce Jesus's resurrection to the disciples. A frightening angel accompanied by cataclysmic events, bewildered women, and excited disciples had each announced Jesus's resurrection.

Much as angels heralded to shepherds the Messiah's birth, the event of the angel's announcement of Jesus's resurrection bears a follower's reflection. These things, these momentous turnings of history, bear more than their mere occurrence. People announce everything, from the birth of babies and graduation or marriage of children to the opening of stores and anniversary of companies. Centennials and bicentennials gain even greater announcement, memorial, and celebration. Wouldn't the greatest event ever in the history of humankind bear greater announcement? Christ's resurrection wouldn't warrant merely a small notice in the newspaper or social media. Every follower should instead celebrate the correct image of a brilliant angel, alit like lightning and so fearsome as to stupefy and freeze toughened guards, whose lives depended on securing the tomb, descending to the tomb to roll back its large stone, accompanied by earthquake. The simple notice that the angel bore, *he rose just as he said*, would forever change the meaning of being human. If faith in Christ's resurrection is to mean what it should mean, then stop at that moment. *See* the angel. *Feel* if not the fear then the stupefaction at the news that the angel bore that the Son of God rose from death. Do not let that moment pass without announcement, without at least a momentary bewilderment at how profoundly the world and human existence had changed. Yes, the women would very soon see Jesus himself, as would the disciples. But their shocked joy at the angel's news preceded that meeting. God gave followers that moment. Know it, reflect on it, and deeply relish it.

He had such a hard time appreciating fully what Jesus's resurrection meant that he felt as if he had to take it a step at a time. Fortunately, the Gospels allowed him to do exactly that. His sense of frank bewilderment over Jesus's resurrection was exactly why he so much appreciated the details of these scenes of Jesus's disciples and followers discovering it. He thought again of the angel telling the women that Christ rose. He thought of how the angel might have appeared as the angel descended from heaven, the brilliance of its appearance, and the shaking earth that accompanied it. He considered how the guards reacted in stupor and how the women responded to the angel's news in what must have been wild joy as they hurried away. They clearly believed the angel's news, and of course, who wouldn't when the news announcer was so fearsome? These announcement events in some way made him more secure in his knowledge of what the resurrection meant. Who can know and appreciate resurrection abstractly? To rise again from the dead is something so shocking and yet also so organic that he felt that he needed to embrace it not so much intellectually but emotionally, almost viscerally as the women might have done in that moment. Before he could think deeply of Jesus walking, talking, and eating again, he had to think first of the women's frantic joy at the announcement. He had to have the anticipation of the angel pulling the theater's great curtain back before he could once again see Jesus. He needed, and had, an announcement.

156 Appearing.

Matthew 28:9; *see also* Matthew 28:17; Mark 16:9; Luke 24:13, 24:39; John 20:16; Acts 1:3.

The Gospels of course clearly record that Jesus appeared in resurrection, allowing many to confirm the occurrence of that most-momentous event. The first example, recorded in Matthew's Gospel, finds the women returning to the tomb as just described in the above section. Promptly after the angel announced that Jesus had risen and instructed the joyous women to go quickly tell the disciples, the account states that *Jesus met them*. Jesus appeared to the women, presumably outside or near the tomb. The women not only had the angel's announcement but actually saw Jesus, indeed clasped Jesus's feet in worship as the account further records. Another account records that Mary Magdalene, the one whom Jesus had cleansed of demons, was the first to see Jesus, immediately after she turned away from the two angels at the tomb. Another account also records that Mary Magdalene was the first of the women to see Jesus. The same account mentions that Jesus next appeared to two disciples *walking in the country*, who promptly returned to report his resurrection to the other disciples. A different account provides the detail that these disciples had been walking the seven miles from Jerusalem to Emmaus when Jesus appeared to walk and talk at length with them, even though the two only later recognized Jesus. Jesus then appeared twice to the disciples in the upper room to which they had retired in secret, as a subsequent section studies. He also appeared to three of the disciples as they fished and then had a meal with them. The disciples also saw and worshiped Jesus on the mountain in Galilee where he had sent them and where he gave them the Great Commission. The book of Acts confirms that over a period of forty days, Jesus made many appearances after resurrection and before his ascension.

The image of Jesus appearing suddenly to his disciples and followers is of enormous significant for followers when looking to Jesus. Resurrection implies appearing. One supposes that Jesus could have risen and returned to the Father without having shown himself to anyone. Someone then, maybe an angel or the Holy Spirit, might have informed one or more disciples or followers that indeed Christ had risen, from which news of the resurrection would then flow. That construct is probably what many persons who do not follow Christ, and possibly a few who do, believe of the faith, which is that no one *really* saw Christ who never *really* appeared to anyone. Yet we have the Gospel record that he did appear, the many occurrences of which absolutely confirmed Christ's resurrection. *Appearing* becomes an important part of resurrection, maybe the most important part for those who mistrust others' reports, even the announcement of angels. Yet putting aside the question of confidence in the resurrection, Jesus's appearances provide followers with important images for reflection. One need not reflect solely on Jesus's ministry and miracles. One may just as readily recall and contemplate Jesus in resurrection. Followers may indeed too infrequently think of the resurrected Jesus, where, when, and to whom he appeared. The number and impact of his appearances, the communications he shared in them, and the reactions of those who observed them should all encourage followers toward mature practices of the faith. *This thing is real*, might just be an appropriate reflective response, one that followers may need daily, even hourly. Jesus's appearances confirm the authenticity and suggest the impact of his resurrection.

She trusted in Jesus's resurrection, no doubt. She had none of the significant questions that others sometimes expressed about just what had happened after Christ's burial, whether Christ returned to visible life, and who had actually seen him. The Gospels answered those questions for her. Still, she found that she hadn't drawn much on Jesus's resurrection, not nearly so much as she had his ministry and miracles. So she began to recall them in some earnest. In doing so, she realized how much she loved the account of the two on the road to Emmaus, of doubting Thomas, and of course when Jesus appeared and ascended. She realized that she knew and could draw more deeply on details of each of those events, even though she hadn't thought of these events as often as she could have. Yet the account that she most missed having studied and contemplated was that of the women appearing at the tomb. As she reflected on it, she began to imagine the special light at dawn in which the scene must have occurred. She began nearly to smell the garden at that early hour and wondered whether the air might have been warm or cool. Then she imagined Jesus, appearing as if a gardener, and the shock and incredible delight of the women as they recognized him. She hoped that she would remember this scene in her later years, maybe even as she passed toward her own resurrection, reaching for and clasping the feet of the resurrected Jesus.

157 Disguised.

John 20:14; *see also* Mark 16:11; Luke 24:16; John 21:4.

The Gospels record the curious fact that Jesus did not make his identity readily apparent whenever he appeared but instead sometimes at first went disguised or unrecognized. As a section above mentions, one account records that Mary Magdalene was the first to see Jesus after his resurrection. In that instance, Mary had just turned away from the tomb where she had seen the two angels in white. The account records that as she turned, she saw a figure whom she did not recognize to be Jesus, thinking instead that he was the gardener who maintained the tomb. Calling her *woman* as if she might be a stranger, and thus leaving some possible implication that he was not yet ready for Mary to recognize him, Jesus asked Mary why she cried and for whom she looked. Still not realizing that she was facing Jesus, Mary, who had already told the angels that someone must have *taken her Lord* from the empty tomb, replied to Jesus that if he, the suspected gardener, had taken the body, then she would go bring the body back. Jesus then addressed her *Mary*, his doing so causing Mary to recognize him, shout *Teacher*, and apparently to clutch at Jesus, who told her instead to go tell the disciples that he was returning to the Father. In another Gospel account, the two disciples walking the seven miles from Jerusalem to Emmaus, one of those disciples named Cleopas, had Jesus just suddenly join them, walk with them, and explain the scriptures to them as to why Jesus had to suffer as the two disciples had just seen that he did. Yet somehow, during that extended conversation, the two disciples did not recognize Jesus. The account states cryptically that they *were kept* from recognizing Jesus, although by what means the account does not suggest. When Jesus asked what the two were discussing, Cleopas even turned to Jesus asking if he *was only a visitor to Jerusalem* such that he didn't know what had happened to *Jesus of Nazareth*. The two couldn't identify Jesus even when wondering who he was and when telling Jesus about the *powerful prophet* Jesus whom their women had just reported as resurrected after crucifixion. Only when Jesus broke bread with them later did their *eyes open*, as the account records, so that they then recognized Jesus, even though they acknowledged to one another that their hearts had burned within them while Jesus had opened the scriptures to them. The three disciples Peter, James, and John also did not recognize Jesus when he first appeared on the shore while they fished, until he had helped them make a miraculous catch. Jesus went disguised or unrecognized.

The image of Jesus disguised from, or at least unrecognized by those who had known and followed him closely, is another important one on which followers may reflect. The accounts give no clear indication of why those who knew and saw Jesus did not at first recognize him. That one account records that they *were kept* from recognizing Jesus may indicate some intention on Jesus's part to remain unrecognized. If instead they failed to recognize Jesus out of emotion or distraction, then Jesus must at least have assented that he would remain unrecognized at least for a time. That inference raises the question of why he would so assent. Here, the accounts may be more help. Jesus's having allowed himself to go unrecognized gives readers the opportunity to note the observers' reactions, to read of how they addressed Jesus's crucifixion and apparent resurrection without yet knowing that they were looking at him. Readers thus see Mary reacting to Jesus, whom she mistook as the gardener, as if he had *not* risen and as if she still needed to find and attend to his still-dead body. The account suggests that her fervor and confusion may have moved Jesus to call her name *Mary*, or possibly that he used her name in gentle rebuke for failing to see his prophesied resurrection, or simply for her to recognize him. One hardly knows, the account permitting and possibly encouraging one to consider each as possibilities, granting greater room for reflection. How would we respond, and indeed how *do* we respond, to resurrection? And more significantly, how would Jesus see our response? The two disciples on the road to Emmaus received Jesus's rebuke for their disbelief, while Mary received what sounded much more like consolation. Going disguised or at least unrecognized enabled Jesus to observe, judge, and comment in some respect on their reactions, just as he might observe, judge, and have responses to our own. Reflect on your reaction to the resurrection, but know that Jesus may be your hidden observer.

Of all of the precious scenes of Jesus after his resurrection, she felt that she treasured the scene of Mary meeting whom she thought to be the gardener but was actually Jesus at the tomb more than any of them. This scene became her touchstone. She could see her life reflected in this one scene, how she had for a time sought the Lord's dead body when he stood beside her living, when she had not yet embraced the life and confidence of resurrection. She now knew that even then, when she felt the Lord to be dead or distant, he had instead been right behind her, right beside her, disguised by her own lack of confidence in the resurrection. He had waited for her to recognize him as living. Bemused, he had answered her questions, those confused questions that she had put to him as if he was merely the gardener, with his own questions. *Why do you cry? For whom do you look?* Yet then, he had called her name. The Lord of all creation had called *her* name. And his doing so had caused her to turn more directly toward him, to look more clearly at him, to rely more fully on him for what she sought, only to discover that it was *him*, her Lord Savior. Every time that she thought again of the scene at the tomb with the gardener, these things, these personal, life-history, life-changing things were what she thought. She had life verses and memory verses, but this scene was her life scene, the one through which she lived her life, clutching at the body of the risen Lord, while he urged her to go tell others that he had indeed risen.

158 **Doubted.**

John 20:25; *see also* Mark 16:11; Luke 24:11; John 20:3.

Although an angel announced Jesus's resurrection, and Jesus then appeared to the women and to two disciples on the road to Emmaus, other disciples continued to doubt and disbelieve in the resurrected Jesus, until they also saw Jesus, touched him, conversed with him, and ate with him. The Gospels record that when Mary Magdalene saw Jesus, she promptly went and told the disciples, whom she found mourning and weeping. The account also records that the disciples *did not believe* her report. A parallel account records that the disciples felt that the women's words seemed like *nonsense*. That same account credits the disciple Peter with running to the empty tomb after hearing the women's report. Although that account records that Peter discovered nothing but the linen cloth in which Joseph had wrapped Jesus's body, it also records that Peter left the empty tomb not believing the women's report but instead *wondering what had happened*. Another account records both Peter and John racing to the tomb. While that account, *John's account*, records that John *believed*, John also records that even he still did not understand that Jesus had risen according to the scriptures. The disciples had the same unbelieving response when the two disciples returned from Emmaus with the same news that they had just seen and indeed walked and spoken at length with the resurrected

Jesus. Once again, the account states that the disciples *did not believe them either*. Only when Jesus appeared to those disciples did they then believe. Even the most dedicated disciples doubted Jesus's resurrection after its announcement and reports of his appearance from other followers whom they knew and presumably trusted. Among those disciples, Thomas doubted most, saying to the other disciples who had already seen Jesus that he would have to put his hands into Jesus's nail marks and into Jesus's pierced side to believe that Jesus had risen. The account records that one week later, Jesus appeared again in the upper room, telling the awestruck Thomas to do exactly as he said he would require. Jesus added that he had now believed because he had seen but that God would bless those who believed without seeing.

Scenes of the disciples doubting first-hand reports, made by their close confidantes, that the Father had resurrected the Son may both trouble and reassure followers in reflection. The troubling aspect of the disciples' doubt and disbelief is that they directed it toward the central prophecy of their Master. If the women and other witnesses had reported something inconsistent with or irrelevant to Jesus's prophecy that he would die and rise again in three days, then one might better understand the disciples' reluctance to accept their reports. Those reports would then have had no endorsement from Jesus. Yet the witnesses reported just what Jesus had told the disciples would happen. The disciples were not only lacking in faith but stubbornly so, even on the second report. On the other hand, one suspects that the disciples' response might have been the response of most anyone, even ardent followers like the disciples. Resurrection is a stunning, bewildering development. The disciples were also still weeping and mourning over Jesus's death, plainly disheartened, even miserable, which may have contributed to their disbelief in the reports of resurrection. One might hardly blame the disciples for their doubt as a natural reaction to the most extraordinary event that they would ever witness. But Jesus did blame them for their doubting reaction, as the next section shows. Followers reflecting on the disciples' doubt over the resurrection should consider carefully Jesus's response to their doubt.

He had a strong commitment to the practical, clinical, rational, and real. He had never been into fantasy, myth, the occult, or the surreal. He had no interest in fables and felt that he needed no comfort from anything, instead prepared in all respects to take what little or much the world gave him. In those characteristics, he imagined himself to be much like Peter, James, John, and the other disciples, several of them hardworking fishermen, others likely tradesmen, and the one tax collector Matthew. In what the Gospels disclosed of them in their thoughts about and reactions to Jesus, they hadn't seemed easily led into fantasy, either. They had seemed to have had nothing practical or material to gain and instead much practical and material to lose in following Jesus. As he reflected on how the disciples had doubted Jesus's resurrection, he realized that the disciples' sturdy practicality may have been in part why Jesus chose them rather than others who would more-readily have entertained the fantastic, bizarre, odd, or unreal. He understood why the disciples had doubted reports of Jesus's resurrection because he also had for a long time been unsure of the reality of resurrection, which still seemed strange, otherworldly, almost eerie, or nearly dreamlike. He supposed that as much as he knew and trusted in Jesus's resurrection now, as the Spirit had informed him over good time ever more deeply in the nature, mission, and life of Jesus, the resurrection may still remain bewildering. He wouldn't doubt any longer like the disciples had briefly doubted, but he accepted for now that he could continue to regard resurrection with astonishment and wonder.

159 **Rebuking.**

Mark 16:14; *see also* Luke 24:25.

The Gospels record that Jesus rebuked the disciples who had not believed the first-hand reports of Jesus's resurrection from both the women who had seen Jesus at the tomb and the disciples who had walked with Jesus on the road to Emmaus. The account recording that both Mary Magdalene and the two disciples returning from Emmaus had told the disbelieving disciples, who did not believe until Jesus appeared also to them, ends stating specifically that Jesus *rebuked* those disciples. The account further gives the reason for Jesus's rebuke that the disciples' *stubborn refusal* to believe had demonstrated their *lack of faith*. In so saying, Jesus was both acknowledging that accepting first-hand reports nonetheless requires some measure of faith while also communicating that the disciples should have had that faith. Yes, believing accounts of resurrection takes faith, given the extraordinary nature of resurrection. Yet of all things in which disciples should have faith, of all things against which their belief should not be stubborn, those things would be events fulfilling the prophetic statements of the Master. One might not believe accounts that some unknown miscreant had risen, but disciples should believe accounts confirming the prophecy of their own Lord in resurrection. Stubbornness is no asset when applied against the prophecies of one's own Master. Jesus also rebuked the two disciples who had walked the road to Emmaus with him, saying that they had been *foolish* and *slow of heart to believe* the prophecies about him. The resurrected Jesus showed that he remained concerned about the attitude of his followers when he rebuked his disciples for their lack of faith.

Followers may draw reliable guidance from reflecting on scenes of Jesus rebuking the disciples for doubting first-hand reports that Jesus had risen. As just suggested in the prior section, the disciples might have felt natural cause to disbelieve because of the wonder of resurrection. Yet natural reactions are precisely what Jesus may have been cautioning against when rebuking the disciples. Jesus's rebuke unquestionably implies that the disciples should have had different attitudes than they exhibited. The disciples should not have reacted naturally as others who had *not* heard Jesus's prophecy and did *not* know, trust, and follow Jesus would naturally react. Jesus expects followers to behave differently from those who do not know, trust, and follow him. God's words must mean something to followers. They must guide the follower's thought, action, and reaction. Followers should thus accept Jesus's willingness to admonish the disciples as fair warning that natural reactions aside, followers must *exercise* and *apply* faith. Followers must set aside stubbornness against anything that Jesus says particularly *about his resurrection*. Notice, too, how Jesus treated the two on the road to Emmaus that Jesus first explained the scriptures to them and then rebuked them for not believing the prophecies about him. Followers should likewise explain the faith to those who do not know Jesus and who thus react naturally against his resurrection that they, too, may embrace the fact of the resurrection and know, trust, and follow Jesus.

That Jesus rebuked the disciples for not believing multiple first-hand reports of his resurrection somewhat disconcerted him. One might have thought that Jesus would understand their shock, doubt, and surprise. Why didn't Jesus just appear, resolve the resurrection question once and for all, and get it over with? Yet as he kept reflecting on Jesus's admonishment, his *rebuke* of the disciples, he realized that the doubt that the disciples faced imminently is like the doubt that many today face chronically, indeed that he had faced himself. Although he supposed that Jesus could do so, he knew that Jesus would not be appearing again and again to every generation of followers on into the future. Certainly, he had not seen Jesus, at least not while knowing it. But he believed, or wanted to believe, as firmly in Jesus's resurrection as if he had seen Jesus. He realized then that in some way, Jesus had helped future followers by inviting the disciples to rely on their faith and then rebuking them for their not having done so. The same would be true today. Although he had not seen Jesus, he didn't want to suffer Jesus's rebuke for a stubborn lack of faith. After all, Jesus said that he would do it, and then many witnesses confirmed in bewilderment and at fatal risk that he *had* done it. No, he decided, he was not going to be in the camp of stubborn disbelief. He had learned the lesson of the disciples' stubborn lack of faith and of Jesus's rebuke.

160 Greeting.

Matthew 28:9.

Jesus did not simply appear in resurrection, as a distant or fixed image. The Gospels record Jesus greeting others in resurrection, recognizing, identifying, and welcoming them. One account records that Jesus first told the women *greetings*, when he met the women at the tomb, in an appearance that the prior section describes. Jesus acknowledged the women in a way that implied that he knew them and that they would know him, as the women clearly did in coming to him and clasping his feet in worship. Indeed, Jesus added *not to be afraid*, which the women were then apparently not given their approach and worship. Jesus then referred to the disciples as *his brothers* in another clear indication of close relationship.

The image of Jesus in resurrection greeting his disciples and followers should be another specific encouragement for followers in reflection. Jesus need not have deigned to acknowledge anyone in resurrection. He might instead simply have shown his glory on his way to the Father. Individual or group greetings, welcoming interaction with others, and recognizing and displaying familiarity with those who observed him, all seem unnecessary to resurrection itself but also hugely welcome additions. That Jesus continued to know, locate, and warmly acknowledge the women who had cared for him, individual disciples, and possibly others humanizes resurrection. Jesus didn't become a force or thought in resurrection, or a distant if great deity. He remained personal and personable, and interested in personal relationship, much as he had been before burial. Although followers may draw different impressions from the accounts, to some followers, post-resurrection Jesus will seem in some way nearly as familiar, warm, and engaging as he did in his public ministry and miracles. One message seems clear, which is that followers may still expect personal relationship, care, and interest from Jesus in resurrection. Followers seem not to have lost anything in the relationship, and instead gained much for reflection, from Jesus's resurrection. He knows your name, even in resurrection.

He had grown to the point of wanting to be constantly at the feet of the Master, to be a disciple. For a time, the thought of following Jesus had primarily been to him a confession of faith, knowledge of doctrine, and practice of commands, habits, and disciplines. He still valued those things, still feeling them to be important to this journey that he had long followed. Yet he now more than anything wanted to follow and be close to the Master more so than to practice the Master's disciplines. Proximity, companionship, and fellowship, even friendship, were his primary pursuits beyond those habits and practices that had for a good time supported his journey toward the Master. As he contemplated Jesus in resurrection, who was the only Jesus whom he could now know, he thought again of the scenes of the resurrected Jesus. He could readily imagine walking and talking with someone and only later realizing, like the two on the road to Emmaus, that the person had carried Jesus's love, Spirit, word, and image. He could readily imagine Jesus speaking to him as Jesus had spoken to the disciples and then to Thomas, bringing schools of fish toward him as he had for the fishing disciples, and restoring him as Jesus had restored Peter. The more that he pondered the scenes and images of Jesus in resurrection, the closer that he felt to him, and the more that he trusted and heavier that he leaned on the good Lord Jesus.

¹⁶¹ Conversing.

Luke 24:17; *see also* Matthew 28:18; Luke 24:45; Acts 1:3.

Jesus did not simply appear in resurrection while also recognizing and greeting his disciples and followers, as a grand king might wave to followers in passing. The Gospels instead record the resurrected Jesus communicating and conversing closely with others. To the women at the tomb, Jesus gave the specific instructions to return to the disciples, whom Jesus called *his brothers*, to tell them to meet him in Galilee. Of the two disciples walking to Emmaus, Jesus inquired what they were discussing. The account then records that the two gave Jesus what reads like an excited description of the crucifixion and empty-tomb events, to which Jesus replied with what the account suggests might have been a lengthy exposition of the scriptures as the three walked to Emmaus. At the exposition's end, Jesus prepared to depart but relented when the two urged him strongly to stay with them. Jesus remained until breaking bread with them, when the two finally recognized Jesus who then promptly disappeared from their sight. When greeting more of the disciples in the upper room, Jesus first convinced them that he was real but then stayed to *open their minds* by once again explaining the scriptures. At the mountain in Galilee to which Jesus sent the disciples, Jesus gave them the Great Commission to go make disciples of all nations. God did not resurrect Jesus merely to show his power, honor his Son, and fulfill the prophecies of Jesus's rising again but also to enable Jesus to once again teach, preach, and converse with his disciples, which he did so repeatedly and richly. The book of Acts confirms that in his several appearances over forty days, Jesus spoke about the kingdom of God.

The scenes of Jesus guiding, directing, and conversing with the disciples and other followers after his resurrection are frankly extraordinary ones on which followers may reflect. Jesus would seemingly have accomplished more than enough in resurrection, particularly once he had appeared to confirm his resurrection, so that none might doubt, and moreover once he had also acknowledged his disciples and other followers, whom he would thus have specifically encouraged. Yet Jesus did more in resurrection. He tarried sufficiently to engage the disciples and followers much as he had taught, guided, and directed them during his ministry. His doing so establishes something important beyond the extraordinary fact of new life from the dead. Resurrected life was not to be a tableau, representation, picture, or mere image, even if a living image made from one who previously was dead. Resurrected life was to be engaged life, life in which the resurrected Jesus would *interact personally* with his followers communicating on important, actually *eternal*, subjects. Followers might gain one thing from a resurrected Lord merely from the fact of resurrection. They gain something qualitatively different and greater in a resurrected Lord who speaks, guides, directs, and communicates personally. Study the scenes of the resurrected Jesus communicating with his followers. Let the resurrected Lord's Spirit communicate with you.

She very much liked the thought of walking and talking with Jesus. She didn't want to be foolish about things, didn't want to mumble to herself and have others rightly think her crazy. On the other hand, she had the sense of conversing with Jesus, or as she understood the practice more precisely, with his Holy Spirit, the Counselor or Comforter whom Jesus sent after his ascension. Because she had a harder time picturing the Holy Spirit, though, she tended to think of herself conversing with the resurrected Lord, the one about whose words and actions she could read and reflect at the end of the Gospels. Those scenes seemed in some gentle respect to endorse her growing practice of talking with Jesus. Indeed, her talk was not just talk. She was also learning to listen. The resurrected Lord had listened and responded to the two on the road to Emmaus and the disciples including especially Thomas and Peter. *They* had conversed, and so why couldn't *she* also converse with Jesus? She appreciated that he had ascended, and yet she also knew that he had sent the Comforter and Counselor whom she knew was to bring to her the words and life of Jesus. So she just kept walking and talking with Jesus, and listening to Jesus, with no apologies. Others might think her muttering, but she wasn't going to miss speaking with her Lord.

¹⁶² Opposed.

Matthew 28:12.

While the scenes and events of the resurrection encourage followers greatly, those scenes nonetheless include continuing opposition to Jesus. The Gospels record that after the angel rolled back the stone from the entrance to the tomb and announced Jesus's resurrection, some of the tomb's guards reported everything to the chief priests. The chief priests then met with the elders, the account states, *to devise a plan* to frustrate and counteract the resurrection story. The chief priests and elders bribed the soldiers liberally to say that the disciples had stolen Jesus's body while the soldiers slept. This fabrication would have gotten the soldiers in the worst trouble with the governor who assigned them to guard the tomb. So the chief priests and elders assured the soldiers that if the governor heard and believed the fabrication, they would explain things to the governor to keep the soldiers out of trouble. The soldiers took the large bribe and did as the chief priests and elders had instructed. The account ends by recording that the fabrication continued to receive wide circulation among the Jews.

The image of Jesus opposed even in resurrection is in some respects a strange, almost bizarre or absurd one for followers in reflection. The risen Lord is so clearly beyond opposition. Without knowing the prophecies and seeing the miracles, one might have questioned anyone making the claims that Jesus made, as even the disciples and other followers failed to grasp fully what Jesus had said about his resurrection. Resurrection is simply that improbable, astounding, staggering, and extraordinary. To grasp it, one must nearly see it, or afterward receive highly reliable report of it such as the disciples gave in offering to die for it. Jesus accomplished so much in resurrection that for the chief priests and elders to continue to oppose him, *to oppose a resurrected Lord*, reduces them to absurdly small-minded proportion. They continued to plot and scheme to protect their position even in the knowledge that the Messiah whom they had crucified had risen, announced by a lightning-clad angel. Jesus had made the world anew, but they continued to cling to the old world that his resurrection had made meaningless. The question that the opposition of the chief priests and elders to the resurrected Lord raises, though, is to what *we* foolishly cling in the face of resurrection. Followers do well to reflect on the foolishness of opposition to Jesus resurrected.

Whenever he thought of how the religious leaders had continued to oppose Jesus *even after his resurrection*, he thought of his own acquaintances today who didn't seem to acknowledge Jesus, who didn't profess faith, who when he heard them speak of spiritual things spoke in ways that made clear their unbelief. He understood their sense of superiority. They were rational or wanted others to think them so, he could easily tell. They were scientific, modern, relieved of superstition, needing no comfort from fables, they told him in so many words. Yet from his perspective, they seemed too like the ancient religious leaders who refused to encounter the resurrected Jesus, who felt that they had too much to give up by embracing resurrected life. He felt that in one sense they were dead right. The moment that he had realized that Jesus walked again, spoke again, ate again, was the moment that he had to give up everything that he had believed, everything that he had pursued, and everything that he had held too tight. He just hoped and prayed that they, too, would see how much better off they would be also giving up all to which they were holding too tightly. One has to let go of that which one grasps, he thought, in order to open the hand to far greater gifts that come with resurrected life.

163 **Physical.**

Luke 24:39.

The Gospels plainly record that the resurrected Jesus had a physical body that others could not just see but also touch. As already shown in a prior section, the women who met Jesus outside the tomb after the dawn announcement of his resurrection *clasped his feet* in worship. The women touched the resurrected Jesus's physical body. Another Gospel records details of Jesus appearing to the doubting disciples in the upper room in which they had taken seclusion. They were still talking about the extraordinary news that the two disciples had just brought them from Emmaus, and still doubting that the news was true, when Jesus stood among them wishing them peace. Jesus's appearance startled the disciples who thought him to be a ghost. Jesus first told them not to trouble themselves, reminding them also not to doubt. He then urged the disciples to recognize him by looking at his hands and feet, the implication being that they bore the marks of crucifixion. Yet Jesus then specifically told the disciples to *touch him*. Even as he did so, Jesus reminded the disciples that a ghost *does not have flesh and bones*, Jesus added, *as you see I have*. He then extended his hands and feet. The account continues, though, that the disciples still did not believe Jesus's resurrection, although now, the account clarifies, because of *amazement and joy*. No matter the disciples' response, Jesus nonetheless had a physical, material body in resurrection and wanted others to know it.

The image of the resurrected Jesus as a physical, touchable being is hugely significant for followers in their reflections on resurrection. Naively, or from the standpoint of one unfamiliar with Jesus's prophetic role, one supposes that resurrection could mean just about anything. Many who are unfamiliar with or unaccepting of the scriptures may construe resurrection in other ways, some for instance to mean release, annihilation, or incorporation into some collective spirit beyond. Scenes of the physically resurrected Jesus dispel those constructions. Resurrection involves a physical body. Jesus still, or once again, had human structure and form. Jesus also made quite clear the nature of his human structure, which was specifically that he had *flesh and bones*. Beyond those very important clarifying considerations, though, Jesus's physicality appears to have played another important role for the disciples that Jesus himself acknowledged. Everyone has some experience with ghosts or similar apparitions, whether perceived or imagined, or at least in dramatic (or even comedic) representations. Jesus did not want the disciples believing that he was merely an apparition, even as he expressly broached the possibility that *ghost* is what the disciples saw and would construe. Jesus used his physical body to dispel any notion that he was a vision, dream, specter, or apparition. He was instead *real*, living flesh and blood, even though he plainly had other powers to appear and disappear.

He was so glad that Jesus had done with the disciples in the upper room what he did. He nearly breathed an audible sigh of relief every time that he thought of Jesus extending his hands and feet while telling the disciples to touch him and saying that he was *flesh and blood*. That one scene, one on which he reflected often, gave him a clarity about resurrection that all of the doctrine could never quite give, however sound that doctrine might be. All that he needed to understand resurrection seemed to be in that one scene in the upper room with the disciples. Like others, nearly daily, and at least weekly, he had news of serious illnesses or deaths or brushes with death, or discussions about the recently or long-ago departed, that in one way or another raised the question of resurrection. He could not think about death without thinking about resurrection, as he imagined was true for any other follower and maybe a good number of those who do not follow the Lord. He would often briefly think what *resurrection* really meant, especially when hearing others make direct or oblique references to *being with the Lord* or other similar phrases. Yet no sooner would he wonder than the answer would appear in the form of this one scene with Jesus saying to *look at my hands* and *look at my feet.* He could hear Jesus saying that *ghosts are not flesh and blood like me*, even imagining that Jesus would be smiling at the disciples' joy and amazement. Thank God, he would always think, for the Gospels.

164 Identifiable.

Luke 24:39; *see also* John 20:20.

These accounts reveal another key characteristic of Jesus's resurrection. Jesus was not only in physical form in his resurrection but in a form that the disciples would recognize *as him*. Even though he sometimes went unrecognized for a time, the Gospel accounts generally indicate that when or soon after he appeared, Jesus looked enough like he did before his death and resurrection for those who knew him to recognize him once again. As just shown in the prior section, the Gospels record Jesus appearing to the women outside the tomb, the two on the road to Emmaus, and the disciples in the upper room in physical form, but notably, also in form recognizable *as Jesus*. Indeed, he still or once again bore the marks of his crucifixion, showing his hands and feet to allow the disciples to confirm his identity. One account records that he showed his hands *and side*, again the inference being that the distinguishing marks of his crucifixion, including the side that the soldier pierced, helped the disciples to accept that he was indeed Jesus. As that account states, upon showing his hands and side, the disciples were *overjoyed* at recognizing their Lord. Jesus's resurrection was not just real and not just to a physical body but to a body looking much like his before-resurrection body, enough for others to know him.

The image of Jesus urging the disciples to look at him and touch him to confirm not just that he was living in resurrection but also that he *was Jesus* is an important one for followers' reflection. One supposes that Jesus could have looked like many things in resurrection, as indeed at other times he may have done or may in the future do. He appeared as a gardener and has appeared or will appear as a slain Lamb and glorious King. Yet he also appeared as he did before his death in a way that those who knew him would recognize his appearance after resurrection. That Jesus remained Jesus in form after his resurrection may be of little consequence to more-recent followers who never knew Jesus's before-resurrection identity. We draw images of Jesus only from popular portrayals or from our imagination, although one suspects that the resurrected Jesus could still, if he wished, appear in ways that modern followers would nonetheless recognize as Jesus. We, too, should in some way be readily able to identify Jesus when the Father determines that his time to reappear has come. Yet another significance of Jesus's post-resurrection identity may be that followers can reasonably expect to also retain aspects of their own identity in resurrection. When followers wonder what body they will occupy, or who they will be, or what form they will take in resurrection, these scenes of Jesus urging his disciples to recognize him by his physical appearance give clues to the answers. We may not know how we will appear, but these scenes at least suggest that we will appear in some essential way as ourselves, not our old corrupt selves, and instead surely as new resurrected selves, but in any case as ourselves. The image of the resurrected Jesus in form identifiable as Jesus is a very helpful image worth a follower's substantial reflection.

While he mainly directed his reflections to Jesus, including at times Jesus's very-heartening resurrection, he nonetheless thought from time to time about what his own resurrection would be like. He suspected that too much such reflection would be unwise. The Gospels didn't give him much in that way on which to reflect. Yet the Gospels clearly did expect him to believe not only in Jesus's resurrection but also his own resurrection with Jesus someday. So he figured that the Spirit might accept and even guide his little and tentative confirming thought. His first surprise and satisfaction in those reflections was that he should probably expect to be much of whom he currently was. Oh, no, he wouldn't be the corrupted and corruptible person he now was, nor with his current aches, irritations, annoyances, and pains. He would, though, be himself, he figured, in large part from the fact that Jesus was still himself in appearance *even including the nail marks*. His surprise over this keeping-your-own-identity thing, every time he thought of his own resurrection, was that he couldn't quite see any part of his identity being in heaven. He realized that he just felt that the whole thing, his *whole* person and identity, needed God's transformation in order that he bear the saving image of Christ. He decided to leave to God how heaven could possibly preserve any identifiable part of him, knowing that he was only getting in because of Christ. His satisfaction with the keeping-your-own-image construct, though, was that he knew that he would still exist. He wouldn't be a mindless, faceless minion but instead still able to see, love, and follow Christ.

165 Functional.

Luke 24:40; *see also* John 21:9.

Another significant and quite-intentional disclosure that the Gospels make about Jesus's resurrection is that his resurrected body was also *functional*. The fact that Jesus's body was physical has import as described above, just as does the fact that he still bore his own body in identifiable form. Yet add to those attributes, both addressed above, the fact that Jesus wanted his disciples to know that he could *eat*, reflecting again that he was *real* rather than an apparition or immaterial presence, force, or form. The Gospels record that when Jesus visited the disciples in the upper room for the first time, he first urged that he was flesh and blood, even showing his hands and feet. But when the disciples still did not believe, then because of their joy and amazement, Jesus specifically asked them for *something to eat*. The context plainly shows that Jesus did so not because he was hungry but to show that he was *real*. The disciples responded to Jesus's request by handing him a piece of broiled fish. The account records that Jesus took the fish and ate the fish *in their presence*, again to demonstrate his material presence and rule out apparitional form. Apparitions don't eat real food. Jesus then brought home directly the point that he was making by eating, saying that he told them before his crucifixion that he would fulfill all prophecy including that he would die and then rise again in three days. Jesus ate again later with three disciples on the seashore. When the disciples landed their boat on the shore, Jesus had bread and a coal fire burning with fish on it. He told the disciples to bring more fish from the full net of fish that he had just helped them miraculously catch. Jesus told the disciples to *come have breakfast* with him, handing them bread and fish, while waiting to finish the meal before he addressed Peter over his restoration. The account even states that although they knew that the Lord had appeared to them a third time, *none dared ask him* to confirm it, instead simply eating the meal with him as if in its own confirmation. Reflect on Jesus eating, and you may gain an even clearer sense of the reality of his resurrection. He intended his eating to do so for the disciples.

The image of Jesus eating has power and purpose all its own. Function confirms reality. Dreams often seem real, but in a dream, not much of anything *works*. One seldom, for instance, eats or drinks in a dream, certainly not in a way that consumes real food. Even if one did eat or drink in a dream, the consumption would only be imaginary. If while one dreamt of eating a plate of food or piece of broiled fish happened to be on the adjacent nightstand, then the food or fish would still be there when one woke from the dream. Likewise, apparitions do not consume real food. Eating with another is one of the simplest but also clearest of ways to appreciate their life and humanity. Something happens when one breaks bread with another that does not happen when the two merely converse. Jesus seemed to have something like this connection in mind when urging the disciples to give him something to eat so that they could come to their senses about his presence. Prospects look good that resurrected followers will also eat, indeed of the fruit of the tree of life. Followers may expect not only to have physical bodies and personal identities in heaven but also to have those bodies function in kingdom-consistent ways.

Oddly, but maybe not so oddly, some of her favorite Gospel scenes were of Jesus and the disciples eating. She loved thinking of the wedding banquet when Jesus turned water into wine. She also loved the scene of the disciples picking grain heads on which to snack while Jesus admonished the religious leaders that when doing so they hadn't violated the Sabbath. She liked the scene of Jesus eating and drinking with tax collectors and other sinners but also the scenes of Jesus invited to dine in the homes of the religious leaders. Jesus ate. Yet of all the scenes that she most enjoyed of Jesus and the disciples eating, she enjoyed the post-resurrection scenes. The thought of the resurrected Jesus eating broiled fish to show the disciples the reality of his resurrection somehow enthralled her. She wanted to know who had bought and cooked the fish, and where the piece of fish had been, whether in a serving bowl or on someone's plate, when a disciple picked it up and gave it to Jesus. She also loved, maybe even more, the scene of Jesus preparing food for the disciples on the seashore. How exquisite that food must have tasted to the disciples! She wondered whether the Lord would feed her in heaven, even as she knew that she would love to serve and feed the Lord.

¹⁶⁶ Ascended.

Luke 24:51; *see also* Psalm 24:7; Acts 1:9.

The Gospels also record the resurrected Jesus ascending into heaven as that which marks a clear final stage of Jesus's resurrection. In one account, the resurrected Jesus had finally appeared to the disciples gathered in the upper room. There, Jesus had urged the disciples to recognize his resurrection from the flesh-and-blood body he still or now inhabited, nail marks included, and then confirmed that reality by eating their own real food in front of the disciples. The account then records that Jesus then led the disciples out to Bethany's vicinity, after once again explaining to the disciples how his resurrection fulfilled the prophecies. Near Bethany, Jesus raised his hands in blessing over the disciples. The account records that while blessing the disciples in just this manner, Jesus *left them*, taken up into heaven. The account then records the disciples' worship of the departed Jesus. The account ends documenting the disciples returning in great joy to Jerusalem to await the promised coming of the Holy Spirit. The book of Acts repeats that the Father took Jesus up *before their very eyes* until a cloud hid Jesus from their sight. As the disciples continued to stare intently into the sky, two angels appeared asking why they stood looking into the sky when Jesus, whom the Father had just taken into heaven, would return. So the disciples did as Jesus had told them, returning to their upper room in Jerusalem to await the Holy Spirit.

The image of the resurrected Jesus ascending into heaven after having appeared to his disciples, the women, and other followers marks a special turning point for followers' reflection. The scene is one that from earth may carry a note of sorrow, as Jesus departed for a time, but is one that from heaven and for all on earth simultaneously carries exquisite joy, the height and culmination of the greatest of all possibility. How often do followers think of that moment, prophesied so magnificently in Psalm 24 and interpreted in such splendor by Handel's *Messiah*, of the Son returning to the Father in glory? Yes, lift up those ancient gates that the King of glory, the Lord almighty, may enter. Imagine how every angel in heaven must have strained to observe every glorious detail of that momentous instant, one of those very few instances in history that has no equal or parallel, indeed one that held no greater joy than any other moment in the universe's history could hold, as the Father finally and formally greeted the Son who has now accomplished all that the Father could ever ask of him. We see so little of heaven from earth until the Spirit opens our eyes to its wonder. The moment of Jesus's ascension is that perfect moment of wonder. Let the image of the ancient gates of heaven opening only for the Son be your frequent, deep, and immensely inspiring reflection, one that no sadness or loss, however deep and wounding, could ever fully restrain. Keep constantly in mind the one greatest hope that resurrection offers. Lift up your heads, ye ancient gates, as the King of glory enters.

He had always felt something magic in Handel's *Messiah* far beyond its hauntingly uplifting vocal crescendos. He of course knew that the song, that song which he felt somehow was much more than a song, was about his beloved Lord. Yet he took quite a while to realize that spectacular moment that the song portrayed, the one that his heart so deeply and so often embraced, and to connect the song's special moment with the specific scripture prophesying that moment. He hadn't realized the song's forty-plus movements each based on Bible passages, from his perspective all organized to highlight that moment of Christ's return to the Father. He had never needed the song to make him cry in heart-swelling and joyous reflection over that moment. He had read the Gospels' ascension accounts so many times, often without pausing to reflect on their hidden heaven side. The accounts themselves seemed earthbound, their perspectives that of their recorders looking heavenward to the ascending Lord. Yet the Spirit had shown him time and again that the moment also had an earthward view from heaven. He easily imagined from the psalm that those ancient gates between heaven and earth that had closed so long ago, marked so gloriously with flaming swords, must have taken such command from the Father to open. He wished that he could have been there among the angels to exult as creation had never before quite exulted. Whenever he reflected on this scene, he could not think of another scene or image that held equal exultation. He only hoped that heaven would still hold in ringing ear, in ancient echo, just a little bit of that triumph and jubilation when he snuck, skulked, crept, crawled, or whatever God had him do, through that same gate.

8

His Revelation

Transfigured. Luke 9:29.   ***Returning.*** Luke 17:20.
Unexpected. Matthew 25:13.   ***Impersonated.*** Luke 21:8.
Gathering. Mark 13:27.   ***Enthroned.*** Matthew 25:31.
Rewarding. Matthew 25:29.

Jesus's revelation as the Son of God come to save humankind would like the other stages of Jesus's life need to unfold in ways that humankind could understand and embrace it. First, though, one needs to distinguish Jesus's revelation from prior stages, in part because his revelation overlapped with other stages of his life including especially his calling, public ministry, and miracles. When Peter acknowledged that Jesus was the Christ, the very Son of God, and Jesus affirmed that Peter was indeed correct, the event marked a turning point. Jesus had by then clearly heard and accepted his full calling. One could even say that Peter's statement was an outside endorsement akin to revelation, just as one could say the same about the Father's voice coming down like thunder in recognition of Jesus's baptism. Both events were also to some degree revelations of Jesus's Son of God role. Both events, though, involved Jesus's participation to a greater degree than other more-clearly revelatory events that followed. Thus, this part instead takes Jesus's transfiguration as the first full revelation of Jesus as the Son of God. A revelation is, shall we agree, a disclosure of the previously hidden essence of a thing or, in Jesus's case, of a person, a very special divine person. This part concludes the book with a collection of revelations of Jesus's divine attributes, beginning with his spectacular transfiguration.

[167] Transfigured.

Luke 9:29; *see also* Matthew 17:2; Mark 9:2; Revelation 1:13.

The Gospels record the confirmation of Jesus's calling in his mountainside transfiguration before his three closest disciples Peter, John, and James. Toward the end of Jesus's public ministry, as his movement toward his Jerusalem trial, conviction, and sentence accelerated, Jesus took the three disciples alone up a mountain to pray. The multiple Gospel accounts of the event record that as he prayed, Jesus became as bright as a flash of lightning, while Moses and Elijah appeared in like splendor talking alongside him about Jesus's impending departure. The extraordinary event roused the sleepy disciples just as Moses and Elijah were leaving, which Peter tried nonsensically to delay by offering to build them shelters. But a cloud instead enveloped the disciples, who only heard a voice saying to *listen to my chosen Son*. When the cloud dissipated, there stood Jesus alone. The account ends saying that when Jesus and the disciples descended the mountain, the disciples kept the extraordinary event to themselves, only telling about it later. Jesus's momentary transfiguration in the midst of his public ministry would foreshadow the glory in which the disciple John's vision captured Jesus in Revelation, the Son of Man dressed in a robe with golden sash, hair white as snow, eyes blazing like fire, and face as brilliant as the sun. His feet glowed like bronze in a furnace, his voice sounded like rushing waters, his hand held seven stars, and his mouth revealed a sword. Jesus confirmed then that he was both First and Last, the Living One whose eternal resurrection gave him the keys over death. God has transfigured Jesus.

The image of Jesus transfigured into lightning brightness and surrounded by Moses and Elijah, and after resurrection appearing as brilliant as the sun and like glowing bronze, satisfies something important for followers. So much of the Gospels have to do with Jesus moving about nearly as an ordinary person would, walking, resting, eating, drinking, and even tiring and sleeping. Jesus's ordinary movements among ordinary people can seem to belie his extraordinary status as the Son of God. Many do not see Jesus for who he is and was. Some who overlook Jesus's divinity do so because he was not only divine but also a man, and as a man, subject to the ordinariness of human existence, things like eating and drinking with which every person is familiar. To some, a God-man is a contradiction so strong that it is incapable of resolution. Indeed, more of us should probably feel that tension to a greater degree. By resolving it too easily, we lose the sense both of who God is and of what he did when becoming a man. Jesus's transfiguration, though, connects God with man. Humans do not simply begin to glow like lightning. God in man would on the other hand make man glow. When they saw Jesus as bright as lightning, the disciples saw the marriage of the human with the divine, what a God-man really must look like. When the disciples saw Moses and Elijah speaking with the lightning-bright God-man Jesus, they had confirmation of the historical, national, and prophetic context for the God-man's appearance. Reflect richly on the extraordinary scene of Jesus's transfiguration. While the Bible records equally remarkable post-resurrection and Revelation images of Jesus, Jesus's transfiguration in the midst of his public ministry carries its own special meaning.

She didn't feel that she needed the transfiguration scene, but she sure appreciated it. Actually, whenever she thought of it, she had to sort of shift her perspective from what she could imagine happening with and around Jesus to something that she really could not imagine. She could imagine Jesus's miracles, which in one respect or another all seemed at least somewhat natural even if also extraordinary, surely the miracle healings but also calming stormy seas and multiplying bread. Yet whenever she thought of the transfiguration, she had to substitute her natural imagination of things happening in the world to something from entirely outside of her world, which she realized was probably the scene's point. Maybe Jesus needed a meeting with Moses and Elijah right then, maybe to finish some unfinished business for which the three disciples just happened to be along for the figurative ride. But to her, the transfiguration seemed instead meant to show the disciples and, through their eyes, the world that the divine could enter the world, indeed could inhabit a human. And when God did take on human form, he might for the most part cloak his glory to protect the eyes and fragile minds of those who saw him, just as he hid Moses in the cleft of the rock, but at some point he might also decide to let his glory break out. She just wanted so badly to be able to imagine what Jesus had looked like, lightning-bright in his glory.

168 Returning.

Luke 17:20; *see also* Matthew 24:27; Mark 13:26; John 14:3; Revelation 20:1.

The scriptures reveal that the kingdom of God will come with Jesus's return. One Gospel records the religious leaders asking Jesus when the kingdom of God would come. Jesus replied not to go looking for it because the kingdom was already within them. To his disciples, though, Jesus turned and said that the Son of Man, while suffering first and then gone for a time, would then be *like the lightning* lighting up the sky. On the day that God reveals the Son of Man, no one should turn back for anything. God will take the ones who look only to him while leaving those who turn back. Another Gospel account records Jesus confirming that although he will return, no one will know the hour when he does so. The Son of Man will come *in clouds with great power and glory*, sending his angels to gather the elect from all over the earth. Another Gospel account records Jesus saying during the Last Supper that he was leaving to prepare a place for his disciples but that he would be returning to take each of them to be with him in that place. Revelation prophecies Christ's return for a thousand-year reign on earth, when those who had lost their lives testifying for Christ would reign with him. Jesus is returning.

The image of Jesus returning is one on which followers should duly reflect. While the Spirit of Christ is in the world, guiding followers into righteousness and helping them discern their many good works, the world is nonetheless imperfect, incomplete. By delaying his return, Jesus gives more the opportunity to see and accept him that he should not lose one whose heart desires him. While everyone must treat the question with its due urgency, none of us knowing when our own hour will come, Jesus will not return before that time when the greatest number will have had that opportunity to elect him. Christ's return, though, must come. What would the world be but continuing chaos and disorder without it? Indeed, who would Christ be without his return? He is the one great King of kings, not another king of some kings. Every knee must bow for Christ to be as his Father has ordained him. Without his return, Jesus would not have ruled to the extent that the Father would have him rule. He must hold all authority, not just some authority. Jesus must show his glory before all, like lightning filling the skies, not just before some, in an upper room or ascending into heaven. He must see the final defeat of his adversary who failed to tempt him but who still tempts others. The kingdom must come.

He admitted to himself that he found it harder to reflect on Jesus's return than on things that Jesus had already done as the Gospels recorded them. He could take a Gospel account, imagine well how the event had actually been, and then draw inspiration from his reflection. These things he simply could not do, though, with the prophecy of Jesus's return. Jesus's return was certain, he knew and accepted. His problem was not one of disbelief but instead of imagination. He did not trust his imagination and felt that he had less of it than others, and so he turned to the imagination of others to reflect on Christ's return. He found great hope and joy in those reflections. He found things that the scriptures intimated, even if he could not be sure that those things would actually someday be just as others imagined them. Those imaginations, though, were still helpful in giving him a clearer sense of what Christ's return could mean, the incredible glory of the kingdom fully come, even if no one knew precisely what the kingdom would actually be like or what his return would precisely mean. He just wanted more inspiration that it would be special, maybe special *beyond imagination*, even if he needed someone else's imagination to help him appreciate just how special.

169 Unexpected

Matthew 25:13; *see also* Mark 13:35; Luke 12:35.

Although Jesus's return is certain, the Gospels record Jesus saying that his return would also be unexpected, when many have not prepared. When during his final week in Jerusalem Jesus instructed his disciples about events to come, he was particularly clear about his followers needing to be prepared for his return. Because God would delay Jesus's return, no one would know the hour of his return, and many false prophets and false Christs would appear before his return, followers might have the tendency to relax their watch. To ensure that his followers remained prepared for his return, Jesus told the disciples the parable of the ten virgins waiting to meet the bridegroom, the figure of the returning Christ. Five of the virgins were wise for having kept their lamps filled with oil, taken as a figure of the Holy Spirit. Five virgins were foolish for letting oil run out of their lamps while the bridegroom delayed in coming. The bridegroom returned at midnight when the foolish virgins had no light to come out to meet him and had left to buy more. The bridegroom took the wise virgins to the wedding banquet, leaving the foolish virgins shut out for not knowing them. Jesus concluded the parable with the admonition to *keep watch, not knowing the day or hour* that he would return. Jesus's return would be unexpected.

The image of Jesus returning unexpectedly, on a day and at an hour when no one knew he would return, provides a good reminder for followers to remain in the Spirit. To keep watch is to maintain a mental and spiritual attitude of expectation. Vigilance is by definition difficult to maintain because it indicates heightened awareness, something more than the usual. One cannot be naturally vigilant because vigilance is unnatural. At some point, the vigilance wears off, returning one's senses to normal. The artificial or *supernatural* quality of vigilance or awareness may be precisely that to which Jesus refers in his parable. The Holy Spirit's role is to bring Jesus to our attention, to be his comforter, counselor, and guide for us, not just for our general wellbeing as might a therapist, coach, or valet, but instead to keep us close to Jesus. Jesus's admonition to *keep watch* suggests some form of discipline, and likely not so much a natural discipline such as physical exercise, but instead a spiritual discipline that keeps the follower attuned to the Holy Spirit. Followers practice spiritual disciplines like confession, repentance, thanksgiving, fasting, prayer, worship, and study of God's word not out of tradition or because they feel good but rather to keep close to the Holy Spirit, attuned and sensitive to the Spirit's movements. We do so to keep watch for Jesus, ready for the unexpected hour of his return.

She felt at times that her habits kept her attuned to the Holy Spirit while at other times they didn't keep her aware, sensitive, and attuned. For a time, she thought that the question of whether she was close to the Spirit was mostly one of how busy she was or was not, the less busy the closer to the Spirit, the busier the farther away. But she soon found that being busy or not wasn't really the problem with keeping her spiritual lamp filled. She discerned instead that spiritual fullness had more to do with the little practices in which she engaged or did not engage. When she was regularly memorizing scripture, she just felt much more attuned to what the Spirit might be saying and doing in and around her. When she was active in a Bible study, or in a vital service ministry at church, or in a special season of worship, she again felt the Spirit moving. On the other hand, whether she was busy or not, when she was spiritually listless or aimless and lacking in any particular spiritual design or discipline, she felt less connected, less attuned. She knew that making a system out of the question wasn't really the answer. One didn't find Jesus following a formal method. Yet she kept thinking of his caution to *keep watch* and, from that caution, felt that he must have meant that she should be *doing* something with purpose or design. And so the things of which she decided to do more were those things that kept her attuned to the Spirit, more Bible study, more memorizing scripture, more prayer, and more worship. She wanted to be ready for his return.

¹⁷⁰ Impersonated.

Luke 21:8; *see also* Matthew 24:5; Mark 13:5, 13:22.

As to Jesus's returning, the scriptures reveal Jesus as warning that others will impersonate him to fool followers about his return. Impostors will imitate, mimic, and impersonate Jesus without having his authority or even being his follower. Jesus taught about the timing of his return during his final week in Jerusalem, as he prepared his followers for his arrest, conviction, and crucifixion. Gospel accounts record Jesus's disciples remarking at the temple's beauty, to which Jesus replied that adversaries would throw down every stone of the temple.

When his disciples asked *when* the desolation that Jesus had described would take place, Jesus warned them not to let others deceive them. He then prophesied that many others would come claiming that they did so in Jesus's name or even that they were he, false Christs and instead impostors. Others would claim that the time for Christ's return was near. Jesus warned his disciples, though, not to follow those who made such claims to know when he would return. Wars, earthquakes, famine, and pestilences should not frighten the disciples, Jesus continued, because many terrible things must happen before his return. Enemies of the faith would arrest, imprison, and try the disciples, who should still not worry but instead simply speak the words that Jesus would give them. Eventually, though, after all of the impostors, rumors, and horrors, Jesus would return *in a cloud with power and great glory* to redeem his followers.

The image of Jesus as one whom others would imitate provides an important caution for followers. Enemies of the faith know Jesus's authority and power just as well, indeed sometimes better, than followers discern and rely on Jesus's authority and power. Impostors, charlatans, and defrauders will imitate and coopt anything good, anything authoritative, or anything having power, so why wouldn't they pose or postulate the moment of Jesus's return? In that sense, that Christ would have imitators in no sense undermines but rather endorses his power and authority. If he had no impostors and imitators, then one would reasonably question his influence, for as the saying goes, imitation is the sincerest form of flattery. Impostors should not trouble or distract followers, who should instead ignore false Christs and false prophecies of his return, just as Jesus cautioned. By cautioning followers against false Christs and false prophets, Jesus also means to inoculate followers against misleading assertions, to set us on our guards against false representations and images, of which we should expect plenty. Jesus must have known that his followers would long for his return so earnestly that their longing might deceive them. Jesus wants us instead standing guard against deception even while remaining prepared for his return. We should both expect and yet not be troubled or misled by Jesus's impersonation.

The accomplishment had taken quite a while, but she finally felt that she had a reasonably good grasp on what Jesus meant about anticipating his return. She understood clearly that she should be both watchful but also cautious. She should be sure of his return while not letting her confidence mislead her into believing that she knew its timing and certainly not mislead her into following an impostor. She was glad that Jesus had warned his followers about false Christs and false prophecies of his return. She had actually seen many such false prophecies and suspected that she had seen a few who appeared to be claiming some status like a false Christ. She also suspected that she would see more false prophecies and false Christs in the future. Every year did seem to bring more world calamity or at least more news or rumors of world calamity. She found anticipating the world's nearing end to be all too easy these days, given the wars and rumors of war, and the other natural and man-made disasters dominating the headlines. She also felt that the threats of all kinds, while more numerous, also seemed more insidious, more disruptive, direr. Yet she also appreciated Jesus's caution not to be anxious. She knew her eternal destination. She could watch the world's accelerating pace, indeed the way in which it appeared to be accelerating toward its demise, without fearing for herself and other followers, and without jumping to any conclusions over the moment of Jesus's return. Most of all, she felt that with the Holy Spirit in her heart to guide her, she could now identify and avoid impostors.

171 Gathering.

Mark 13:27; *see also* Matthew 24:31.

The scriptures reveal that on his return Jesus will gather his followers to him. Jesus gathers his elect. The Gospels record Jesus speaking many things to his disciples during his last week in Jerusalem, about what was to come. On one such occasion, Jesus had just left the temple area and retired to the Mount of Olives where he and his disciples could still see the temple. Jesus told the disciples about the *abomination that causes desolation* and the hard times that his followers would endure. Jesus encouraged the disciples, though, that God would shorten those desolate days so that his elect would survive. Then, when the distress had ended and Jesus was to return, neither the sun nor moon would shine. Stars would fall and planets shake. People would see Jesus coming in clouds with power and glory. At that moment of his second coming, Jesus would send angels to *gather his elect* from all over the earth and throughout the heavens, wherever the angels might find them. Jesus's return would mean the salvation of his followers, all of whom Jesus would have the angels gather to him no matter where those followers might be. Jesus would be a gatherer, assembler, and convener, drawing or rounding up his flock into the great kingdom of heaven.

The image of Jesus gathering his elect from the four corners of the earth should be powerful encouragement to his followers. One sometimes gets the inaccurate sense that following Jesus requires strenuous pursuit more so than simple faith, when to the contrary Jesus may well be the pursuer. God draws the elect to his Son, followers having only to acknowledge their need for Jesus and their faith in his redemption and resurrection. While we have the liberty and will to accept Jesus, God knows whom we will choose, whether we will choose his Jesus or not. When Jesus speaks of angels gathering his elect, he means that God drew all to him, that only some chose to follow, and that God knew who. Jesus also means, though, that having made the choice to follow Jesus, followers would then have angels gathering them to him. Significantly, those who stand firm in faith to the end will not have to find Jesus. When he says that his angels with gather the elect, Jesus seems clearly to mean that he will find his followers. That he *gathers* his elect is thus hugely important. We have only to stand firm in faith, without fear that we will somehow miss locating the returning Jesus. Followers should highly value not only that Jesus is faithful to his followers to the end but also that Jesus is a gatherer.

Once in a while, he would wonder about Jesus's return, coming in a cloud with power and glory. While he was interested in what Jesus might look like and how he would return in that cloud, he was just as interested in whether he would see or miss it. Would he have to be looking up, looking east, or looking west? Would he have to be near Jerusalem? Or would Jesus be visible to all at once? He also sometimes wondered how Jesus would gather his followers to him. Would he have to make his way to where Jesus appeared, having the means, time, and ability to somehow step up or step forward? Then he remembered that Jesus said that his angels would gather his followers to him from the corners of the earth and end of the heavens. He found something deeply reassuring in the thought that Jesus would in effect come and get him. He didn't want to live with the anxiety that Jesus would leave him behind, like having the right ticket, documents, or qualifications but missing the ride to the airport. He didn't want any struggle about joining Jesus because he didn't trust that he would be able to struggle, sensing instead that in any such struggle, he of all people would lose, relinquishing his place to others, not wanting to compete for Jesus's favor or attention. When the day of Jesus's return came, he didn't want any apocalyptic scene to unfold in which he, his family, and his fellow believers had to face many new obstacles to joining Jesus. He just wanted to rely on Jesus.

172 Enthroned.

Matthew 25:31; *see also* Matthew 19:28; Luke 1:32; Revelation 3:21, 4, 5.

The scriptures reveal Jesus taking the throne of God. God will enthrone Jesus above all and as ruler of all. One Gospel account heralding Jesus's coming reveals that the Lord God would give the Son of the Most High the throne of David. Another Gospel account records that during his final week in Jerusalem, Jesus told the disciples that when coming in his glory, the Son of Man *will sit on his throne in heavenly glory* where God will gather all the nations before him. The same Gospel records Jesus at an earlier time revealing to his disciples that he would take that glorious throne *at the renewal of all things*, when he would rule over all. Revelation through the Spirit reveals God on heaven's throne, appearing as if he was of jasper and ruby, encircled by an emerald rainbow, with the throne giving off lightning and thunder. God held a scroll that only Jesus, looking like a slain lamb and standing at the throne's center, could open. When Jesus took the scroll from God, worthy to do so because of his sacrifice for all nations, all then worshiped Jesus. Significantly, Jesus further revealed in one Gospel account that the disciples who had followed him would also sit on thrones in judgment. Revelation also quotes Jesus as saying that he would give the victorious the right to *sit with him on his throne* in just the way that he sat down victorious with his Father on the Father's throne. Jesus will be enthroned and will provide thrones for his disciples.

The image of Jesus as enthroned on God's seat in heaven may epitomize for many followers how they should ultimately think of Jesus. The image of Jesus as the slain lamb taking God's mighty throne gives followers endless opportunity for reflection. A throne represents both divinity and rule, both reverential awe and also recognition of the absolute power and authority to govern. A throne is also a seat for a person. The image of God on his throne thus makes divinity and governance personal in both the Father and Son. God is not a force but a person who authors and authorizes force. The scene of the Father passing his authority to Jesus at the throne could be no clearer as to why the Father did so in that the Son had given his life for all. One cannot too greatly exaggerate God's splendor, at which Revelation only hints with jasper, rubies, and emeralds, or the fearsomely powerful aspects of God's throne, at which Revelation again only hints with lightning and thunder. Imagination may here justly run wild. Yet followers also cannot miss the extraordinary juxtaposition of a slain lamb, what must be among the least or weakest of all possible images, approaching and taking that throne. The love of God for all persons lives luxuriously in that exquisite tension between the Father's absolute power and the Lamb's absolute vulnerability. The Lamb took the throne. Followers may forever reflect that the Lamb took the throne.

He wasn't much for science fiction, although one could not avoid seeing at least some images of it. The images that he saw were indeed fearsome, even freakishly so. Each depiction seemed to outdo the prior one, the powers growing ever greater, scarier, and stranger. He'd had dreams a little like that, of incomprehensibly fearsome, uncontrollable, and inescapable powers, as he assumed everyone does. Although he made no effort to investigate, preserve, or replicate those dreams and images, not wanting to waste his time and mental energy on frivolous and distracting speculation, he still in some way valued those dreams and images. He needed an appropriate sense of God's grandness. He needed a degree of reverence, awe, and mystery mixed with a healthy dose of very highly respectful fear. He also needed to connect those feelings, attitudes, and emotions to his image of Jesus. He wanted to know Jesus both as a friendly brother *and* as a fearsome God. He found the image of the slain lamb taking the lightning-and-thunder throne by scroll, while far from anything that he might have created in his own weak imagination, somehow exactly the kind of rich representation, allegory, or imagery that he needed. After all, it was biblical. He could and should rely on it for deep reflection. Let the Lamb take the throne, he smiled in realization.

¹⁷³ Rewarding.

Matthew 25:29; *see also* Luke 19:12.

While the scriptures reveal Jesus taking the throne for his having completed his salvation mission, the scriptures also reveal Jesus rewarding those who follow him in active pursuit and service of his mission. One Gospel account records Jesus reassuring the disciples during his final week in Jerusalem that if they remained dressed and ready for service through the difficult times ahead, then God would reward them generously. Jesus illustrated with the parable of the talents. The servant who put his master's property and money to work while the master was away, and who earned the master more money, received back his master's thanks *well done* and many more things in his care. Indeed, the master had the servant *share in his happiness*. But the servant who believed his master hard and who hid his master's money rather than put it to work received only his master's chastisement. Jesus concluded the parable with the lesson that those who do much will receive more, even an *abundance*, while those who do little will lose what little they have. Jesus continued the same lesson by revealing that when he sat on his throne in heavenly glory, he would separate those who served him from those who did not and then give his servants their kingdom inheritance, blessed by his Father. Jesus rewards.

The image of Jesus giving due reward to his followers for their effective service should encourage followers to continue in their fruitful labors. Natural disposition is to please one's self, to acquire and accumulate for one's own security, satisfaction, and benefit. Yet we see and hear from Jesus that the more that followers give up their lives for his life and mission, the more that Jesus rewards them for doing so. Life is so often like that twist, enigma, or conundrum. Pursue one's own gain while ignoring his gain, and one loses all, but pursue his gain while ignoring one's own, and one gains all. Hate one's life and gain, while love one's life and lose it. Repeatedly, followers learn that direct pursuit of one's own benefit is not the way to meaningful riches. Instead of pursuing riches directly, Jesus indicates that followers should desire to *inherit*, as he puts it. Succinctly, Jesus's reference to *inheritance* means to acquire the property of another through that other's passing. You could work hard all of your life and maybe accumulate a little, but haven't you instead wanted to inherit riches that others have earned, invested, and accumulated for generations? Getting into right relationship with Jesus gives a follower Jesus's riches, kingdom riches that are immeasurably greater than anything earthly that one could acquire and accumulate. Jesus rewards and does so not miserly, by the hour so to speak, but with a kingdom inheritance. Go for the greater reward. Reflect on your inheritance.

She liked the sense of inheriting something. Oh, she was fine with working for her daily keep. She liked labor, liked to keep busy. She wasn't lazy and wasn't looking for a handout, didn't want to rely on others when she could care for herself. Indeed, she preferred to provide and care for others, to be the giver more so than one who received. Yet what she didn't particularly like was trying to accumulate the fruits of her labor into something in which she put her security. She was prudent about savings, prudent about retirement planning, as any good steward should be. Still, she had a stronger sense that her security was not in the money that she earned, put aside, invested, and gradually accumulated. Maybe she had a little temporal security in those accounts and funds, but she wasn't so interested in temporal security. She instead wanted *eternal* security. She wanted a kingdom reward. No, she wanted a kingdom *inheritance*. She didn't want her own money. She wanted *God's* riches and not because she wanted to be rich but instead because she wanted to be rich *toward God*. That ambition to please and serve God was why she kept thinking more about an inheritance than earned income. If she worked and was prudent, then things would take care of themselves. But if she worked for God, then he would take care of her. She liked the image of that kind of an eternal inheritance.

Conclusion

When looking to Christ, we become whom he made us to be. Followers often hear that their identity is *in Christ*. Each of us has our unique image *in him*, as he intended us to be when imagining or conceiving and creating us in his image through his Holy Spirit. If indeed we find our image in him, then the question arises as to the pursuit and process of that discovery. How do we best become whom he made us to be? Again, the answer must lie *in his image*. We must in some progressively greater sense contemplate, come to know, and then subsume, incorporate, or take on his image. Of course, the Holy Spirit guides and vitalizes that process. We do not. Our pursuit without the Spirit's influence would be vanity, of which nothing in this context could be worse. Yet the Spirit guides the follower in truth through the *word* of Christ. Followers find and embrace the Spirit *in the word*. Thus a study of what the word reflects in the image of Christ would seem to be a worthwhile, indeed the key, pursuit and process of Christ-image discovery. Contemplate Jesus richly, and you may be taking on his image.

The many accounts, records, images, and scenes that the Bible give us of Jesus reflect not just events of his life but also attributes or conditions of his character. Each small three-paragraph summary in this book of many of those scenes revealing Jesus's character bears a one-word title, meant to capture that attribute, condition, or character. Every person has character of some kind. No person has had the full character of Christ. While we are each unique, Christ's life reflected a character so utterly distinct from any life to have gone before or come since that any thinking person, follower or not, must stand in awe. Many have received baptism, none but Christ with the dove-like Spirit's descent. Many have healed others, none but Christ so often, completely, generously, and instantly. Many have suffered, none but Christ so utterly with such clarity and generosity of purpose. The greatest, most informative, and most influential character study one could ever make would be of Christ. One would do so by knowing what the events of his life revealed of his character.

Many of the above sections may seem like simple recounts of events in Jesus's life. They are not or at least don't intend to be. Rather, the title of each section reflects not merely an event in Christ's life or an activity in which he engaged but also *attributes* of Christ, meaning characteristics that he possesses that are part of his eternal identity. That we have a *crucified* Lord is hugely significant as to who Christ is and who we become as his followers, the cross having such significance both as the cruelest of death mechanisms but also an arms-open-wide symbol. Yet moreover, Jesus's crucifixion was not incidental, as if the governor arrested him randomly off the street for sacrifice. No, we also follow a *convicted* Lord, albeit one whom the religious leaders falsely convicted, and a *sentenced* Lord, although again a sentence that should have been ours rather than his. Conviction for our sin and sentence for our punishment are not simply events in Jesus's life but also attributes of the Christ whom we follow. Reflecting on these events not simply as stations along the way in the most significant moment in history but especially as our Lord's *attributes* enables us to draw more deeply from him in contemplation. We open the door to becoming ourselves in his image.

Epilogue

They had each reflected on Jesus, looked to Jesus, throughout much of their adult lives together. In some seasons, their gazing on their Lord was frequent, nearly constant, while other seasons seemed to draw them away from him, though never too far. They never stopped looking to Christ because they each knew that their living depended on him. Without him, they knew that they had no life and were only walking dead, not really living but dying. So in all seasons, they kept looking to Jesus. While they looked together to Jesus for many years, even decades, their perspectives of Jesus nevertheless changed frequently, richly, kaleidoscopically, even though Jesus never changed. As they went through the seasons and stages of their lives, facing challenges and welcoming blessings, they learned to let go of things to which they had clung but had never needed, particularly things that clouded their view of their Lord. Thus over the years, while their natural sight grew weaker, their sight of their Lord grew clearer and more keen. They each saw his movement and heard his words, sensed his presence, and even felt his healing touch more frequently. The more that they looked toward Jesus, searching for another view or glimpse of Jesus, the more that his beloved Holy Spirit showed them of him. And the more that they saw of Jesus, the greater their anticipation became for joining him in resurrection in his kingdom.

Table of Attributes

Abandoned	292
Accessible	223
Alien	46
Allegorical	155
Anointed	75
Announced	327
Appealed	302
Appearing	329
Appointer	136
Arrested	294
Ascended	349
Astonished	210
Astonishing	214
Authoritative	103
Avenger	20
Aware	52
Baptized	60
Besieged	275
Betrayed	287
Broken	289
Builder	96
Burdened	306
Buried	315
Calming	174
Celebrant	200
Celebrated	101
Centered	68
Childlike	162
Christ	90
Commander	16
Commissioner	113
Compassionate	212
Conceived	29
Condemned	279
Conferrer	323
Consecrated	38

Consolation	40
Contender	12
Convener	138
Conversing	340
Convicted	298
Counteractive	151
Crowned	21
Crucified	308
Defender	158
Deliverer	18
Denouncing	256
Disguised	331
Dispatcher	141
Divider	168
Doubted	334
Drawing	208
Dutiful	242
Egalitarian	158
Enthroned	362
Expositor	149
Facilitator	195
Family	83
Fasted	62
Fearsome	216
Flesh	31
Forgiving	166
Friend	186
Fruitful	246
Fulfillment	81
Functional	347
Gathering	360
Glorified	325
Glorifying	111
Good	99
Greeting	338
Grown	54
Guarded	277
Guest	10
Harvester	134
Hated	285
Healer	191
Humble	248
Identifiable	345
Immersed	58
Impersonated	358
Inclusive	160
Inscrutable	85

Insurgent	48
Intercessor	145
Interpreter	98
Joyous	94
Judge	77
King	39
Knowing	206
Lawgiver	14
Leader	116
Liberator	154
Life	88
Living	319
Merciful	226
Mourned	312
Named	36
Offending	260
Opposed	342
Partaker	147
Participant	130
Passionate	73
Path	107
Persecuted	263
Persistent	176
Physical	343
Pierced	314
Poured	290
Powered	66
Preacher	118
Priest	7
Proclaimed	34
Prophetic	267
Protector	23
Provider	230
Pursuer	164
Ready	178
Rebuking	336
Receptive	236
Redeemer	44
Refugee	265
Refusing	258
Rescuer	193
Resolute	269
Responder	25
Responding	221
Resting	143
Restorative	250
Restorer	187

Returned	50
Returning	355
Revealer	79
Rewarding	364
Savior	182
Scriptural	105
Scourged	304
Secretive	228
Sentenced	300
Separated	310
Serving	184
Shepherd	92
Shrewd	180
Signifier	132
Superior	240
Supported	70
Surprising	124
Swaddled	32
Teacher	120
Tested	64
Testifier	198
Testing	232
Terrifying	234
Therapeutic	238
Threatened	273
Transfigured	353
Transient	321
Tried	296
Troubled	283
Unequivocal	252
Unexpected	356
Unschooled	122
Vanquisher	218
Verified	172
Vine	109
Visitor	202
Warrior	128
Watchful	271
Weeping	281
Willing	204
Word	6
Worker	244
Worshiper	126

www.ingramcontent.com/pod-product-compliance
Lightning Source LLC
Chambersburg PA
CBHW071144300426
44113CB00009B/1075